THE

DINOSAUR
■ DATA BOOK ■

THE

DINOSAUR DATA BOOK

The definitive, fully illustrated encyclopedia of dinosaurs

David Lambert and the Diagram Group

AVON BOOKS ◆ NEW YORK

Other Avon Books by
The Diagram Group

A FIELD GUIDE TO DINOSAURS

THE DINOSAUR DATA BOOK is an original publication of Avon Books. This work has never before appeared in book form.

AVON BOOKS
A division of
The Hearst Corporation
105 Madison Avenue
New York, New York 10016

The Diagram Group

Project director	Jane Robertson
Editor	Sylvia Worth
Sub editors	Damian Grint, Randal Gray
Designer	Richard Hummerstone
Restorations artist	Graham Rosewarne
Artists	Ashley Best, Darren Bennett, Brian Hewson, Pavel Kostal, Lee Lawrence, Paul McCauley, Philip Patenall, Micky Pledge
Indexer	David Harding

Acknowledgments

The producers of this book wish to thank the following museums for providing details of their collections:

Academy of Natural Sciences, Philadelphia, Pennsylvania, USA
Academy of Sciences of the M.P.R., Ulan-Bator, Mongolia
American Museum of Natural History, New York City, New York, USA
Argentine Museum of Natural Sciences, Buenos Aires, Argentina
Australian Museum, Sydney, New South Wales, Australia
Bavarian State Institute for Paleontology and Historical Geology, Munich, West Germany
Bernard Price Institute for Paleontological Research, University of the Witwatersrand, Johannesburg, South Africa
Bernissart Museum, Bernissart, Hainaut, Belgium
Birmingham Museum and Art Gallery, Birmingham, UK
British Museum (Natural History), London, UK
Buffalo Museum of Science, Buffalo, New York, USA
Carnegie Museum of Natural History, Pittsburgh, Pennsylvania, USA
Civic Museum of Natural History, Venice, Italy
Chengdu College of Geology, Chengdu, Sichuan, China
Cleveland Museum of Natural History, Cleveland, Ohio, USA
Denver Museum of Natural History, Denver, Colorado, USA
Dinosaur Museum, Dorchester, Dorset, UK
Dinosaur National Monument, Jensen, Utah, USA
Earth Science Museum, Brigham Young University, Provo, Utah, USA
Field Museum of Natural History, Chicago, Illinois, USA
Geological and Paleontological Institute, Münster, West Germany
Geological Museum at the University of Wyoming, Laramie, Wyoming, USA
Gunma Prefectural Museum of History, Maebashi, Gunma, Japan
Institute and Museum for Geology and Paleontology, University of Tübingen, Tübingen, West Germany
Institute of Vertebrate Paleontology and Paleoanthropology, Beijing, China
Ipswich Museum, Ipswich, Suffolk, UK
Iwaki City Museum of Coal and Fossils, Iwaki, Fukushima, Japan
Kitakyushu Museum of Natural History, Kitakyushu, Fukuoka, Japan
Leicestershire Museum, Leicester, UK
Maidstone Museums and Art Gallery, Maidstone, Kent, UK
M.S.U. Museum, Michigan State University, East Lansing, Michigan, USA
Museum of Comparative Zoology, Harvard University, Cambridge, Massachusetts, USA
Museum of Natural History, Princeton University, Princeton, New Jersey, USA
Museum of Paleontology, University of California, Berkeley, California, USA
Museum of the Rockies, Montana State University, Bozeman, Montana, USA
National Museum of Natural History, Paris, France
National Museum of Natural History, Smithsonian Institution, Washington, D.C., USA
National Museum of Natural Science, Taichung, Taiwan
National Museum of Natural Sciences, Madrid, Spain
National Museum of Natural Sciences, Ottawa, Canada
National Science Museum, Tokyo, Japan
Natural History Museum, Humboldt University, Berlin, East Germany
Natural History Museum of Los Angeles County, Los Angeles, California, USA
Osaka Museum of Natural History, Osaka, Japan
Paleobiology Institute, Academy of Sciences, Warsaw, Poland
Paleontological Institute, Moscow, Russia
Paleontological Museum, Uppsala University, Uppsala, Sweden
Peabody Museum of Natural History, Yale University, New Haven, Connecticut, USA
Pratt Museum of Natural History, Amherst, Massachusetts, USA
Provincial Museum of Alberta, Edmonton, Alberta, Canada
Queensland Museum, Fortitude Valley, Queensland, Australia
Redpath Museum, McGill University, Montreal, Canada
Royal Institute of Natural Sciences, Brussels, Belgium
Royal Museum of Scotland, Edinburgh, UK
Royal Ontario Museum, Toronto, Ontario, Canada
Science Museum of Minnesota, Saint Paul, Minnesota, USA
Sedgwick Museum, Cambridge University, Cambridge, UK
Senckenberg Natural History Museum, Frankfurt, West Germany
South African Museum, Cape Town, South Africa
State Museum for Natural History, Stuttgart, West Germany
Takikawa Museum of Art and Natural History, Takikawa, Hokkaido, Japan
Toyohashi Museum of Natural History, Toyohashi, Aichi, Japan
Tyrrell Museum of Paleontology, Drumheller, Alberta, Canada
University Museum, Oxford, UK
University of Michigan Exhibit Museum, Ann Arbor, Michigan, USA
Utah Museum of Natural History, University of Utah, Salt Lake City, Utah, USA

Foreword

Concise, comprehensive, and up-to-date, the *Dinosaur Data Book* answers almost every question anyone aged 11 upward could ask about these fascinating prehistoric creatures, the land's most successful-ever backboned animals. Here you will find all dinosaurs known when we went to press (dozens named since 1980), how their bodies worked, how they lived and died, the world they occupied, how their bones were fossilized, who discovered them and where, where to see them on display, and more . . .

Text and captions explain scientific terms in simple language. Key information figures in the hundreds of easily grasped illustrations – "field guide" pictures, maps, and time lines, length lines, family trees, and diagrams simplifying complex scientific studies.

There are seven chapters with brief introductions. Two chapters are A to Z guides. In others, bold headings signal pages on special topics.

Chapter 1: The Age of Dinosaurs introduces dinosaurs, explains how they evolved and what made them special, describes their close kin and their world, and speculates on why they disappeared.

Chapter 2: The A to Z of Dinosaurs names and briefly describes all known genera (more than 440 by 1990) and all higher ranks of dinosaurs plus related reptile groups, with translations of their names. (Pages 20- 21 and Chapter 3 show how dinosaurs are ranked and classified.)

Chapter 3: Dinosaurs Classified describes all major groups of dinosaurs and individual families, with their listed genera.

Chapter 4: Dinosaur Life explains how dinosaurs were built and how their bodies worked; then how they moved, fed, fought, bred, and died.

Chapter 5: Dinosaurs Worldwide reveals how dinosaurs formed fossils; how scientists discover, excavate, and study these; how museums clean, preserve, and reconstruct the bones; where these were found around the world; and which museums show or store which dinosaurs.

Chapter 6: Dinosaurologists is a unique A to Z guide to who found, named, or described which dinosaurs and when; and who thought up important theories about the ways in which they lived.

Chapter 7: Dinosaurs Revived shows how artists, sculptors, writers, and motion-picture makers have shaped people's notions of the dinosaurs; how scientists' ideas of these have changed; and how dinosaurs themselves might have evolved had they survived until today.

There follows a descriptive list of books on dinosaurs, and an index.

The producers of this book warmly thank all those who made it possible, especially our two general consultants; Dr Michael Benton, Dr Peter Galton, George Olshevsky, and Masahiro Tanimoto; and museum curators around the world who checked information on local finds and museum collections. Of course the responsibility for stated facts (some controversial) is ours.

Contents

Chapter 1
THE AGE OF DINOSAURS

10	Introduction	**24**	Birds
12	Introducing dinosaurs	**26**	Dinosaur family tree
14	Before the dinosaurs	**28**	Triassic time
16	Evolving reptiles	**30**	Jurassic time
18	Arrival of the dinosaurs	**32**	Cretaceous time
20	What were the dinosaurs?	**34**	End of an age
22	Pterosaurs		

Chapter 2
THE A TO Z OF DINOSAURS

36 Introduction
38 A to Z listings

Chapter 3
DINOSAURS CLASSIFIED

106	Introduction	**136**	Saurischians 2: sauropodomorphs and segnosaurs
108	Two great groups	**148**	Ornithischians 1: ornithopods
110	Saurischians 1: theropods (with Herrerasaurs)	**158**	Ornithischians 2: five suborders

Chapter 4
DINOSAUR LIFE

172	Introduction	**196**	Skin and scales
174	Bony scaffolding	**198**	Color and camouflage
176	Muscles	**200**	Keeping warm
178	Heart-lung system	**202**	Moving around
180	Heads	**204**	Feeding
182	Brains and intelligence	**206**	Attack
184	Sight, smell, and hearing	**208**	Defense
186	Necks	**210**	Winning a mate
188	Arms and hands	**212**	Eggs
190	Digestive systems	**214**	Young dinosaurs
192	Hips, legs, and feet	**216**	Life expectancy
194	Tails		

Chapter 5
DINOSAURS WORLDWIDE

218 Introduction
220 How dinosaurs were fossilized
222 Discovery and excavation
224 Dating fossil dinosaurs
226 Preparing fossils
228 Understanding fossils
230 North American dinosaurs 1
232 North American dinosaurs 2
234 North American museums 1
236 North American museums 2
238 European dinosaurs 1
240 European dinosaurs 2
242 European museums 1

244 European museums 2
246 Asian dinosaurs 1
248 Asian dinosaurs 2
250 Asian dinosaurs 3
252 Asian dinosaurs 4
254 Asian museums 1
256 Asian museums 2
258 South American dinosaurs
260 South American museums
261 African dinosaurs 1
262 African dinosaurs 2
263 African museums
264 Dinosaurs down under

Chapter 6
DINOSAUROLOGISTS

266 Introduction
268 Alphabetical list of dinosaurologists

Chapter 7
DINOSAURS REVIVED

286 Introduction
288 Popular misconceptions
290 Dinosaurs in art
292 Dinosaurs rebuilt
294 Dinosaurs in fiction

296 Dinosaurs in comics
298 Movie dinosaurs 1
300 Movie dinosaurs 2
302 Dinosaurs old and new
304 If dinosaurs lived on . . .

306 Books on dinosaurs
311 Index

Chapter 1

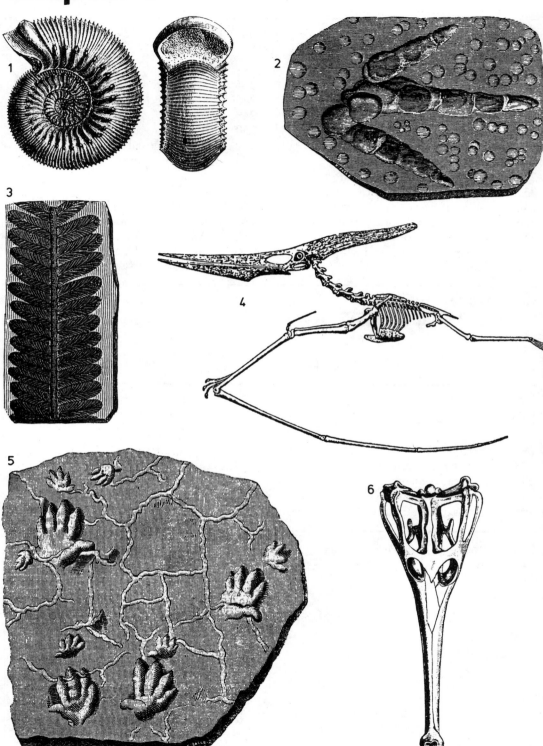

THE AGE OF DINOSAURS

After an overview of dinosaurs, these pages trace the origins of backboned animals leading to the rise of reptiles and the Mesozoic Era or Age of Dinosaurs. We see how dinosaurs themselves evolved and how they differed from all other reptiles. A glance at their close kin pterosaurs and birds leads to a grand family tree of dinosaurs and their relations. Then come brief accounts of the lands, climates, plants, and animals that shared the world with dinosaurs through the three periods of Mesozoic time.

The chapter ends with a selection of solutions to prehistory's greatest riddle: why dinosaurs died out 65 million years ago.

Fossils (not to scale) represent the three periods of the Age of Dinosaurs.
1 A Jurassic ammonite.
2 Birdlike footprint of a Triassic dinosaur.
3 Part of a Triassic fern.
4 Skeleton of the Cretaceous flying reptile *Pteranodon*.
5 Tracks of the Triassic thecodont *Chirotherium*.
6 Skull of *Steneosaurus*, a Jurassic crocodilian.

Introducing dinosaurs

Eight dinosaurs among the
longest or heaviest of their
kind, with one of the
smallest dinosaurs. All but
3, **7**, and **9** ate plants.
1 *Lambeosaurus*, a
hadrosaur: 49ft (15m).
2 *Ankylosaurus*, an armored
dinosaur: 35ft (10.7m).
3 *Tyrannosaurus*, a
theropod: 7 US tons (6.4
tonnes).
4 *Stegosaurus*, a plated
dinosaur: 30ft (9m).
5 "Ultrasaurus," a
sauropod: 55 US tons (50
tonnes).
6 *Diplodocus*, a sauropod:
87ft 6in (27m).
7 *Spinosaurus*, a theropod:
50ft (15m).
8 *Triceratops*, a horned
dinosaur: 30ft (9m).
9 *Compsognathus* a
theropod: 2ft (60cm).

Dinosaurs were the most successful backboned animals that ever
lived on land. They appeared about 230 million years ago, and
flourished 40 times longer than the time elapsed since our own
ancestors emerged from apes. Living when all continents lay
joined, dinosaurs spread around the globe, evolving a diversity of
sizes, shapes, and ways of life. There were immense four-legged
plant-eaters taller than a five-floor building, as heavy as six
elephants, and longer than a row of buses. There were four-legged
plant-eaters with built-in body armor of bony shields, plates, or
horns. There were bipedal plant-eaters, too. All lived at risk from
two-legged flesh-eaters equipped with fangs and claws. The largest
predators weighed as much as an elephant and, if living now, might
easily have swallowed people whole. Yet not all dinosaurs were
huge. Some grew little bigger than a chicken. Large and small,
dinosaurs played the parts now occupied by mammal herbivores
and carnivores.

As time passed, old types of dinosaur died out and new ones took
their place. Meanwhile dinosaurs ruled everywhere, killing most
animals big enough to rival them for food and living space. At last
the dinosaurs themselves mysteriously perished about 65 million
years ago. Only then could mammals start evolving into forms
much larger than a rat.

What kinds of creatures were the dinosaurs that dominated continents so long? Most scientists believe they formed a group or two groups of reptiles. Indeed their name means "terrible lizards" or "terrible reptiles." Like today's cold-blooded reptiles, dinosaurs had a scaly skin and tail; they even sprang from the same reptile group that gave rise to the crocodiles. Yet, unlike any ordinary reptiles, they walked with limbs erect. Some were more intelligent than living reptiles. And small flesh-eating dinosaurs gave rise to birds. All this convinces certain scientists that dinosaurs had been as active, brainy, and warm-blooded as most mammals are.

By 1990 hunters of old bones had dug up the remains of thousands of dinosaurs belonging to about 440 genera – at least one quarter named since 1980. Each year ancient rocks release more members of this zoo of prehistoric wildlife and fresh glimpses of the fascinating ways in which it lived.

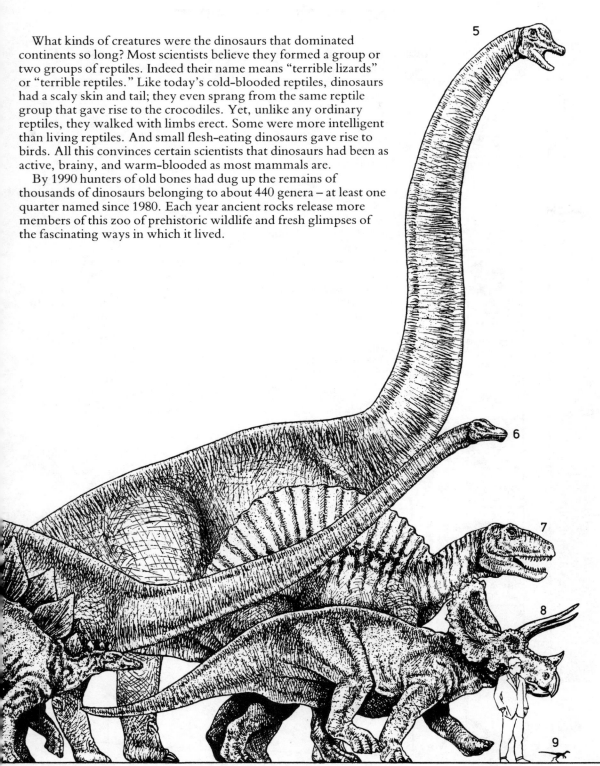

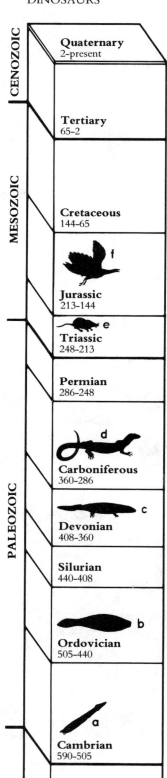

Before the dinosaurs

Dinosaurs – the largest animals that ever walked on land – had their origins in living things too small for us to see. Bit by bit, such minute simple life forms gave rise to big complex ones through accumulating changes in their genes: the tiny units in each body cell deciding how an organism grows and handing on the same instructions to its young. Random genetic changes happen all the time but only those persist that help an organism and its offspring to survive. So, over many million years, evolved millions of different kinds of living thing, each adapted for living in a particular natural environment.

Life seemingly began when sunshine and lightning brewed biochemical compounds from elements in the young Earth's seas and suffocating atmosphere 4000 million years ago. The first living cells were probably self-replicating blobs of jelly. These grew by eating available proteins. Then they split in two to reproduce. As cells multiplied, they began using up the protein foods. But certain cells evolved the knack of harnessing the energy in sunlight to manufacture food from water's plentiful supply of simple chemicals. Early food-makers gave rise to plants, which gave off oxygen as waste. Oxygen in turn made the Earth's atmosphere fit for the first animals to breathe, and plants supplied their food.

Geological column
Seen left are the main time units of Earth history since complex animals became abundant 590 million years ago. The Paleozoic, Mesozoic, and Cenozoic eras are subdivided into named periods. Numbers give their spans in millions of years ago. Letters **b**, **c**, **d**, **e**, **f** identify five types of vertebrate (backboned animal), shown when they first appeared.
a Primitive chordate (vertebrate ancestor)
b Fish
c Amphibian
d Reptile
e Mammal
f Bird

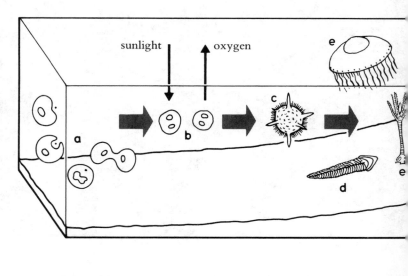

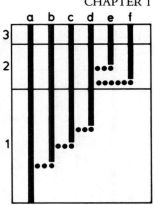

About 590 million years ago the seas began to teem with worms, jellyfish, and other creatures made of many cells of different kinds, each specialized to feed, move, breed, or in some other way. Now began the Paleozoic Era, Earth's "Age of Ancient Life." Its 340 million years or so saw new complex kinds of animal appear. First, sea creatures such as trilobites built shells to guard and reinforce their soft bodies. Later came fishes – backboned animals supported by an inside skeleton. Unlike a crab's carapace, a fish's skeleton allows free movement of the body, and a growing fish has no need to shed its skeleton from time to time.

Freshwater fishes with fleshy fins and lungs began to haul themselves ashore to escape enemies or hunt the snails and insects feeding on the plants now growing on dry land. About 350 million years ago one kind of lobe-finned fish gave rise to the first four-legged animal – a sprawling, salamander-like amphibian. Amphibians can breathe, feed, and move about on land, but have to lay their soft-shelled eggs in water to prevent them drying up.

More than 100 million years passed before descendants of the first amphibians evolved into the dinosaurs.

Evolving vertebrates
Above: Simplified vertebrate family tree.
a Primitive chordates
b Fishes
c Amphibians
d Reptiles
e Birds
f Mammals
1 Paleozoic Era
2 Mesozoic Era
3 Cenozoic Era

Vertebrates emerging
Arrows trace the origins of land vertebrates.
a Early living cells consuming ready-made food.
b Early plants making food and giving off oxygen with help from sunlight.
c Early one-celled "animals" breathing oxygen and eating plants.

d Worms: among the first many-celled animals.
e Jellyfish and echinoderms: invertebrates from worms.
f Chordates: with a notochord (skeletal rod).
g Fish: first vertebrates.
h Amphibians: with limbs evolved from fins.

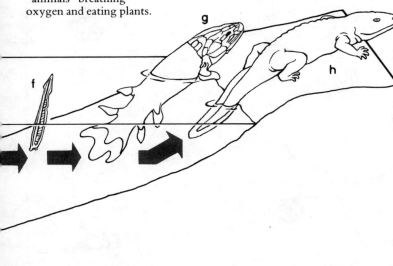

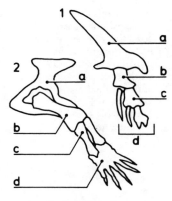

Evolving limbs (*above*)
1 Bones supporting a pelvic fin in a Devonian lobe-finned fish.
2 Corresponding bones as evolved in the hind limb of a Permian amphibian.
a Pelvis (hip bones)
b Femur (thigh bone)
c Tibia and fibula
d Pes (foot)

©DIAGRAM

Evolving reptiles

Dinosaurs sprang from the class of backboned animals called Reptilia ("crawlers"). Typical reptiles are cold-blooded with waterproof scaly skin and sprawling limbs. Females lay eggs fertilized inside their bodies, and tough skins or hard shells stop the eggs drying up when laid. Early reptiles were the first backboned creatures equipped to breed on land.

Small lizardlike reptiles evolved from amphibians at least 340 million years ago. From such pioneers evolved several reptile groups identified by differences in the skull behind the eyes. The primitive anapsids ("without arch") had skulls without a hole behind each eye, as do testudinates (the turtles). Synapsids ("with arch") had one hole behind each eye. Diapsids ("double arch") had two holes behind each eye.

Big synapsid herbivores and flesh-eaters dominated lands in Late Paleozoic time. From early sprawling kinds called pelycosaurs ("basin lizards") evolved the mammal-like therapsids ("mammal arch") with mammal-like teeth. Some were hairy and warm-blooded, and one gave rise to mammals.

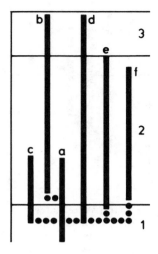

Major groups 1
Above: Evolutionary tree grouping reptiles mainly by holes in the skull behind the eye. But skull-hole similarities mask major differences in body build between **a** and **b** and **e** and **f**.
a, **b** Anapsids (no hole), but **b** is now renamed Testudinates.
c Synapsids (low hole)
d Diapsids (two holes)
e, **f** "Euryapsids" (high hole), now reclassified as (**e**) sauropterygians and (**f**) ichthyopterygians or simply called diapsids.
1 Paleozoic Era
2 Mesozoic Era
3 Cenozoic Era

Major groups 2
Right: Skull types of beasts representing groups of reptiles named above.
A Pareiasaur (anapsid)
B Turtle (testudinate)
C Pelycosaur (synapsid)
D Crocodile (diapsid)
E Plesiosaur (sauropterygian)
F Ichthyosaur (ichthyopterygian)

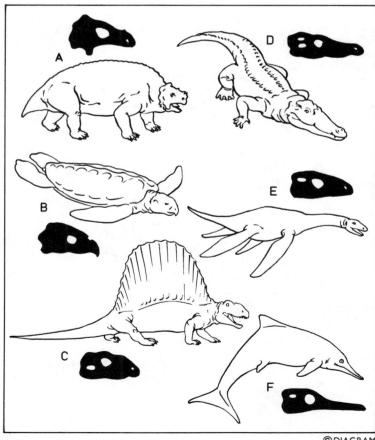

©DIAGRAM

That event happened when mass extinction wiped out scores of old-established lines of animals 248 million years ago and new ones quickly took their place. This watershed in evolution replaced the Paleozoic Era with the Mesozoic Era ("Age of Middle Life") which lasted until 65 million years ago. Also called the Age of Dinosaurs, the Mesozoic Era is subdivided into the Triassic, Jurassic, and Cretaceous geological periods, described briefly on pages 28–33.

As synapsids fizzled out, diapsids diversified and multiplied. One group gave rise to lizards, snakes, and probably those now–extinct seagoing reptiles plesiosaurs, although these had lost the lower hole behind the eye and were once grouped with the extinct "fish lizards" ichthyosaurs as euryapsids ("broad arch"). A second diapsid group, the archosauromorphs, gave rise to the archosaurs or "ruling reptiles" that dominated life on land in Mesozoic times. It was this subgroup that contained the dinosaurs.

Diverse diapsids
Below: Land-based diapsids of the late Paleozoic (**1**) and early Mesozoic (**2**). Items **j-m** were archosaurs.
a Araeoscelids
b Coelurosauravids
c Thalattosaurs
d Eosuchians
e Sphenodonts
f Snakes and lizards
g Protorosaurs
h Rhynchosaurs
i Trilophosaurs
j Thecodonts
k Crocodilians
l Pterosaurs
m Dinosaurs

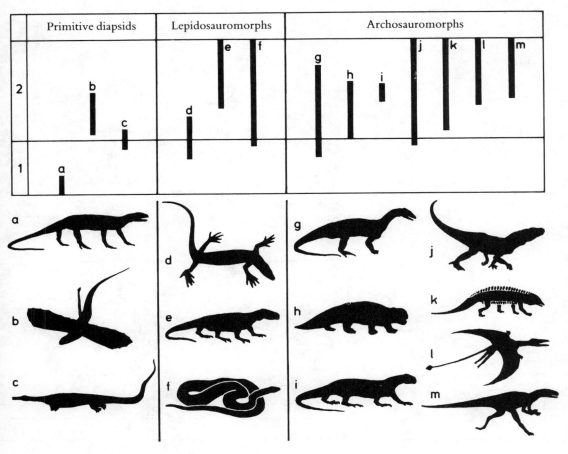

Arrival of the dinosaurs

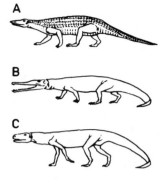

Discovering which kind of animal gave rise to dinosaurs came from carefully comparing bones of the variety of archosauromorphs that lived in early Mesozoic times. Strange offshoots included piglike rhynchosaurs ("beaked lizards") with toothless tonglike jaws, and weird long-necked protorosaurs ("first lizards"), perhaps living in the sea. But the four groups of archosaurs were crocodilians, pterosaurs ("winged lizards"), thecodonts ("socket toothed"), and dinosaurs.

All had an opening in the skull in front of each eye, perhaps to hold a gland for helping blood shed surplus salt. That would have been an aid for creatures living in the deserts thought to dominate much land early on in Mesozoic times. However, some archosaurs were built to stand and walk more upright and swing limbs to and fro more effectively than others. Hind limb and ankle joints point to the ancestors of dinosaurs among that complex group the thecodonts.

Early thecodonts included sprawling, crocodile-like proterosuchians ("primordial crocodiles") with big, less spawling erythrosuchid ("crimson crocodile") predators. At least three thecodont groups – plant-eating aetosaurs ("old lizards"), carnivorous phytosaurs ("plant lizards"), and rauisuchians ("Rau's crocodiles") – had the type of ankle found in crocodiles.

Three thecodonts
Above: These thecodonts with "crocodile normal" ankles might have branched off from the line that led to dinosaurs. Each was about 10ft (3m) long.
A *Stagonolepis,* an armored plant-eating aetosaur.
B *Parasuchus,* a crocodile-like predatory phytosaur with nostrils above its eyes.
C *Ticinosuchus,* a predatory rauisuchian.

Dinosaurs from thecodonts
Numbered animals below show likely trends that gave rise to the dinosaurs. Items **2** through **5** were thecodonts.
1 Lizardlike ancestral archosaur.
2 Large sprawling proterosuchian.

3 Large semi-sprawling erythrosuchid.
4 The small early ornithosuchian *Euparkeria* with semi-improved gait; walking (**a**), running (**b**).
5 Little *Lagosuchus,* with a fully improved gait like that of dinosaurs.
6 *Staurikosaurus,* an early dinosaur.

Crocodiles probably evolved from a thecodont such as one of these. Ornithosuchian ("bird crocodile") thecodonts like little early *Euparkeria* and the lagosuchids ("rabbit crocodiles") shared a second type of ankle. Evolved perhaps from sprawling thecodonts, they raised their bodies off the ground, thrust their whole limbs down and back, and so produced a lengthy stride. *Lagosuchus* had short front limbs but could have run on hind limbs, balancing the body with the tail. Anatomical changes in lagosuchids or close kin very likely gave rise both to the flying pterosaurs and to the dinosaurs with their fully upright stance and gait.

About 230 million years ago the first dinosaurs were two-legged flesh-eaters no heavier than a big dog. Quite likely able to outrun the thecodonts, these might have outcompeted them for food. By 213 million years ago, dinosaurs small and large, carnivorous and herbivorous, had spread around the world and started dominating life on land.

Dinosaurs would flourish for 165 million years. If you compressed into 12 months all time elapsed since life grew plentiful on Earth, it is as if the dinosaurs appeared in early August and died out in late November. By comparison, humankind appeared late on 31 December, a mere eyeblink ago.

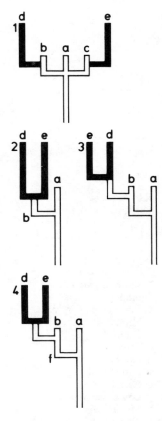

A The sprawling gait of early thecodonts: knees stuck out sideways.
B The semi-improved gait of many later thecodonts: knees more tucked in.
C The fully improved gait of lagosuchids and dinosaurs: knees fully tucked in and legs held directly below the body. Gait change possibly began with semiaquatic beasts that thrust long hind limbs down and back to start swimming. Yet proterosuchians themselves were too big to give rise to thecodonts that led to dinosaurs. New discoveries might fill in the missing evolutionary links.

Alternative origins
Above: Four ways in which both great groups of dinosaurs (saurischians and ornithischians) described on page 108 might have evolved from thecodonts.
1 From two thecodonts.
2 From one thecodont.
3 Ornithischian dinosaurs from saurischian dinosaurs.
4 Both groups from a dinosaur more primitive than either. This now seems likeliest.
a Ancestral archosaurs
b,c Thecodonts
d Saurischian dinosaurs
e Ornithischian dinosaurs
f Primitive dinosaur

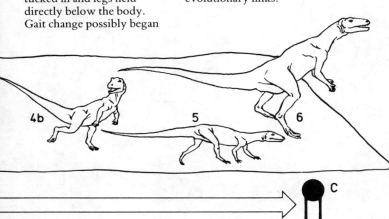

©DIAGRAM

19

What were the dinosaurs?

Scientists studying the bones of dinosaurs now know just what set apart these archosaurs or "ruling reptiles" from all other animals including some theropods once throught to be dinosaurs.

Key features are details in the bones of hips, thighs, legs, and feet. In dinosaurs, but not in sprawling archosaurs, these bones transmitted body weight straight down through the limbs. Each thigh bone (femur) turned in sharply at the top, and its ball-like end (head) fitted into a deep hole – a fully open (perforate) socket (acetabulum) in the hip bones. A strong ridge (the supra-acetabular crest) above the socket stopped the thigh bone slipping out. Low down on the thigh bone a sharp ridge (the fourth trochanter) anchored muscles that pulled the leg back for walking, and more knobs (the greater and lesser trochanters) anchored other muscles. The knee joint lay in a straight line between hip and foot, not at an angle as in sprawling archosaurs. The main leg bone (tibia) had a twist, a prominent cnemial (lower leg) crest, and a notch that interlocked with ankle bones. Unlike almost all other archosaurs except pterosaurs and lagosuchids, the ankle formed a simple

Key features
Illustrations (*right*) stress key dinosaur features mentioned in the text. (See also pages 192–193.)
A Frontal view of *Tyrannosaurus* hind limbs.
B Limb in schematic frontal view.
C Limb in side view.
a Hip bones
b Femur
c Tibia
d Fibula
e Astragalus
f Calcaneum
g Lower tarsal bones
h Metatarsals
i Phalanges
j Interned femur head
k Fully open acetabulum
l Supra–acetabular crest
m Trochanters
n Knee joint in straight line between hip and foot
o Cnemial crest
p High ankle joint with simple hinge between upper (**e**, **f**) and lower (**g**) tarsal bones
q Long foot bones
r Long middle toe
s Weight borne on toes

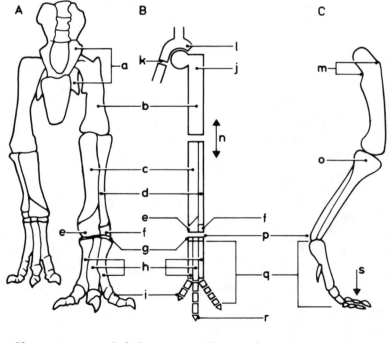

From class to species
Right: How a dinosaur is classified. Dinosaurs are usually placed in two orders but cladistics shows they were one group. (See also pages 108–109.)

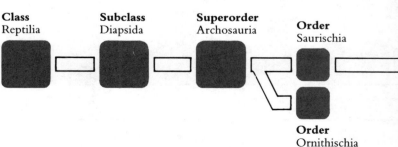

Class	Subclass	Superorder	Order
Reptilia	Diapsida	Archosauria	Saurischia
			Order Ornithischia

hinge. Both upper ankle bones (astragalus and calcaneum) closely joined the tibia, and part of the astragalus, the chief ankle bone, rose to fit into a pit in the tibia. Other ankle bones formed part of the foot. The middle toe was the longest, and many later dinosaurs had short outer toes or none at all. Their high ankles and long foot bones prove that dinosaurs usually walked on their toes and not flat-footedly.

Inturned femur head, fully open acetabulum, fourth trochanter low on the femur, prominent cnemial crest, and ascending process (rising projection) on astragalus – together these comprise a derived or advanced set of characters (features) found in dinosaurs but not in other archosaurs. Additional sets of derived characters help scientists to split dinosaurs into successively more advanced groups. Each group of dinosaurs, or other animals with shared features not found in any other group, is called a clade. Some clades consist of just one species. The study of clades is cladistics, and family trees based on clades are cladograms. Cladistics is changing the ways in which scientists group, or classify, dinosaurs.

Dinosaurs derived
Based on a cladogram devised by Michael Benton this diagram (*left*) shows derived characters influencing gait as branches coming off the archosaur stem.
A Archosauria (fourth trochanter)
B Ornithosuchia (perforated acetabulum, supra-acetabular crest, femur with inturned head and sharp flange as fourth trochanter, knee bending 90°, weight borne on toes)
C Ornithodira (Bipedal, with longer shin than thigh, ankle joint a simple hinge, rising process on astragalus, reduced fibula, and long closely bunched middle foot bones)
D Pterosauria (Femur with offset head, distinct neck, and two "knuckles" at the lower end)
E Dinosauria (Fully open acetabulum, low fourth trochanter, prominent cnemial crest, and marked ascending process on astragalus)
F Reduced ischial and pubic hip bone contact
G Twisted tibia
H Three or more sacral vertebrae (connected to hip bones) and spiky or crested third trochanter
a Other archosaurs
b *Ornithosuchus*
c *Lagosuchus*
d Pterosaurs
e *Herrerasaurus*
f *Staurikosaurus*
g *Pisanosaurus*
h Later dinosaurs

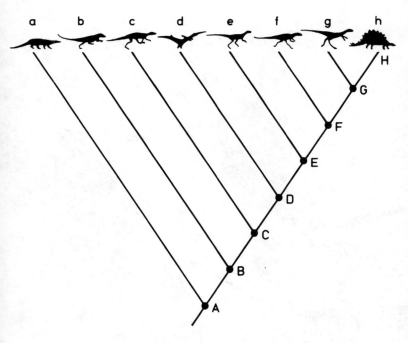

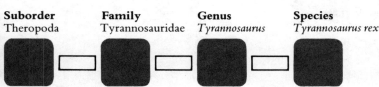

Suborder	Family	Genus	Species
Theropoda	Tyrannosauridae	*Tyrannosaurus*	*Tyrannosaurus rex*

Pterosaurs

Close kin of the dinosaurs dominated Mesozoic skies. Evolved perhaps from "protodinosaurs" like *Lagosuchus*, pterosaurs ("winged lizards") were the first backboned animals to fly. They had light, hollow bones, and fairly narrow skin wings stretched between immensely long fourth-finger bones and tail. Brain development assured keen eyesight and skilled wing control. Sparrow-sized species flew actively; giants even larger than a condor soared and glided. At least some pterosaurs evidently had a furry body; perhaps all were warm blooded as birds and mammals are.

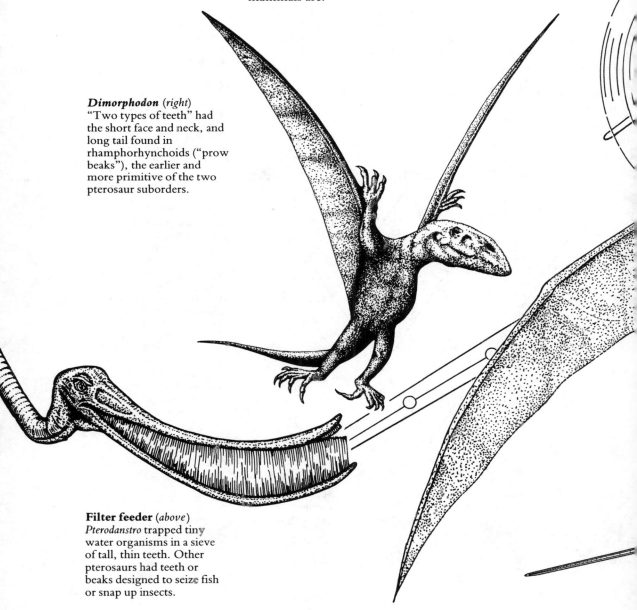

Dimorphodon (*right*)
"Two types of teeth" had the short face and neck, and long tail found in rhamphorhynchoids ("prow beaks"), the earlier and more primitive of the two pterosaur suborders.

Filter feeder (*above*)
Pterodanstro trapped tiny water organisms in a sieve of tall, thin teeth. Other pterosaurs had teeth or beaks designed to seize fish or snap up insects.

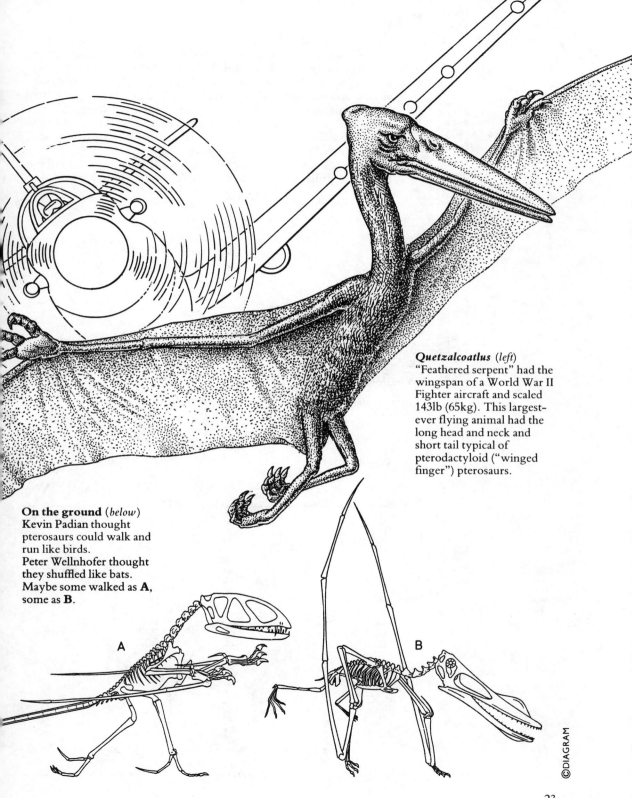

Quetzalcoatlus (*left*)
"Feathered serpent" had the
wingspan of a World War II
Fighter aircraft and scaled
143lb (65kg). This largest-
ever flying animal had the
long head and neck and
short tail typical of
pterodactyloid ("winged
finger") pterosaurs.

On the ground (*below*)
Kevin Padian thought
pterosaurs could walk and
run like birds.
Peter Wellnhofer thought
they shuffled like bats.
Maybe some walked as **A**,
some as **B**.

A

B

©DIAGRAM

Birds

Even closer to the dinosaurs than pterosaurs were birds. Indeed the skeletons of early birds and small predatory dinosaurs appear almost identical. Modern birds still feature dinosaur-like toes and ankles, and the birds' efficient hearts and body temperature control support the theory that at least small predatory dinosaurs had been warm-blooded just as birds and mammals are. Most scientists now reckon that theropod dinosaurs gave rise to birds in Late Jurassic times, about 150 million years ago.

The first known Mesozoic birds had feathered wings and tail but retained reptilian features: teeth, clawed fingers, solid not hollow

Birds and dinosaurs
Archaeopteryx (**A**) and *Compsognathus* (**B**) showed remarkable similarities.
a Bony tail core
b Simple ankle joint
c Long legs
d Short body
e No enlarged breastbone
f Teeth in long, slim jaws
g Slim, flexible neck
h Long, clawed fingers

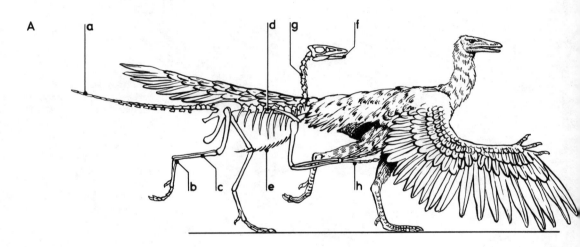

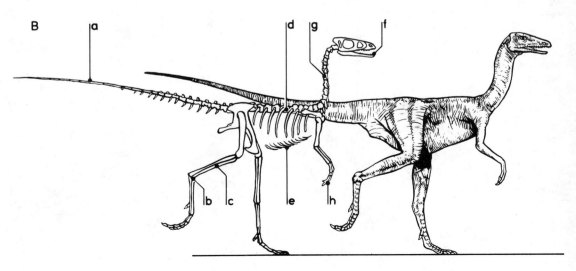

bones, and a bony tail core. Birds' feathers apparently evolved from frayed scales, at first perhaps better shaped to insulate the body than for use in flapping flight. Awkward early fliers such as *Archaeopteryx* seemingly gave rise in Cretaceous times to more modern looking yet still toothy waterbirds. Two of the best known of these probable fish-eaters were ternlike *Ichthyornis* ("fish bird"), and flightless diving *Hesperornis* ("western bird"), both from the shallow sea then bisecting North America. Toothed birds died out as the Mesozoic Era ended. But by then there were emerging loons, flamingoes, and other groups of truly modern waterbirds.

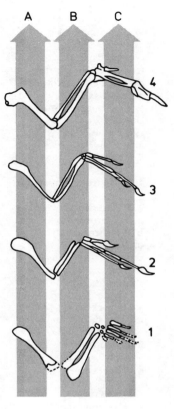

Early birds
Illustrations depict five early kinds of bird.
A *Ichthyornis* ("fish bird"), a small, toothed tern-like seabird from Late Cretaceous North America.
B *Baptornis* ("diving bird"), a flightless, toothed diving bird like *Hesporornis*, from Late Cretaceous North America.
C Flamingo
D Pelican
E Heron
(**CDE** are modern types perhaps evolved before the Mesozoic Era ended.)

Wings from arms
Four diagrams of bones trace the evolution of a bird's wing from a thecodont's arm and hand.
A Upper arm bone
B Forearm bones
C Bones of the hand
1 Primitive thecodont
2 Theropod dinosaur
3 *Archaeopteryx*
4 Pigeon, a modern bird. Its forearm and hand bones have become relatively long and finger bones have become one long structure strong enough to help support a wing capable of powerful flight.

© DIAGRAM

Dinosaur family tree

Ruling reptiles
This family tree shows the
likely evolution of
dinosaurs, birds,
crocodilians, and pterosaurs
from within the mixed
group of early archosaurs
called thecodonts. For
explanations of names see
chapters 2 and 3.
A Triassic Period
B Jurassic Period
C Cretaceous Period

1 Ancestral archosaurs

2 Thecodonts
a   Proterosuchians
b   Erythrosuchids
c   Rauisuchians
d   Aetosaurs
e   Phytosaurs (alias
     parasuchians)
f   Ornithosuchids
g   Euparkeriids
h   Lagosuchids

3 Crocodilians

4 Pterosaurs

5 Dinosaurs
i   Herrerasaurs

5A Saurischian dinosaurs
(**j-m** are flesh-eaters
collectively called theropods)
j   Deinonychosaurs
k   Oviraptorosaurs
l   Ornithomimosaurs
m   Carnosaurs and
     coelurosaurs
n   Segnosaurs
o   Prosauropods
p   Sauropods

**5B Ornithischian
dinosaurs**
q   Fabrosaurids
r   Scelidosaurs
s   Stegosaurs
t   Ankylosaurs
u   Ornithopods
v   Heterodontosaurids
w   Ceratopsians
x   Pachycephalosaurs

6 Birds

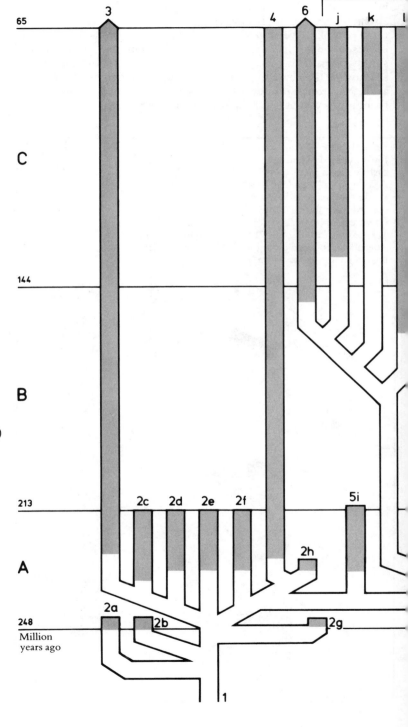

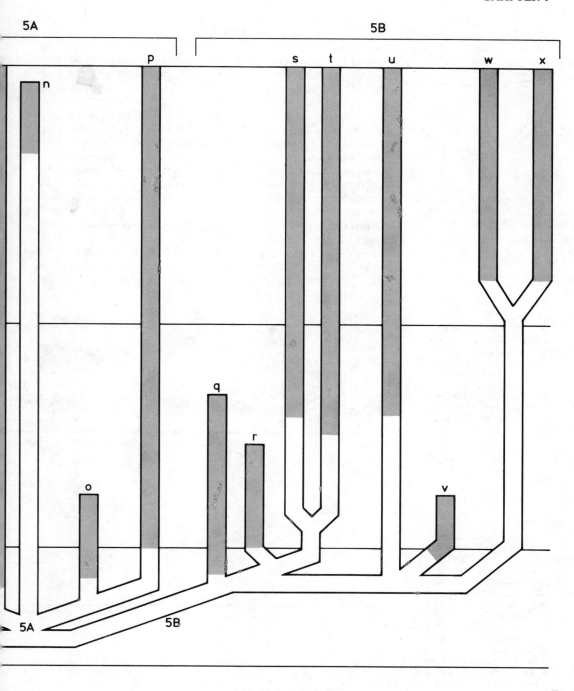

Tinted areas indicate solid fossil evidence

©DIAGRAM

Triassic world
Continents lay jammed
together. (Lines mark the
Equator and 30- and 60-
degree lines of latitude.)

Triassic time

The Triassic period (248–213 million years ago) marked the dawning of the Age of Dinosaurs. *Trias* ("three") refers to three rock layers laid down in Germany in Triassic times.

Lands and climates Landmasses lay fused together in the supercontinent Pangaea ("All Earth"), though this showed early signs of splitting into Laurasia (North America, Europe, and Asia) and Gondwana (South America, Africa, India, Antarctica, and Australia). Their eastern ends lay separated by a gulf, the Tethys Sea. The land was generally warm, but inland regions formed vast deserts cut off from rain-bearing oceanic winds.

Plants No grasses or other flowering plants had yet evolved. Moisture-loving ferns and horsetails grew by pools and streams. Taller plants included tree-like cycadeoids and cycads. Dry land supported ginkgoes and tall conifers resembling monkey puzzle trees and swamp cypress.

Dinosaurs Evolving it appears from lagosuchid thecodonts no bigger than a rabbit, the first known dinosaurs were late Middle Triassic predators no heavier than a big bull terrier. But by the end of Triassic time flesh-eating dinosaurs included beasts as heavy as a cow. Meanwhile, some early predatory dinosaur very likely gave

Triassic life
Right: Some plants and
animals of Triassic times
(not to the same scale).
Therapsids were advanced
mammal-like reptiles.
Protorosaurs and
rhynchosaurs belonged to
the reptile group that gave
rise to the thecodonts and
dinosaurs.

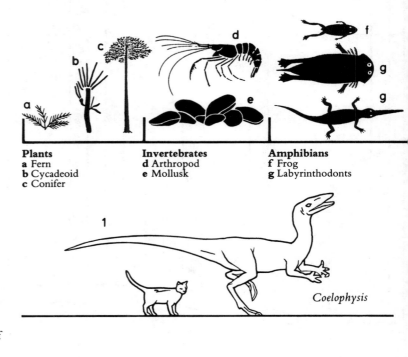

Plants	Invertebrates	Amphibians
a Fern	d Arthropod	f Frog
b Cycadeoid	e Mollusk	g Labyrinthodonts
c Conifer		

1

Coelophysis

Triassic dinosaurs
There were at least three
dinosaur suborders in
Triassic times. Shown right
is one example of each and
dinosaurs perhaps in other
major groups.
1 Theropoda
2 Herrerasauria (an order of
  primitive flesh-eating
  dinosaurs)
3 Sauropodomorpha
4 Suborder uncertain
(family Fabrosauridae)
5 Ornithopoda (if
Pisanosaurus was a
heterodontosaurid and
these were
ornithopods)

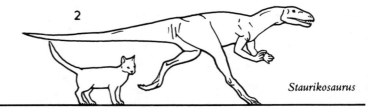

2

Staurikosaurus

rise to the first plant-eating dinosaurs. From small bipedal prosauropod plant-eaters like *Thecodontosaurus* emerged four-legged long-necked beasts as big as a bus. Yet bird-hipped dinosaurs, with teeth better than prosauropods' for chewing leaves, were late starters and stayed small throughout Triassic time. Without ocean barriers to stop them, dinosaurs might have colonized the world by 225 million years ago.

Other animals Triassic times followed the disappearance of many sprawling reptiles and amphibians that had ruled the land for millions of years. Advanced mammal-like reptiles now gave rise to mammals but themselves died out, perhaps killed off by thecodonts, reptiles in that new, successful group the archosaurs. Then thecodonts went too. Some experts think dinosaurs had wiped out these competitors; others believe thecodonts died off from some other cause. Either way, dinosaurs, pterosaurs, and crocodilians – all archosaurs or "ruling reptiles" – largely dominated life on land through Mesozoic time. Other novelties included frogs, salamanders, turtles, lizards, and, at sea, big reptiles that included those dolphin-like "fish lizards" ichthyosaurs.

Dinosaur families
Anchisaurids
Blikanasaurids
Coelophysids
Fabrosaurids
Halticosaurids
Herrerasaurids
Heterodontosaurids
Melanorosaurids
Plateosaurids
Staurikosaurids

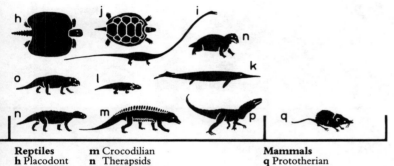

Reptiles
h Placodont
i Protorosaur
j Turtle
k Ichthyosaur
l Cotylosaur
m Crocodilian
n Therapsids
o Rhynchosaur
p Thecodont

Mammals
q Prototherian

Anchisaurus

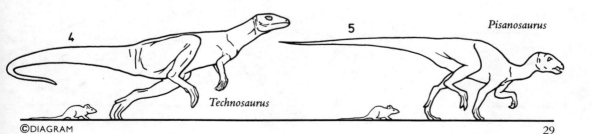
Technosaurus
Pisanosaurus

Jurassic time

Jurassic world
Continents were breaking
up and drifting apart.

Jurassic life
Right: Some plants and
animals of Jurassic times
(not to the same scale).

Jurassic dinosaurs
Shown below are examples
from dinosaur suborders
living in Jurassic times.
1 Theropoda
2 Sauropodomorpha
3 Suborder uncertain
(family Fabrosauridae)
4 Ornithopoda
5 Scelidosauria
6 Stegosauria
7 Ankylosauria
8 Pachycephalosauria

The Jurassic Period (213–144 million years ago) formed the middle
of the Age of Dinosaurs. Its name comes from rocks laid down in
what became the Jura Mountains of France and Switzerland.
Lands and climates Rifting of the Earth's crust released great lava
flows, opened the Atlantic Ocean, and split the supercontinent
Pangaea into (northern) Laurasia and (southern) Gondwana, itself
already breaking up. Yet, until late on, dinosaurs evidently still
crossed the world unhindered. Old mountains were now worn
away to stubs, and shallow seas invaded much of North America
and Europe, so seaborne winds brought rain to deserts that had
once been deep inland. Climates almost everywhere were warm or
mild.
Plants Tree-like cycads and stubby, palm-like cycadeoids, also
ginkgoes, ferns, and tree ferns clothed river banks in forest. Tall
sequoias and other conifers throve on drier ground.
Dinosaurs New kinds now replaced old ones, less well equipped
for eating leaves or killing prey. Some groups enormously
increased in size. Prosauropods gave way to the immense,
long-necked, high-browsing sauropods, the land's largest-ever

Plants	Invertebrates	Fishes
a Conifer	**d** Tentaculate	**g** Bony fish
b Cycadeoid	**e** Arthropod	**h** Chondrichthyan
c Ginkgo	**f** Mollusks	

Compsognathus

Diplodocus

Fabrosaurus

Dryosaurus

herbivores. Meanwhile small bipedal bird-hipped plant-eaters like
Fabrosaurus gave rise to bigger beasts with toothless beaks and
cheek teeth ideal for cropping and chewing low leafy plants or
fungi. The bird-footed group of bird-hipped dinosaurs now ranged
from small lively hypsilophodontids to bulky camptosaurids.
There were also early bone-heads and four-legged plated and
armored dinosaurs.

Most herbivores lived at risk from megalosaurids, allosaurids, or
other huge sharp-fanged predators. Smaller hunters including
coelurids and compsognathids scavenged at their kills or darted
after early birds and lizards. Birds themselves seemingly evolved
from predators resembling little *Compsognathus*.

Other animals Dominated by the dinosaurs, no land animals
could rival these for size. Jurassic mammals were largely small
nocturnal burrowers or climbers. Skin-winged, furry-bodied
pterosaurs flapped and glided through the air. Large freshwater
animals included prehistoric crocodilians. Shallow seas were home
to more big prehistoric reptiles – especially the ichthyosaurs and
short-necked plesiosaurs, both with limbs evolved as flippers.

Dinosaur families
Allosaurids
Anchisaurids
Archaeopterygids
Barapasaurids
Brachiosaurids
Camarasaurids
Camptosaurids
Ceratosaurids
Cetiosaurids
Chaoyoungosaurids
Coelophysids
Coelurids
Compsognathids
Dicraeosaurids
Diplodocids
Dryosaurids
Euhelopodids
Eustreptospondylids
Fabrosaurids
Halticosaurids
Heterodontosaurids
Hypsilophodontids
Huayangosaurids
Megalosaurids
Melanorosaurids
Nodosaurids
Ornithomimids
Plateosaurids
Scelidosaurids
Scutellosaurids
Stegosaurids
Titanosaurids
Torvosaurids
Yunnanosaurids
Vulcanodontids

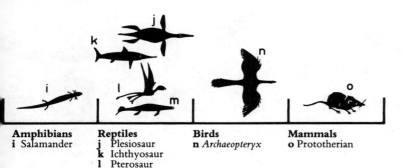

Amphibians
i Salamander

Reptiles
j Plesiosaur
k Ichthyosaur
l Pterosaur
m Crocodilian

Birds
n *Archaeopteryx*

Mammals
o Prototherian

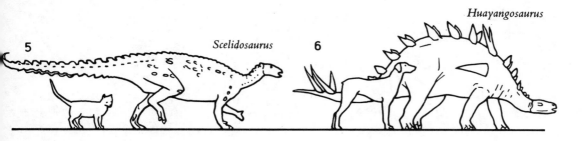

5 *Scelidosaurus*
6 *Huayangosaurus*

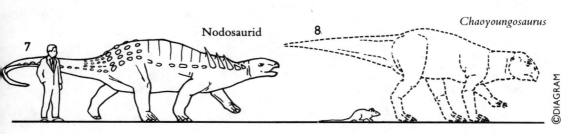

7 Nodosaurid
8 *Chaoyoungosaurus*

©DIAGRAM

31

Cretaceous time

Cretaceous world
Most continents had almost reached today's positions. India was still an island.

Cretaceous life
Right: Some Cretaceous plants and animals (not to the same scale).

Cretaceous dinosaurs
Shown below are examples from the dinosaur suborders living in Cretaceous times.
1 Theropoda
2 Sauropodomorpha
3 Segnosauria
4 Ornithopoda
5 Stegosauria
6 Ankylosauria
7 Pachycephalosauria
8 Ceratopsia

The Cretaceous Period (144–65 million years ago) marked the last and longest part of the Age of Dinosaurs. Its name comes from the Latin *creta* ("chalk"), for chalky layers accumulated on the beds of some shallow, warm Cretaceous seas.

Lands and climates Invading shallow seas helped split the northern supercontinent Laurasia into Asiamerica (East Asia with western North America) and Euramerica (Europe with eastern North America). Mountains grew. Clearcut seasons emerged. Southern continents formed islands, isolating different groups of dinosaurs.

Plants Flowering plants diversified. By Late Cretaceous times, hickories, oaks, and magnolias thrived in North America.

Dinosaurs Toothless birdlike dinosaurs appeared and tyrannosaurids, the heaviest known land predators, were ranged against new and powerfully protected plant-eaters: the armored ankylosaurs and horned ceratopsians. Low-browsing horned and

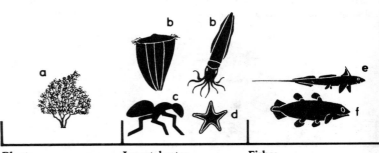

Plants
a Flowering plant

Invertebrates
b Mollusks
c Arthropod
d Echinoderm

Fishes
e Chondrichthyan
f Sarcopterygian

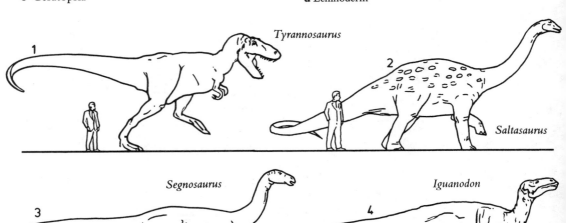

Tyrannosaurus

Saltasaurus

Segnosaurus

Iguanodon

duck-billed dinosaurs with jaws and teeth for chewing tough-leaved plants now heavily outnumbered long-necked, high-browsing sauropods. But rifting continents isolated some newer groups of dinosaurs. Thus large horned dinosaurs are known only from North America. Yet duck-billed dinosaurs occur in South and North America, and armored dinosaurs lived as far south as Antarctica and Australia. As the Cretaceous ended, the dinosaurs' diversity diminished and all became extinct.

Other animals Dinosaurs shared Late Cretaceous western North America with the largest known pterosaur *Quetzalcoatlus* ("feathered serpent"), and with modern-looking frogs, salamanders, turtles, lizards, snakes, crocodiles, waterbirds, and small mammals including opossums. Those great flippered lizards mosasaurs and the long-necked plesiosaurs were now the chief seagoing reptiles.

Dinosaur families
Abelisaurids
Allosaurids
Ankylosaurids
Aublysodontids
Avimimids
Baryonychids
Brachiosaurids
Caenagnathids
Camarasaurids
Camptosaurids
Ceratopsids
Cetiosaurids
Chubutisaurids
Coelurids
Deinocheirids
Diplodocids
Dromaeosaurids
Dryosaurids
Dryptosaurids
Enigmosaurids
Euhelopodids
Eustreptospondylids
Garudimimids
Hadrosaurids
Homalocephalids
Hypsilophodontids
Iguanodontids
Ingeniids
Itemirids
Lambeosaurids
Megalosaurids
Noasaurids
Nodosaurids
Ornithomimids
Oviraptorids
Pachycephalosaurids
Protoceratopsids
Psittacosaurids
Segnosaurids
Spinosaurids
Stegosaurids
Therizinosaurids
Thescelosaurids
Titanosaurids
Troodontids
Tyrannosaurids

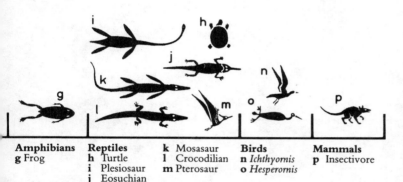

Amphibians
g Frog

Reptiles
h Turtle
i Plesiosaur
j Eosuchian
k Mosasaur
l Crocodilian
m Pterosaur

Birds
n *Ichthyornis*
o *Hesperornis*

Mammals
p Insectivore

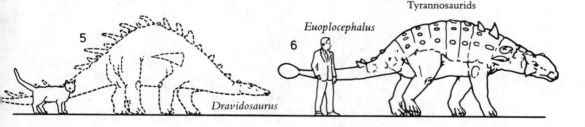

5 *Dravidosaurus*

6 *Euoplocephalus*

7 *Homalocephale*

8 *Torosaurus*

End of an age

About 65 million years ago dinosaurs, plesiosaurs, pterosaurs, and many other animals of land or sea became extinct. Just why remains a mystery that many scientists have sought to solve.

Most explanations prove badly flawed, among them these: dinosaurs evolved such awkward bodies that they could not move or breed; predatory dinosaurs ate the rest then starved; tiny mammals gobbled up the dinosaurs' eggs; new kinds of plants poisoned the dinosaurs; infectious germs caused a fatal dinosaur pandemic. These notions ignore the fact that dinosaurs were well designed for life in Mesozoic times, and fail to show why other creatures disappeared.

The most likely explanation is a drastic global change. Certain scientists have blamed deadly radiation from exploding stars or let in from the Sun by brief reversal of the Earth's magnetic field. By the 1980s evidence from rocks worldwide hinted at the Earth's collision with a massive asteroid or shower of asteroids – mini planets up to 6 miles (10km) across. Dust and moisture hurled into the air would have darkened the sky and chilled the world for months, killing countless plants and animals. Were dinosaurs

Mass extinctions
A diagram traces the rise and fall of 12 groups of backboned animals including dinosaurs.
A Paleozoic Era
B Mesozoic Era
C Cenozoic Era
1 Turtles
2 Ichthyosaurs
3 Plesiosaurs
4 Lizards and snakes
5 Birds
6 Saurischian dinosaurs
7 Ornithischian dinosaurs
8 Pterosaurs
9 Crocodilians
10 Thecodonts
11 Mammals
12 Mammal-like reptiles

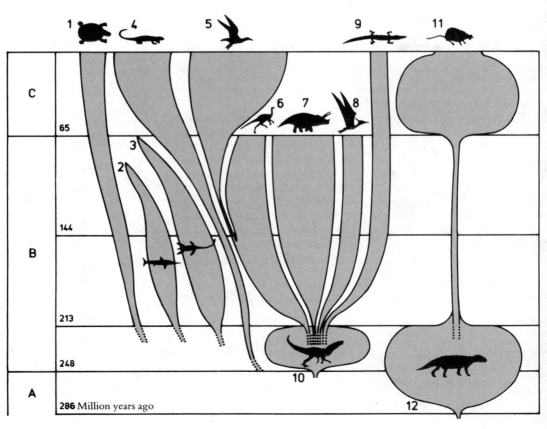

cold-blooded, most would have been too large to burrow to escape frost. Were they warm-blooded, without hair or feathers they could not have stored body heat. After the dust settled, moisture remaining in the air would have trapped the Sun's warmth near the ground. Overheating would have killed many creatures that had survived the cold.

By the 1990s some scientists believed a deadly global dust cloud had sprung up not from asteroid impact but from the vast volcanic eruptions that built India's great Deccan Plateau.

Yet other experts think dinosaurs and other creatures fizzled out quite slowly as shifting continents, rising mountains, and shrinking shallow seas chilled oceans and some lands and helped the spread of new creatures capable of outcompeting old.

Whatever happened, the Mesozoic Era ended and the Cenozoic began as birds and mammals took over from the dinosaurs and pterosaurs. But birds are arguably feathered theropods and there are more kinds of birds than mammals, so, in a way, The Age of Dinosaurs goes on.

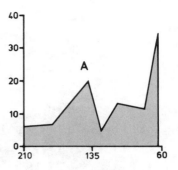

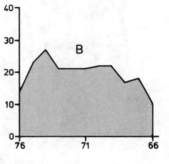

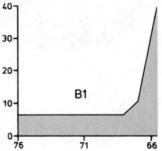

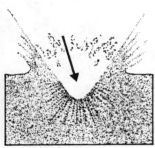

Bomb from space
Debris thrown up by an immense meteorite (a fallen asteroid) could have shut out sunlight, chilling lands and killing plants, so robbing dinosaurs and some other animals of vital warmth and nourishment.

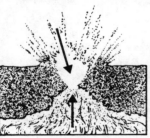

Asteroids and volcanoes
An asteroid punching through a weak spot in the Earth's crust might have triggered an immense volcanic eruption. Volcanic dust clouds causing global cooling might have finished off the dinosaurs.

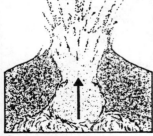

Volcanic devastation
A vast blob of molten rock rising from the Earth's core maybe sparked off an immense volcanic eruption that killed off the dinosaurs. Welling up at intervals, such blobs might cause periodic mass extinctions.

Two views of extinction
Diagrams based on conflicting evidence show two views of how dinosaurs declined and disappeared.
Vertical scales show numbers of genera.
Horizontal scales show millions of years ago.
A Rapid disappearance as if by some catastrophe.
B Gradual dinosaur decline, as if due to climatic change.
B1 Rise of mammals, perhaps enabled by climatic change to compete effectively with dinosaurs.

35

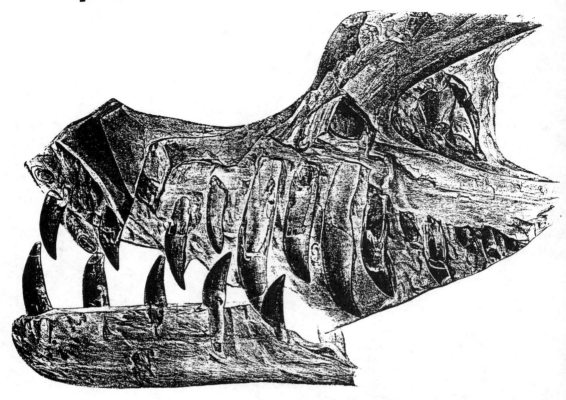

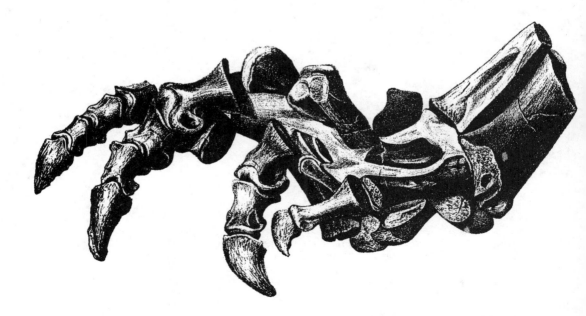

THE A TO Z OF DINOSAURS

Entries list all dinosaur genera known when this chapter went to press, plus families, higher groups, and many of the dinosaurs' kin and contemporaries.

For most dinosaurs we can explain scientific names, classify, locate in time and place, and give a brief description. But some are undescribed and many are known only from teeth or scraps of bone. For these, descriptions must be partly guesswork, and dinosaurs of doubtful identity are mainly shown as silhouettes.

Chironyms (handy unofficial names) appear in quotes where no official name exists. "Former names" (more properly called synonyms or invalid names) include discarded chironyms, names preoccupied by other animals, and duplications. (Many a "new" dinosaur proves a kind already given another name. Only the first formally published name is valid.)

Above: Part of the jaws of a *Megalosaurus*. Big, curved, pointed teeth help to show this was a large flesh-eating dinosaur.
Below: The right foot of a *Scelidosaurus*, a plant-eating dinosaur. Both illustrations figured in Sir Richard Owen's *A History of British Fossil Reptiles* (1849–84). Its British author gave dinosaurs the collective name they bear today.

Bars next to dinosaurs show likely lengths: 1½in (3.8cm)≈80ft (24m). A few sauropods were even longer than that.

Aachenosaurus – Aepisaurus

Abrictosaurus

Acanthopholis

Adasaurus

Aegyptosaurus

Aepisaurus

0   80ft (24m)

Aachenosaurus "Aachen lizard" Supposed hadrosaurid ornithopod that proved to be a piece of petrified wood.

Abelisaurids The family Abelisauridae INFRAORDER Carnosauria SUBORDER Theropoda ORDER Saurischia. Main entry in Chapter 3.

Abelisaurus "Abel's lizard" FAMILY Abelisauridae
INFRAORDER Carnosauria SUBORDER Theropoda ORDER Saurischia
TIME Late Cretaceous PLACE Patagonia, Argentina
DESCRIPTION A large flesh–eater with a deep, lightly built, mobile skull 2ft 11in (85cm) long. *Abelisaurus* probably weighed about 1.5 tons. It was named in 1985.

Abrictosaurus "awake lizard" FAMILY Heterodontosauridae
SUBORDER Ornithopoda ORDER Ornithischia
TIME Early Jurassic PLACE Lesotho, southern Africa
DESCRIPTION A small, speedy, bipedal plant-eater about 4ft (1.2m) long. This early ornithischian dinosaur's tuskless skull suggests it might have been a female *Heterodontosaurus*.

Acanthopholis "thorn bearer" FAMILY Nodosauridae
SUBORDER Ankylosauria ORDER Ornithischia
TIME Early and Late Cretaceous PLACE southern England
DESCRIPTION An armored dinosaur about 18ft (5.5m) long with neck spikes, rows of raised plates down the body, and maybe tail plates. Identity doubtful.

Acrocanthosaurus "top spined lizard" FAMILY Allosauridae?
INFRAORDER Carnosauria SUBORDER Theropoda ORDER Saurischia
TIME Early Cretaceous PLACE Oklahoma and Texas
DESCRIPTION A large flesh–eater maybe up to 40ft (12m) long and weighing 2-3 tons. Spines more than 12in (30cm) high rising from its backbone produced a ridge or low skin sail that ran from neck to tail, perhaps serving as a radiator or identifying flag.

Adasaurus "Ada (a demon) lizard" FAMILY Dromaeosauridae
INFRAORDER Deinonychosauria SUBORDER Theropoda
ORDER Saurischia
TIME Late Cretaceous PLACE southern Mongolia
DESCRIPTION A lightweight predator about 7ft (2m) long and weighing about 33lb (15kg). Each foot had a switchblade toe claw. The backward pointing pubic bones produced a hip structure more like that of birds than typical saurischian dinosaurs.

Aegyptosaurus "Egyptian lizard" FAMILY Titanosauridae
INFRAORDER Sauropoda SUBORDER Sauropodomorpha
ORDER Saurischia
TIME Late Cretaceous PLACE northern Africa
DESCRIPTION A sauropod estimated to have reached a length of 52ft 6in (16m). It is only known from limb bones found in Egypt (but lost in World War II) and bones from northwest Africa.

Aeolosaurus "wind lizard" FAMILY Titanosauridae
INFRAORDER Sauropoda SUBORDER Sauropodomorpha
ORDER Saurischia TIME Late Cretaceous PLACE Argentina
DESCRIPTION Large four-legged plant-eater seemingly with long neck and tail. Formally described in 1988.

Aepisaurus "elephant lizard" FAMILY Titanosauridae
INFRAORDER Sauropoda SUBORDER Sauropodomorpha
ORDER Saurischia
TIME Early Cretaceous PLACE southern France

DESCRIPTION Apparently a relatively small sauropod up to 49ft (15m) long, but known mainly from an arm bone. Identity doubtful.

Aetonyx "old claw" A former name of *Massospondylus*.

Aetosaurs "old lizards" SUBORDER Aetosauria ORDER Thecodontia TIME Late Triassic PLACE Europe and North and South America DESCRIPTION Armored relatives of dinosaurs up to 10ft (3m) long, with small, leaf-shaped teeth; the only plant-eating thecodonts.

Aetosaurs

Agathaumas "marvelous" FAMILY Ceratopsidae SUBORDER Ceratopsia ORDER Ornithischia TIME Late Cretaceous PLACE Wyoming, USA DESCRIPTION This horned dinosaur was named from limb bones, vertebrae and other bones that do not clearly separate it from all other horned dinosaurs. Some scientists have thought it might be *Triceratops* or *Brachyceratops*. Identity doubtful.

Agrosaurus "field lizard" FAMILY Anchisauridae INFRAORDER Prosauropoda SUBORDER Sauropodomorpha ORDER Saurischia TIME Early Jurassic? PLACE Queensland, Australia DESCRIPTION Small herbivorous dinosaur known from a claw and a few bones. Once thought to be *Thecodontosaurus*.

Agrosaurus

Alamosaurus "Alamo lizard" FAMILY Titanosauridae INFRAORDER Sauropoda SUBORDER Sauropodomorpha ORDER Saurischia TIME Late Cretaceous PLACE Montana, New Mexico, Texas, Utah DESCRIPTION A sauropod up to 69ft (21m) long and weighing up to 30 tons. The name comes from its fossils in the Ojo Alamo Formation. This last known sauropod was North America's only known titanosaurid.

Alamosaurus

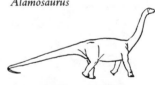

Albertosaurus "Alberta lizard" FAMILY Tyrannosauridae INFRAORDER Carnosauria SUBORDER Theropoda ORDER Saurischia TIME Late Cretaceous PLACE Canada, USA, and ? Mexico DESCRIPTION Like *Tyrannosaurus* but less immense, with a lower, longer-snouted skull, and more backward-pointing teeth. It grew up to 26ft (8m) long and some individuals weighed over 2 tons. There might have been smaller, lighter species, too.

Albisaurus "white lizard" FAMILY unknown INFRAORDER unknown SUBORDER perhaps Theropoda ORDER perhaps Saurischia TIME Early Late Cretaceous PLACE Czechoslovakia DESCRIPTION Known only from scrappy fossils that have been called variously theropod, iguanodontid, and non dinosaur.

Alectrosaurus "eagle lizard" FAMILY Tyrannosauridae INFRAORDER Carnosauria SUBORDER Theropoda ORDER Saurischia TIME Late Cretaceous PLACE China, Mongolia, and ?USSR DESCRIPTION A large flesh-eater resembling a smaller version of *Albertosaurus* It was about 16ft (5m) long, weighed maybe less than half a ton, and had short, sharp teeth, slim shoulder blades, and long slender hind limbs. Maybe close kin of *Alioramus*.

Albertosaurus

Algoasaurus "Algoa lizard" FAMILY Camarasauridae INFRAORDER Sauropoda SUBORDER Sauropodomorpha ORDER Saurischia TIME Early Cretaceous PLACE Algoa Bay, South Africa

© DIAGRAM

39

Alioramus – Ammosaurus

Alioramus

Aliwalia

Allosaurus

Alocodon

Altispinax

DESCRIPTION A small sauropod, whose 19in (50cm) thigh bone suggests a total length of only 30ft (9m). Experts formerly assigned its scanty, problematic remains to the Titanosauridae.

Alioramus "other branch" FAMILY Tyrannosauridae
INFRAORDER Carnosauria SUBORDER Therapoda ORDER Saurischia
TIME Early Late Cretaceous PLACE Mongolia
DESCRIPTION An unusual tyrannosaurid about 20ft (6m) long and maybe weighing three quarters of a ton. Its large, low head had a slim, straight lower jaw, and a series of short crests above the snout. The teeth were long, curved, and sharp.

Aliwalia "Aliwal" FAMILY ? SUBORDER? ORDER Herrerasauria
TIME Late Triassic PLACE near Aliwal North, South Africa
DESCRIPTION One of the earliest large flesh-eating dinosaurs, perhaps weighing 1.5 tons, as much as *Allosaurus*. The only fossils certainly from *Aliwalia* are bits of thigh bone found a century ago but not properly identified until 1985.

Allosaurids The family Allosauridae
INFRAORDER Carnosauria SUBORDER Theropoda
ORDER Saurischia. Main entry in Chapter 3.

Allosaurus "different lizard" FAMILY Allosauridae
INFRAORDER Carnosauria SUBORDER Theropoda ORDER Saurischia
TIME Late Jurassic PLACE North America, Africa, Australia, maybe Asia
DESCRIPTION Large flesh-eater about 36ft (11m) long and weighing about 1.5 tons. The big head, S-shaped "bulldog" neck, and bulky body were balanced by a long, deep, tail; powerful hind limbs with clawed feet; and short strong three-fingered forelimbs with large, sharp claws. The top of the head had bony ridges and bumps, and jaws held serrated, blade-like teeth. This was the most abundant predator in Late Jurassic North America.

Alocodon "wing tooth" FAMILY Fabrosauridae (Hypsilophodontidae?)
SUBORDER Ornithopoda? ORDER Ornithischia
TIME Late Jurassic PLACE Portugal
DESCRIPTION Small, light, bipedal plant-eater, maybe with five-fingered hands. Perhaps 3ft 3in (1m) long, but known only from the wing- shaped teeth from which it gets its name.

Altispinax "high spines" FAMILY Megalosauridae
INFRAORDER Carnosauria SUBORDER Theropoda ORDER Saurischia
TIME Early Cretaceous PLACE southeast England and Germany
DESCRIPTION Large flesh-eater perhaps 26ft (8m) long, with tall spines rising from its backbone to support a skin sail serving as radiator or identifying flag. Identity doubtful (partly based on other theropods' remains) and name liable to change.

Amargasaurus "Amarga lizard" FAMILY Dicraeosauridae
INFRAORDER Sauropoda SUBORDER Sauropodomorpha
ORDER Saurischia
TIME Early Cretaceous PLACE La Amarga in Argentina
DESCRIPTION Bulky plant-eater to be described, but evidently with high, forked spines projecting from some vertebrae.

Ammosaurus "sand lizard" FAMILY Plateosauridae
INFRAORDER Prosauropoda SUBORDER Sauropodomorpha
ORDER Saurischia

0   80ft (24m)

TIME Early Jurassic PLACE Connecticut and Arizona, USA
DESCRIPTION Prosauropod about 8ft (2.4m) long. It was a browser
with a small head, long neck, bulky body, small feet, big hands
with large thumb claws, and a long tail. It mainly walked on all
fours but might have stood on hind limbs to feed.

Ammosaurus

Amphibians The vertebrate class Amphibia, including frogs, toads,
and salamanders. Many of these backboned, cold-blooded animals
live on land but most must lay their unprotected, shell-less eggs in
water. Prehistoric amphibians gave rise to reptiles ancestral to
dinosaurs, birds, modern reptiles, and mammals.

Amphicoelias "with hollow-ended vertebrae"
FAMILY Diplodocidae INFRAORDER Sauropoda
SUBORDER Sauropodomorpha ORDER Saurischia
TIME Late Jurassic PLACE Colorado, USA
DESCRIPTION Large four-footed plant-eater with long neck and tail:
a long sauropod with slender limbs, but known from incomplete
remains. Identity doubtful.

Amphicoelias

Amphisaurus "double lizard" A former name of *Anchisaurus*.

Amtosaurus "Amtgay lizard" FAMILY Ankylosauridae?
SUBORDER Ankylosauria? ORDER Ornithischia
TIME Late Cretaceous PLACE Bayn Shire, Mongolia
DESCRIPTION Probably an armored dinosaur about 23ft (7m) long
but known only from part of a skull. This might have come from
the armored dinosaur *Talarurus* or even from a hadrosaur.

Amygdalodon "almond tooth" FAMILY Cetiosauridae
INFRAORDER Sauropoda SUBORDER Sauropodomorpha
ORDER Saurischia
TIME Mid Jurassic PLACE southern Argentina
DESCRIPTION Large four-footed plant-eater with a long neck and
tail; one of the more "advanced" of those primitive sauropods the
cetiosaurids. Its known remains are vertebrae, fragments of bone,
and distinctive almond-shaped teeth.

Amtosaurus

Anapsids The subclass Anapsida: reptiles without holes in the sides
of the skull behind the eyes. Some were the first-known reptiles.
Anapsids include the extinct captorhinomorphs, millerosaurs,
procolophonoids, pareiasaurs, and mesosaurs, and, arguably,
turtles. Prehistoric anapsids gave rise to other reptile groups and,
indirectly, to the birds and mammals.

Anatosaurus "duck lizard" A name once given to the hadrosaurs
Edmontosaurus and "Anatotitan."

"Anatotitan" "giant duck" FAMILY Hadrosauridae
SUBORDER Ornithopoda ORDER Ornithischia
TIME Late Cretaceous PLACE North America
DESCRIPTION A duck-billed dinosaur perhaps 40ft (12.2m) long,
once called *Anatosaurus*, being formally described.

Anchiceratops

Anchiceratops "similar horned face" FAMILY Ceratopsidae
SUBORDER Ceratopsia ORDER Ornithischia
TIME Late Cretaceous PLACE Alberta, Canada
DESCRIPTION A long-frilled horned dinosaur measuring about 16ft
(4.8m). It had a massive head with a horny beak, two long horns
above the eyes, a short nose horn, and a long bony frill (with bony
studs only at the back) covering the shoulders.

©DIAGRAM

Anchisaurids The family Anchisauridae

Anchisaurus – Apatosaurus

Anchisaurus

Ankylosaurus

Anserimimus

Antarctosaurus

Apatosaurus

0   80ft (24m)

INFRAORDER Prosauropoda SUBORDER Sauropodomorpha
ORDER Saurischia. See also Chapter 3.

Anchisaurus "near lizard" FAMILY Anchisauridae
INFRAORDER Prosauropoda SUBORDER Sauropodomorpha
ORDER Saurischia
TIME Early Jurassic PLACE northeast USA and ?China
DESCRIPTION Small, lightweight prosauropod about 7ft (2.1m) long
and weighing 60lb (27kg). It had a small, slim-snouted head with
ridged teeth suitable for shredding leaves, a long neck, body, and
tail, and large, curved thumb claws. It probably walked on all
fours, but could have reared to feed.

Ankylosaurids The family Ankylosauridae
SUBORDER Ankylosauria ORDER Ornithischia. See also Chapter 3.

Ankylosaurs The armored dinosaurs
SUBORDER Ankylosauria ORDER Ornithischia. See also Chapter 3.

Ankylosaurus "fused lizard" FAMILY Ankylosauridae
SUBORDER Ankylosauria ORDER Ornithischia
TIME Late Cretaceous PLACE Canada (Alberta) and USA (Montana)
DESCRIPTION A "living tank" up to 35ft (10.7m) long with an
armored head and horny beak; neck, shoulders, and back encased in
tough skin reinforced by raised, bony plates and spikes; four
powerful limbs; and a tail armed with a bony club.

Anodontosaurus "toothless lizard" Name once given to a fossil
find that proved to be the armored dinosaur *Dyoplosaurus*.

Anoplosaurus "unarmored lizard" FAMILY Iguanodontidae
SUBORDER Ornithopoda ORDER Ornithischia
TIME Early Cretaceous PLACE eastern England
DESCRIPTION A large plant-eater that is only poorly known from
worn and broken bones. Identity doubtful.

Anserimimus "goose mimic" FAMILY Ornithomimidae
INFRAORDER Ornithomimosauria SUBORDER Theropoda
ORDER Saurischia
TIME Late Cretaceous PLACE southern Mongolia
DESCRIPTION An ostrich dinosaur with narrow hand claws;
described in 1988 from part of a skeleton including hand, foot, and
shoulder bones but no skull.

Antarctosaurus "southern lizard" FAMILY Titanosauridae
INFRAORDER Sauropoda SUBORDER Sauropodomorpha
ORDER Saurischia
TIME Late Cretaceous PLACE South America; ?India; Kazakhstan,
USSR
DESCRIPTION Huge, heavy, four-footed plant-eater with short, steep
face, large eyes, bulky body, and slim hind limbs. It might have
measured more than 60ft (18m) and weighed 40-50 tons.

Anthodon "flower tooth" Name once given to the stegosaur now
called *Paranthodon*.

Antrodemus "strongly framed" Name (based on half a hollowed
tail vertebra) given in 1870 to a theropod, perhaps the same kind as
subsequently named *Allosaurus*. Identity doubtful.

Apatodon "deceptive tooth" Name once given to remains (now
lost) suspected to belong to *Allosaurus*. Identity doubtful.

Apatosaurus "deceptive lizard" FAMILY Diplodocidae
INFRAORDER Sauropoda SUBORDER Sauropodomorpha

ORDER Saurischia
TIME Late Jurassic PLACE USA (Colorado, Oklahoma, Utah, Wyoming) and maybe Mexico
DESCRIPTION Huge four-footed plant-eater up to 70ft (21m) long, 14ft 6in (4.5m) high at the shoulder, and weighing more than 20 tons. It had a small, low head, long thick neck, relatively short heavy body, heavy legs, and long, whiplash tail.

Aragosaurus "Aragon lizard" FAMILY Camarasauridae
INFRAORDER Sauropoda SUBORDER Sauropodomorpha
ORDER Saurischia
TIME Early Cretaceous PLACE Teruel, eastern Spain
DESCRIPTION Huge, four-footed plant-eater with short, deep head, long neck, bulky body, and long tail. Named in 1987 from fossils including a shoulder blade and tail bones. This represents the first discovery in Spain of a hitherto unknown dinosaur.

Aralosaurus

Aralosaurus "Aral lizard" FAMILY Hadrosauridae
SUBORDER Ornithopoda ORDER Ornithischia
TIME Late Cretaceous PLACE near the Aral Sea, Kazakhstan, USSR
DESCRIPTION Early duck-billed dinosaur known from an incomplete skull with a *Hadrosaurus*-like low bulge in front of the eyes. Reportedly it revealed hitherto unknown differences between hadrosaurs' upper and lower teeth.

Archaeopterygids The family Archaeopterygidae
INFRAORDER Coelurosauria SUBORDER Theropoda ORDER Saurischia
Main entry in Chapter 3.

Archaeopteryx

Archaeopteryx "ancient wing" FAMILY Archaeopterygidae
INFRAORDER Coelurosauria SUBORDER Theropoda ORDER Saurischia
TIME Late Jurassic PLACE Bavaria, West Germany
DESCRIPTION A crow-sized "feathered dinosaur," also considered the first known bird. It was 3ft (about 1m) long, with sharp teeth, long, bony tail core, and clawed fingers on wings; the sole known member of its family. See Chapter 3.

Archaeornis "ancient bird" Name once used for *Archaeopteryx*.

Archaeornithomimus "ancient bird mimic" FAMILY
Ornithomimidae INFRAORDER Ornithomimosauria
SUBORDER Theropoda ORDER Saurischia
TIME Mid Early to Early Late Cretaceous
PLACE north China and eastern North America
DESCRIPTION An early ostrich dinosaur known from fragments including curved claws possibly more primitive than those of later ostrich dinosaurs.

Archaeornithomimus

Archosaurs "ruling lizards" or "ruling reptiles" The superorder Archosauria: reptiles including past and present crocodilians and the extinct thecodonts, pterosaurs, and dinosaurs. All belong within the infraclass Archosauromorpha, along with the extinct protorosaurs and trilophosaurs.

Arctosaurus "Arctic lizard" FAMILY unknown INFRAORDER
unknown SUBORDER Sauropodomorpha? ORDER Saurischia?
TIME Late Triassic? PLACE Cameron Island, Canada
DESCRIPTION Known only from one vertebra, arguably not a dinosaur's, found north of the Arctic Circle. Identity doubtful.

Argyrosaurus "silver lizard" FAMILY Titanosauridae
INFRAORDER Sauropoda SUBORDER Sauropodomorpha

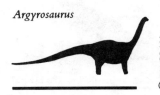
Argyrosaurus

© DIAGRAM

Aristosuchus

Arrhinoceratops

Arstanosaurus

Asiatosaurus

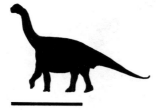

Astrodon

0   80ft (24m)

Aristosaurus – Atlantosaurus

ORDER Saurischia
TIME Late Cretaceous   PLACE Argentina and Uruguay
DESCRIPTION huge four-footed plant-eater maybe 70ft (21m) long. It had a long neck and tail, and massive limbs, with thigh bones measuring 6ft 6in (2.1m). Its name comes from the Latin *argentum* (Argentina means "land of silver.")

Aristosaurus "best lizard" Name once given to a prosauropod now considered to be *Massospondylus*.

Aristosuchus "best crocodile" Name once given to a coelurid now considered to be *Calamospondylus*.

"Arkanosaurus" See "Arkansaurus."

"Arkansaurus" "Arkansas lizard" FAMILY Ornithomimidae
INFRAORDER Ornithomimosauria SUBORDER Theropoda
ORDER Saurischia
TIME Cretaceous PLACE Arkansas, USA
DESCRIPTION An ostrich dinosaur named from foot bones and awaiting formal identification; possibly a specimen of *Archaeornithomimus*. Identity doubtful.

Armored dinosaurs The SUBORDER Ankylosauria. See Chapter 3.

Arrhinoceratops "no nose-horned face" FAMILY Ceratopsidae
SUBORDER Ceratopsia ORDER Ornithischia
TIME Late Cretaceous PLACE Alberta, Canada
DESCRIPTION A horned dinosaur with long, pointed brow horns, a short nose horn, and a bony neck frill lightened by two "windows" and rimmed by bony studs.

Arstanosaurus "Arstan lizard" FAMILY Hadrosauridae?
SUBORDER Ornithopoda ORDER Ornithischia
TIME Late Cretaceous PLACE Kazakhstan, USSR
DESCRIPTION Young, flat-headed, duck-billed dinosaur described in 1982 from several fossils including a bit of upper jaw that might come from a horned dinosaur.

Asiatosaurus "Asian lizard" FAMILY Camarasauridae
INFRAORDER Sauropoda SUBORDER Sauropodomorpha
ORDER Saurischia
TIME Early Cretaceous PLACE Mongolia and China
DESCRIPTION Large four-footed plant-eater with long neck and tail; named mainly from teeth. Identity doubtful.

Astrodon "star tooth" FAMILY Brachiosauridae
INFRAORDER Sauropoda SUBORDER Sauropodomorpha
ORDER Saurischia
TIME Early Cretaceous PLACE USA, and maybe South Africa and England
DESCRIPTION Large four-footed plant-eater with long neck and tail; a relatively small sauropod but maybe more than 33ft (10m) long. Largely known by spoon-shaped teeth. Some supposed finds are juveniles of other genera.

Atlantosaurus "Atlas lizard" FAMILY Diplodocidae?
INFRAORDER Sauropoda SUBORDER Sauropodomorpha
ORDER Saurischia
TIME Late Jurassic PLACE Colorado, USA
DESCRIPTION Huge four-footed plant-eater 75 feet (23m) long, with long neck and tail. The best *Atlantosaurus* fossils proved to be *Apatosaurus*. Others are of doubtful identity.

Atlascopcosaurus "Atlas Copco lizard" FAMILY Hypsilophodontidae
SUBORDER Ornithopoda ORDER Ornithischia
TIME Early Cretaceous PLACE Victoria, Australia
DESCRIPTION Small, agile bipedal plant-eater up to 9ft (2.7m) long, known from teeth and partial upper jaw. Named in 1989 to honor the Atlas Copco Corporation whose gear aided excavation.

Aublysodon "?blunt tooth" FAMILY Aublysodontidae
INFRAORDER Carnosauria SUBORDER Theropoda ORDER Saurischia
TIME Late Cretaceous PLACE Montana, USA; Alberta, Canada; China
DESCRIPTION Big-game hunter akin to *Tyrannosaurus* but far lighter at about 440lb (200kg), with slim lower jaw, sharp snout, and smooth, not serrated, front fangs.

Aublysodontids The family Aublysodontidae
INFRAORDER Carnosauria
SUBORDER Theropoda ORDER Saurischia
TIME Late Cretaceous PLACE Montana, USA; and China (Xinjiang)
DESCRIPTION Small big-game hunters akin to *Tyrannosaurus*. *Aublysodon* weighed maybe 440lb (200kg); *Shanshanosaurus* was about 8ft (2.5m) long. Skeletons are incompletely known.

Austrosaurus "southern lizard" FAMILY Cetiosauridae
INFRAORDER Sauropoda SUBORDER Sauropodomorpha
ORDER Saurischia
TIME Early-Mid Cretaceous PLACE Queensland, Australia
DESCRIPTION Large, four-footed plant-eater some 50ft (15m) long with long neck and tail, and relatively long front limbs due to elongated "wrist" bones. A relatively primitive sauropod.

Avaceratops "Ava horned face" FAMILY Ceratopsidae
SUBORDER Ceratopsia ORDER Ornithischia
TIME Late Cretaceous PLACE Montana, USA
DESCRIPTION Small horned dinosaur (juvenile?) about 8ft (2.5m) long, with one short nose horn and a short bony neck frill. Named in 1986 for the wife of its discoverer.

Avalonianus "of Avalon" Supposed prosauropod dinosaur identified from a tooth, now thought to be an ornithosuchid thecodont's.

Avimimids The family Avimimidae INFRAORDER Oviroptorosauria SUBORDER Theropoda ORDER Saurischia. Main entry in Chapter 3.

Avimimus "bird mimic" FAMILY Avimimidae
INFRAORDER Oviroptorosauria SUBORDER Theropoda ORDER Saurischia
TIME Late Cretaceous PLACE southern Mongolia and China
DESCRIPTION The most birdlike dinosaur: a 5ft (1.5m) long biped, with short, deep head, toothless beak, long neck and tail, long hind limbs, and maybe feathered wings.

Avipes "bird foot" FAMILY Coelophysidae INFRAORDER Coelurosauria SUBORDER Theropoda ORDER Saurischia
TIME Late Triassic PLACE Thuringia, East Germany
DESCRIPTION Small bipedal predator maybe 4ft (1.2m) long, known from three fused birdlike foot bones. Identity doubtful.

Avisaurids The family Avisauridae INFRAORDER Coelurosauria SUBORDER Theropoda ORDER Saurischia. Proposed family of theropod dinosaurs (perhaps birds) based on *Avisaurus*.

Atlantosaurus

Atlascopcosaurus

Aublysodon

Austrosaurus

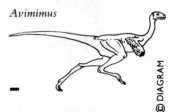
Avimimus

© DIAGRAM

Avisaurus – Barsboldia

Bactrosaurus

Avisaurus "bird lizard" FAMILY Avisauridae INFRAORDER
Coelurosauria? SUBORDER Theropoda? ORDER Saurischia?
TIME Late Cretaceous PLACE Montana, USA
DESCRIPTION Supposedly one of the last small predatory dinosaurs,
a primitive form named in 1984 but only known from fused foot
bones. Some think they came from a prehistoric type of bird.

Azendohsaurus "Azendoh lizard" FAMILY uncertain
INFRAORDER Prosauropoda SUBORDER Sauropodomorpha
ORDER Saurischia
TIME Early Late Triassic PLACE Morocco
DESCRIPTION Four-footed plant-eater about 6ft (1.8m) long, with
long neck and tail. One of the earliest dinosaurs, known only from
teeth and a scrap of jaw once thought a fabrosaurid's.

Bahariasaurus

Bactrosaurus "Bactrian lizard" FAMILY Lambeosauridae
SUBORDER Ornithopoda ORDER Ornithischia
TIME Early Late Cretaceous PLACE Central and East Asia
DESCRIPTION Relatively small duck-billed dinosaur 13-20ft (4-6m)
long, with a hadrosaurid-type flat head, lambeosaurid-type high-
spined vertebrae, and traces of iguanodontid ancestry.

Bagaceratops "small horned face" FAMILY Protoceratopsidae
SUBORDER Ceratopsia ORDER Ornithischia
TIME Late Cretaceous PLACE Mongolia
DESCRIPTION Tiny, squat horned dinosaur 3ft 3in (1m) long, with a
small nose horn and short neck frill.

Bahariasaurus "Baharije lizard" FAMILY uncertain
INFRAORDER uncertain SUBORDER Theropoda ORDER Saurischia
TIME Late Cretaceous PLACE Egypt, and maybe Algeria and Niger
DESCRIPTION Known from 4ft (1.2m) hip bones but lightly built;
perhaps related to the ornithomimids.

Barapasaurids The family Barapasauridae
INFRAORDER Sauropoda SUBORDER Sauropodomorpha
ORDER Saurischia. Known from primitive *Barapasaurus*, arguably in
the family Cetiosauridae.

Barapasaurus

Barapasaurus "big leg lizard" FAMILY Cetiosauridae (or arguably
Barapasauridae) INFRAORDER Sauropoda SUBORDER
Sauropodomorpha ORDER Saurischia
TIME Early Jurassic PLACE central India
DESCRIPTION huge four-footed plant-eater up to 60ft (18m) long,
with short deep head, saw-edged spoon-shaped teeth, long neck,
bulky body, slim limbs, and long tail; a primitive sauropod with
some prosauropod-like bones. Known from a number of
individuals.

Barosaurus "heavy lizard" FAMILY Diplodocidae INFRAORDER
Sauropoda SUBORDER Sauropodomorpha ORDER Saurischia
TIME Late Jurassic PLACE South Dakota and Wyoming, USA; and
Tanzania
DESCRIPTION Huge four-footed plant-eater (perhaps *Amphicoelias*)
75-90ft (23-27m) long, with low head, 30ft (9m) neck, bulky body,
and long tail. Tail shorter and neck longer than in *Diplodocus*.

Barosaurus

0   80ft (24m)

Barsboldia "Barsbold" FAMILY Lambeosauridae
SUBORDER Ornithopoda ORDER Ornithischia
TIME Late Cretaceous PLACE Mongolia

DESCRIPTION A large duck-billed dinosaur named in 1981 in honor
of Mongolian paleontologist **Rinchen Barsbold**.

Baryonychids The family Baryonychidae INFRAORDER
Carnosauria SUBORDER Theropoda ORDER Saurischia. Family
created to contain *Baryonyx*. Main entry in Chapter 3.

Baryonyx "heavy claw" FAMILY Baryonychidae
INFRAORDER Carnosauria SUBORDER Theropoda ORDER Saurischia
TIME Early Cretaceous PLACE southeast England
DESCRIPTION Large fish-eater about 30ft (9m) long, more than 10ft
(3m) tall, and weighing about 2 tons. It had a long, low
crocodile-like head, and relatively long arms, seemingly with great
claws on the thumbs. Named in 1986.

Baryonyx

Basutodon "Basuto tooth" Supposed theropod dinosaur identified
from a tooth now thought to be an ornithosuchid thecodont's.

Bellusaurus "?lizard" FAMILY Cetiosauridae INFRAORDER
Sauropoda SUBORDER Sauropodomorpha ORDER Saurischia
TIME Middle Jurassic PLACE Junggar Basin, northwest China
DESCRIPTION Very small sauropod about 16ft (5m) long with
relatively short neck and tail, and evidently small, deep head with
steeply sloping face. All finds might be of juveniles.

Basutodon

Betasuchus "B crocodile" FAMILY uncertain
INFRAORDER uncertain SUBORDER Theropoda
ORDER Saurischia
TIME Late Cretaceous PLACE southeast Netherlands
DESCRIPTION Known from a slim thigh bone; reputedly sole proof
of a European ostrich dinosaur. Identity doubtful.

Bird-hipped dinosaurs See Ornithischians.

Birds The class Aves: warm-blooded, backboned animals with
feathers. Some scientists see birds as a subclass of the class
Dinosauria or as a subdivision of the theropod dinosaurs.

Blikanasaurids The family Blikanasauridae
INFRAORDER Prosauropoda SUBORDER Sauropodomorpha ORDER
Saurischia. A family created to contain the unusual prosauropod
Blikanasaurus.

Betasuchus

Blikanasaurus "Blikana lizard" FAMILY Blikanasauridae
INFRAORDER Prosauropoda SUBORDER Sauropodomorpha
ORDER Saurischia
TIME Late Triassic PLACE Transkei, South Africa
DESCRIPTION Large, bulky, four-footed plant-eater with stockier
hindlimbs and stronger ankle bones than other prosauropods.

Bone-headed dinosaurs See **Pachycephalosaurids**;
Homalocephalids.

Borogovia "borogove" FAMILY Troodontidae
INFRAORDER Coelurosauria SUBORDER Theropoda ORDER Saurischia
TIME Late Cretaceous PLACE Mongolia
DESCRIPTION Small, speedy, carnivorous dinosaur with a sickle-
clawed foot; identified from its unusual foot bones and named in
1987 for Lewis Carroll's fictional borogoves.

Bothriospondylus "excavated vertebrae" FAMILY Brachiosauridae
INFRAORDER Sauropoda SUBORDER Sauropodomorpha
ORDER Saurischia
TIME Mid Jurassic-Early Cretaceous PLACE Europe and Madagascar
DESCRIPTION Four-footed plant-eater 49-66ft (15-20m) long maybe

Bothriospondylus

©DIAGRAM

Brachiosaurus

Brachylophosaurus

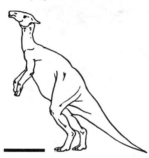

Bradycneme

Callovosaurus

0   80ft (24m)

Brachiosaurids – Callovosaurus

with bulky body, and long neck and tail. Identity doubtful.
Brachiosaurids The family Brachiosauridae
INFRAORDER Sauropoda SUBORDER Sauropodomorpha
ORDER Saurischia. See Chapter 3.
Brachiosaurus "arm lizard" FAMILY Brachiosauridae
INFRAORDER Sauropoda SUBORDER Sauropodomorpha
ORDER Saurischia
TIME Late Jurassic PLACE Colorado, USA; Tendaguru, Tanzania
DESCRIPTION One of the largest, tallest dinosaurs, about 82ft (25m)
long, 52ft (16m) high and weighing 50 tons: a massive four-footed
plant-eater with nostrils high on the head, long "giraffe neck,"
longer forelimbs than hindlimbs, and short tail. See also its East
African subgenus *Giraffatitan*.
Brachyceratops "short horned face" FAMILY Ceratopsidae
SUBORDER Ceratopsia ORDER Ornithischia
TIME Late Cretaceous PLACE Alberta, Canada; and Montana, USA
DESCRIPTION Horned dinosaur up to 13ft (4m) long, with short face,
curved nose horn, small horns above the eyes, and short neck frill;
mainly known from small, young specimens.
Brachylophosaurus "short-crested lizard" FAMILY Hadrosauridae
SUBORDER Ornithopoda ORDER Ornithischia
TIME Late Cretaceous PLACE Alberta, Canada; and Montana, USA
DESCRIPTION Primitive duck-billed dinosaur about 23ft (7m) long,
with long forelimbs, deep snout, low nasal crest, and (between the
eyes) a bony plate forming a short backward-pointing spike.
Brachypodosaurus "short-foot lizard" FAMILY Nodosauridae?
SUBORDER Ankylosauria? ORDER Ornithischia
TIME Late Cretaceous PLACE Central India
DESCRIPTION Known only from the short, strong bone of the left
upper "arm," this beast might be a stegosaur.
Brachyrophus "short ? " Probably *Camptosaurus*.
Bradycneme "heavy shin" FAMILY Dromaeosauridae INFRAORDER
Deinonychosauria SUBORDER Theropoda ORDER Saurischia
TIME Late Cretaceous PLACE Transylvanian Romania
DESCRIPTION Known only from part of a lower leg bone with
distinctive ankle joint. Once thought to be a fossil owl.
Brontosaurus "thunder lizard" Name once used for *Apatosaurus*, a
heavy sauropod with a supposedly thunderous tread.

Caenagnathids The family Caenagnathidae
INFRAORDER Oviraptorosauria SUBORDER Theropoda ORDER
Saurischia. Main entry in Chapter 3.
Caenagnathus "recent jaw" *Chirostenotes* or valid name of a
dinosaur related to that theropod.
Calamosaurus "reed lizard" A former name of *Calamospondylus*.
Calamospondylus "quill vertebrae" FAMILY Coeluridae
INFRAORDER Coelurosauria SUBORDER Theropoda ORDER Saurischia
TIME Early Cretaceous PLACE southern England
DESCRIPTION Known only from fragments of a small, two-legged,
flesh-eater, often known as *Aristosuchus*.
Callovosaurus "Callovian lizard" FAMILY Camptosauridae
SUBORDER Ornithopoda ORDER Ornithischia
TIME Mid Jurassic PLACE southern England

DESCRIPTION Bipedal/quadrupedal plant–eater 11ft 6in (3.5m) long; an early camptosaurid named in 1980 from a thigh bone found in rocks of Callovian age.

Camarasaurids The family Camarasauridae
INFRAORDER Sauropoda SUBORDER Sauropodomorpha
ORDER Saurischia. See Chapter 3.

Camarasaurus "chambered lizard" FAMILY Camarasauridae
INFRAORDER Sauropoda SUBORDER Sauropodomorpha
ORDER Saurischia
TIME Late Jurassic PLACE Colorado, Utah, western USA
DESCRIPTION Four-footed plant-eater 30–60ft (9–18m) long and weighing up to 20 tons; with relatively large, deep head, short neck, and short tail. Long forelimbs meant the back was almost level. The commonest North American sauropod of its time.

Camarasaurus

Camelotia "of Camelot" FAMILY Melanorosauridae
INFRAORDER Prosauropoda SUBORDER Sauropodomorpha
ORDER Saurischia
TIME Late Triassic PLACE Somerset, southwest England
DESCRIPTION Large prosauropod known by bones from back, tail, hips, and hindlimb. The Northern Hemisphere's only known melanorosaurid, named in 1985 from King Arthur's legendary court Camelot, supposedly in Somerset.

Camptonotus "bent ?back?" A former name of *Camptosaurus*.

Camptosaurids The family Camptosauridae
SUBORDER Ornithopoda ORDER Ornithischia. Main entry in Chapter 3.

Camptosaurus "bent lizard" FAMILY Camptosauridae
SUBORDER Ornithopoda ORDER Ornithischia
TIME Late Jurassic to Early Cretaceous PLACE western North America and western Europe
DESCRIPTION Bulky bipedal/quadrupedal plant-eater 16–23ft (about 5–7m) long, with much longer legs than arms, four-toed feet, and hoof-like claws on toes and fingers. Known from young and adults.

Camptosaurus

Campylodon "bent tooth" A former name of *Campylodoniscus*.

Campylodoniscus "bent toothed" FAMILY Titanosauridae
INFRAORDER Sauropoda SUBORDER Sauropodomorpha
ORDER Saurischia
TIME Late Cretaceous PLACE southern Argentina
DESCRIPTION Large four-footed plant-eater probably with long neck and tail, but known only from part of a jaw. Identity doubtful.

Carcharodontosaurus

Carcharodontosaurus "*Carcharodon* (a shark) lizard"
FAMILY unknown INFRAORDER uncertain SUBORDER Theropoda
ORDER Saurischia
TIME Early and Early Late Cretaceous PLACE North Africa
DESCRIPTION Large two-legged flesh-eater about 26ft (8m) long, supposedly with huge head and sharklike fangs, yet lightly built and perhaps related to the ostrich dinosaurs.

Cardiodon "heart tooth" A former name of *Cetiosaurus*.

Carnosaurs "meat-eating lizards" The dinosaur infraorder Carnosauria SUBORDER Theropoda ORDER Saurischia.
An artificial grouping of all large flesh-eating dinosaurs. See also Chapter 3.

© DIAGRAM

Carnotaurus

Cathetosaurus

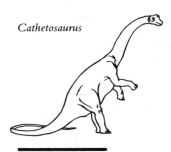

Centrosaurus

Ceratosaurus

Cetiosaurus

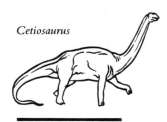

0   80ft (24m)

Carnotaurus – Cetiosaurus

Carnotaurus "meat-eating bull" FAMILY Abelisauridae
INFRAORDER Carnosauria SUBORDER Theropoda ORDER Saurischia
TIME Early Cretaceous PLACE southern Argentina
DESCRIPTION Large, bizarrely "bull-headed," two-legged flesh-
eater, 25ft (7.5m) long and weighing a ton. It had long, slim legs, a
slim scaly body, very short arms, and a short, deep head, with
broad horns jutting out above the eyes. Described in 1985.
Cathetosaurus "upright lizard" FAMILY Camarasauridae
INFRAORDER Sauropoda SUBORDER Sauropodomorpha
ORDER Saurischia
TIME Late Jurassic PLACE Colorado, USA
DESCRIPTION Large four-footed plant-eater with long neck and tail;
evidently capable of rearing on hind limbs and tail to feed.
Excavated 1967; described 1988.
Caudocoelus "tail hollow" A former name of *Teinurosaurus*.
Caulodon "stem tooth" A former name of *Camarasaurus*.
Centrosaurus "horned lizard" The horned dinosaur renamed
Eucentrosaurus in 1989 after the discovery that another animal might
already bear the name *Centrosaurus*.
Cerapods "horned feet" The nanorder Cerapoda, proposed in 1986
to include ornithopods, ceratopsians, etc. See also Chapter 3.
Ceratops "horned face" FAMILY Ceratopsidae
SUBORDER Ceratopsia ORDER Ornithischia
TIME Late Cretaceous PLACE Colorado and Montana, USA
DESCRIPTION Small horned dinosaur with a short three-horned head
and short neck frill. Identity doubtful.
Ceratopsians Horned dinosaurs and their kin
SUBORDER Ceratopsia ORDER Ornithischia. See also Chapter 3.
Ceratopsids The family Ceratopsidae SUBORDER Ceratopsia
ORDER Ornithischia. See also Chapter 3.
Ceratosaurs "horned lizards" The Ceratosauria, a proposed
suborder of flesh-eating dinosaurs including many large and small
forms previously divided into carnosaurs and coelurosaurs.
Ceratosaurids The family Ceratosauridae
INFRAORDER Carnosauria. See also Chapter 3.
Ceratosaurus "horned lizard" FAMILY Ceratosauridae
INFRAORDER Carnosauria SUBORDER Theropoda ORDER Saurischia
TIME Late Jurassic PLACE North America and East Africa
DESCRIPTION Large two-legged flesh-eater 15-20ft (4.6-6m) long
and weighing up to 1 ton. It had a massive head with big blade-like
fangs and short blade-shaped horns above nose and eyes; small
bony plates running down its back; short, strong arms; four fingers
(three clawed); three-clawed feet; and deep, broad tail.
Cetiosaurids The family Cetiosauridae INFRAORDER Sauropoda
SUBORDER Sauropodomorpha ORDER Saurischia. See Chapter 3.
Cetiosauriscus "whale lizard" FAMILY Diplodocidae
INFRAORDER Sauropoda SUBORDER Sauropodomorpha
ORDER Saurischia
TIME Late Jurassic PLACE southern England and maybe Switzerland
DESCRIPTION Large four-footed plant-eater about 49ft (15m) long,
with whiplash tail. A primitive diplodocid sauropod.
Cetiosaurus "whale lizard" FAMILY Cetiosauridae
INFRAORDER Sauropoda SUBORDER Sauropodomorpha

ORDER Saurischia
TIME Middle to Late Jurassic PLACE western Europe; North Africa
DESCRIPTION Large four-footed plant-eater up to 60ft (18m) long or
more, with blunt head, spoon-shaped teeth, solid spongy-textured
backbone not hollowed out for lightness, moderately long neck
and relatively short tail. The first sauropod discovered.

Changdusaurus "Changdu lizard" FAMILY Stegosauridae
SUBORDER Stegosauria ORDER Ornithischia
TIME Jurassic PLACE China
DESCRIPTION Four-legged plant-eater probably with spikes or plates
down its back. In the mid 1980s this plated dinosaur's name figured
briefly in a Chinese summary of Jurassic dinosaur and other fossil
finds from China.

Chasmosaurus

Chaoyoungosaurids The family Chaoyoungosauridae
SUBORDER Pachycephalosauria?
ORDER Ornithischia. Perhaps ancestral to the pachycephalosaurs
("bone-heads") and psittacosaurs ("parrot lizards"). See
Chaoyoungosaurus and *Xuanhuasaurus*.

Chaoyoungosaurus "Chaoyoung lizard" FAMILY
Chaoyoungosauridae SUBORDER Pachycephalosauria?
ORDER Ornithischia
TIME Late Jurassic PLACE Liaoning, east China
DESCRIPTION Small, two-legged plant-eater known from a skull
with bony projections foreshadowing *Psittacosaurus*'s; three-lobed
teeth in the front upper jaw; and some canine-type teeth. Described
in 1983 from a fossil found in Chaoyoung County.

Chasdernbergia

Chasmosaurus "cleft lizard" FAMILY Ceratopsidae
SUBORDER Ceratopsia ORDER Ornithischia
TIME Late Cretaceous PLACE Alberta, Canada; New Mexico, USA
DESCRIPTION Large four-legged plant-eater, a 2.5 ton horned
dinosaur 17ft (5.2m) long, with horny beak, small nose horn, blunt
brow horns, and long neck frill lightened by huge holes. Different
sexes or species had long or short brow-horns.

Chassternbergia "Charles Sternberg" FAMILY Nodosauridae
SUBORDER Ankylosauria ORDER Ornithischia
TIME Late Cretaceous PLACE Alberta, Canada; Montana, USA
DESCRIPTION Large, four-footed armored plant-eater similar to (and
perhaps) *Edmontonia*. Named in 1988 after a dinosaur hunter.

"Chendusaurus" Perhaps *Changdusaurus*.

Cheneosaurus "goose lizard" A name once given to *Hypacrosaurus*.

"Chengdusaurus" Perhaps *Changdusaurus*.

Chialingosaurus

Chialingosaurus "Chia-ling lizard" FAMILY Stegosauridae
SUBORDER Stegosauria ORDER Ornithischia
TIME Mid Jurassic PLACE Chia-ling River, southern China
DESCRIPTION Four-legged plant-eater about 13ft (4m) long, with
two rows of small, spiky plates along back and tail; slimmer than
Kentrosaurus and with relatively long forelimbs.

Chiayuesaurus "Chia-yü lizard" FAMILY Camarasauridae?
INFRAORDER Sauropoda SUBORDER Sauropodomorpha
ORDER Saurischia
TIME Late Cretaceous PLACE Chia-yü-kuan, northwest China
DESCRIPTION Large four-legged plant-eater probably with long neck
and tail, but only known from teeth. Identity doubtful.

Chiayuesaurus

©DIAGRAM

Chienkosaurus – Chubutisaurids

Chilantaisaurus

Chienkosaurus "Chien-ko lizard" Supposed carnosaur named from four teeth: three crocodilian, one from *Szechuanosaurus*.

Chilantaisaurus "Ch'i-lan-t'ai lizard" FAMILY Allosauridae INFRAORDER Carnosauria SUBORDER Theropoda ORDER Saurischia TIME Late Cretaceous PLACE northwest and south China DESCRIPTION Large two-legged flesh-eater weighing maybe 4 tons, with massive arms, clawed, three-fingered hands, powerful hind limbs, and a weaker brow ridge than *Allosaurus*. Perhaps close kin to the tyrannosaurids' ancestors.

"Chindesaurus" "ghost lizard" FAMILY Staurikosauridae SUBORDER? ORDER Herrerasauria
TIME Early Late Triassic PLACE Chinde Point, Arizona, USA DESCRIPTION Heavy-boned 200lb (90.7kg) bipedal flesh-eater about 10-13ft (3-4m) long, publicized in 1985 as the "oldest... dinosaur" and described in 1989.

Chingkankousaurus "Ch'ing-kang-kou lizard" FAMILY Tyrannosauridae INFRAORDER Carnosauria SUBORDER Theropoda ORDER Saurischia
TIME Late Cretaceous PLACE eastern China DESCRIPTION Large two-legged flesh-eater known from a slender shoulder blade, perhaps from *Tarbosaurus*. Identity doubtful.

Chinshakiangosaurus "Kinsha-kiang lizard" FAMILY Melanorosauridae INFRAORDER Prosauropoda SUBORDER Sauropodomorpha ORDER Saurischia
TIME Early Jurassic PLACE Kinsha-kiang (upper Yangtze River) southern China
DESCRIPTION Large four-footed plant-eater with long neck and tail. Formerly thought to be a cetiosaurid sauropod, now considered closer to the prosauropod *Melanorosaurus*.

Chinshakiangosaurus

Chirostenotes "slender hands" FAMILY Caenagnathidae INFRAORDER Oviraptorosauria SUBORDER Theropoda ORDER Saurischia
TIME Late Cretaceous PLACE Alberta, Canada DESCRIPTION Small, lightly built, two-legged flesh-eater (or maybe plant-eater) about 7ft (2m) long. Each hand had three long, narrow fingers armed with long, narrow claws. There was probably a long, deep toothless beak. *Caenagnathus* (and some say *Macrophalangia*) was in fact *Chirostenotes*.

Chondrosteosaurus "bony cartilage lizard" FAMILY Titanosauridae INFRAORDER Sauropoda SUBORDER Sauropodomorpha ORDER Saurischia
TIME Early Cretaceous PLACE Isle of Wight, England DESCRIPTION Large four-footed plant-eater with long neck and tail, known only from distinctive vertebrae. Identity doubtful.

Chondrosteus "bony cartilage" Former name of *Chondrosteosaurus*.

Chuandongocoelurus "Chuandong hollow tail" FAMILY Coeluridae INFRAORDER Coelurosauria SUBORDER Theropoda ORDER Saurischia TIME Middle Jurassic PLACE Sichuan, China DESCRIPTION Small, light, two-legged flesh-eater named in 1984.

Chubutisaurids The family Chubutisauridae INFRAORDER Sauropoda SUBORDER Sauropodomorpha ORDER Saurischia Family created to contain the seemingly unusual sauropod *Chubutisaurus*.

Chirostenotes

0   80ft (24m)

Chubutisaurus "Chubut lizard" FAMILY Chubutisauridae?
INFRAORDER Sauropoda SUBORDER Sauropodomorpha
ORDER Saurischia
TIME Late Cretaceous PLACE Chubut province, southern Argentina
DESCRIPTION Huge four-legged plant-eater perhaps 75ft (about
23m) long, with deeply hollowed vertebrae, probably long neck
but short tail, and supposedly longer hindlimbs than forelimbs.
One expert suggests it was a brachiosaurid. Identity doubtful.

Chubutisaurus

Chungkingosaurus "Chungking lizard" FAMILY Stegosauridae
SUBORDER Stegosauria ORDER Ornithischia
TIME Early Late Jurassic PLACE Sichuan, south-central China
DESCRIPTION Four-legged plant-eating dinosaur 10-13ft (3-4m)
long, with small, deep, narrow head and two rows of large, thick,
plate-like spines running down the back. Named in 1983.

Cionodon " ? tooth" FAMILY Hadrosauridae
SUBORDER Ornithopoda ORDER Ornithischia
TIME Late Cretaceous PLACE Colorado, USA
DESCRIPTION Large duck-billed dinosaur named from a few bones of
the back, arm, foot, and upper jaw. Identity doubtful.

Clasmodosaurus

Cladeiodon "branch tooth" Supposed theropod dinosaur named
from a tooth now thought to be from a teratosaurid thecodont.

Claorhynchus "broken beak" Now thought to be *Triceratops*.

Claosaurus "broken lizard" FAMILY Hadrosauridae
SUBORDER Ornithopoda ORDER Ornithischia
TIME Late Cretaceous PLACE Kansas and Wyoming, USA
DESCRIPTION Small, early duck-billed dinosaur; a plant-eater 12ft
(3.7m) long with long hind limbs, slender feet and body, and
evidently rows, not batteries, of teeth behind the toothless beak.

Coelophysid

Clasmodosaurus "fragment tooth lizard" FAMILY uncertain
INFRAORDER Sauropoda SUBORDER Sauropodomorpha
ORDER Saurischia
TIME Late Cretaceous PLACE southern Argentina
DESCRIPTION Known from fossil teeth. Identity uncertain.

Clevelanotyrannus "Cleveland tyrant" Former name of
Nanotyrannus.

Coelophysids The family Coelophysidae INFRAORDER
Coelurosauria SUBORDER Theropoda ORDER Saurischia. Main
entry in Chapter 3.

Coelophysis "hollow form" FAMILY Coelophysidae
INFRAORDER Coelurosauria SUBORDER Theropoda ORDER Saurischia
TIME Late Triassic PLACE southwestern and eastern USA
DESCRIPTION–Small, early, two-legged flesh-eating dinosaur up to
10ft (3m) long and weighing 60lb (27kg) or more. It had a small,
low head with long jaws rimmed by small, sharp teeth, a snaky
neck, long tail, long, slim legs, and short, three-fingered hands
with claws. The bones were light and hollow.

Coelophysis

Coelosaurus "hollow lizard" A former name of *Ornithomimus*.

Coelurids The family Coeluridae INFRAORDER Coelurosauria
SUBORDER Theropoda ORDER Saurischia. Main entry in Chapter 3.

Coeluroides "Coelurid form" FAMILY Coeluridae
INFRAORDER Coelurosauria SUBORDER Theropoda ORDER Saurischia
TIME Late Cretaceous PLACE India; and maybe Kazakhstan, USSR
DESCRIPTION Probably a small, two-legged flesh-eater, about 7ft

Coeluroides

©DIAGRAM

Coelurus

Coloradisaurus

Compsognathus

Corythosaurus

0   80ft (24m)

Coelurosaurs – Craspedodon

(2.1m) long, though has been called a theropod as large as *Allosaurus*. Only known from several vertebrae. Identity doubtful.

Coelurosaurs "hollow tail lizards" The infraorder Coelurosauria SUBORDER Theropoda ORDER Saurischia. An artificial grouping of many families of small flesh-eating dinosaurs. See Chapter 3.

Coelurus "hollow tail" FAMILY Coeluridae
INFRAORDER Coelurosauria SUBORDER Theropoda ORDER Saurischia
TIME Late Jurassic PLACE Wyoming, USA
DESCRIPTION Small, light, two-legged flesh-eater about 6ft (1.8m) long, seemingly with long hands and small sharp teeth.

Colonosaurus "hill lizard" Supposed theropod dinosaur known from a jaw now identified as from the toothed bird *Ichthyornis*.

Coloradia "Colorados" A preliminary name for *Coloradisaurus*.

Coloradisaurus "Colorados lizard" FAMILY Plateosauridae
INFRAORDER Prosauropoda SUBORDER Sauropodomorpha
ORDER Saurischia
TIME Late Triassic PLACE Argentina
DESCRIPTION Bipedal/quadrupedal plant-eater about 13ft (4m) long, with relatively short snout, blunt teeth, and long neck and tail. Named from the Los Colorados rock formation.

Compsognathids The family Compsognathidae
INFRAORDER Coelurosauria SUBORDER Theropoda ORDER Saurischia. Main entry in Chapter 3.

Compsognathus "pretty jaw" FAMILY Compsognathidae
INFRAORDER Coelurosauria SUBORDER Theropoda ORDER Saurischia
TIME Late Jurassic PLACE southwest Germany; southeast France
DESCRIPTION Tiny, swift, two-legged flesh-eater with small head, sharp teeth, long neck, long legs and tail, short arms and two-fingered hands tipped with claws. At 2ft (60cm) and 6½lb (3kg), a birdlike predator among the smallest of all dinosaurs.

Compsosuchus "pretty crocodile" FAMILY Allosauridae?
INFRAORDER Carnosauria? SUBORDER Theropoda ORDER Saurischia
TIME Late Cretaceous PLACE central India
DESCRIPTION Probably a large, two-legged meat-eater but known only from a neck vertebra. Usually considered a coelurid dinosaur but probably an allosaurid.

Conchoraptor "conch thief" FAMILY Oviraptoridae
INFRAORDER Oviraptorosauria SUBORDER Theropoda
ORDER Saurischia
TIME Late Cretaceous PLACE Southern Mongolia
DESCRIPTION Two-legged, birdlike hunter, or maybe herbivore, less than 5ft (1.5m) long, with short deep head, large eyes, and toothless beak resembling a parrot's. Lack of head crest at first suggested a young *Oviraptor*. *Conchoraptor* was named in 1986.

Corythosaurus "helmet lizard" FAMILY Lambeosauridae
SUBORDER Ornithopoda ORDER Ornithischia
TIME Late Cretaceous PLACE Alberta, Canada
DESCRIPTION Large bipedal/quadrupedal plant-eater with toothless beak, batteries of grinding cheek teeth and hollow "cocked hat" head crest flattened from side to side. Females and young had smaller crests. Some species really might be *Hypacrosaurus*.

Craspedodon "edge tooth" FAMILY Iguanodontidae
SUBORDER Ornithopoda ORDER Ornithischia

TIME Late Cretaceous PLACE Belgium
DESCRIPTION Large bipedal/quadrupedal plant-eater with toothless
beak and maybe spiky thumbs. A late survivor in its family, but
known only from cheek teeth flattened from side to side and
strongly ridged for effective chewing. Identity doubtful.

Crataeomus "mighty shoulder" FAMILY Nodosauridae
SUBORDER Ankylosauria ORDER Ornithischia
TIME Late Cretaceous PLACE Austria and Romania
DESCRIPTION Perhaps small armored dinosaur some 6ft (1.8m) long,
but to be redescribed. Fossils included a shoulder blade that might
be from the armored dinosaur *Danubiosaurus*.

Craterosaurus

Craterosaurus "bowl lizard" FAMILY Stegosauridae
SUBORDER Stegosauria ORDER Ornithischia
TIME Early Cretaceous PLACE southern England
DESCRIPTION Four-legged plant-eating dinosaur about 13ft (4m)
long, maybe with rows of plates or spines down back and tail.
Known by a vertebra with a bowl-shaped dip. Identity doubtful.

Creosaurus "flesh lizard" Former name of *Allosaurus*.

Crocodilians The order Crocodylia SUPERORDER Archosauria
DESCRIPTION Large, long-snouted, carnivorous aquatic reptiles –
close kin of dinosaurs and, like them, dating from Triassic times.
Of six suborders, only one, the Eusuchia, survives.

Crocodilian

Cryptodraco "hidden dragon" FAMILY Nodosauridae
SUBORDER Ankylosauria ORDER Ornithischia
TIME Late Jurassic PLACE eastern England
DESCRIPTION Four-legged armored dinosaur known from a large
thigh bone whose identity for long remained a mystery.

Cryptosaurus "hidden lizard" Former name of *Cryptodraco*.

Cumnoria "from Cumnor" Former name of *Camptosaurus*.

Dacentrurus "pointed tail" FAMILY Stegosauridae
SUBORDER Stegosauria ORDER Ornithischia
TIME Mid to Late Jurassic PLACE England, France, and Portugal
DESCRIPTION Four-legged plant-eating dinosaur about 15ft (4.4m)
long, with relatively low back and long forelimbs, and two rows of
spikes down back and tail.

Dacentrurus

Dachongosaurus "Dachong lizard" FAMILY Cetiosauridae
INFRAORDER Sauropoda SUBORDER Sauropodomorpha
ORDER Saurischia
TIME Jurassic PLACE Yunnan, southern China
DESCRIPTION Large, four-legged plant-eater with long neck and tail;
in widespread early family of sauropods. Named in 1986.

Dachungosaurus See *Dachongosaurus*.

Damalasaurus "Damala lizard" FAMILY Brachiosauridae
INFRAORDER Sauropoda SUBORDER Sauropodomorpha
ORDER Saurischia
TIME Jurassic PLACE China
DESCRIPTION Very large, four-legged plant-eating dinosaur;
member of a family typically built like giant giraffes, with long
forelimbs, shoulders higher than hips, downward sloping back,
and neck considerably longer than tail. Named in 1986.

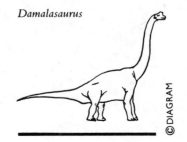

Damalasaurus

©DIAGRAM

Danubiosaurus "Danube lizard" FAMILY Nodosauridae
SUBORDER Ankylosauria ORDER Ornithischia

Daspletosaurus – Dianchungosaurus

Daspletosaurus

TIME Late Cretaceous PLACE Eastern Europe
DESCRIPTION Small, four-legged armored dinosaur known by some from fossils also credited to *Crataeomus* and *Struthiosaurus*.

Daspletosaurus "frightful lizard" FAMILY Tyrannosauridae INFRAORDER Carnosauria SUBORDER Theropoda ORDER Saurischia
TIME Late Cretaceous PLACE Alberta, Canada
DESCRIPTION Two-legged flesh-eater about 28ft (8.5m) long and weighing up to 3 tons or more, with massive head, dagger-like fangs, short, flexible neck, short body, short arms, two-fingered hands, massive legs, clawed toes and fingers, and long, strong tail. Close kin to (some say was) *Tyrannosaurus*.

Datousaurus "Datou lizard" FAMILY Cetiosauridae INFRAORDER Sauropoda SUBORDER Sauropodomorpha ORDER Saurischia
TIME Middle Jurassic PLACE Zigong in Sichuan, China
DESCRIPTION Four-legged plant-eater 15ft (4.6m) long, with long neck and tail, strongly built skull, spoon-shaped teeth, and more advanced backbone than in some other early sauropods.

Deinocheirids The family Deinocheiridae INFRAORDER Ornithomimosauria SUBORDER Theropoda ORDER Saurischia. Main entry in Chapter 3.

Deinocheirus

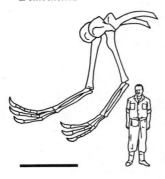

Deinocheirus "terrible hand" FAMILY Deinocheiridae INFRAORDER Ornithomimosauria SUBORDER Theropoda ORDER Saurischia
TIME Late Cretaceous PLACE southern Mongolia
DESCRIPTION Two-legged predatory or plant-eating dinosaur weighing maybe 6 tons, known only from two arms some 8ft (2.4m) long, each with three fingers tipped with long, curved claws.

Deinodon "terrible tooth" Dinosaur known only from Late Cretaceous teeth found in Montana. Perhaps *Albertosaurus*.

Deinonychosaurs The infraorder Deinonychosauria SUBORDER Theropoda ORDER Saurischia A grouping of the families Dromaeosauridae and Troodontidae (Saurornithoididae).

Deinonychus

Deinonychus "terrible claw" FAMILY Dromaeosauridae INFRAORDER Deinonychosauria SUBORDER Theropoda ORDER Saurischia
TIME Early Cretaceous PLACE western USA, and maybe South Korea
DESCRIPTION Moderately sized but formidably armed big-game hunter 8–11ft (2.4–3.4m) long. It had a long, low head, bladelike teeth, large, clawed hands, muscular legs with clawed toes including a huge sickle-shaped "switchblade" claw on the second toe, and a long tail with bony rodlike stiffeners.

Denversaurus

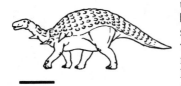

Denversaurus "Denver lizard" FAMILY Nodosauridae SUBORDER Ankylosauria ORDER Ornithischia
TIME Late Cretaceous PLACE South Dakota, USA
DESCRIPTION Four-legged armored plant-eater about 15ft (4.6m) long, with eye far back, snout fairly short and head steeply angled for low-browsing. Named in 1988 from a squashed skull. Some consider it was *Edmontonia*.

Dianchungosaurus "Dianchung lizard" FAMILY Heterodontosauridae?

0   80ft (24m)

SUBORDER Ornithopoda   ORDER Ornithischia
TIME Early Jurassic   PLACE Yunnan, southern China
DESCRIPTION Small, early bipedal bird–hipped dinosaur named in 1982 in a Chinese publication. Perhaps identical to the later named *Tianchungosaurus*, in a "new" pachycephalosaur family.

Diapsids

Diapsids The subclass Diapsida: reptiles with two holes in the sides of the skull behind the eyes. Diapsids include lepidosaurs (eg lizards, snakes) sauropterygians (eg the extinct plesiosaurs), archosaurs (eg crocodilians and the extinct thecodonts, dinosaurs, and pterosaurs), and probably ichthyosaurs.

Diceratops "two-horned face" A former name of *Triceratops*.

Diclonius "two stems"   FAMILY Hadrosauridae
SUBORDER Ornithopoda   ORDER Ornithischia
TIME Late Cretaceous   PLACE Montana, USA
DESCRIPTION Big bipedal plant-eater with a toothless beak. Named from (mostly) hadrosaur cheek teeth. Identity doubtful.

Dicraeosaurus

Dicraeosaurids The family Dicraeosauridae
INFRAORDER Sauropoda   SUBORDER Sauropodomorpha   ORDER Saurischia. Family created to contain the sauropod *Dicraeosaurus*.

Dicraeosaurus "forked lizard"   FAMILY Dicraeosauridae or Diplodocidae   INFRAORDER Sauropoda
SUBORDER Sauropodomorpha   ORDER Saurischia
TIME Late Jurassic   PLACE Tendaguru, Tanzania
DESCRIPTION Four-legged plant-eater 43-66ft (13-20m) long but relatively slim, weighing only about 6 tons. It had a long tail but relatively shorter neck than *Diplodocus*, and high forked spines that rose from nearly solid vertebrae.

Didanodon "two ? teeth" A former name of *Lambeosaurus*.

Dilophosaurus "two ridged lizard"   FAMILY Halticosauridae?
INFRAORDER Coelurosauria?   SUBORDER Theropoda   ORDER Saurischia
TIME Early Jurassic   PLACE Arizona, USA
DESCRIPTION Slender, early bipedal flesh-eating dinosaur up to 20ft (6m) long and weighing nearly half a ton, with a pair of fragile bony crests along its head. If a coelophysid, as some suppose, its large size was apparently exceptional.

Dilophosaurus

Dimodosaurus "two mode lizard" A former name of *Plateosaurus*.

Dinodocus "terrible beam"   FAMILY Brachiosauridae
INFRAORDER Sauropoda   SUBORDER Sauropodomorpha
ORDER Saurischia
TIME Early Cretaceous   PLACE Kent, southeast England
DESCRIPTION Very large four-legged plant-eater about 72ft (22m) long, probably with very long neck, relatively shorter tail, slim forelimbs, and shoulders higher than the hips. Known only from broken bones of hips and limbs. Identity doubtful.

Dinosaurs "terrible lizards" Prehistoric, mainly large, backboned land animals. Dinosaurs have been considered as one group or two groups, for example: (1) ORDER Dinosauria (1841); (2) ORDERS Saurischia and Ornithischia (1888); (3) CLASS Dinosauria (1974) with subclasses Saurischia, Ornithischia, and Aves (birds). Most paleontologists now think dinosaurs formed a natural unit, but differ on its subdivisions. Accordingly this book follows the established (artificial) classification: ORDERS Saurischia and

Dinodocus

©DIAGRAM

Diplodocus

Diplotomodon

Dolichosuchus

Dravidosaurus

0   80ft (24m)

Dinosaurus – Dromaeosaurus

Ornithischia SUPERORDER Archosauria INFRACLASS
Archosauromorpha CLASS Reptilia. (For dinosaur features, time
lines, and family trees see **Chapters** 1 and 3.)
Dinosaurus "terrible lizard" A former name of *Plateosaurus*.
Diplodocids The family Diplodocidae INFRAORDER Sauropoda
SUBORDER Sauropodomorpha ORDER Saurischia. Main entry
Chapter 3.
Diplodocus "double beam" FAMILY Diplodocidae
INFRAORDER Sauropoda SUBORDER Sauropodomorpha
ORDER Saurischia
TIME Late Jurassic PLACE Colorado, Montana, Utah and Wyoming,
USA
DESCRIPTION Immensely long four-legged plant-eater with low,
sloping head, snaky neck, slim limbs, and finely tapered whiplash
tail. One of the longest dinosaurs, up to 87ft 6in (27m) long, yet
weighing 12 tons or less.
Diplotomodon "double cutting tooth" FAMILY Dryptosauridae?
INFRAORDER Carnosauria SUBORDER Theropoda ORDER Saurischia
TIME Late Cretaceous PLACE New Jersey, USA
DESCRIPTION Large two-legged flesh-eater named on the basis of a
tooth similar to teeth of *Dryptosaurus*. Identity doubtful.
Diracodon "double ? tooth" FAMILY Stegosauridae
SUBORDER Stegosauria ORDER Ornithischia
TIME Late Jurassic PLACE western United States
DESCRIPTION Large four-legged plant-eater, probably with two
rows of plates down its back. Long identified with *Stegosaurus*.
Dolichosuchus "long crocodile" FAMILY Halticosauridae?
INFRAORDER Coelurosauria SUBORDER Theropoda ORDER Saurischia
TIME Late Triassic PLACE southwest West Germany
DESCRIPTION Large two-legged flesh-eater known only from a leg
bone. Identity doubtful; perhaps *Halticosaurus*.
Doryphosaurus "?back bearer lizard" Former name of *Kentrosaurus*.
Dracopelta "armored dragon" FAMILY Nodosauridae
SUBORDER Ankylosauria ORDER Ornithischia
TIME Late Jurassic PLACE western Portugal
DESCRIPTION Small, four-legged, armored plant-eater with five
types of armor; about 7ft (2m) long. Best preserved of the early
armored dinosaurs. Named in 1980.
Dravidosaurus "Dravidanadu lizard" FAMILY Stegosauridae
SUBORDER Stegosauria ORDER Ornithischia
TIME Late Cretaceous PLACE southern India
DESCRIPTION Four-legged plant-eater – a small plated dinosaur 10ft
(3m) long with rows of plates and bulging spines. This "lizard from
south India" was the last known stegosaurid dinosaur.
Dromaeosaurids The family Dromaeosauridae
INFRAORDER Deinonychosauria SUBORDER Theropoda
ORDER Saurischia. Main entry in Chapter 3.
Dromaeosaurus "running lizard" FAMILY Dromaeosauridae
INFRAORDER Deinonychosauria SUBORDER Theropoda
ORDER Saurischia
TIME Late Cretaceous PLACE Alberta, Canada
DESCRIPTION Agile two-legged flesh-eater about 6ft (1.8m) long,
with a big head, powerful jaws, large fangs and probably a short

retractable sickle claw on each second toe.

Dromiceiomimus "emu mimic" FAMILY Ornithomimidae
INFRAORDER Ornithomimosauria SUBORDER Theropoda
ORDER Saurischia

Dromiceiomimus

TIME Late Cretaceous PLACE Alberta, Canada
DESCRIPTION An ostrich dinosaur 11ft 6in (3.5m) long and weighing
220lb (100kg), with big, keen eyes, toothless beak, long neck and
tail, short back, slim arms with three-fingered hands, and long legs
capable of running at up to 40mph (64.4kph).

Dromicosaurus "?emu lizard" A former name of *Massospondylus*.

Dryosaurids The family Dryosauridae SUBORDER Ornithopoda
ORDER Ornithischia. Main entry in Chapter 3.

Dryosaurus "oak lizard" FAMILY Dryosauridae
SUBORDER Ornithopoda
ORDER Ornithischia

Dryosaurus

TIME Mid–Late Jurassic PLACE England, Romania, Tanzania, USA
DESCRIPTION Two-legged plant-eater 10–13ft (3–4m) long, with
horny beak, grinding cheek teeth, five-fingered hands, long
three-toed legs, and tendon-stiffened tail.

Dryptosaurids The family Dryptosauridae
INFRAORDER Carnosauria SUBORDER Theropoda ORDER Saurischia
Main entry in Chapter 3.

Dryptosauroides "*Dryptosaurus* form" FAMILY uncertain
INFRAORDER Carnosauria SUBORDER Theropoda ORDER Saurischia
TIME Late Cretaceous PLACE central India
DESCRIPTION Large, two-legged flesh-eater known from spinal
bones once thought megalosaurid or dryptosaurid. Identity
doubtful.

Dryptosaurus "wounding lizard" FAMILY Dryptosauridae
INFRAORDER Carnosauria SUBORDER Theropoda ORDER Saurischia
TIME Late Cretaceous PLACE western and eastern North America
DESCRIPTION Slimly built, two-legged big-game hunter more than
20ft (6m) long and weighing 1.5 tons; with curved fangs, strong
arms, large curved claws on fingers, and a unique type of ankle.

Dryptosaurus

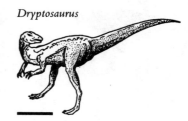

Duck-billed dinosaurs Large, two-legged plant-eaters with a
toothless, duck-like beak and batteries of cheek teeth.
See **Hadrosaurids** and **Lambeosaurids**.

Dynamosaurus "powerful lizard" A former name of *Tyrannosaurus*.

Dyoplosaurus "double-armed lizard" FAMILY Ankylosauridae
SUBORDER Ankylosauria ORDER Ornithischia
TIME Late Cretaceous PLACE Alberta, Canada
DESCRIPTION Large, armored, four-legged plant-eater with a
toothless beak, small cheek teeth, armor-plated body and tail
ending in a bony club. Often held to be *Euoplocephalus*.

Dysalotosaurus "uncatchable lizard" A former name of *Dryosaurus*.

Dysganus "?unbright" FAMILY Ceratopsidae
SUBORDER Ceratopsia ORDER Ornithischia
TIME Late Cretaceous PLACE Montana, USA
DESCRIPTION Four-legged, horned, plant-eating dinosaur known
only from isolated teeth. Identity doubtful.

Dystrophaeus "wasted one" FAMILY Cetiosauridae
INFRAORDER Sauropoda SUBORDER Sauropodomorpha
ORDER Saurischia

©DIAGRAM

Dyoplosaurus

Echinodon

Edmontosaurus

Elaphrosaurus

Elmisaurus

0   80ft (24m)

Dystylosaurus – Embasaurus

TIME Late Jurassic PLACE Utah, USA
DESCRIPTION Large four-legged plant-eater with long neck and tail; known by scrappy bits of fossil bone. Identity doubtful.

Dystylosaurus "two beam lizard" FAMILY Brachiosauridae?
INFRAORDER Sauropoda SUBORDER Sauropodomorpha
ORDER Saurischia
TIME Late Jurassic PLACE Colorado, USA
DESCRIPTION Very large four-legged plant-eater known from a spinal bone more than 3ft 3in (1m) tall described in 1985. Its owner might have resembled the huge sauropod *Brachiosaurus*.

Echinodon "spiny tooth" FAMILY Scutellosauridae?
SUBORDER Scelidosauria? ORDER Ornithischia
TIME Late Jurassic PLACE Colorado, USA; and southern England
DESCRIPTION Perhaps a tiny bipedal/quadrupedal plant-eater only 2ft (60cm) long, known from jaw bones and distinctive teeth, some long and sharp. Many still consider it a fabrosaurid.

Edmontonia "of Edmonton" FAMILY Nodosauridae
SUBORDER Ankylosauria ORDER Ornithischia
TIME Late Cretaceous PLACE Alberta, Canada
DESCRIPTION Large, four-legged armored plant-eater perhaps 23ft (7m) long. Some identify it with *Panoplosaurus*.

Edmontosaurus "Edmonton lizard" FAMILY Hadrosauridae
SUBORDER Ornithopoda ORDER Ornithischia
TIME Late Cretaceous PLACE Alberta, Canada; and Montana and New Jersey, USA
DESCRIPTION Large flat-headed duck-billed dinosaur up to 42ft 6in (13m) long and weighing nearly 3½ tons; a bipedal/quadrupedal plant-eater with toothless beak and batteries of cheek teeth.

Efraasia "E. Fraas" A prosauropod (now know to be a young *Sellosaurus*) named after Eberhard Fraas, its discoverer.

Elaphrosaurus "lightweight lizard" FAMILY Ornithomimidae
INFRAORDER Ornithomimosauria SUBORDER Theropoda
ORDER Saurischia
TIME Late Jurassic/Early Cretaceous PLACE Africa; N America
DESCRIPTION Reputedly an ancestral ostrich dinosaur about 11ft 6in (3.5m) long, with light, hollow bones, but shorter arms and legs (and a slower running speed) than later ornithomimids.

Elmisaurids The family Elmisauridae, named in 1981 but now incorporated in the Caenagnathidae.

Elmisaurus "foot lizard" FAMILY Caenagnathidae
INFRAORDER Oviraptorosauria SUBORDER Theropoda
ORDER Saurischia
TIME Late Cretaceous PLACE Mongolia and Alberta, Canada
DESCRIPTION Small, lightly built two-legged predator (or maybe herbivore) perhaps 7ft (2m) long, known from slender hands and birdlike feet with fused cannon bones.

Elosaurus "small lizard" In fact a young *Apatosaurus*.

Embasaurus "Emba lizard" FAMILY Megalosauridae
INFRAORDER Carnosauria SUBORDER Theropoda ORDER Saurischia
TIME Early Cretaceous PLACE Kazakhstan, USSR
DESCRIPTION Large two-legged flesh-eater named from two vertebrae found near the Emba River. Identity doubtful.

Enigmosaurids The family Enigmosauridae
SUBORDER Segnosauria ORDER Saurischia? Family created to contain
the Mongolian segnosaur *Enigmosaurus*.

Enigmosaurus

Enigmosaurus "mysterious lizard" FAMILY Enigmosauridae
SUBORDER Segnosauria ORDER Saurischia?
TIME Late Cretaceous PLACE southeast Mongolia
DESCRIPTION Lightly built predator (or herbivore?) perhaps 23ft
(7m) long, known from skull, jaws, and hip bones. The pubis had a
shoelike outer end and it slanted back against the ischium, as
usually found in ornithischians. Named in 1983.

Eoceratops "early horned face" FAMILY Ceratopsidae
SUBORDER Ceratopsia ORDER Ornithischia
TIME Late Cretaceous PLACE Alberta, Canada
DESCRIPTION Four-legged plant-eating dinosaur with a skull 3ft
(90cm) long, short bony neck frill, forward curving nose horn,
short backward pointing brow horns, deep toothless beak, and
sharp cheek teeth. Perhaps a young *Ceratops* or *Chasmosaurus*.

Eoceratops

Eolosaurus See *Aeolosaurus*.

Epachtosaurus Argentinian titanosaurid sauropod named but not
described in 1986.

Epanterias " ? " FAMILY Allosauridae ? INFRAORDER Carnosauria
SUBORDER Theropoda ORDER Saurischia
TIME Late Jurassic PLACE Colorado and Oklahoma, USA
DESCRIPTION Immense bipedal flesh-eater 50ft (15m) long with
dagger-like fangs, "elastic" jaws, and crouching walk. Perhaps just
a very large *Allosaurus*.

Erectopus "upright foot" FAMILY Megalosauridae?
INFRAORDER Carnosauria SUBORDER Theropoda ORDER Saurischia
TIME Early Cretaceous PLACE northeast France
DESCRIPTION Fairly large two-legged predator mainly known from
limb bones. A strange thigh bone implying upright posture seems
akin to finds (to be described) from southern France.

Erlikosaurus

Erlikosaurus "Erlik's (a king of the dead's) lizard" FAMILY
Segnosauridae SUBORDER Segnosauria ORDER Saurischia?
TIME Late Cretaceous PLACE southeast Mongolia
DESCRIPTION Bipedal predator (or herbivore?) about 16ft (5m) long,
with long neck and tail; short sharp teeth behind a slim toothless
beak; broad feet each with four, clawed, forward facing toes; and
short but massive arms. Smaller than *Segnosaurus*, it had a larger
beak, more teeth, and narrower claws on its feet.

Erythrosuchids "red crocodiles" See *Proterosuchians*.

Euacanthus "good spine" *Polacanthus*.

Eucamerotus "well chambered?" A former name of
Chondrosteosaurus.

Eucentrosaurus

Eucentrosaurus "well horned lizard" FAMILY Ceratopsidae
SUBORDER Ceratopsia ORDER Ornithischia
TIME Late Cretaceous PLACE Alberta, Canada; ?and Montana, USA
DESCRIPTION Four-legged plant-eating dinosaur 20ft (6m) long,
with a long forward-curving nose horn, small brow horns, and a
bony neck frill with two "hooks" jutting forward from its rear.
Formerly *Centrosaurus*; tentatively renamed in 1989.

Eucercosaurus "well tailed lizard" A former name of *Anoplosaurus*.

Eucnemesaurus "good leg lizard" A former name of *Euskelosaurus*.

©DIAGRAM

Euhelopodids – Fabrosaurus

Euhelopus

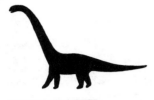

Euoplocephalus

Eustreptospondylus

Fabrosaurus

Euhelopodids The family Euhelopodidae
INFRAORDER Sauropoda SUBORDER Sauropodomorpha
ORDER Saurischia. Main entry in Chapter 3.

Euhelopus "good marsh foot" FAMILY Euhelopodidae
INFRAORDER Sauropoda SUBORDER Sauropodomorpha
ORDER Saurischia
TIME Late Jurassic PLACE Shantung, eastern China
DESCRIPTION Large four-legged plant-eater 33–50ft (10–15m) long
and weighing up to 25 tons. It had a small head, spoon-shaped
teeth, very long neck, bulky body, forelimbs and hindlimbs of
equal length, long tail, and distinctive vertebrae.

Euoplocephalus ("well armored head") FAMILY Ankylosauridae
SUBORDER Ankylosauria ORDER Ornithischia
TIME Late Cretaceous PLACE Alberta, Canada; and maybe China
DESCRIPTION Four-legged armored plant-eater up to 23ft (7m) long
and weighing about 2 tons, with broad beaked head with bony
horns, massive limbs, bony plates and studs protecting back, and
raised tail ending in a bony club.

Euornithopoda "good bird feet" Proposed ornithischian
hypoorder including heterodontosaurs, hypsilophodonts, and
iguanodonts.

Euparkeriids "good Parkers" The family Euparkeriidae (named for
British scientist W.K. Parker)
SUBORDER Ornithosuchia ORDER Thecodontia
TIME Early to Late Triassic PLACE perhaps worldwide
Not dinosaurs but small, agile Triassic thecodonts: advanced
archosaurs close to the ancestry of dinosaurs.

Euryapsids Obsolete collective term for reptiles including
plesiosaurs and ichthyosaurs that were probably **diapsids.**

Euskelosaurus "primitive leg lizard" FAMILY Plateosauridae
INFRAORDER Prosauropoda SUBORDER Sauropodomorpha ORDER
Saurischia
TIME Late Triassic PLACE South Africa
DESCRIPTION Four-legged plant-eater up to 20ft (6m) long, with
long neck and tail and bulky body; abundant in its day.

Eustreptospondylids The family Eustreptospondylidae proposed
controversially to include big flesh-eating dinosaurs such as
Eustreptospondylus and *Piatnitzkysaurus* from other families.

Eustreptospondylus "well curved vertebrae" FAMILY
Megalosauridae
INFRAORDER Carnosauria SUBORDER Theropoda ORDER Saurischia
TIME Middle Jurassic PLACE England and France
DESCRIPTION Two-legged flesh-eater up to 23ft (7m) long, with
large head, sharp "steak-knife" teeth, short arms, and "old-
fashioned" hip bones. See also **Eustreptospondylids**.

Fabrosaurids The family Fabrosauridae SUBORDER
uncertain ORDER Ornithischia. Main entry in Chapter 3.

Fabrosaurus "Fabre's lizard" FAMILY Fabrosauridae
SUBORDER uncertain ORDER Ornithischia
TIME Early Jurassic PLACE Lesotho, Africa
DESCRIPTION Primitive ornithischian: a light, long-legged plant-
eater 3ft 4in (1m) long, with small arms, five-fingered hands, long

0   80ft (24m)

tail, and ridged teeth rimming jaws. (*Lesothosaurus*?)

Fenestrosaurus "window lizard" A former name of *Oviraptor*.

Frenguellisaurus "Frenguelli lizard" FAMILY Staurikosauridae?
SUBORDER ? ORDER Herrerasauria
TIME Late Triassic PLACE northwest Argentina
DESCRIPTION Primitive carnivorous dinosaur weighing about 770lb
(350kg), with a long, low head, strong jaws armed with fangs,
birdlike shoulder blade and upper arm, and a *Staurikosaurus*-like hip
bone. Some think it was a herrerasaurid.

Fulgurotherium "lightning beast" FAMILY Hypsilophodontidae
SUBORDER Ornithopoda ORDER Ornithischia
TIME Early Cretaceous PLACE New South Wales, Australia
DESCRIPTION Two-legged plant-eater only 7ft (2m) long, with a
horny beak, short arms, and long hind limbs. Known only from
part of a thigh bone. (Perhaps was *Kangnasaurus*.)

"Futabasaurus" "Futaba lizard" Unofficial name for a Japanese
theropod, to be described.

Gadolosaurus A former name of *Arstanosaurus*.

Gallimimus "fowl mimic" FAMILY Ornithomimidae
INFRAORDER Ornithomimosauria SUBORDER Theropoda
ORDER Saurischia
TIME Late Cretaceous PLACE southern Mongolia
DESCRIPTION Tall birdlike ostrich dinosaur with large eyes,
toothless beak, thin arms, clawed "hands," long slim legs, slender
S-shaped neck and slim, stiffly held tail. At up to 20ft (6m), the
longest known of all the ostrich dinosaurs.

Garudimimids The family Garudimimidae
INFRAORDER Ornithomimosauria SUBORDER Theropoda
ORDER Saurischia. Main entry in Chapter 3.

Garudimimus "Garuda (a mythological bird) mimic" FAMILY
Garudimimidae INFRAORDER Ornithomimosauria
SUBORDER Theropoda ORDER Saurischia
TIME Late Cretaceous PLACE southern Mongolia
DESCRIPTION Tall birdlike ostrich dinosaur with brow hornlet,
rounded tip to its toothless beak, shorter toes than other ostrich
dinosaurs, and old-fashioned features in skull and feet.

Gasosaurus "gas lizard" FAMILY Megalosauridae?
INFRAORDER Carnosauria SUBORDER Theropoda ORDER Saurischia
TIME Middle Jurassic PLACE Sichuan, China
DESCRIPTION Fairly small two-legged flesh-eater 13ft (4m) long and
8ft 3in (2.5m) high, with curved, serrated fangs, powerful legs, and
perhaps three-clawed hands. Named (1985) to mark the petroleum
industry's contribution to its discovery.

Genyodectes "biting jaw" FAMILY uncertain
INFRAORDER Carnosauria SUBORDER Theropoda ORDER Saurischia
TIME Late Cretaceous PLACE Chubut, southern Argentina
DESCRIPTION Large, two-legged, flesh-eating dinosaur known by a
snout tip with long, slim teeth. Some consider it an abelisaurid.

Geranosaurus "crane lizard" FAMILY Heterodontosauridae
SUBORDER Ornithopoda ORDER Ornithischia
TIME Early Jurassic PLACE Cape Province, South Africa
DESCRIPTION Plant-eater 4ft (1.2m) long, with grinding cheek teeth,

Fulgurotherium

Gallimimus

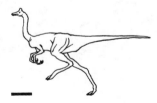

Garudimimus

Genyodectes

©DIAGRAM

Gigantosaurus – "Hadrosauravus"

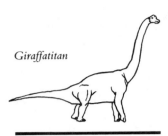

Giraffatitan

Gorgosaurus

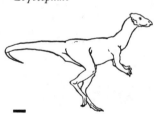

Goyocephale

Gravitholus

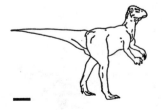

small tusks, and long slim legs. Bipedal/quadrupedal?

Gigantosaurus "giant lizard" A former name of *Pelorosaurus*.

Gigantoscelus "giant leg" A former name of *Euskelosaurus*.

Gilmoreosaurus "Gilmore's lizard" FAMILY Hadrosauridae
SUBORDER Ornithopoda ORDER Ornithischia
TIME Late Cretaceous PLACE China
DESCRIPTION Large bipedal/quadrupedal plant-eater with duck-like
beak and batteries of grinding cheek teeth; an early and seemingly
primitive and relatively small Asian hadrosaurid.

Giraffatitan "gigantic giraffe" GENUS *Brachiosaurus*
FAMILY Brachiosauridae INFRAORDER Sauropoda
SUBORDER Sauropodomorpha ORDER Saurischia
TIME Late Jurassic PLACE Tendaguru, Tanzania
DESCRIPTION One of the largest, tallest dinosaurs: an immense
giraffe-like creature 82ft (25m) long, 52ft (16m) high, and weighing
50 US tons (45 metric tons). Lightly built African subgenus of
(see also) *Brachiosaurus*. Named in 1988.

Gongbusaurus "Gongbu lizard" FAMILY Fabrosauridae
SUBORDER uncertain ORDER Ornithischia
TIME Early Later Jurassic PLACE Sichuan and Xinjiang, China
DESCRIPTION Two-legged plant-eater 5ft (1.5m) long, known from
partial skeletons. Named in 1983.

Gorgosaurus "terrible lizard" FAMILY Tyrannosauridae
INFRAORDER Carnosauria SUBORDER Theropoda ORDER Saurischia
TIME Late Cretaceous PLACE Alberta, Canada
DESCRIPTION Huge two-legged flesh-eater with massive head and
jaws but small, two-fingered arms. Some think it *Albertosaurus*.

Goyocephale "decorated head" FAMILY Homalocephalidae
SUBORDER Pachycephalosauria ORDER Ornithischia
TIME Late Cretaceous PLACE Mongolia
DESCRIPTION Bone-headed dinosaur, a two-legged plant-eater with
pairs of small, stabbing front teeth and a low-domed head, with a
thick, rough skull. Described in 1982.

Gravisaurus "heavy lizard" Iguanodontid ornithischian from
Niger, named but not described.

Gravitholus "heavy dome" FAMILY Pachycephalosauridae
SUBORDER Pachycephalosauria ORDER Ornithischia
TIME Late Cretaceous PLACE Alberta, Canada
DESCRIPTION Bone-headed dinosaur, a two-legged plant-eater
perhaps 10ft (3m) long, with a thick, broad, dome-shaped skull
with small pits and a large depression.

Gresslyosaurus "Gressly's lizard" A former name of *Plateosaurus*.

Griphosaurus "griffin lizard" A former name of *Archaeopteryx*.

Gryponyx "griffin claw" A former name of *Massospondylus*.

Gryposaurus "griffin lizard" FAMILY Hadrosauridae
SUBORDER Ornithopoda ORDER Ornithischia
TIME Late Cretaceous PLACE Alberta, Canada
DESCRIPTION Large bipedal/quadrupedal plant-eater, a duck-billed
dinosaur that some identify with *Hadrosaurus*.

Gyposaurus " ? " A former name of *Anchisaurus*.

"Hadrosauravus" Large, beaked, bipedal/quadrupedal plant-eater: a
duck-billed dinosaur being formally named and described.

0   80ft (24m)

Hadrosaurids The family Hadrosauridae
SUBORDER Ornithopoda ORDER Ornithischia. Main entry in
Chapter 3.
Hadrosaurs The **hadrosaurids** and **lambeosaurids.**
Hadrosaurus "big lizard" FAMILY Hadrosauridae
SUBORDER Ornithopoda ORDER Ornithischia
TIME Late Cretaceous PLACE Alberta, Canada; and New Jersey,
Montana, New Mexico, USA
DESCRIPTION Large bipedal/quadrupedal plant-eater 26-32ft (8-10m)
long, with toothless beak and batteries of cheek teeth.

Hadrosaurus

Halticosaurids The family Halticosauridae
INFRAORDER Coelurosauria? SUBORDER Theropoda ORDER
Saurischia. Poorly known family of early, two-legged, flesh-eating
dinosaurs. Some consider it includes *Dilophosaurus, Dolichosuchus,
Halticosaurus, Liliensternus, Tanystrosuchus,* and *Walkeria.*
Halticosaurus "nimble lizard" FAMILY Halticosauridae
INFRAORDER Coelurosauria? SUBORDER Theropoda
ORDER Saurischia
TIME Late Triassic PLACE southern Germany and maybe France
DESCRIPTION Two-legged early flesh-eater about 18ft (5.5m) long,
with big head, short arms, and four- or five-fingered hands.

Halticosaurus

Haplocanthosaurus "single-spined lizard" FAMILY Cetiosauridae
INFRAORDER Sauropoda SUBORDER Sauropodomorpha
ORDER Saurischia
TIME Late Jurassic PLACE Western USA
DESCRIPTION Very large four-legged plant-eater up to 72ft (21.5m)
long, with long neck and back, solid, single-spined vertebrae,
relatively long forelimbs and high shoulders, and short tail.
Haplocanthus "single spine" A former name of *Haplocanthosaurus.*
Harpymimus "harpy mimic" FAMILY Garudimimidae
INFRAORDER Ornithomimosauria SUBORDER Theropoda
ORDER Theropoda
TIME Mid Cretaceous PLACE Mongolia
DESCRIPTION Two-legged predator or omnivore weighing about
276lb (125kg). A primitive ostrich dinosaur with teeth in its beak,
slim neck, clawed fingers, long legs, and long tail. Named 1984.

Haplocanthosaurus

Hecatasaurus "Hecate (a goddess of the Underworld) lizard"
Former name of *Telmatosaurus.*
Heishansaurus "Mt. Hei lizard" FAMILY Ankylosauridae?
SUBORDER Ankylosauria? ORDER Ornithischia
TIME Late Cretaceous PLACE China
DESCRIPTION Armored (or possibly bone-headed) dinosaur known
from scrappy fossils including a thick skull roof.
Helopus "marsh foot" A former name of *Euhelopus.*
Heptasteornis "seven mountains bird" FAMILY Troodontidae
INFRAORDER Deinonychosauria SUBORDER Theropoda
ORDER Saurischia
TIME Latest Late Cretaceous PLACE Romania
DESCRIPTION Poorly known – probably a small, light, two-legged
predator with large eyes, sharp teeth, clawed, grasping hands,
stiffened tail, and switchblade sickle claw on each second toe.
Herrerasaurids The family Herrerasauridae SUBORDER **Herrerasauria?**
ORDER **Herrerasauria.** Main entry in Chapter 3.

Harpymimus

©DIAGRAM

Herrerasaurus

Heterodontosaurus

Homalocephale

Hoplitosaurus

0   80ft (24m)

Herrerasaurs The order Herrerasauria. Group of primitive, early dinosaurs, including the **herrerasaurids, staurikosaurids,** and *Aliwalia.*

Herrerasaurus "Herrera lizard" FAMILY Herrerasauridae
SUBORDER ? ORDER Herrerasauria
TIME Early Late Triassic PLACE northwest Argentina
DESCRIPTION Two-legged flesh-eater about 10ft (3m) long, with sharp teeth, short, birdlike, folding arms, longer thighs than shins, four-toed feet, and hip bones with saurischian and ornithischian features. One of the earliest known dinosaurs, arguably too primitive to be saurischian or ornithischian.

Heterodontosaurids The family Heterodontosauridae
SUBORDER Ornithopoda ORDER Ornithischia. Main entry in Chapter 3.

Heterodontosaurus "different teeth lizard"
FAMILY Heterodontosauridae SUBORDER Ornithopoda
ORDER Ornithischia
TIME Early Jurassic PLACE southern Africa
DESCRIPTION Early bipedal/quadrupedal plant-eater 3ft 11in (1.2m) long, with small, sharp cutting teeth, short, curved tusks (perhaps only in the males), and close-packed, grinding cheek teeth that chewed from side to side as well as up and down.

Heterosaurus "different lizard" *Iguanodon.*

Hierosaurus "sacred lizard" Probably *Nodosaurus.*

Hikanodon " ? " A former name of *Iguanodon.*

"Hironosaurus" "Hirono-machi lizard" FAMILY Hadrosauridae?
SUBORDER Ornithopoda ORDER Ornithischia
TIME Late Cretaceous PLACE Fukushima, Japan
DESCRIPTION Unofficially named large, bipedal/quadrupedal plant-eater probably with duck-like beak and batteries of cheek teeth; known only from scanty fossil remains.

"Hisanohamasaurus" "Hisano-hama lizard" FAMILY Diplodocidae?
INFRAORDER Sauropoda SUBORDER Sauropodomorpha
ORDER Saurischia
TIME Late Cretaceous PLACE Fukushima, Japan
DESCRIPTION Unofficially named large, four-legged plant-eater maybe with long neck and tail; only known from pencil-shaped teeth.

Homalocephale "even head" FAMILY Homalocephalidae
SUBORDER Pachycephalosauria ORDER Ornithischia
TIME Late Cretaceous PLACE Mongolia
DESCRIPTION Bipedal plant-eater about 10ft (3m) long with a large, flat, fairly smooth skull roof with nodes along the back.

Homalocephalids The family Homalocephalidae
SUBORDER Pachycephalosauria ORDER Ornithischia. Main entry in Chapter 3.

Honghesaurus Early unofficial name of *Yandusaurus.*

Hoplitosaurus "armed lizard" FAMILY Nodosauridae
SUBORDER Ankylosauria ORDER Ornithischia
TIME Early Cretaceous PLACE South Dakota, USA
DESCRIPTION Four-legged armored plant-eater protected by flat, keeled, round, spined, and triangular armor plating. Known from scanty remains. Some think it was *Polacanthus.*

Hoplosaurus "weapon lizard" A former name of *Struthiosaurus*.

Hortalotarsus " ? foot" A former name of *Massospondylus*.

Huayangosaurids The family Huayangosauridae SUBORDER Stegosauria ORDER Ornithischia. Main entry in Chapter 3.

Huayangosaurus "Huayang lizard" FAMILY Huayangosauridae SUBORDER Stegosauria ORDER Ornithischia
TIME Middle Jurassic PLACE Sichuan, China
DESCRIPTION Primitive plated dinosaur 13ft (4m) long: a four-legged plant-eater with deep, short-snouted head with front upper teeth, distinctive skeleton, two rows of narrow, pointed bony plates down neck and back, and tail and shoulder spines.

Huayangosaurus

"Hughenden sauropod" FAMILY Brachiosauridae?
INFRAORDER Sauropoda SUBORDER Sauropodomorpha
ORDER Saurischia
TIME Early Cretaceous PLACE Queensland, Australia
DESCRIPTION Huge four-legged plant-eater about 66ft (20m) long or more, perhaps resembling a gigantic giraffe but known only from one incomplete spinal bone. Might be *Austrosaurus*.

"Hughenden sauropod"

Hulsanpes "Khulsan foot" FAMILY Dromaeosauridae
INFRAORDER Deinonychosauria SUBORDER Theropoda
ORDER Saurischia
TIME Late Cretaceous PLACE Mongolia
DESCRIPTION Small two-legged predator known from foot bones.

Hylaeosaurus "woodland lizard" FAMILY Nodosauridae
SUBORDER Ankylosauria ORDER Ornithischia
TIME Early Cretaceous PLACE southeast England
DESCRIPTION Four-legged, armored plant-eater 13ft (4m) long, with rows of big curved plates guarding its back. Named for fossil remains perhaps of *Polacanthus* and *Polacanthoides*.

Hylaeosaurus

Hypacrosaurus "nearly the highest lizard" FAMILY Lambeosauridae
SUBORDER Ornithopoda ORDER Ornithischia
TIME Late Cretaceous PLACE Canada, USA, and ?Mexico
DESCRIPTION Bipedal/quadrupedal plant-eater 30ft (9m) long, with a high-ridged back. The short, tall skull had a toothless beak, batteries of cheek teeth, and a less rounded "cocked hat" crest than *Corythosaurus*, with a spike jutting down at the back.

Hypacrosaurus

Hypselosaurus "high ridge lizard" FAMILY Titanosauridae
INFRAORDER Sauropoda SUBORDER Sauropodomorpha
ORDER Saurischia
TIME Late Cretaceous PLACE southern France and northern Spain
DESCRIPTION Four-legged plant-eater 40ft (12m) long with long neck and whiplash tail; a likely source of fossil sauropod eggs twice as large as ostrich eggs, found in southern France.

Hypsibema "high step" FAMILY Hadrosauridae? INFRAORDER Ornithopoda SUBORDER Ornithischia ORDER Saurischia
TIME Late Cretaceous PLACE North Carolina and Missouri, USA
DESCRIPTION Poorly known dinosaur based on fossils from at least two kinds of beast, one an ornithischian.

Hypsilophodon "high ridge tooth" FAMILY Hypsilophodontidae
SUBORDER Ornithopoda ORDER Ornithischia
TIME Early Cretaceous PLACE USA, England, Portugal
DESCRIPTION Small, speedy two-legged plant-eater 4ft 6in-7ft 6in (1.4-2.3m) long. It had a horny beak with teeth, self-sharpening

Hypsilophodon

© DIAGRAM

67

Iguanodon

Indosuchus

Ingenia

Inosaurus

0   80ft (24m)

Hypsilophodontids – Inosaurus

cheek teeth, cheek pouches, short arms with five-fingered hands, long shins, long, four-toed feet, and a tendon-stiffened tail.

Hypsilophodontids The family Hypsilophodontidae SUBORDER Ornithopoda ORDER Ornithischia. Main entry in Chapter 3.

Hypsirophus "high ?" A former name of *Stegosaurus*.

Ichthyosaurs "fish lizards" The subclass Ichthyopterygia. Not dinosaurs but extinct dolphin–like marine reptiles with fins and a vertical tail. TIME Early Triassic through Late Cretaceous.

Iguanasaurus "iguana lizard" A former name of *Iguanodon*.

Iguanodon "iguana tooth" FAMILY Iguanodontidae SUBORDER Ornithopoda ORDER Ornithischia TIME Early Cretaceous PLACE western North America, western Europe, Romania, and Mongolia DESCRIPTION Large bipedal/quadrupedal plant-eater up to 29ft 6in (9m) long and weighing up to 5 tons, with toothless beak, tight-packed, ridged cheek teeth, hooflike claws, and spiky thumbs.

Iguanodontids The family Iguanodontidae SUBORDER Ornithopoda ORDER Ornithischia. Main entry in Chapter 3.

Iliosuchus "crocodile hipped" FAMILY Megalosauridae? INFRAORDER Carnosauria SUBORDER Theropoda ORDER Saurischia TIME Mid Jurassic PLACE Oxfordshire, England DESCRIPTION Two-legged flesh-eater known only from an ilium (upper hip bone). Possibly *Piatnitzkysaurus*.

Indosaurus "Indian lizard" FAMILY Abelisauridae? INFRAORDER Carnosauria SUBORDER Theropoda ORDER Saurischia TIME Late Cretaceous PLACE Madhya Pradesh, central India DESCRIPTION Large, two–legged broad-headed flesh-eater known from a massive, thick braincase.

Indosuchus "Indian crocodile" FAMILY Abelisauridae? INFRAORDER Carnosauria SUBORDER Theropoda ORDER Saurischia TIME Late Cretaceous PLACE Madhya Pradesh, central India DESCRIPTION Large, two-legged flesh-eater known from part of a skull somewhat like *Tyrannosaurus*'s but smaller and more primitive with more and shorter sharply tapered teeth.

Ingenia named for Ingenia-Khuduk FAMILY Oviraptoridae or Ingeniidae INFRAORDER Oviraptorosauria SUBORDER Theropoda ORDER Saurischia TIME Late Cretaceous PLACE southwest Mongolia DESCRIPTION Small, two-legged birdlike predator, omnivore, or herbivore perhaps 4ft 6in (1.4m) long, probably with a toothless beak like *Oviraptor* but with stubbier fingers (the first the longest) armed with less sharply curved claws. Named in 1981.

Ingeniids The family Ingeniidae INFRAORDER Oviraptorosauria SUBORDER Theropoda ORDER Saurischia. Family created in 1986 for the unusual oviraptorosaurid *Ingenia*.

Inosaurus "In (In Tedreft) lizard" FAMILY Coeluridae INFRAORDER Coelurosauria SUBORDER Theropoda ORDER Saurischia TIME Early Cretaceous PLACE In Tedreft and In Abangarit, Niger

DESCRIPTION Two–legged predator about 7ft (2.1m) long. Identity doubtful.

Ischisaurus "Ischigualasto lizard" FAMILY Herrerasauria SUBORDER ? ORDER Herrerasauridae
TIME Early Late Triassic PLACE northwest Argentina
DESCRIPTION Small two–legged predator about 7ft (2m) long – one of the earliest dinosaurs. Some consider it too primitive to identify as either saurischian or ornithischian.

Ischisaurus

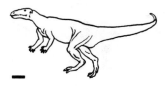

Ischyrosaurus "?hip lizard" A former name of *Pelorosaurus*.

Itemirids The family Itemiridae INFRAORDER Carnosauria SUBORDER Theropoda ORDER Saurischia. Family containing *Itemirus*.

Itemirus "Itemir lizard" FAMILY Itemiridae
INFRAORDER Carnosauria SUBORDER Theropoda ORDER Saurischia
TIME Late Cretaceous PLACE Itemir, Kyzylkym Desert, USSR
DESCRIPTION Small, maybe speedy, two–legged flesh-eater with keen sight and well-developed sense of balance. Known from a braincase with features found in *Dromaeosaurus* and *Tyrannosaurus*.

Jaxartosaurus "Jaxartes lizard" FAMILY Lambeosauridae
SUBORDER Ornithopoda ORDER Ornithischia
TIME Late Cretaceous PLACE Kazakhstan, USSR; Xinjiang, China
DESCRIPTION Bipedal/quadrupedal plant-eater 30ft (9m) long, with toothless beak and batteries of cheek teeth; poorly known.

Jaxartosaurus

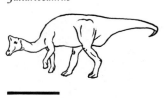

Jiangjunmiaosaurus "Jiangjunmiao lizard" FAMILY Megalosauridae
INFRAORDER Carnosauria SUBORDER Theropoda ORDER Saurischia
TIME Late Jurassic? PLACE Xinjiang, China
DESCRIPTION Large two–legged flesh-eater maybe with a crested skull; discovered in 1983. See also **"Monolophosaurus"**

Jubbulpuria "from Jabalpur" FAMILY Coeluridae
INFRAORDER Coelurosauria SUBORDER Theropoda ORDER Saurischia
TIME Late Cretaceous PLACE Madhya Pradesh, central India
DESCRIPTION Tiny two–legged flesh-eater, about 4ft (1.2m) long, known from little more than two spinal bones. Identity doubtful.

Jubbulpuria

Jurapteryx "Jura wing" An archaeopterygid named in 1985 from a redescribed fossil *Archaeopteryx*; probably just *Archaeopteryx*.

"Kagasaurus" "Kaga lizard" FAMILY Megalosauridae?
INFRAORDER Carnosauria SUBORDER Theropoda ORDER Saurischia
TIME Early Cretaceous PLACE Shiramine-mura in Ishihawa, Japan
DESCRIPTION Unofficially named, large two–legged flesh-eater, only known from its big, sharp teeth. Identity doubtful.

Kakuru

Kaijiangosaurus "Kaijiang lizard" FAMILY Megalosauridae?
INFRAORDER Carnosauria SUBORDER Theropoda ORDER Saurischia
TIME Middle Jurassic PLACE Kaijiang County in Sichuan, China
DESCRIPTION Large two–legged flesh-eater with compressed fangs and distinctive bones in head, neck, arm, and thighs. Named 1984.

Kakuru "rainbow serpent" FAMILY Coeluridae?
INFRAORDER Coelurosauria SUBORDER Theropoda ORDER Saurischia
TIME Early Cretaceous PLACE central South Australia
DESCRIPTION Small two–legged flesh-eater about 8ft (2.4m) long, known only from a shin bone largely changed to opal.

Kangnasaurus "very slender lizard" FAMILY Dryosauridae

Kangnasaurus

© DIAGRAM

Kelmayisaurus

Kentrosaurus

Kritosaurus

Labocania

0   80ft (24m)

"Katsuyamasaurus" – Labocania

SUBORDER Ornithopoda ORDER Ornithischia
TIME Cretaceous PLACE Namaqualand, South Africa
DESCRIPTION Fairly small bipedal plant-eater known from a thigh
bone and a tooth; once thought to be an iguanodontid.

"Katsuyamasaurus" "Katsuyama lizard" FAMILY Allosauridae
INFRAORDER Carnosauria SUBORDER Theropoda ORDER Saurischia
TIME Early Cretaceous PLACE Katsuyama in Fukui, Japan
DESCRIPTION Unofficially named, large two-legged flesh-eater
known only from a lower arm bone. Identity doubtful.

Kelmayisaurus "Kelmayi lizard" FAMILY Megalosauridae
INFRAORDER Carnosauria SUBORDER Theropoda ORDER Saurischia
TIME Early Cretaceous PLACE Xinjiang, China DESCRIPTION Large
two-legged flesh-eater known from such scrappy fossils as a
toothless lower jaw. Identity doubtful.

Kentrosaurus "spiky lizard" FAMILY Stegosauridae
SUBORDER Stegosauria ORDER Ornithischia
TIME Late Jurassic PLACE Tendaguru, Tanzania
DESCRIPTION Four-legged plant-eater 17ft (5m) long, with two rows
of short triangular plates above neck and shoulders, tall narrow
spines above back and tail, and a pair of shoulder spikes.

Kentrurosaurus "spiky tail lizard" Former name of *Kentrosaurus*.

"Kitadanisaurus" "Kitadani lizard" FAMILY Coeluridae?
INFRAORDER Coelurosauria? SUBORDER Theropoda
ORDER Saurischia
TIME Early Cretaceous PLACE Katsuyama in Fukui, Japan
DESCRIPTION Unofficially named, small two-legged predator
known only from a tooth. Identity doubtful.

Koreanosaurus "Korean lizard" FAMILY Dromaeosauridae?
INFRAORDER Deinonychosauria? SUBORDER Theropoda
ORDER Saurischia
TIME Cretaceous PLACE North Gyeongsang-do, South Korea
DESCRIPTION Small, two-legged flesh-eater (*Deinonychus*?), known
only from a thigh bone first thought to be an ornithopod's.

Kotasaurus "Kota lizard" FAMILY Vulcanodontidae?
INFRAORDER Sauropoda SUBORDER Sauropodomorpha
ORDER Saurischia
TIME Early Jurassic PLACE central India
DESCRIPTION Large four-legged plant-eater with long neck and tail:
a primitive sauropod to be formally described.

Kritosaurus "noble lizard" FAMILY Hadrosauridae
SUBORDER Ornithopoda ORDER Ornithischia TIME Late Cretaceous
PLACE Alberta, Canada; New Mexico, USA; Mexico; Argentina
DESCRIPTION Large bipedal/quadrupedal plant-eater 30ft (9m) long
and weighing about 3 tons, with broad flat head, humped snout,
toothless beak, and batteries of cheek teeth.

Kunmingosaurus "Kunming lizard" FAMILY Cetiosauridae
INFRAORDER Sauropoda SUBORDER Sauropodomorpha
ORDER Saurischia
TIME Early Jurassic? PLACE Yunnan, China
DESCRIPTION Large four-legged plant-eater with long neck and tail:
an early sauropod named in 1986.

Labocania "La Bocana (having red lips)" FAMILY uncertain

INFRAORDER Carnosauria SUBORDER Theropoda ORDER Saurischia
TIME Late Cretaceous PLACE Baja California (La Bocana Roja rock formation), Mexico
DESCRIPTION Two-legged flesh-eater with a massive head. Apart from the jaws it somewhat resembled *Tyrannosaurus*.

Laevisuchus

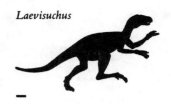

Labrosaurus "?lip lizard" A former name of *Allosaurus*.
Laelaps "terrible leaper" A former name of *Dryptosaurus*.
Laevisuchus "slim, or light, crocodile" FAMILY Caenagnathidae?
INFRAORDER Oviraptorosauria? SUBORDER Theropoda
ORDER Saurischia
TIME Late Cretaceous PLACE Madhya Pradesh, central India
DESCRIPTION Two-legged flesh-eater about 7ft (2.1m) long, known from three neck bones somewhat like those of *Microvenator*.

Lagosuchus

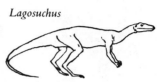

Lagerpetonids "rabbit reptiles" The family Lagerpetonidae
SUBORDER Ornithosuchia ORDER Thecodontia
TIME Earliest Late Triassic PLACE Argentina
DESCRIPTION Rabbit-sized reptile "protodinosaurs" with dinosaur-like hindlimbs. They included *Lagerpeton* and *Lewisuchus*.
Lagosuchids "rabbit crocodiles" The family Lagosuchidae
SUBORDER Ornithosuchia ORDER Thecodontia
TIME Earliest Late Triassic PLACE Argentina
DESCRIPTION Rabbit-sized, bipedal/quadrupedal "protodinosaurs" with long rabbitlike legs and hands capable of grasping prey. Head, neck, shoulders, and ankles showed features found in their possible descendants, dinosaurs and pterosaurs. Lagosuchids included *Lagosuchus* and *Pseudolagosuchus*.

Lambeosaurus

Lambeosaurids The family Lambeosauridae
SUBORDER Ornithopoda ORDER Ornithischia. Main entry in Chapter 3.
Lambeosaurus "Lambe's lizard" FAMILY Lambeosauridae
SUBORDER Ornithopoda ORDER Ornithischia
TIME Late Cretaceous PLACE Alberta, Canada; Montana, USA; Baja California, Mexico
DESCRIPTION Bipedal/quadrupedal plant-eater with pebbly skin, toothless beak, batteries of cheek teeth, and hatchet-shaped skull crest with backward pointing bony spike perhaps anchoring a neck frill. One of the largest hadrosaurs, up to 49ft (15m) long.
Lametasaurus "Lameta lizard" FAMILY Titanosauridae
INFRAORDER Sauropoda SUBORDER Sauropodomorpha
ORDER Saurischia
TIME Late Cretaceous PLACE Madhya Pradesh, central India
DESCRIPTION Large four-legged plant-eater, named from fossils mixed with theropod remains and bits of crocodilian body armor.

Lametasaurus

Lanasaurus "wool lizard" FAMILY Heterodontosauridae
SUBORDER Ornithopoda ORDER Ornithischia
TIME Early Jurassic PLACE Orange Free State, South Africa
DESCRIPTION Small bipedal/quadrupedal plant-eater with self-sharpening teeth; new replaced old in groups of three.
Lancangjiangosaurus "Lancangjian lizard" FAMILY Brachiosauridae
INFRAORDER Sauropoda SUBORDER Sauropodomorpha
ORDER Saurischia
TIME Middle Jurassic PLACE Sichuan?, China
DESCRIPTION Very large four-legged plant-eater somewhat like a

©DIAGRAM

Lanasaurus

Lancangosaurus – Lexovisaurus

Lapparentosaurus

huge giraffe with massive limbs; described in 1986.

Lancangosaurus "Lancang lizard" A former name of *Datousaurus*.

Laopteryx "fossil wing" Supposed archaeopterygid, now known to be a pterosaur.

Laosaurus "fossil lizard" FAMILY Hypsilophodontidae or Dryosauridae SUBORDER Ornithopoda ORDER Ornithischia
TIME Late Jurassic PLACE Wyoming, USA
DESCRIPTION Small, long-legged bipedal plant-eater poorly known from spinal bones. Perhaps identical to *Othnielia* or *Dryosaurus*.

Laplatasaurus "La Plata lizard" FAMILY Titanosauridae
INFRAORDER Sauropoda SUBORDER Sauropodomorpha
ORDER Saurischia
TIME Late Cretaceous PLACE Argentina, ?India, and ?Madagascar
DESCRIPTION Very large four-legged plant-eater about 60ft (18m) long, with long neck and tail and maybe bony plates embedded in its skin; slimmer but maybe larger than *Titanosaurus*.

Lapparentosaurus "Lapparent's lizard" FAMILY Cetiosauridae
INFRAORDER Sauropoda SUBORDER Sauropodomorpha
ORDER Saurischia
TIME Middle Jurassic PLACE northern Madagascar
DESCRIPTION Large four-legged plant-eater with long neck and tail and more primitive vertebrae than most cetiosaurids.

Leptoceratops

Leaellynosaura "Leaellyn's lizard" FAMILY Hypsilophodontidae
SUBORDER Ornithopoda ORDER Ornithischia
TIME Early Cretaceous PLACE Victoria, Australia
DESCRIPTION Small, speedy two-legged plant-eater with large eyes. A juvenile? Two scientists named it after their daughter in 1989.

Leipsanosaurus " ? lizard" Former name of *Struthiosaurus*.

Lepidosaurs "scaly reptiles" Not dinosaurs but reptiles including lizards, snakes, and *Sphenodon* (the tuatara).
SUPERORDER Lepidosauria INFRACLASS Lepidosauromorpha
SUBCLASS Diapsida.

Leptoceratops "slim horned face" FAMILY Protoceratopsidae
SUBORDER Ceratopsia ORDER Ornithopoda
TIME Late Cretaceous PLACE Canada, USA, Mongolia
DESCRIPTION Quadrupedal and maybe bipedal plant-eater only 6ft (1.8m) long and weighing 120lb (55kg), with big head, parrot-like beak, flat, solid neck frill, and no horns.

Leptospondylus "slim vertebrae" A former name of *Massospondylus*.

Lesothosaurus

Lesothosaurus "Lesotho lizard" FAMILY Fabrosauridae
SUBORDER uncertain ORDER Ornithischia
TIME Early Jurassic PLACE Lesotho
DESCRIPTION Early two-legged plant-eater only 3ft 4in (1m) long, with pointed front teeth, cheek teeth like tiny serrated arrowheads, small cheeks, flexible neck, long tail, long legs (especially shins), and short arms. Was perhaps *Fabrosaurus*.

Lexovisaurus

Lexovisaurus "Lexovii lizard" FAMILY Stegosauridae
SUBORDER Stegosauria ORDER Ornithischia
TIME Middle Jurassic PLACE England and France
DESCRIPTION Four-legged plant-eater 17ft (5m) long, probably with two rows of narrow, short plates on neck and back, and long paired spines on the tail and shoulders. Named for the Lexovii, an ancient

0   80ft (24m)

tribe that lived in France.

Likhoelesaurus "Li Khoele lizard" FAMILY Melanorosauridae
INFRAORDER Prosauropoda SUBORDER Sauropodomorpha
ORDER Saurischia
TIME Late Triassic PLACE Lesotho
DESCRIPTION One of the first large four-legged plant-eaters,
formerly misidentified from teeth belonging to a theropod.

Liliensternus "(Herr von) Lilienstern" FAMILY Halticosauridae?
INFRAORDER Coelurosauria SUBORDER Theropoda ORDER Saurischia
TIME Late Triassic PLACE Germany
DESCRIPTION Two-legged predator about 16ft (5m) long, with
features seen in *Coelophysis* and *Dilophosaurus*. Named in 1984, it
might be part *Halticosaurus* part *Sellosaurus*.

Limnosaurus "pool? lizard" A former name of *Telmatosaurus*.

Lizard-hipped dinosaurs See **Saurischians**.

Loncosaurus "Lonco lizard" FAMILY Iguanodontidae or
Hypsilophodontidae? SUBORDER Ornithopoda?
ORDER Ornithischia?
TIME Late Cretaceous PLACE southern Argentina
DESCRIPTION Bipedal or bipedal/quadrupedal plant-eater described
from an ornithopod thigh bone mixed up with theropod teeth. If
named from just the teeth, *Loncosaurus* was a theropod.

Longosaurus "Long's lizard" FAMILY Coelophysidae
INFRAORDER Coelurosauria SUBORDER Theropoda ORDER Saurischia
TIME Late Triassic PLACE New Mexico, USA
DESCRIPTION Two-legged predator up to 10ft (3m) long, with low,
long head, small, sharp teeth, snaky neck, four-fingered hands
(fourth fingers much reduced), effectively three-toed feet, and long
tail. Named in 1984. Maybe just a long-necked *Coelophysis*.

Lophorhothon "crested snout" FAMILY Hadrosauridae
SUBORDER Ornithopoda ORDER Ornithischia
TIME Late Cretaceous PLACE Alabama, USA
DESCRIPTION Bipedal/quadrupedal plant-eater maybe up to 49ft
(15m) long, with toothless beak, batteries of cheek teeth, and a
bony hump above the short snout. Known only from a juvenile.

Loricosaurus "armored lizard" FAMILY Titanosauridae
INFRAORDER Sauropoda SUBORDER Sauropodomorpha
ORDER Saurischia
TIME Late Cretaceous PLACE southern Argentina
DESCRIPTION Large four-legged plant-eater with long neck and tail,
only known from bony plates embedded in its skin.

Lufengocephalus "Lufeng head" FAMILY Fabrosauridae?
SUBORDER uncertain ORDER Ornithischia?
TIME Early Jurassic PLACE Yunnan, China
DESCRIPTION Probably a small, early bipedal plant-eater; possibly a
prosauropod (*Lufengosaurus* or *Tawasaurus*).

Lufengosaurus "Lufeng lizard" FAMILY Plateosauridae
INFRAORDER Prosauropoda SUBORDER Sauropodomorpha
ORDER Saurischia
TIME Early Jurassic PLACE China (Sichuan, Yunnan, Tibet)
DESCRIPTION Bipedal/quadrupedal plant-eater up to 20ft (6m) long,
with small head, widely spaced teeth, long neck, heavy body,
broad feet, long, clawed fingers and massive, clawed thumbs.

Likhoelesaurus

Loncosaurus

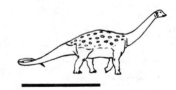
Loricosaurus

Lufengosaurus

©DIAGRAM

73

Lukousaurus – Majungatholus

Macrophalangia

Lukousaurus "Lukou lizard" FAMILY Coelophysidae
INFRAORDER Coelurosauria SUBORDER Theropoda ORDER Saurischia
TIME Early Jurassic PLACE Yunnan, China
DESCRIPTION Two-legged predator about 6ft 6in (2m) long, with
little brow horns. Might be a thecodont or crocodilian.
Lusitanosaurus "Lusitania lizard" FAMILY Scelidosauridae
SUBORDER Scelidosauria ORDER Ornithischia
TIME Early Jurassic PLACE Portugal
DESCRIPTION Low-slung, four-legged plant-eater protected by bony
studs. Known only from part of an upper jaw and teeth.
Lycorhinus "wolf snout" FAMILY Heterodontosauridae
SUBORDER Ornithopoda ORDER Ornithischia
TIME Early Jurassic PLACE Cape Province, South Africa
DESCRIPTION Small, maybe bipedal/quadrupedal, plant-eater with
sharp front teeth, small curved tusks, and grinding cheek teeth.

Macrurosaurus

Macrodontophion "large tooth snake" Supposed megalosaurid
dinosaur, but probably a crocodilian.
TIME Jurassic PLACE south European Russia
DESCRIPTION Big flesh-eater known only from a large, curved tooth
with a rounded top.
Macrophalangia "big phalanges" (end toe or finger bones)
FAMILY Caenagnathidae INFRAORDER Oviraptorosauria
SUBORDER Theropoda ORDER Saurischia
TIME Late Cretaceous PLACE Alberta, Canada
DESCRIPTION Two-legged predator, herbivore, or omnivore 7ft
(2m) long with longer foot bones than *Elmisaurus*, and probably a
deep head and toothless beak. Some consider it *Chirostenotes*.
Macrurosaurus "long tail lizard" FAMILY Titanosauridae
INFRAORDER Sauropoda SUBORDER Sauropodomorpha
ORDER Saurischia
TIME Early Cretaceous PLACE near Cambridge, eastern England
DESCRIPTION Four-legged plant-eater about 40ft (12m) long, with
bulky body, long neck, and long tail. Known from 40 tail bones.
"Madsenius" A proposed new allosaurid theropod to be formally
named and described.
Magnosaurus "great lizard" Possibly *Megalosaurus*.
Magyarosaurus "Magyar lizard" Probably *Titanosaurus*.
Maiasaura "good mother lizard" FAMILY Hadrosauridae
SUBORDER Ornithopoda ORDER Ornithischia
TIME Late Cretaceous PLACE Montana, USA
DESCRIPTION Bipedal/quadrupedal plant-eater about 30ft (9m) long,
with short, broad, toothless beak, batteries of cheek teeth in
shallow jaws, and a short bony crest between the eyes. Found near
nests 7ft (2m) across, with fossil young of different ages.
Majungasaurus "Majunga lizard" FAMILY Abelisauridae?
INFRAORDER Carnosauria SUBORDER Theropoda ORDER Saurischia
TIME Late Cretaceous PLACE Madagascar and maybe Egypt
DESCRIPTION Fairly large two-legged predator known from teeth, a
partial jaw and bones from the spine.
Majungatholus "Majunga dome" FAMILY Pachycephalosauridae
SUBORDER Pachycephalosauria ORDER Ornithischia
TIME Late Cretaceous PLACE Majunga in northwest Madagascar

Maiasaura

Majungatholus

0   80ft (24m)

DESCRIPTION Two-legged plant-eater perhaps only 4ft 6in (1.4m) long, with a domed skull rimmed by knobs and grooves; first known bone-head from the ancient southern supercontinent Gondwana.

"Maleevosaurus" A Mongolian tyrannosaurid theropod to be formally named.

Maleevus "Maleev" FAMILY Ankylosauridae SUBORDER Ankylosauria ORDER Ornithischia TIME Late Cretaceous PLACE ?Mongolia DESCRIPTION Four-legged armored plant-eater with broad head and bony tail club. Named in 1987. Once mistaken for *Pinacosaurus*.

Mamenchisaurids The Mamenchisauridae, a proposed family of sauropods based on *Mamenchisaurus*. But see its entry.

Mamenchisaurus "Mamenchi lizard" FAMILY Euhelopodidae? INFRAORDER Sauropoda SUBORDER Sauropodomorpha ORDER Saurischia TIME Late Jurassic PLACE Sichuan, Gansu and ?Xinjiang, China DESCRIPTION Very large four-legged plant-eater maybe up to 89ft (27m) long, with the world's longest known neck perhaps measuring up to 49ft (15m), with 19 vertebrae (more than any other known dinosaur), many overlapped by long, thin, reinforcing bony struts. Perhaps a mamenchisaurid, but tall, blunt snout and spoon-shaped teeth suggest it was a euhelopodid.

Mammal-like reptiles See **Synapsids.**

Mammals The class Mammalia: warm-blooded hairy backboned animals whose females suckle their young. Mammals evolved from **Synapsids** early in the Age of Dinosaurs.

Mandschurosaurus "Manchurian lizard" FAMILY Hadrosauridae SUBORDER Ornithopoda ORDER Ornithischia TIME Late Cretaceous PLACE northern China, Laos, Mongolia DESCRIPTION Two-legged plant-eater 26ft (8m) long with flat head, toothless beak, and batteries of cheek teeth.

Manospondylus "sparse vertebrae" A former name of *Tyrannosaurus*

Marginocephalia "bordered heads" Proposed ornithischian hypoorder to include pachycephalosaurs and ceratopsians.

Marmarospondylus "marble vertebrae" *Bothriospondylus*.

Marshosaurus "Marsh's lizard" FAMILY Allosauridae? INFRAORDER Carnosauria? SUBORDER Theropoda ORDER Saurischia TIME Late Jurassic PLACE Utah, USA DESCRIPTION Two-legged predator up to 16ft (5m) long, probably with large head, curved, sharp, serrated teeth, and powerful legs.

Massospondylus "massive vertebrae" FAMILY Plateosauridae INFRAORDER Prosauropoda SUBORDER Sauropodomorpha ORDER Saurischia TIME Early Jurassic PLACE southern Africa and North America DESCRIPTION Bipedal/quadrupedal plant-eater 13ft (4m) long, with long neck and tail, bulky body, massive hands, rounded front teeth, flat-sided back teeth, and possibly a horny lower beak.

Megacervixosaurus "big neck lizard" FAMILY Diplodocidae INFRAORDER Sauropoda SUBORDER Sauropodomorpha ORDER Saurischia TIME Late? Cretaceous PLACE Tibet, China

Mamenchisaurus

Mandschurosaurus

Marshosaurus

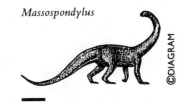
Massospondylus

©DIAGRAM

Megalosaurus

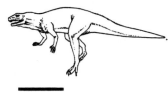

Melanorosaurus

Metriacanthosaurus

Microceratops

0   80ft (24m)

Megadactylus – Microhadrosaurus

DESCRIPTION Very large four-legged plant-eater, probably with long neck, bulky body, and whiplash tail. Named in 1983.

Megadactylus "big finger" A former name of *Anchisaurus*.

Megalosaurids The family Megalosauridae
INFRAORDER Carnosauria SUBORDER Theropoda ORDER Saurischia. Main entry in Chapter 3.

Megalosaurus "great lizard" FAMILY Megalosauridae
INFRAORDER Carnosauria SUBORDER Theropoda ORDER Saurischia
TIME Maybe Early Jurassic through Early Cretaceous PLACE Europe and maybe Africa, Asia, and South America
DESCRIPTION Large, heavily built two-legged predator 30ft (9m) long and weighing a ton or more. It had a large head, short, strong neck, curved, flattened, saw-edged teeth, strong arms, powerful legs, long tail, and formidable toe and finger claws.

Melanorosaurids The family Melanorosauridae
INFRAORDER Prosauropoda SUBORDER Sauropodomorpha ORDER Saurischia. Main entry in Chapter 3.

Melanorosaurus "black mountain lizard" FAMILY Melanorosauridae INFRAORDER Prosauropoda
SUBORDER Sauropodomorpha ORDER Saurischia
TIME Late Triassic PLACE South Africa
DESCRIPTION Four-legged plant-eater about 40ft (12m) long, with small head, long neck, bulky body, elephantine legs, and long tail. One of the largest of prosauropods.

Metriacanthosaurus "moderately spined lizard" FAMILY Megalosauridae? INFRAORDER Carnosauria SUBORDER Theropoda ORDER Saurischia
TIME Early Jurassic PLACE southern England
DESCRIPTION Two-legged predator 26ft (8m) long. Vertebrae with spines up to 10in (26cm) long perhaps supported a skin sail.

Microceratops "tiny horned face" FAMILY Protoceratopsidae SUBORDER Ceratopsia ORDER Ornithischia
TIME Late Cretaceous PLACE China (Gansu, Inner Mongolia, and Shanxi)
DESCRIPTION One of the tiniest dinosaurs, a 30in (76cm) long, mainly bipedal plant-eater with a horny beak, small neck frill, long hind limbs, slim feet, and quite long forelimbs.

Microcoelus "tiny hollow" FAMILY Titanosauridae?
INFRAORDER Sauropoda SUBORDER Sauropodomorpha
ORDER Saurischia
TIME Late Cretaceous PLACE Argentina
DESCRIPTION Large four-legged plant-eater with long neck and tail, but known only from an arm bone and bones from tail and back. Identity doubtful (might be the same as *Saltasaurus*).

Microdontosaurus "tiny tooth lizard" FAMILY Diplodocidae?
INFRAORDER Sauropoda? SUBORDER Sauropodomorpha
ORDER Saurischia
TIME Middle Jurassic PLACE Tibet, China
DESCRIPTION Large four-legged plant-eater with long neck and tail and evidently pencil-like teeth. Named in 1983, it has been called both a sauropod and a prosauropod.

Microhadrosaurus "tiny *Hadrosaurus*" FAMILY Hadrosauridae
SUBORDER Ornithopoda ORDER Ornithischia

TIME Late Cretaceous PLACE Guangdong, China
DESCRIPTION Bipedal/quadrupedal plant-eater with toothless beak
and batteries of cheek teeth: one of the smallest hadrosaurs, about
8ft 2in (2.5m) long. Named in 1979, but identity doubtful.

Micropachycephalosaurus "tiny thick-headed lizard" FAMILY
Homalocephalidae SUBORDER Pachycephalosauria
ORDER Ornithischia
TIME Late Cretaceous PLACE Shandong, China
DESCRIPTION One of the tiniest known dinosaurs: a bipedal,
bone-headed plant-eater about 20in (51cm) long, with a flattened
dome-shaped skull. Given its immensely long name in 1978.

Microvenator "tiny hunter" FAMILY Caenagnathidae
INFRAORDER Oviraptorosauria SUBORDER Theropoda
ORDER Saurischia
TIME Early Cretaceous PLACE Montana, USA; and Tibet, China
DESCRIPTION Two-legged birdlike predator or herbivore 4ft (1.2m)
long, with small head, maybe deep toothless beak, long neck and
tail, three-fingered hands, short arms, and long strong legs.

"Mifunesaurus" "Mifune lizard" FAMILY Megalosauridae?
INFRAORDER Carnosauria SUBORDER Theropoda ORDER Saurischia
TIME Late Cretaceous PLACE Mifune in Kumamoto, Japan
DESCRIPTION Unofficially named large two-legged predator, known
only from a single tooth.

Minmi "Minmi" FAMILY Nodosauridae SUBORDER Ankylosauria
ORDER Ornithischia
TIME Early Cretaceous
PLACE Minmi Crossing in Queensland, Australia
DESCRIPTION Four-legged armored plant-eater only 7ft (2m) long
with bony plates within the body wall; the Southern Hemisphere's
first undoubted armored dinosaur to get a name (in 1980).

Mochlodon "bar tooth" A discontinued name for *Rhabdodon*.

Mongolosaurus "Mongolian lizard" FAMILY Diplodocidae?
INFRAORDER Sauropoda SUBORDER Sauropodomorpha
ORDER Saurischia
TIME Early Cretaceous PLACE Mongolia
DESCRIPTION Big four-legged plant-eater with bulky body and long
neck and tail. Known from scrappy fossils. Identity doubtful.

Monkonosaurus "Monko lizard" FAMILY Stegosauridae
SUBORDER Stegosauria ORDER Ornithischia
TIME Early Cretaceous PLACE Tibet, China
DESCRIPTION Four-legged plant-eater probably with two rows of
plates jutting from its neck and back, and long sharp spines
projecting from the tail and shoulders. Named in 1983.

Monoclonius "one horned" FAMILY Ceratopsidae
SUBORDER Ceratopsia ORDER Ornithischia
TIME Late Cretaceous PLACE Alberta to Mexico, North America
DESCRIPTION Four-legged plant-eater 18ft (5.5m) long, with a
massive head featuring a large nose spike, two small brow horns,
and a short bony neck frill edged by bony studs.

"Monolophosaurus" "one ridge lizard" *Jiangjunmiaosaurus*.

Montanoceratops "horned face of Montana"
FAMILY Protoceratopsidae SUBORDER Ceratopsia
ORDER Ornithischia

Microvenator

Minmi

Monoclonius

Montanoceratops

© DIAGRAM

Morinosaurus – Nemegtosaurus

"Moshisaurus"

Mussaurus

Muttaburrasaurus

Nanosaurus

Nemegtosaurus

0   80ft (24m)

TIME Late Cretaceous PLACE Montana, USA
DESCRIPTION Bulky four-legged plant–eater about 6ft (1.8m) long, with parrotlike beak, large bony neck frill, prominent nose horn, and longer forelimbs but smaller head than *Leptoceratops*.

Morinosaurus "? lizard" A former name of *Pelorosaurus*.

Morosaurus "stupid lizard" A former name of *Camarasaurus*.

Mosasaurs "Meuse lizards" The family Mosasauridae SUPERFAMILY Varanoidea SUBORDER Lacertilia ORDER Squamata. Not dinosaurs but marine Late Cretaceous lizards up to 33ft (10m) long.

"Moshisaurus" "Moshi lizard" FAMILY Euhelopodidae?
INFRAORDER Sauropoda SUBORDER Sauropodomorpha
ORDER Saurischia
TIME Early Cretaceous PLACE Moshi in Iwate, Japan
DESCRIPTION Unofficially named large four-legged plant–eater (perhaps the immensely long-necked *Mamenchisaurus*?) known only from part of a humerus (upper arm bone).

Mussaurus "mouse lizard" FAMILY Plateosauridae
INFRAORDER Prosauropoda SUBORDER Sauropodomorpha
ORDER Saurischia
TIME Late Triassic PLACE southern Argentina
DESCRIPTION At 8in (20cm), one of the tiniest known dinosaurs; a prosauropod hatchling. Adults were probably 10ft (3m), bipedal/quadrupedal, and with long neck, bulky body, and long tail.

Muttaburrasaurus "Muttaburra lizard" FAMILY Camptosauridae or Iguanodontidae SUBORDER Ornithopoda ORDER Ornithischia
TIME Mid-Late Cretaceous PLACE Queensland and New South Wales, Australia
DESCRIPTION Bipedel/quadrupedal plant–eater 23ft (7m) long, with broad low head, shearing teeth, hollow upward-bulging muzzle, hooflike claws, and large flattened thumb spike. Named in 1981.

Nanotyrannus "tiny tyrant" FAMILY Tyrannosauridae
INFRAORDER Carnosauria SUBORDER Theropoda ORDER Saurischia
TIME Late Cretaceous PLACE Montana, USA
DESCRIPTION Two-legged flesh-eater about 16ft (5m) long, with long low head, forward-facing eyes, and small curved fangs. Named in 1988.

Nanosaurus "dwarf lizard" FAMILY Fabrosauridae
SUBORDER uncertain ORDER Ornithischia
TIME Late Jurassic PLACE Colorado and Utah, USA
DESCRIPTION Bipedal plant–eater a mere 3ft (90cm) long, with long hind limbs, short arms, slender neck, long stiffened tail, and lower jaw tip formed of toothless bone.

Nanshiungosaurus "Nanshiung lizard" FAMILY uncertain
SUBORDER Segnosauria? ORDER Saurischia?
TIME Late Cretaceous PLACE Nanxiong Formation, Shandong, China
DESCRIPTION Poorly known dinosaur 13ft (4m) long with saurischian type hip apart from pubis, angled backward as in segnosaurs and ornithischians. Some think it was a small unusual sauropod.

Nemegtosaurus "Nemegt lizard" FAMILY Diplodocidae
INFRAORDER Sauropoda SUBORDER Sauropodomorpha

ORDER Saurischia
TIME Late Cretaceous PLACE south Mongolia and Xinjiang, China
DESCRIPTION Big four-legged plant-eater with low sloping head,
pencil-shaped teeth, and maybe long neck and whiplash tail.

Neosaurus "new lizard" A former name of *Parrosaurus*.

Neosodon "new ? tooth" A former name of *Pelorosaurus*.

Neuquensaurus "lizard from Neuquén" Argentinian titanosaurid
sauropod named in 1986, but to be formally described.

Ngexisaurus

Ngexisaurus "Ngexi lizard" FAMILY Coeluridae
INFRAORDER Coelurosauria SUBORDER Theropoda ORDER Saurischia
TIME Middle Jurassic PLACE Tibet, China
DESCRIPTION Lightly built two-legged predator, named in 1983.

Nipponosaurus "Japanese lizard" FAMILY Lambeosauridae
SUBORDER Ornithopoda ORDER Ornithischia
TIME Late Cretaceous PLACE Sakhalin Island (once Japanese), USSR
DESCRIPTION bipedal/quadrupedal plant-eater with toothless beak
and batteries of cheek teeth – a small hadrosaur with a domed crest
on its broad, deep, short head. Perhaps a young individual in a
lambeosaurid genus known by another name. Identity doubtful.

Nipponosaurus

Noasaurids The family Noasauridae
INFRAORDER Coelurosauria SUBORDER Theropoda ORDER
Saurischia. Created in 1980 to contain the unusual small theropod
Noasaurus. Main entry in Chapter 3.

Noasaurus "northwest Argentina lizard" FAMILY Noasauridae
INFRAORDER Coelurosauria SUBORDER Theropoda ORDER Saurischia
TIME Late Cretaceous PLACE northwest Argentina
DESCRIPTION Lightly built two-legged predator about 8ft (2.4m)
long; each foot with a sickle claw that could be raised like a
dromaeosaurid's but by a unique retractor tendon. Skull design
suggests its ancestors were large flesh-eating dinosaurs.

Noasaurus

Nodosaurids The family Nodosauridae SUBORDER Ankylosauria
ORDER Ornithischia. Main entry in Chapter 3.

Nodosaurus "node lizard" FAMILY Nodosauridae
SUBORDER Ankylosauria ORDER Ornithischia
TIME Late Cretaceous PLACE Kansas and Wyoming, USA
DESCRIPTION Four-legged armored dinosaur 18ft (5.5m) long, with
relatively narrow snout and no tail club. Big and small plates ran
down the back and flanks in alternate rows, and skin bore large
knobby plates between the ribs.

Nodosaurus

Nothosaurs "false lizards" ORDER Nothosauria SUPERORDER
Sauropterygia INFRACLASS Lepidosauromorpha SUBCLASS
Diapsida. Not dinosaurs but long-necked, lizardlike aquatic reptiles
up to 13ft (4m) long, that flourished in Mid and Late Triassic seas.

Notoceratops "southern horned face" FAMILY Protoceratopsidae
SUBORDER Ceratopsia ORDER Ornithischia
TIME Late Cretaceous PLACE southern Argentina
DESCRIPTION Four-legged plant-eater with parrotlike beak and
perhaps the makings of a nose horn and bony neck frill; known
only from part of a lower jawbone.

Nothosaur

Nuthetes "monitor (lizard)" FAMILY Coeluridae? INFRAORDER
Coelurosauria? SUBORDER Theropoda ORDER Saurischia
TIME Late Cretaceous PLACE southern England
DESCRIPTION Small two-legged predator that might have been a

©DIAGRAM

Nyasasaurus

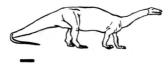

Omeisaurus

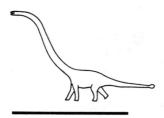

Opisthocoelicaudia

Ornatotholus

Nyasasaurus – Ornithischians

young megalosaurid. Identity doubtful.

Nyasasaurus "Nyasa lizard" FAMILY Anchisauridae
INFRAORDER Prosauropoda SUBORDER Sauropodomorpha
ORDER Saurischia
TIME Middle Triassic PLACE Lake Nyasa, Tanzania
DESCRIPTION Seemingly a very early bipedal/quadrupedal plant-
eating dinosaur 7ft (2.1m) long with small head, long neck, slim
hands and feet, and huge thumb claws. Some question its identity.

Ohmdenosaurus "Ohmden lizard" FAMILY Cetiosauridae
INFRAORDER Sauropoda SUBORDER Sauropodomorpha
ORDER Saurischia
TIME Late Early Jurassic PLACE Ohmden, southwest West Germany
DESCRIPTION Four-legged plant-eater 13ft (4m) long, probably with
long neck and tail and bulky body; a very small early sauropod
identified on the basis of one complete shin bone.

Oligosaurus "scanty lizard" A former name of *Rhabdodon*.

Omeisaurus "Omei lizard" FAMILY Euhelopodidae
INFRAORDER Sauropoda SUBORDER Sauropodomorpha
ORDER Saurischia
TIME Late Jurassic PLACE near Mt Omei in Sichuan, China
DESCRIPTION Very large four-legged plant-eater up to 66ft (20m)
long, with short deep head, spoon-shaped teeth, immensely long
neck, bulky body with back highest at the hips, pillar-like legs, and
long tapering tail with a clubbed tip. Several species known.

Omosaurus "scapula lizard" A former name of *Dacentrurus*.

Onychosaurus "nail lizard" A former name of *Rhabdodon*.

Opisthocoelicaudia "tail vertebrae cupped at the back" FAMILY
Camarasauridae
INFRAORDER Sauropoda SUBORDER Sauropodomorpha
ORDER Saurischia
TIME Late Cretaceous PLACE southern Mongolia
DESCRIPTION Large four-legged plant-eater 40ft (12m) long, with
level back, equally long forelimbs and hindlimbs, and short tail
held stiffly off the ground. Head and neck unknown.

Oplosaurus "armored lizard" A former name of *Pelorosaurus*.

Orinosaurus "iron rust lizard" A former name of *Euskelosaurus*.

Ornatotholus "ornate dome" FAMILY Pachycephalosauridae
SUBORDER Pachycephalosauria ORDER Ornithischia
TIME Late Cretaceous PLACE Alberta, Canada
DESCRIPTION Two-legged plant-eater about 6ft 6in (2.5m) long with
a thick, low-domed skull: a bone-headed dinosaur once thought to
be a female *Stegoceras*. Named in 1983.

Ornithischians "bird-hipped dinosaurs" The order Ornithischia
SUPERORDER Archosauria INFRACLASS Archosauromorpha SUBCLASS
Diapsida CLASS Reptilia
TIME Late Triassic through Cretaceous PLACE All continents
DESCRIPTION Plant-eating dinosaurs with birdlike hip bones, extra
bone at the lower jaw tip, horny bill or beak, leaf-shaped teeth,
bony tendons along the spine, and other features. Ornithischians
included the ornithopods, stegosaurs, ankylosaurs,
pachycephalosaurs and ceratopsians. See also **Dinosaurs** and
Chapter 3.

Ornithoides "bird form" A former name of *Saurornithoides*.

Ornitholestes "bird robber" FAMILY Coeluridae
INFRAORDER Coelurosauria SUBORDER Theropoda ORDER Saurischia
TIME Late Jurassic PLACE Wyoming, USA
DESCRIPTION Lightweight two–legged predator 6ft 6in (2m) long, with small head, low nasal horn, strong grasping hands each with three long clawed fingers, long legs, and finely tapered tail.

Ornitholestes

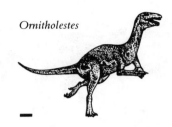

Ornithomerus "having bird parts" Former name of *Rhabdodon*.

Ornithomimids The family Ornithomimidae
INFRAORDER Ornithomimosauria SUBORDER Theropoda ORDER Saurischia. So-called ostrich dinosaurs. Main entry in Chapter 3.

Ornithomimoides "bird form mimic" FAMILY Coeluridae?
INFRAORDER Coelurosauria? SUBORDER Theropoda
ORDER Saurischia
TIME Late Cretaceous PLACE Madhya Pradesh, India
DESCRIPTION Two-legged predator perhaps 7ft (2.1m) long, known only from five spinal bones. Identity doubtful.

Ornithomimosaurs The infraorder Ornithomimosauria
SUBORDER Theropoda ORDER Saurischia. Large, birdlike dinosaurs including deinocheirids, garudimimids and ornithomimids. See too Chapter 3.

Ornithomimus

Ornithomimus "bird mimic" FAMILY Ornithomimidae
INFRAORDER Ornithomimosauria SUBORDER Theropoda
ORDER Saurischia
TIME Late Cretaceous PLACE North America and Tibet
DESCRIPTION Ostrich dinosaur about 11ft 6in (3.5m) long, with small head, toothless beak, long curved neck, thinner arms than *Struthiomimus*, three clawed fingers on each hand, long sprinter's legs, and long tail occupying more than half its length.

Ornithopods "bird-feet" The suborder Ornithopoda
ORDER Ornithischia. Bipedal and bipedal/quadrupedal plant-eating bird-hipped dinosaurs: heterodontosaurids, hypsilophodontids, dryosaurids, thescelosaurids, camptosaurids, iguanodontids, hadrosaurids, and lambeosaurids. Main entry in Chapter 3.

Ornithopsis "birdlke structure" A former name of *Pelorosaurus*.

Ornithosuchians "bird crocodiles" The suborder Ornithosuchia
ORDER Thecodontia SUPERORDER Archosauria
TIME Triassic PLACE perhaps worldwide
DESCRIPTION Arguably the closest kin of dinosaurs and pterosaurs, containing ancestors of both. They included the euparkeriids, lagosuchids, and ornithosuchids.

Ornithosuchus

Ornithosuchids "bird crocodiles" The family Ornithosuchidae
ORDER Thecodontia TIME Late Triassic PLACE perhaps worldwide
DESCRIPTION Bipedal and quadrupedal flesh-eating reptiles that were close kin to (some were once identified as) dinosaurs. They included *Avalonianus*, *Basutodon*, *Ornithosuchus*, and *Zatomus*.

Ornithotarsus "bird ankle" A former name of *Hadrosaurus*.

Orodromeus "mountain runner" FAMILY Hypsilophodontidae
SUBORDER Ornithopoda ORDER Ornithischia
TIME Late Cretaceous PLACE Montana, USA
DESCRIPTION Small two-legged plant-eater about 8ft (2.5m) long, with a horny beak, short arms, long agile legs, and long stiffened tail. Found with eggs and young. Named in 1988.

Orodromeus

©DIAGRAM

Oshanosaurus

Othnielia

Ouranosaurus

Oviraptor

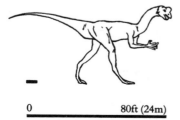

Orosaurus – Pachycephalosaurs

Orosaurus "mountain lizard" A former name of *Euskelosaurus*.

Orthogoniosaurus "straight angle lizard" FAMILY Megalosauridae?
INFRAORDER Carnosauria SUBORDER Theropoda ORDER Saurischia
TIME Late Cretaceous PLACE Madhya Pradesh, India
DESCRIPTION Two-legged flesh-eater known only from a single
tooth of unusual design. Identity doubtful.

Orthomerus "having straight parts" FAMILY Hadrosauridae
SUBORDER Ornithopoda ORDER Ornithischia
TIME Late Cretaceous PLACE Netherlands and maybe USSR
DESCRIPTION Large bipedal/quadrupedal plant-eater with toothless
beak and batteries of cheek teeth; a duck-billed dinosaur named
from a thigh bone found in the Netherlands. Identity doubtful.
Most "*Orthomerus*" material came from *Telmatosaurus*.

Oshanosaurus "Oshan lizard" FAMILY Cetiosauridae
INFRAORDER Sauropoda SUBORDER Sauropoda ORDER Saurischia
TIME Early Jurassic PLACE Yunnan, China
DESCRIPTION Large four-legged plant-eater with bulky body and
long neck and tail; an early sauropod named in 1986.

Ostrich dinosaurs See **Ornithomimosaurs**.

Othnielia "Othniel" FAMILY Hypsilophodontidae
SUBORDER Ornithopoda ORDER Ornithischia
TIME Late Jurassic PLACE Colorado, Utah, Wyoming, USA
DESCRIPTION Two-legged plant-eater only 4ft 6in (1.4m) long, with
small head, big eyes, horny beak, teeth enameled on both sides,
short arms, long legs and long tail. Named for **Othniel C. Marsh**.

Ouranosaurus "brave monitor lizard" FAMILY Iguanodontidae
SUBORDER Ornithopoda ORDER Ornithischia
TIME Early Cretaceous PLACE Sahara Desert, Niger
DESCRIPTION Bipedal/quadrupedal plant-eater 23ft (7m) long, with
long flat head, toothless beak, cheek teeth, and skin sail (a radiator?)
rising from its back and tail.

Oviraptor "egg thief" FAMILY Oviraptoridae
INFRAORDER Oviraptorosauria SUBORDER Theropoda
ORDER Saurischia
TIME Late Cretaceous PLACE southern Mongolia
DESCRIPTION Birdlike predator or herbivore about 6ft (1.8m) long,
with short deep crested head, short deep beak with two teeth in the
mouth roof, strong arms, long legs, curved claws on its three-
fingered hands and three-toed feet, and heavy tail.

Oviraptorids The family Oviraptoridae
INFRAORDER Oviraptorosauria SUBORDER Theropoda ORDER
Saurischia. They included birdlike *Conchoraptor* and *Oviraptor*.
Main entry in Chapter 3.

Oviraptorosaurs The infraorder Oviraptorosauria
SUBORDER Theropoda ORDER Saurischia. Weird, birdlike dinosaurs
including the oviraptorids, ingeniids, caenagnathids, and
avimimids.

Ovoraptor "egg thief" A former name of *Velociraptor*.

Pachycephalosaurids The family Pachycephalosauridae
SUBORDER Pachycephalosauria ORDER Ornithischia. Main entry in
Chapter 3.

Pachycephalosaurs The suborder Pachycephalosauria

ORDER Ornithischia. Bipedal and bipedal/quadrupedal bird-hipped dinosaurs: plant-eaters including the chaoyoungosaurids, homalocephalids and pachycephalosaurids.

Pachycephalosaurus "thick-headed lizard" FAMILY Pachycephalosauridae SUBORDER Pachycephalosauria ORDER Ornithischia
TIME Late Cretaceous PLACE Alberta, Canada; Wyoming, USA
DESCRIPTION Largest bone-headed dinosaur: a two-legged plant-eater 15ft (4.6m) long with a high-domed braincase 10in (25cm) thick, low spiky snout, and sharp knobs at the back of the head.

Pachycephalosaurus

Pachyrhinosaurus "thick-nosed lizard" FAMILY Ceratopsidae SUBORDER Ceratopsia ORDER Ornithischia
TIME Late Cretaceous PLACE Alberta, Canada
DESCRIPTION Heavily built four-legged plant-eater up to 18ft (5.5m), with a deep face, parrotlike beak, thick rough bony bulge above the muzzle, and spiky horn rising from the middle of a short bony neck frill rimmed by hornlets varying in shape and size.

Pachysauriscus "thick little lizard" Former name of *Plateosaurus*.
Pachysaurops "thick lizard form" *Plateosaurus*.
Pachysaurus "thick lizard" Former name of *Plateosaurus*.
Pachyspondylus "thick vertebrae" Former name of *Massospondylus*.
Palaeopteryx "ancient wing" Bird or deinonychosaurian theropod, known only from part of an arm bone.
Palaeoscincus "ancient skink" FAMILY Nodosauridae SUBORDER Ankylosauria ORDER Ornithischia
TIME Late Cretaceous PLACE Montana, USA
DESCRIPTION four-legged armored plant-eater maybe some 23ft (7m) long. Known only from worn teeth; identity doubtful.

Pachyrhinosaurus

Paleopods "ancient feet" The suborder Paleopoda ORDER Saurischia. A former grouping of those early dinosaurs the herrerasaurids, staurikosaurids, and prosauropods.

Panoplosaurus "fully armored lizard" FAMILY Nodosauridae SUBORDER Ankylosauria ORDER Ornithischia
TIME Late Cretaceous PLACE Alberta to Texas, North America
DESCRIPTION Tanklike four-legged plant-eater 23ft (7m) long with bony plates encasing back and bony armor fused to skull. Its short head had a short plump snout and relatively broad beak.

Panoplosaurus

Paranthodon "beside *Anthodon*" FAMILY Stegosauridae SUBORDER Stegosauria ORDER Ornithischia
TIME Early Cretaceous PLACE Cape Province, South Africa
DESCRIPTION Four-legged plant-eater 17ft (5m) long, with two rows of plates or spikes or both jutting up from neck, back and tail. Known from a partial jaw with ridged, *Kentrosaurus*-like teeth.

Parasaurolophus "beside *Saurolophus*" FAMILY Lambeosauridae SUBORDER Ornithopoda ORDER Ornithischia
TIME Late Cretaceous PLACE Alberta, Canada; and Utah and New Mexico, USA
DESCRIPTION Bipedal/quadrupedal plant-eater 33ft (10m) long, with toothless beak and batteries of cheek teeth. From its head a 5ft (1.5m) curved hollow tube (a hooter?) projected back above the shoulders. Maybe a skin frill joined tube to back.

Parasaurolophus

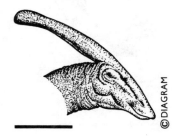

Parasuchians "like crocodiles" The suborder Parasuchia

©DIAGRAM

Parksosaurus – Pentaceratops

Paronychodon

Parrosaurus

Patagosaurus

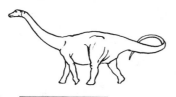

Peishansaurus

Pentaceratops

0   80ft (24m)

ORDER Thecodontia SUPERORDER Archosauria
TIME Late Triassic PLACE mainly Northern Hemisphere
DESCRIPTION Crocodile-like relatives of crocodiles and dinosaurs up
to 20ft (6m), with nostrils far back.

Parksosaurus "Parks's lizard" FAMILY Hypsilophodontidae
SUBORDER Ornithopoda ORDER Ornithischia
TIME Late Cretaceous PLACE Alberta, Canada
DESCRIPTION Two-legged plant-eater 8ft (2.4m) long with a small
head, large eyes, horny beak, ridged cheek teeth, short arms, long
sprinters' shins and feet, and long tendon-stiffened tail.

Paronychodon "alongside the nail tooth" FAMILY Troodontidae?
INFRAORDER Deinonychosauria SUBORDER Theropoda
ORDER Saurischia
TIME Late Cretaceous PLACE Montana, USA
DESCRIPTION Two-legged predator maybe 6ft 6in (2m) long, with
small head, large eyes, long arms, stiffened tail, and sickle-shaped
retractable second toe claw; but known only from teeth with
distinctive radiating ridges. Identity doubtful.

Parrosaurus "Parr's lizard" FAMILY Camarasauridae
INFRAORDER Sauropoda SUBORDER Sauropodomorpha
ORDER Saurischia
TIME Late Cretaceous PLACE Missouri, USA
DESCRIPTION Large plant-eater probably with relatively shorter neck
and tail than many sauropods.

Parrot lizards See **Psittacosaurids**.

Patagosaurus "Patagonian lizard" FAMILY Cetiosauridae
INFRAORDER Sauropoda SUBORDER Sauropodomorpha
ORDER Saurischia
TIME Late Jurassic PLACE southeast Argentina
DESCRIPTION Very large four-legged plant-eater with long neck,
fairly long tail, bulky body, and more advanced spinal bones than
those of some cetiosaurids.

Pectinodon "comb tooth" A former name of *Troodon*.

Peishansaurus "Mt. Pei lizard" FAMILY Ankylosauridae?
SUBORDER Ankylosauria? ORDER Ornithischia
TIME Late Cretaceous PLACE northwest China
DESCRIPTION Possibly a four-legged armored plant-eater with a tail
club, but known only from part of a small lower jaw. Some think it
was a bone-headed dinosaur. Identity doubtful.

Pelorosaurus "monstrous lizard" FAMILY Brachiosauridae
INFRAORDER Sauropoda SUBORDER Sauropodomorpha
ORDER Saurischia
TIME Late Jurassic-Early Cretaceous PLACE western Europe
DESCRIPTION Very large four-legged plant-eater perhaps 80ft (24m)
long, with giraffe-like neck, back sloping down from shoulders to
hips, and seemingly small, flat, six-sided tubercles in its skin.

Pentaceratops "five-horned face" FAMILY Ceratopsidae
SUBORDER Ceratopsia ORDER Ornithischia
TIME Late Cretaceous PLACE New Mexico
DESCRIPTION Four-legged plant-eater 20ft (6m) long. The massive
head 7ft 6in (2.3m) long had a parrotlike beak and huge bony neck
frill, two long and pointed brow horns, a small nose horn, and a
pair of bony, hornlike outgrowths on the cheeks.

Phaedrolosaurus "gleaming whole lizard" FAMILY
Dromaeosauridae INFRAORDER Deinonychosauria
SUBORDER Theropoda ORDER Saurischia
TIME Early Cretaceous PLACE Xinjiang, China
DESCRIPTION Two-legged predator thought to resemble or be an
ancestor of *Deinonychus*. Identity doubtful.

Phaedrolosaurus

Phyllodon "leaf tooth" FAMILY Hypsilophodontidae
SUBORDER Ornithopoda ORDER Ornithischia
TIME Late Jurassic PLACE central Portugal
DESCRIPTION Tiny bipedal plant-eater maybe 3ft (90cm) long with
horny beak, cheek teeth, short arms, long legs, and stiff tail.

Phytosaurs "plant lizards" See **Parasuchians**.

Piatnitzkysaurus "Piatnitzky's lizard" FAMILY Allosauridae
INFRAORDER Carnosauria SUBORDER Theropoda ORDER Saurischia
TIME Middle/Late Jurassic PLACE southern Argentina
DESCRIPTION Bipedal predator about 14ft (4.3m) long; smaller,
more primitive, and with relatively longer arms than *Allosaurus*.

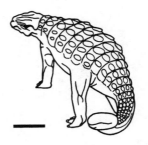
Pinacosaurus

Picrodon "sharp tooth" Supposed theropod dinosaur identified
from a pointed tooth now thought to be an ornithosuchid
thecodont's.

Pinacosaurus "plank lizard" FAMILY Ankylosauridae
SUBORDER Ankylosauria ORDER Ornithischia
TIME Late Cretaceous PLACE Mongolia and northern China
DESCRIPTION Four-legged armored plant-eater 18ft (5.5m) long,
slimly built, with rounded beak, small feet, and bony tail club.

Pisanosaurus "Pisano's lizard" FAMILY Heterodontosauridae?
SUBORDER Ornithopoda? ORDER Ornithischia
TIME Early Late Triassic PLACE northwest Argentina
DESCRIPTION Tiny bipedal (or bipedal/quadrupedal) plant-eater
perhaps 3ft (90cm) long; known from pointed teeth, and bits of
backbone, jaw, leg and foot. The earliest known ornithischian.

Pisanosaurus

Piveteausaurus "Piveteau's lizard" FAMILY Megalosauridae
INFRAORDER Carnosauria SUBORDER Theropoda ORDER Saurischia
TIME Mid Jurassic PLACE northern France
DESCRIPTION Two-legged predator perhaps up to 36ft (11m) long
and weighing up to 2 tons. It had lower bumps above the eyes but a
longer braincase than *Allosaurus*, yet one scientist thinks its scanty
remains came from a dinosaur weighing only 110lb (50kg).

Plated dinosaurs See **Stegosaurs**.

Plateosauravus "flat lizard ancestor" *Euskelosaurus*.

Plateosaurids The family Plateosauridae
INFRAORDER Prosauropoda SUBORDER Sauropodomorpha
ORDER Saurischia. See Chapter 3.

Plateosaurus "flat lizard" FAMILY Plateosauridae
INFRAORDER Prosauropoda SUBORDER Sauropodomorpha
ORDER Saurischia
TIME Late Triassic PLACE western Europe and maybe Argentina
DESCRIPTION Bipedal/quadrupedal plant-eater about 26ft (8m) long,
with small head, pointed leaflike teeth, fairly short neck, bulky
body, and long tail. *Plateosaurus* might have reared to browse.

Plateosaurus

Plesiosaurs "near lizards" ORDER Plesiosauria SUPERORDER
Sauropterygia SUBCLASS Diapsida. Not dinosaurs but two
superfamilies of predatory marine Mesozoic reptiles that swam

©DIAGRAM

Pleurocoelus – Priodontognathus

with flippers. Plesiosauroids were up to 39ft (12m) long, with small heads, snaky necks, and barrel-shaped bodies. Pliosaurs were up to 56ft (17m) long, with massive heads and short necks.

Pleurocoelus "hollow side" FAMILY Brachiosauridae
INFRAORDER Sauropoda SUBORDER Sauropodomorpha
ORDER Saurischia
TIME Early Cretaceous PLACE Perhaps USA, Europe, and Africa
DESCRIPTION Huge, four-legged plant-eater with long neck and tail, identified from deeply hollowed vertebrae and isolated teeth, perhaps of *Astrodon* and *Brachiosaurus*. Identity doubtful.

Pleurocoelus

Pleuropeltus "side shield" A former name of *Struthiosaurus*.

Podokesaurids "swift-footed lizards" The family Podokesauridae, a term for early, mainly lightweight predatory dinosaurs described here as coelophysids and halticosaurids.

Podokesaurus "swift-footed lizard" FAMILY Coelophysidae
INFRAORDER Coelurosauria SUBORDER Theropoda ORDER Saurischia
TIME Early Jurassic PLACE Connecticut, USA
DESCRIPTION Small two-legged predator about 3ft (90cm) long, with long neck, legs, and tail; known only from a fossil skeleton destroyed by fire. Identity doubtful; perhaps *Coelophysis*.

Podokesaurus

Poekilopleuron "varying side" FAMILY Megalosauridae
INFRAORDER Carnosauria SUBORDER Theropoda ORDER Saurischia
TIME Mid Jurassic PLACE northern France
DESCRIPTION Large bipedal flesh-eater up to 30ft (9m) long, with short powerful arms, and five-fingered hands.

Polacanthoides "*Polacanthus* form" FAMILY Nodosauridae
SUBORDER Ankylosauria ORDER Ornithischia
TIME Early Cretaceous PLACE Isle of Wight, southern England
DESCRIPTION Four-legged armored plant-eater maybe 16ft (5m) long, with a distinctive type of shoulder blade.

Polacanthus

Polacanthus "many spines" FAMILY Nodosauridae
SUBORDER Nodosauridae ORDER Ornithischia
TIME Early Cretaceous PLACE Isle of Wight, southern England
DESCRIPTION Four-legged armored plant-eater maybe 13ft (4m) long, with many spines that probably protected flanks and legs.

Polyodontosaurus "many-toothed lizard" A former name of *Troodon*.

Polyonax "many ? " A former name of *Triceratops*.

Poposaurids See **Teratosaurids**.

Prenocephale "sloping head" FAMILY Pachycephalosauridae
SUBORDER Pachycephalosauria ORDER Ornithischia
TIME Late Cretaceous PLACE Mongolia
DESCRIPTION Bone-headed dinosaur: a two-legged plant-eater 8ft (2.4m) long, with rows of bony knobs on the sides of its high-domed braincase and steep narrow face, and sharp front teeth.

Prenocephale

Priconodon "saw cone-shaped tooth" FAMILY Nodosauridae
SUBORDER Ankylosauria ORDER Ornithischia
TIME Early Cretaceous PLACE Maryland, USA
DESCRIPTION Four-legged armored dinosaur perhaps 20ft (6m) long, known from teeth like *Sauropelta*'s. Identity doubtful.

Priodontognathus "saw-toothed jaw" FAMILY Nodosauridae
SUBORDER Ankylosauria ORDER Ornithischia
TIME Late Jurassic or Early Cretaceous PLACE Yorkshire, England

0   80ft (24m)

DESCRIPTION Four-legged armored plant-eater identified from part of an upper jaw with 18 relatively big teeth like *Sauropelta*'s.

Procompsognathus

Probactrosaurus "before *Bactrosaurus*" FAMILY Iguanodontidae SUBORDER Ornithopoda ORDER Ornithischia
TIME Late Cretaceous PLACE China and Mongolia
DESCRIPTION Bipedal/quadrupedal plant-eater 19ft 6in (6m) long, with toothless beak and hooflike claws; despite its flattish head similarities to *Bactrosaurus* suggest it might have been an ancestor of lambeosaurid duck-billed dinosaurs.

Proceratops "first horned face" A former name of *Ceratops*.

Proceratosaurus "before *Ceratosaurus*" FAMILY Coeluridae or Allosauridae INFRAORDER Coelurosauria or Carnosauria SUBORDER Theropoda ORDER Saurischia
TIME Mid Jurassic PLACE southern England
DESCRIPTION Two-legged flesh-eater perhaps weighing 220lb (100kg). The head 1ft (30cm) long had a nose horn, and the front teeth were small and conical.

Prodeinodon

Procerosaurus "first horned lizard" A former name of *Iguanodon*.

Procheneosaurus "before *Cheneosaurus*" See *Corythosaurus*.

Procompsognathids The Procompsognathidae. See **Coelophysids**.

Procompsognathus "before *Compsognathus*" FAMILY Coelophysidae INFRAORDER Coelurosauria SUBORDER Theropoda ORDER Saurischia
TIME Late Triassic PLACE southern West Germany
DESCRIPTION Small primitive predatory dinosaur 4ft (1.2m) long, with long slim head, body, tail, and legs; two short fingers on each five-fingered hand; and the first toe pointing backward.

Prosaurolophus

Prodeinodon "before *Deinodon*" FAMILY Tyrannosauridae? INFRAORDER Carnosauria SUBORDER Theropoda ORDER Saurischia
TIME Early Cretaceous PLACE Mongolia and maybe China
DESCRIPTION Large two-legged flesh-eater originally named from teeth. Identity doubtful, possibly *Alectrosaurus*.

Prosaurolophus "before *Saurolophus*" FAMILY Hadrosauridae SUBORDER Ornithopoda ORDER Ornithischia
TIME Late Cretaceous PLACE Alberta, Canada
DESCRIPTION Bipedal/quadrupedal plant-eater 26ft (8m) long with bumps above the eyes, sloping face, broad toothless duck-bill muzzle, and batteries of grinding cheek teeth.

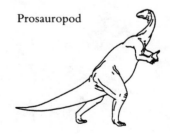
Prosauropod

Prosauropods "before sauropods" The infraorder Prosauropoda SUBORDER Sauropodomorpha ORDER Saurischia
TIME Late Triassic and Early Jurassic PLACE worldwide
DESCRIPTION Early bipedal, bipedal-quadrupedal, and quadrupedal plant-eating dinosaurs with long necks and tails. At least some ground food with gizzard stones. They included anchisaurids, blikanasaurids, plateosaurids, melanorosaurids, and yunnanosaurids. See also Chapter 3.

Proterosuchians "earlier crocodiles" The suborder Proterosuchia ORDER Thecodontia SUPERORDER Archosauria
TIME Late Permian to Late Triassic PLACE worldwide
DESCRIPTION Not dinosaurs but primitive sprawling and semi-sprawling crocodile-like reptiles, perhaps ancestral to later thecodonts, pterosaurs and dinosaurs. They included

Proterosuchian

©DIAGRAM

Protoceratops

Protognathus

Psittacosaurus

Pterosaur

0   80ft (24m)

"Protoavis" – Quaesitosaurus

proterosuchids, erythrosuchids, and proterochampsids.

"Protoavis" "first bird" North American birdlike fossil (perhaps a herrerasaurid theropod) to be formally described and named.

Protoceratops "first horned face" FAMILY Protoceratopsidae SUBORDER Ceratopsia ORDER Ornithischia
TIME Late Cretaceous PLACE China (Inner Mongolia) and Mongolia
DESCRIPTION Four-legged plant-eater 6ft (1.8m) long with big head, parrotlike beak, shearing cheek teeth, broad bony neck frill, thickened bone above the eyes and snout, and bulky body.

Protoceratopsids The family Protoceratopsidae
SUBORDER Ceratopsia ORDER Ornithischia. Main entry in Chapter 3.

Protognathus "early jaw" FAMILY Cetiosauridae
INFRAORDER Sauropoda SUBORDER Sauropodomorpha
ORDER Saurischia
TIME Middle Jurassic PLACE Sichuan, China
DESCRIPTION Large four-legged plant-eater with long neck and tail and sharper, slimmer spoon-shaped teeth than *Shunosaurus*. Named in 1988 from part of a downcurved lower jaw; to be renamed, as a beetle preoccupies the name *Protognathus*.

Protorosaurs "first lizards" The order Protorosauria INFRACLASS Archosauromorpha
TIME Late Permian to Early Jurassic PLACE worldwide?
DESCRIPTION Not dinosaurs but long-necked, lizardlike primitive archosaurs up to 10ft (3m) long.

Protorosaurus "first lizard" A former name of *Chasmosaurus*.

Pseudosuchians "false crocodiles" A supposed group of advanced thecodont reptiles now split among other groups. Some pseudosuchians were close kin to crocodilians, some to dinosaurs.

Psittacosaurids The family Psittacosauridae SUBORDER Ceratopsia ORDER Ornithischia. Main entry in Chapter 3.

Psittacosaurus "parrot lizard" FAMILY Psittacosauridae
SUBORDER Ceratopsia ORDER Ornithischia
TIME Early Cretaceous PLACE China, Mongolia, USSR
DESCRIPTION Bipedal plant-eater only up to 6ft 6in (2m) long, with long legs and tail, short arms with grasping hands, a deep parrotlike beak, nostrils and eyes high on the sides of the head, and bony "cheek horns". The most primitive ceratopsian known.

Pteropelyx "wing ? " FAMILY Lambeosauridae
SUBORDER Ornithopoda ORDER Ornithischia
TIME Late Cretaceous PLACE Montana, USA
DESCRIPTION Large bipedal/quadrupedal plant-eater with toothless beak and batteries of cheek teeth, but known only from a headless skeleton. Perhaps *Corythosaurus* or *Hypacrosaurus*.

Pterosaurs "winged lizards" The order Pterosauria SUPERORDER Archosauria. Airborne relatives of dinosaurs. See Chapter 1.

Pterospondylus "winged vertebrae" FAMILY Coelophysidae
INFRAORDER Coelurosauria SUBORDER Theropoda ORDER Saurischia
TIME Late Triassic PLACE western Europe
DESCRIPTION Small two-legged predator built much like (some consider that it was) *Procompsognathus*.

Quaesitosaurus "unusual lizard" FAMILY Diplodocidae or Dicraeosauridae INFRAORDER Sauropoda SUBORDER

Sauropodomorpha ORDER Saurischia
TIME Late Cretaceous PLACE Mongolia
DESCRIPTION Large four-legged plant–eater with long neck and tail.
Named in 1983. Some think it was *Nemegtosaurus*.

Rapator "plunderer" FAMILY uncertain
INFRAORDER Carnosauria SUBORDER Theropoda ORDER Saurischia
TIME Early Cretaceous PLACE eastern Australia
DESCRIPTION Two-legged flesh-eater perhaps 32ft (10m) long,
known from an abelisaurid-like wrist bone and vertebra.

Rauisuchians "Rau's crocodiles" The suborder Rauisuchia
ORDER Thecodontia SUPERORDER Archosauria
TIME Middle to Late Triassic PLACE worldwide?
DESCRIPTION Not dinosaurs but large four-legged relatives with
crocodile-type ankles; some had an upright stance. They included
rauisuchids and teratosaurids (alias poposaurids). Rauisuchid
Zanclodon and teratosaurid *Teratosaurus* were once considered
dinosaurs.

Rebbachisaurus "Rebbachi lizard" FAMILY Brachiosauridae?
INFRAORDER Sauropoda SUBORDER Sauropodomorpha
ORDER Saurischia
TIME Early Cretaceous PLACE Morocco and Tunisia
DESCRIPTION Very large four-legged plant-eater perhaps built like
an immense giraffe. One species (from Niger) to be described as a
camarasaurid.

Regnosaurus "powerful lizard" FAMILY uncertain
SUBORDER Ankylosauria? ORDER Ornithischia?
TIME Early Cretaceous PLACE England
DESCRIPTION Four-legged plant-eater, an armored dinosaur or
sauropod known only from part of a jaw. Identity doubtful.

Reptiles "creeping animals" The class Reptilia
SUBPHYLUM Vertebrata PHYLUM Chordata. Mainly cold-blooded
backboned animals, with dry scaly waterproof skin, and eggs
fertilized inside the females' bodies. See also **Anapsids**,
Testudinates, **Diapsids**, and **Synapsids**. Diapsids included
dinosaurs.

Revueltosaurus "Revuelto lizard" FAMILY Unknown
SUBORDER Unknown ORDER Ornithischia?
TIME Late Triassic PLACE New Mexico, USA
DESCRIPTION Small *Lesothosaurus*-like plant-eater named in 1989
from teeth including a unique form of incisor.

Rhabdodon "rod tooth" FAMILY Hypsilophodontidae
SUBORDER Ornithopoda ORDER Ornithischia
TIME Late Cretaceous PLACE France, Austria, and Romania
DESCRIPTION Two-legged plant-eater about 13ft (4m) long, longer
and heavier than most hypsilophodontids.

Rhodanosaurus "?rose lizard" A former name of *Struthiosaurus*.

Rhoetosaurus "Rhoetos (a giant of Greek myth) lizard" FAMILY
Cetiosauridae INFRAORDER Sauropoda SUBORDER
Sauropodomorpha ORDER Saurischia
TIME Middle Jurassic PLACE eastern Australia
DESCRIPTION Four-legged plant-eater more than 49ft (15m) long,
with small head, long neck and tail, and bulky body.

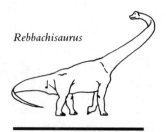

Rebbachisaurus

Revueltosaurus

Rhabdodon

©DIAGRAM

Rhoetosaurus

Rhynchosaurs – Sarcolestes

Riojasaurus

Rhynchosaurs "beaked lizards" The order Rhynchosauria
INFRACLASS Archosauromorpha
TIME Triassic PLACE worldwide
DESCRIPTION Not dinosaurs but piglike reptiles that rooted with
their tusks.

Riojasaurus "Rioja lizard" FAMILY Melanorosauridae
INFRAORDER Prosauropoda SUBORDER Sauropodomorpha
ORDER Saurischia
TIME Late Triassic PLACE La Rioja, Argentina
DESCRIPTION Four-legged plant-eater up to 36ft (11m) long: a heavy
prosauropod with small head, bulky body, long neck and tail, solid
limb bones, and light hollowed-out backbone.

Roccosaurus "Rocco lizard" *Melanorosaurus.*

Saltasaurus

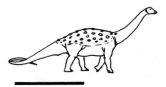

Saichania "beautiful" FAMILY Ankylosauridae
SUBORDER Ankylosauria ORDER Ornithischia
TIME Late Cretaceous PLACE southern Mongolia
DESCRIPTION Armored four-legged plant-eater 23ft (7m) long, with
a bony tail club and bony plates – many knobbed and spiky –
guarding head, neck, back, and belly.

Saltasaurus "Salta lizard" FAMILY Titanosauridae
INFRAORDER Sauropoda SUBORDER Sauropodomorpha
ORDER Saurischia
TIME Late Cretaceous PLACE Salta, northwest Argentina
DESCRIPTION First known armored sauropod: a four-legged plant-
eater 40ft (12m) long, with long neck and tail and bulky broad-
backed body protected by bony plates and hundreds of bony studs.

Saltopus "leaping foot" FAMILY Coelophysidae
INFRAORDER Coelurosauria SUBORDER Theropoda ORDER Saurischia
TIME Late Triassic PLACE northeast Scotland
DESCRIPTION Tiny two-legged predator 2ft (60cm) long and
weighing 2lb (900g), with tiny fourth and fifth fingers on its five-
fingered hands. Arguably the oldest European dinosaur.

Saltopus

"Sanchusaurus" "Sanchu lizard" FAMILY Ornithomimidae?
INFRAORDER Ornithomimosauria? SUBORDER Theropoda
ORDER Saurischia
TIME Early Cretaceous PLACE Gunma, Japan
DESCRIPTION Unofficially named two-legged predator (or maybe
herbivore) known only from a spinal bone apparently like those of
the ostrich dinosaur *Gallimimus.*

Sangonghesaurus "?Sangonghe lizard" FAMILY uncertain
SUBORDER Ankylosauria ORDER Ornithischia
TIME ? PLACE China
DESCRIPTION Four-legged armored plant-eater named in 1983.

Sanpasaurus "Sanpa lizard" FAMILY uncertain
INFRAORDER Sauropoda SUBORDER Sauropodomorpha
ORDER Saurischia
TIME Early/Mid Jurassic PLACE Sichuan, China
DESCRIPTION Large four-legged plant-eater with long neck and tail;
named from scrappy remains of a young animal mixed up with
others from an iguanodontid.

Sarcolestes

Sarcolestes "flesh robber" FAMILY Nodosauridae
SUBORDER Ankylosauria ORDER Ornithischia

0   80ft (24m)

Sarcosaurus – Saurornithoides

Sarcosaurus

TIME Mid Jurassic PLACE Cambridgeshire, England
DESCRIPTION Oldest known armored dinosaur, a four-legged plant-eater protected by bony plates, slabs, and spikes.
Sarcosaurus "flesh lizard" FAMILY Ceratosauridae?
INFRAORDER Carnosauria SUBORDER Theropoda ORDER Saurischia
TIME Early Jurassic PLACE Leicestershire, England
DESCRIPTION Lightly built two-legged predator about 11ft 6in (3.5m) long, known from spinal, hip, and leg bones.
Sauraechinodon "spiny toothed lizard" A former name of *Echinodon*.
Saurischians "lizard-hipped dinosaurs" The order Saurischia
SUPERORDER Archosauria INFRACLASS Archosauromorpha SUBCLASS Diapsida CLASS Reptilia
TIME Late Triassic through Cretaceous PLACE worldwide
DESCRIPTION Dinosaurs mainly with lizardlike hip bones, teeth that rimmed the jaws, and large openings in the skull. Some were the largest, others among the smallest dinosaurs. Some were bipedal others quadrupedal. Some ate plants, others meat. They included theropods, sauropodomorphs and arguably segnosaurs.
See also **Dinosaurs** and Chapter 3.

Sauroplites

Saurolophus "ridged lizard" FAMILY Hadrosauridae
SUBORDER Ornithopoda ORDER Ornithischia
TIME Late Cretaceous PLACE western North America and Mongolia
DESCRIPTION Bipedal/quadrupedal plant-eater 30ft (9m) long, with toothless beak, batteries of cheek teeth, bony spike projecting from the back of the head, and along the face maybe flaps of skin that it could blow up like balloons.
Sauropelta "lizard shield" FAMILY Nodosauridae
SUBORDER Ankylosauria ORDER Ornithischia
TIME Early Cretaceous PLACE Montana, USA
DESCRIPTION Large four-legged armored plant-eater up to 25ft (7.6m) long, with relatively narrow skull, bands of bony shields across its back and very likely spines projecting from its sides.
Saurophagus "lizard eater" A former name of *Allosaurus*.
Sauroplites "lizard hoplite" FAMILY Ankylosauridae
SUBORDER Ankylosauria ORDER Ornithischia
TIME Early Cretaceous PLACE Gansu, China
DESCRIPTION Four-legged armored plant-eater about 20ft (6m) long, with hollow-based armor plates and a bony tail club.
Sauropodomorphs The suborder Sauropodomorpha
ORDER Saurischia. See **Prosauropods** and **Sauropods**.
Sauropods "lizard feet" The infraorder Sauropoda
SUBORDER Sauropodomorpha ORDER Saurischia
TIME Jurassic to Cretaceous PLACE worldwide
DESCRIPTION Mostly immense four-legged plant-eaters with small head, bulky body, and long neck and tail. They included the brachiosaurids, camarasaurids, cetiosaurids, dicraeosaurids, diplodocids, euhelopodids, titanosaurids, and vulcanodontids. Proposed families also include barapasaurids, chubutisaurids, and mamenchisaurids. See also Chapter 3.
Saurornithoides "birdlike lizard" FAMILY Troodontidae
INFRAORDER Deinonychosauria SUBORDER Theropoda
ORDER Saurischia

Sauropod

Saurornithiodes

©DIAGRAM

Saurornithoidids – Segisaurus

Saurornitholestes

TIME Late Cretaceous PLACE Mongolia
DESCRIPTION Two-legged predator 6ft 6in (2m) long, with long low head, keen eyes, relatively big brain, long arms with grasping hands, small retractable sickle claw on each second toe, and long, stiffened tail. Some think it was *Troodon*.
Saurornithoidids See **Troodontids**.
Saurornitholestes "lizard bird-robber" FAMILY Dromaeosauridae
INFRAORDER Deinonychosauria SUBORDER Theropoda
ORDER Saurischia
TIME Late Cretaceous PLACE Alberta, Canada
DESCRIPTION Agile, powerful two-legged predator 6ft (1.8m) long with small saw-edged teeth, grasping hands with sharp claws, and probably a large sharp "switchblade" second toe claw.
Scelidosaurids The family Scelidosauridae
SUBORDER Scelidosauria ORDER Ornithischia. Main entry in Chapter 3.
Scelidosaurs The Scelidosauria, a proposed ornithischian suborder including scelidosaurids and scutellosaurids.

Scelidosaurus

Scelidosaurus "limb lizard" FAMILY Scelidosauridae
SUBORDER Scelidosauria ORDER Ornithischia
TIME Early Jurassic PLACE Arizona, England and Tibet, China
DESCRIPTION Low-slung four-legged plant-eater 13ft (4m) long, with a small head, sturdy legs, long tail, and heavy body shielded by rows of pointed bony studs.
Scleromochlus "hard jumper" FAMILY Scleromochlidae
SUBORDER uncertain ORDER Thecodontia SUPERORDER Archosauria
TIME Late Triassic PLACE Scotland
DESCRIPTION Not a dinosaur but a reptile close to the ancestry of dinosaurs and pterosaurs. It was 1ft (30cm) long, with light bones, and long head, legs, and tail.
Scolosaurus "thorn lizard" A former name of *Dyoplosaurus*. Has been listed also as a former name of *Euoplocephalus*.
Scutellosaurids The family Scutellosauridae
SUBORDER Scelidosauria ORDER Ornithischia
TIME Early to Late Jurassic PLACE North America, Europe, China
DESCRIPTION Small semi-armored bipedal and bipedal/quadrupedal plant-eaters with serrated leaflike teeth and small cheeks. They included *Scutellosaurus*, *Tatisaurus*, and *Trimucrodon*.

Scutellosaurus

Scutellosaurus "small-shield lizard" FAMILY Scutellosauridae
SUBORDER Scelidosauria ORDER Ornithischia
TIME Early Jurassic PLACE Arizona, southwest USA
DESCRIPTION Bipedal/quadrupedal plant-eater 4ft (1.2m) long with long hind limbs, fairly long arms, very long tail, and rows of small, low bony studs running down its back.
Secernosaurus "separate lizard" FAMILY Hadrosauridae
SUBORDER Ornithopoda ORDER Ornithischia
TIME Late Cretaceous PLACE Argentina
DESCRIPTION Bipedal/quadrupedal plant-eater with a crestless head, toothless beak and batteries of cheek teeth: a small duck-billed dinosaur only 10ft (3m) long. With *Kritosaurus*, one of only two duck-billed dinosaurs found in the Southern Hemisphere.

Segisaurus

Segisaurus "Segi Canyon lizard" FAMILY Coelophysidae?
INFRAORDER Coelurosauria SUBORDER Theropoda ORDER Saurischia

0   80ft (24m)

TIME Early Jurassic PLACE Arizona, USA
DESCRIPTION Slim goose-sized predator with slim hands, long legs, birdlike feet, and (unusual features) collarbones. Some put it in its own family, the Segisauridae.

Segnosaurids The family Segnosauridae
SUBORDER Segnosauria ORDER Saurischia? Main entry in Chapter 3.

Segnosaurs The suborder Segnosauria ORDER Saurischia? Strange late dinosaurs with a theropod-type upper hip girdle but somewhat ornithischian-like cheeks, beak, and backward slanting pubic bone. Perhaps more primitive than saurischians or ornithischians, they included enigmosaurids, segnosaurids, and *Nanshiungosaurus*.

Segnosaurus "slow lizard" FAMILY Segnosauridae
SUBORDER Segnosauria ORDER Saurischia?
TIME Late Cretaceous PLACE Mongolia and China
DESCRIPTION Bipedal predator (fish-eater?) or herbivore 30ft (9m) long with cheeks, small sharp cheek teeth, narrow toothless beak, short arms with three sharply clawed fingers, long legs with four-toed feet, and hip bones somewhat like an ornithischian's.

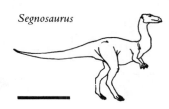
Segnosaurus

"Seismosaurus" "earth-shaking lizard" FAMILY Diplodocidae
INFRAORDER Sauropoda SUBORDER Sauropodomorpha
ORDER Saurischia
TIME Late Jurassic/Early Cretaceous PLACE New Mexico, USA
DESCRIPTION Unofficially named immense four-legged plant-eater with long neck and tail. Early press reports of the world's largest animal claimed a length exceeding 108ft (33m).

Sellosaurus "?saddle lizard" FAMILY Anchisauridae
INFRAORDER Prosauropoda SUBORDER Sauropodomorpha
ORDER Saurischia
TIME Late Triassic PLACE southwest West Germany
DESCRIPTION Lightly built bipedal/quadrupedal plant-eater with small head, fairly long neck, bulky body, long tail, legs longer than arms, and long five-fingered hands with huge thumb claws. An 8ft (2.4m) juvenile was formerly misnamed *Efraasia*.

Sellosaurus

Shamosaurus "Gobi lizard" FAMILY Ankylosauridae
SUBORDER Ankylosauria ORDER Ornithischia
TIME Early Cretaceous PLACE Gobi Desert, Mongolia
DESCRIPTION Four-legged armored plant-eater with heavy body, broad low head with flat bony horns projecting from the back, bony body armor, and bony tail club. Named in 1983.

Shanshanosaurus "Shanshan lizard" FAMILY Aublysodontidae
INFRAORDER Carnosauria SUBORDER Theropoda ORDER Saurischia
TIME Late Cretaceous PLACE Shanshan County in Xinjiang, China
DESCRIPTION Small lightly-built two-legged predator about 8ft (2.5m) long, with short arms, long legs, distinctive snout, slender lower jaw, and large curved teeth.

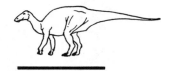
Shantungosaurus

Shantungosaurus "Shantung lizard" FAMILY Hadrosauridae
SUBORDER Ornithopoda ORDER Ornithischia
TIME Late Cretaceous PLACE Shandong, China
DESCRIPTION Bipedal/quadrupedal plant-eater up to 49ft (15m) long, with a flat head, toothless beak, batteries of cheek teeth, fairly short strong arms, massive legs, splayed toes, hooflike nails, and long deep tail. One of the largest hadrosaurids.

Shunosaurus "Shuo lizard" FAMILY Cetiosauridae

©DIAGRAM

Shunosaurus

93

Shuosaurus – Stegoceras

Silvisaurus

INFRAORDER Sauropoda SUBORDER Sauropodomorpha
ORDER Saurischia
TIME Mid Jurassic PLACE Sichuan, China
DESCRIPTION Four-legged plant-eater 33ft (10m) long, with short
deep head, strong spoon-shaped teeth, fairly short neck, bulky
body, and long tail ending in four short spikes and a small bony
club (the first such sauropod described). A well-known Chinese
sauropod, named from Shuo, an old Chinese form of Sichuan.

Shuosaurus A former name of *Shunosaurus*.

Siamosaurus "Siam lizard" FAMILY Spinosauridae?
INFRAORDER Carnosauria SUBORDER Theropoda ORDER Saurischia
TIME Late Jurassic PLACE Phu Pratu Teema, northeast Thailand
DESCRIPTION Large two-legged predator (fish-eater?) known only
from tall semiconical piercing teeth with rounded tops and grooves
and ridges up the sides. Named in 1986.

Silvisaurus "forest lizard" FAMILY Nodosauridae
SUBORDER Ankylosauria ORDER Ornithischia
TIME Early Cretaceous PLACE Kansas, USA
DESCRIPTION Four-legged armored plant-eater 13ft (4m) long, with
big cheek bones, relatively long neck, bony plates protecting the
back, and spines jutting from the shoulders and perhaps the tail.

Sinocoelurus "Chinese coelurid" FAMILY Coeluridae?
INFRAORDER Coelurosauria SUBORDER Theropoda ORDER Saurischia
TIME Late Jurassic PLACE Sichuan, China
DESCRIPTION Small two-legged predator only known from scattered
teeth some think are not from dinosaurs. Identity doubtful.

Spinosaurus

Sinosaurus "Chinese lizard" FAMILY Herrerasauridae
SUBORDER ? ORDER Herrerasauria
TIME Early Jurassic PLACE Yunnan, China
DESCRIPTION Primitive two-legged flesh-eater about 8ft (2.4m)
long, a sharp-toothed predator known mainly from a jaw.

Sphenospondylus "wedged vertebrae" *Iguanodon*.

Spinosaurids The family Spinosauridae INFRAORDER Carnosauria
SUBORDER Theropoda ORDER Saurischia. Main entry in Chapter 3.

Spinosaurus "thorn lizard" FAMILY Spinosauridae
INFRAORDER Carnosauria SUBORDER Theropoda ORDER Saurischia
TIME Late Cretaceous PLACE Egypt and Niger
DESCRIPTION Immense two-legged predator up to 50ft (15m) long
and weighing about 4 tons. A skin fin up to 6ft (1.8m) long ran
down its back, held up by blade-like spines jutting upward from its
vertebrae. It had huge teeth and a vast crocodile-like lower jaw.

Staurikosaurus

Staurikosaurids The family Staurikosauridae SUBORDER ?
ORDER Herrerasauria. Primitive, very early flesh-eating dinosaurs.
Main entry in Chapter 3.

Staurikosaurus "(Southern) Cross lizard" FAMILY Staurikosauridae
SUBORDER ? ORDER Herrerasauria
TIME Latest Middle Triassic PLACE Santa Maria, southern Brazil
DESCRIPTION One of the earliest, most primitive dinosaurs, a
speedy, lightly built two-legged flesh-eater 6ft 6in (2m) long and
weighing 66lb (30kg). It had a fairly large head, sharp teeth, short
arms, long legs and tail, probably five digits on toes and fingers,
and only two vertebrae joining spine to hips.

Stegoceras "horny roof" FAMILY Pachycephalosauridae

Stegoceras

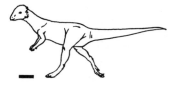

0   80ft (24m)

SUBORDER Pachycephalosauria ORDER Ornithischia
TIME Late Cretaceous PLACE western North America and maybe
northwest China
DESCRIPTION Small bone-headed dinosaur: a two-legged plant-eater
6ft 6in (2.5m) long, with deep short face, mainly sharp teeth, and
thick skull with a domed roof and bony knobs at the back.

Stegopelta "plated shield" Probably *Nodosaurus.*

Stegosaurides "stegosaur form" FAMILY Ankylosauridae
SUBORDER Ankylosauria ORDER Ornithischia
TIME Late Cretaceous PLACE Gansu, China
DESCRIPTION Four-legged armored plant-eater with a bony tail club.
Only known from fragments. Identity doubtful.

Stegosaurids The family Stegosauridae SUBORDER Stegosauria
ORDER Ornithischia. Main entry in Chapter 3.

Stegosaurs The suborder Stegosauria ORDER Ornithischia.
Four-legged plant-eaters with two rows of plates or spines rising
from neck, back, and tail. See **Huayangosaurids** and
Stegosaurids.

Stegosaurus "roof lizard" FAMILY Stegosauridae
SUBORDER Stegosauria ORDER Ornithischia
TIME Late Jurassic PLACE USA (Colorado, Oklahoma, Utah,
Wyoming)
DESCRIPTION Largest known plated dinosaur, a four-legged plant-
eater up to 30ft (9m) long, highest at the hips and with small head,
toothless beak, and two rows of tall bony plates jutting up from
neck, back, and tail. This also had four long spikes.

Stenonychosaurus "narrow claw lizard" A former name of
Troodon.

Stenopelix "narrow pelvis" FAMILY Psittacosauridae or maybe
Protoceratopsidae or even Chaoyoungosauridae
SUBORDER Ceratopsia ORDER Ornithischia
TIME Early Cretaceous PLACE West Germany
DESCRIPTION A probably two-legged plant-eater about 5ft (1.5m)
long with narrow parrotlike beak. Known from hip and leg bones.

Stenotholus "narrow dome" See *Stygimoloch.*

Stephanosaurus "Stephan's lizard" A former name of
Lambeosaurus.

Stereocephalus "solid head" A former name of *Euoplocephalus.*

Sterrholophus " ? " A former name of *Triceratops.*

Stokesosaurus "Stokes's lizard" FAMILY Allosauridae?
INFRAORDER Carnosauria SUBORDER Theropoda ORDER Saurischia
TIME Late Jurassic PLACE Utah, USA
DESCRIPTION Two-legged flesh-eater about 13ft (4m) long with a
short snout and long steak-knife teeth.

Strenusaurus "strenuous lizard" A former name of *Riojasaurus.*

Struthiomimus "ostrich mimic" FAMILY Ornithomimidae
INFRAORDER Ornithomimosauria SUBORDER Theropoda
ORDER Saurischia
TIME Late Cretaceous PLACE Canada (Alberta) and USA (New
Jersey)
DESCRIPTION Ostrichlike predator (or herbivore) 11ft 6in (3.5m)
long, with small head, toothless beak, curved neck, fairly strong
arms, curved claws on fingers, and long legs and tail.

Stegosaurus

Stenopelix

Stokesosaurus

Struthiomimus

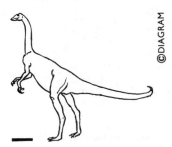

©DIAGRAM

Struthiosaurus

Styracosaurus

Supersaurus

Syntarsus

0   80ft (24m)

Struthiosaurus – Szechuanosaurus

Struthiosaurus "ostrich lizard" FAMILY Nodosauridae
SUBORDER Ankylosauria ORDER Ornithischia
TIME Late Cretaceous PLACE southern France, eastern Austria, and
Romania
DESCRIPTION Four-legged armored dinosaur 6ft (1.8m) long
protected by six kinds of bony or horny armor including shoulder
spines and sharp plates on hips and tail. The smallest known
ankylosaur, evidently a dwarfed island-dwelling form.
Stygimoloch "demon from the River Styx" FAMILY
Pachycephalosauridae SUBORDER Pachycephalosauria
ORDER Ornithischia
TIME Late Cretaceous PLACE Montana, USA
DESCRIPTION Two-legged plant-eater with a thick, narrow high-
domed skull bristling with bony horns and spikes, probably
brandished by rival males. *Stygimoloch* was named in 1983.
Styracosaurus "spiked lizard" FAMILY Ceratopsidae
SUBORDER Ceratopsia ORDER Ornithischia
TIME Late Cretaceous PLACE Alberta, Canada; and Montana, USA
DESCRIPTION Heavily built four-legged plant-eater 18ft (5.5m) long:
a horned dinosaur with short tail, massive head, deep parrotlike
beak, short bony neck frill, stumpy brow horns, and six long
spikes jutting back and outward from around its frill. Some think it
was *Eucentrosaurus* or *Monoclonius*.
Supersaurus "super lizard" FAMILY Diplodocidae INFRAORDER
Sauropoda SUBORDER Sauropodomorpha ORDER Saurischia
TIME Late Jurassic PLACE western Colorado, USA
DESCRIPTION Immense four-legged plant-eater (perhaps *Barosaurus*),
highest at the hips, with very long neck and whiplash tail. It
weighed up to 55 US tons (50 metric tons), measured 80–100ft
(24–30m) – one scientist suggests 138ft (42m) – and stood 54ft
(16.5m) high with head raised on the 39ft (12m) neck. Named in
1985.
Symphyrophus "grown together ?" A former name of
Camptosaurus.
Synapsids The subclass Synapsida. Not dinosaurs but extinct
mammal-like reptiles with one hole in each side of the skull behind
the eyes. Synapsids comprised the (earlier) pelycosaurs and (later)
therapsids. See **Therapsids**.
Syngonosaurus "fused-knee lizard" Former name of *Anoplosaurus*.
Syntarsus "fused ankle" FAMILY Coelophysidae
INFRAORDER Coelurosauria SUBORDER Theropoda ORDER Saurischia
TIME Late Triassic PLACE Zimbabwe and Arizona, USA
DESCRIPTION Slender two-legged predator 10ft (3m) long, with
narrow jaws, short arms with four-fingered hands, and long legs
with fused foot bones. Perhaps hunted prosauropods and lizards.
Syrmosaurus "trail lizard" A former name of *Pinacosaurus*.
Szechuanosaurus "Szechuan lizard" FAMILY Allosauridae?
INFRAORDER Carnosauria SUBORDER Theropoda ORDER Saurischia
TIME Late Jurassic PLACE Sichuan and maybe Xinjiang, China
DESCRIPTION Two-legged predator up to 26ft (8m) long, with a big
head, daggerlike teeth, short three-fingered forelimbs, long
hindlimbs, and a long tail. Like *Allosaurus* but smaller.

Talarurus "basket tail" FAMILY Ankylosauridae
SUBORDER Ankylosauria ORDER Ornithischia
TIME Late Cretaceous PLACE Mongolia
DESCRIPTION Four-legged armored dinosaur 20ft (6m) long, with
hollow spines, bands of thick bony plates guarding back, hips, and
tail, and a bony tail club.

Talarurus

Tanius "of the Tan" FAMILY Hadrosauridae
SUBORDER Ornithopoda ORDER Ornithischia
TIME Late Cretaceous PLACE Shandong, China
DESCRIPTION Flat-headed duck-billed dinosaur: a bipedal/
quadrupedal plant-eater with low bulge between the eyes, toothless
beak and batteries of cheek teeth.

Tanystrosuchus "long vertebra crocodile" Probably *Halticosaurus*.

Tarbosaurus "alarming lizard" FAMILY Tyrannosauridae
INFRAORDER Carnosauria SUBORDER Theropoda ORDER Saurischia
TIME Late Cretaceous PLACE Mongolia
DESCRIPTION Two-legged flesh-eater 19–33ft (5.8–10m) long with
immense head, body and legs, huge jaws armed with terrifying
fangs, and great toe claws; yet tiny arms ending in two-fingered
hands. Like but less immense than North America's *Tyrannosaurus*,
though some consider it a species in that genus.

Tarbosaurus

Tarchia "brainy" FAMILY Ankylosauridae
SUBORDER Ankylosauria ORDER Ornithischia
TIME Late Cretaceous PLACE southern Mongolia
DESCRIPTION Asia's last- and largest-known armored dinosaur: a
four-legged plant-eater 28ft (8.5m) long, with bony plating on its
great broad-snouted skull, rows of plates running down its back,
and a tail armed with a bony club.

Tatisaurus "Ta-Ti lizard" FAMILY Scutellosauridae?
SUBORDER Scelidosauria ORDER Ornithischia
TIME Early Jurassic PLACE Yunnan, China
DESCRIPTION Early bipedal or maybe quadrupedal plant-eater
known from a lower jaw with worn, overlapping teeth. Identity
doubtful; one scientist thinks it was a huayangosaurid plated
dinosaur.

Tarchia

Tawasaurus "Tawa lizard" FAMILY Anchisauridae?
INFRAORDER Prosauropoda? SUBORDER Sauropodomorpha?
ORDER Saurischia
TIME Early Jurassic PLACE Yunnan, China
DESCRIPTION Plant-eating dinosaur named in 1982 from a snout first
identified as ornithischian, but probably prosauropod.

Technosaurus "Tech lizard" FAMILY Fabrosauridae
SUBORDER uncertain ORDER Ornithischia
TIME Early Late Triassic PLACE West Texas, USA
DESCRIPTION Small bipedal plant-eater with leaf-like teeth that
rimmed the jaws and continued to the tip of the front upper jaw.
Named in 1984 (to honor Texas Tech University) from bits of jaw
with teeth, a spinal bone, and an ankle bone. The Northern
Hemisphere's earliest named ornithischian dinosaur.

Technosaurus

Teinchisaurus See *Tenchisaurus*.

Teinurosaurus "extended lizard" FAMILY Coeluridae?
INFRAORDER Coelurosauria SUBORDER Theropoda ORDER Saurischia
TIME Late Jurassic PLACE northern France

©DIAGRAM

Telmatosaurus – Thecospondylus

Telmatosaurus

Tenontosaurus

Teratosaurus

Thecodontosaurus

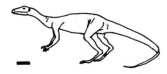

0   80ft (24m)

DESCRIPTION Seemingly a small bipedal flesh-eater, but known only from a tail bone subsequently lost. Identity doubtful.

Telmatosaurus "marsh lizard" FAMILY Hadrosauridae SUBORDER Ornithopoda ORDER Ornithischia TIME Late Cretaceous PLACE Romania, Pyrenees, southern France DESCRIPTION Large bipedal/quadrupedal plant-eater with toothless beak and batteries of cheek teeth; known mainly from a deep skull resembling that of *Hadrosaurus*. Apart from (see also) *Orthomerus*, the only duck-billed dinosaur found in Europe.

Tenantosaurus See *Tenontosaurus*.

Tenchisaurus "?Tenchin lizard" FAMILY uncertain SUBORDER Ankylosauria ORDER Ornithischia TIME Jurassic PLACE ?Tenchin Gomba in Sichuan, China DESCRIPTION Four-legged armored plant-eater named but not described in 1981.

Tenontosaurus "sinew lizard" FAMILY Hypsilophodontidae (or Iguanodontidae?) SUBORDER Ornithopoda ORDER Ornithischia TIME Early Cretaceous PLACE USA (Montana, Oklahoma, Texas) DESCRIPTION Bipedal/quadrupedal plant-eater about 21ft (6.5m) long, with deep head, toothless beak, broad five-fingered hands and four-toed feet, long arms, and a strong deep tail (perhaps swung in defense) far longer than head, neck, and trunk.

Teratosaurids See **Rauisuchians**.

Teratosaurus "monster lizard" Once considered a large early flesh-eating dinosaur, now known to be a teratosaurid thecodont.

Testudinates The subclass Testudinata: reptiles comprising extinct and living turtles, first known from Late Triassic Germany. Often grouped with the **Anapsids**.

Tetanurae "rigid tails" A proposed grouping of all theropod dinosaurs (and birds) except the ceratosaurs with *Liliensternus* and *Procompsognathus*.

Tetragonosaurus "four-knee lizard" Former name of *Corythosaurus*.

Thecocoelurus "socket coelurid" *Calamospondylus*

Thecodontosaurus "socket-toothed lizard" FAMILY uncertain INFRAORDER Prosauropoda SUBORDER Sauropodomorpha ORDER Saurischia TIME Late Triassic PLACE England DESCRIPTION The most primitive prosauropod known: a bipedal plant-eater about 7ft (2.1m) long, with small head, saw-edged spoon-shaped cheek teeth, fairly short neck and arms, huge thumb claws, tiny clawless fourth and fifth fingers, effectively four-toed feet, and long legs and tail.

Thecodonts "socket-toothed" The order Thecodontia SUPERORDER Archosauria INFRACLASS Archosauromorpha CLASS Reptilia TIME Permian through Triassic PLACE worldwide DESCRIPTION Not dinosaurs but (most) quadrupedal reptiles: ancestors and cousins of the dinosaurs, pterosaurs, and crocodilians. Thecodonts included **Aetosaurs**, **Ornithosuchians**, **Parasuchians**, **Proterosuchians**, **Rauisuchians**, and *Scleromochlus*.

Thecospondylus "socket vertebrae" FAMILY uncertain SUBORDER uncertain ORDER uncertain

TIME Early Cretaceous PLACE England
DESCRIPTION Dinosaur known only from a sacrum (spinal bones attached to hips). Could be theropod or ornithischian.

Therapsids "beast openings" The order Therapsida SUBCLASS Synapsida CLASS Reptilia
TIME Permian through Early Jurassic PLACE worldwide
DESCRIPTION Not dinosaurs but advanced mammal-like reptiles; the cynodonts (SUBORDER Cynodontia) included ancestors of mammals.

Therapsid

Therizinosaurids The family Therizinosauridae
INFRAORDER Deinonychosauria? SUBORDER Theropoda? ORDER Saurischia? Dinosaurs known only from arms with huge claws. Main entry in Chapter 3.

Therizinosaurus "scythe lizard" FAMILY Therizinosauridae
INFRAORDER Deinonychosauria? SUBORDER Theropoda?
ORDER Saurischia
TIME Late Cretaceous PLACE southern Mongolia and ?USSR
DESCRIPTION Bipedal or bipedal/quadrupedal flesh-eater (or maybe insect-eater or plant-eater) measuring up to 35ft (10.7m). Known only from powerful arms 8ft (2.4m) long. Fingers ended in immense sickle-shaped claws 2ft (61cm) or more around the outer curve.

Therizinosaurus

Theropods "beast feet" The suborder Theropoda ORDER Saurischia. Bipedal flesh-eating (and maybe some plant-eating) lizard-hipped dinosaurs: deinonychosaurs, ornithomimosaurs, oviraptorosaurs, plus coelurosaurs and carnosaurs (small and large flesh-eaters). See also Chapter 3.

Therosaurus A former name of *Iguanodon*.

Thescelosaurids The family Thescelosauridae. See Chapter 3.

Thescelosaurus "wonderful lizard" FAMILY Thescelosauridae
SUBORDER Ornithopoda ORDER Ornithischia
TIME Late Cretaceous PLACE Canada (Alberta, Saskatchewan) and USA (Montana, Wyoming)
DESCRIPTION Bipedal/quadrupedal plant-eater 11ft (3.4m) long with small head, teeth in the front of the jaws, plump body, five-fingered hands, relatively long thighs, hooflike claws, long tail, and rows of bony studs down the back.

Thescelosaurus

Thespesius "divine" FAMILY Hadrosauridae
SUBORDER Ornithopoda ORDER Ornithischia
TIME Late Cretaceous PLACE South Dakota, USA
DESCRIPTION Large bipedal/quadrupedal plant-eater, a duck-billed dinosaur with toothless beak, batteries of cheek teeth, and a flat head. Resembled (might have been) *Edmontosaurus*.

Thotobolosaurus "Thotobolo lizard" FAMILY Melanorosauridae
INFRAORDER Prosauropoda SUBORDER Sauropodomorpha
ORDER Saurischia
TIME Late Triassic PLACE Lesotho
DESCRIPTION Big four-legged plant-eater with long neck and tail.

Thotobolosaurus

Thyreophorans "shield bearers" the nanorder Thyreophora, proposed in 1986 to include *Scutellosaurus*, *Scelidosaurus*, and the ankylosaurs and stegosaurs.

Tianchungosaurus Dinosaur to be described. Might be *Dianchungosaurus* or in a new family of pachycephalosaurs.

©DIAGRAM

Tichosteus – Triceratops

Tienshanosaurus

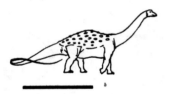

Titanosaurus

Torvosaurus

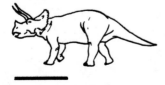

Triceratops

Tichosteus " ? " Probably *Othnielia*.

Tienshanosaurus "Tienshan lizard" FAMILY Euhelopodidae?
INFRAORDER Sauropoda SUBORDER Sauropodomorpha
ORDER Saurischia
TIME Late Jurassic PLACE Xinjiang, China
DESCRIPTION Four-legged plant-eater up to 40ft (12m) long, with
small head, long neck and tail, and bulky body with level back.

Titanosaurids the family Titanosauridae INFRAORDER Sauropoda
SUBORDER Sauropodomorpha ORDER Saurischia. See Chapter 3.

Titanosaurus "titanic lizard" FAMILY Titanosauridae
INFRAORDER Sauropoda SUBORDER Sauropodomorpha
ORDER Saurischia
TIME Late (also Early?) Cretaceous PLACE India and supposedly
Europe, Southeast Asia, and South America
DESCRIPTION Four-legged plant-eater 40ft (12m) long, with small
head, long neck, heavy body probably with a broad low armored
back, and whiplash tail.

Tomodon "cutting tooth" Discontinued name for *Diplotomodon*.

Tornieria "Tornier" FAMILY Diplodocidae
INFRAORDER Sauropoda SUBORDER Sauropodomorpha
ORDER Saurischia
TIME Late Jurassic PLACE Tanzania and perhaps Malawi
DESCRIPTION Four-legged plant-eater with bulky body, small head,
long neck, and long whiplash tail. Possibly immense. Some
Tornieria fossils might represent a new titanosaurid.

Torosaurus "bull lizard" FAMILY Ceratopsidae
SUBORDER Ceratopsia ORDER Ornithischia
TIME Latest Late Cretaceous PLACE North America (Montana
through Texas)
DESCRIPTION Massive four-legged plant-eater 25ft (7.6m) long,
weighing 8–9 US tons (7.3–8.2 metric tons). It had a relatively
larger head than any other animal's, with an immense bony neck
frill, deep parrotlike beak, short nose horn, and two long brow
horns. The body was heavy and the tail short.

Torvosaurids The family Torvosauridae INFRAORDER Carnosauria
SUBORDER Theropoda ORDER Saurischia. Family proposed in 1985
to include big robust flesh-eaters with short strong arms, for
instance *Torvosaurus* and *Xuanhanosaurus*.

Torvosaurus "savage lizard" FAMILY Torvosauridae
INFRAORDER Carnosauria SUBORDER Theropoda ORDER Saurischia
TIME Late Jurassic PLACE Colorado, USA
DESCRIPTION Robustly built two-legged flesh-eater up to 33ft (10m)
and 6 US tons (5.4 metric tons), with short powerful arms, savage
claws, and hip bones much like those of *Megalosaurus*.

Trachodon "rough tooth" FAMILY Hadrosauridae or
Lambeosauridae SUBORDER Ornithopoda ORDER Ornithischia
TIME Late Cretaceous PLACE Montana, USA
DESCRIPTION Large bipedal/quadrupedal plant-eater with toothless
beak and batteries of cheek teeth. Known only from one tooth with
a crown roughened by tiny denticles. Identity doubtful, perhaps
Prosaurolophus or *Corythosaurus*.

Triceratops "three-horned face" FAMILY Ceratopsidae
SUBORDER Ceratopsia ORDER Ornithischia

0   80ft (24m)

TIME Latest Late Cretaceous PLACE western North America
DESCRIPTION Longest horned dinosaur: a four-legged plant-eater up
to 30ft (9m) long and weighing 6 US tons (5.4 metric tons), with
short tail and bulky body. The massive head had a deep narrow
parrotlike beak, brow horns more than 3ft (90cm) long, a short
nose horn, and short solid neck frill rimmed with bony bumps.
The many fossils might come from 15 species or only 2.

Trilophosaurs "three-ridged lizards" The order Trilophosauria
INFRACLASS Archosauromorpha
TIME Triassic PLACE Europe and North America
DESCRIPTION Not dinosaurs but remote relatives: beaked reptiles
with broad, sharp, shearing cheek teeth.

Trimucrodon "three-pointed tooth" FAMILY Scutellosauridae?
SUBORDER Scelidosauria ORDER Ornithischia
TIME Late Jurassic PLACE Portugal
DESCRIPTION Small bipedal or bipedal/quadrupedal plant-eater
known only from three teeth with ridged and pointed crowns.

Troodon "wounding tooth" FAMILY Troodontidae
INFRAORDER Deinonychosauria SUBORDER Theropoda
ORDER Saurischia
TIME Late Cretaceous PLACE Canada (Alberta) and USA (Alaska,
Montana, Wyoming)
DESCRIPTION Lightly built two-legged birdlike predator 6ft 6in (2m)
long. It had slim jaws bristling with pointed saw-edged teeth, long
arms, grasping fingers tipped with large claws, birdlike legs and
feet, a small sickle-shaped second toe claw swung back or forth,
and a stiffened tail. *Troodon* was one of the "brainiest" dinosaurs
with large keen eyes and binocular vision.

Troodontids The family Troodontidae INFRAORDER
Deinonychosauria SUBORDER Theropoda ORDER Saurischia.
Main entry in Chapter 3.

Tsintaosaurus "Tsintao lizard" FAMILY Hadrosauridae
SUBORDER Ornithopoda ORDER Ornithischia
TIME Late Cretaceous PLACE Shandong, China
DESCRIPTION Large duck-billed dinosaur: a bipedal/quadrupedal
plant-eater up to 33ft (10m) long, with toothless beak, batteries of
cheek teeth, and maybe a tall bony spike jutting up between its eyes
– perhaps anchoring a flap of skin above the face. Might be *Tanius*.

Tugulusaurus "Tugulo lizard" FAMILY Coeluridae?
INFRAORDER Coelurosauria? SUBORDER Theropoda
ORDER Saurischia
TIME Early Cretaceous PLACE Xinjiang, China
DESCRIPTION Fairly small two-legged predator, perhaps 11ft 6in
(3m) long, only known from limb bones. Identity doubtful.

Tuojiangosaurus "Tuojiang lizard" FAMILY Stegosauridae
SUBORDER Stegosauria ORDER Ornithischia
TIME Late Jurassic PLACE near Tzekung in Sichuan, China
DESCRIPTION Four-legged plant-eater 23ft (7m) long, with low
head, toothless beak, two rows of triangular plates jutting up from
neck, back and tail, and two shoulder spikes, and four tail-tip
spikes.

Tylocephale "swollen head" FAMILY Pachycephalosauridae
SUBORDER Pachycephalosauria ORDER Ornithischia

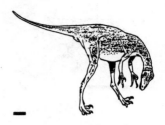

Troodon

Tsintaosaurus

Tuojiangosaurus

Tylocephale

©DIAGRAM

Tyrannosaurus

"Ultrasaurus"

Unquillosaurus

Valdosaurus

0   80ft (24m)

Tylosteus – Valdosaurus

TIME Late Cretaceous PLACE Mongolia
DESCRIPTION Two-legged plant-eater 6ft 6in (2.5m) long with a
thick domed skull highest at the back and rimmed with bony
knobs.
Tylosteus "swollen bone" A former name of *Pachycephalosaurus*.
Tyrannosaurids The family Tyrannosauridae INFRAORDER
Carnosauria SUBORDER Theropoda ORDER Saurischia.
Main entry in Chapter 3.
Tyrannosaurus "tyrant lizard" FAMILY Tyrannosauridae
INFRAORDER Carnosauria SUBORDER Theropoda ORDER Saurischia
TIME Late Cretaceous PLACE western North America and East Asia
DESCRIPTION One of the largest-ever flesh-eating land animals, a
bipedal predator 39ft (12m) long and weighing up to 7 US tons (6.4
metric tons), with huge skull, vast jaws, and 7in (18cm) steak-knife
teeth. The great legs bore enormous claws. Arms were strong but
tiny and ended in two-fingered hands.

Ugrosaurus "ugly lizard" FAMILY Ceratopsidae
SUBORDER Ceratopsia ORDER Ornithischia
TIME Latest Late Cretaceous PLACE Montana, USA
DESCRIPTION Large four-legged plant-eater perhaps up to 30ft (9m)
long, with massive head, short snout with low, rounded bony
boss, narrow parrotlike beak, and evidently long brow horns and
bony neck frill. Named in 1987, but possibly a species of
Triceratops.
Uintasaurus "Uinta lizard" A former name of *Camarasaurus*.
Ultrasaurus "ultra lizard" FAMILY Brachiosauridae
INFRAORDER Sauropoda SUBORDER Sauropodomorpha
ORDER Saurischia
TIME Early Cretaceous? PLACE South Korea
DESCRIPTION Very large four-legged plant-eater built like but
smaller than *Brachiosaurus*. Named in 1983. See too **"Ultrasaurus."**
"Ultrasaurus" "ultra lizard" FAMILY Brachiosauridae
INFRAORDER Sauropoda SUBORDER Sauropodomorpha
ORDER Saurischia
TIME Late Jurassic PLACE Colorado, USA
DESCRIPTION One of the largest-ever land animals, an immense
four-legged plant-eater over 82ft (25m) long and 52ft 6in (16m) tall,
and weighing more than 55 US tons (50 metric tons). It had a small
head on a towering giraffe-like neck, back sloping down from
shoulders to hips, pillar-like limbs, and fairly short tail. Found in
1972 and nicknamed "Ultrasaurus," it was officially so named in
1985, but by then another dinosaur already bore the name. (See
Ultrasaurus). "Ultrasaurus" might be *Brachiosaurus*.
Unquillosaurus "(Río) Unquillo lizard" FAMILY uncertain
INFRAORDER Carnosauria SUBORDER Theropoda ORDER Saurischia
TIME Late Cretaceous PLACE northwest Argentina
DESCRIPTION Huge two-legged predator up to 36ft (11m) long.
Seemingly not tyrannosaurid or megalosaurid. Identity doubtful.

Valdosaurus "Weald lizard" FAMILY Dryosauridae
SUBORDER Ornithopoda ORDER Ornithischia
TIME Early Cretaceous PLACE southern England and Niger

DESCRIPTION Two–legged plant–eater about 10ft (3m) long, evidently built like *Dryosaurus*. Known from a thigh bone.

"Vectensia" "Isle of Wight ?sword" FAMILY Nodosauridae
SUBORDER Ankylosauria ORDER Ornithischia
TIME Early Cretaceous PLACE Isle of Wight, England
DESCRIPTION Four–legged armored dinosaur (perhaps *Hylaeosaurus* or *Polacanthus*) known only from a flat–sided triangular bony spine about 10in (25cm) long described in 1982.

Vectisaurus "Isle of Wight lizard" FAMILY Iguanodontidae
SUBORDER Ornithopoda ORDER Ornithischia
TIME Early Cretaceous PLACE Isle of Wight, England
DESCRIPTION Bipedal/quadrupedal plant–eater 13ft 6in (4m) long, similar to *Iguanodon* (some of its supposed remains came from an *Iguanodon*) but with taller spines jutting from its backbone.

Velocipes "quick foot" FAMILY Coelophysidae?
INFRAORDER Coelurosauria SUBORDER Theropoda ORDER Saurischia
TIME Late Triassic PLACE West Germany
DESCRIPTION Bipedal predator, a fairly small early theropod known only from a leg bone. Identity doubtful.

Velociraptor "quick plunderer" FAMILY Dromaeosauridae
INFRAORDER Deinonychosauria SUBORDER Theropoda
ORDER Saurischia
TIME Late Cretaceous PLACE China, Mongolia, and USSR
DESCRIPTION Ferocious two–legged predator 6ft (1.8m) long with a long low head, relatively big brain, sharp teeth, long arms, long clawed fingers, very long stiffened tail, and long legs. Each foot's second toe bore a formidably large retractable claw.

Volkheimeria "Volkheimer's" FAMILY Cetiosauridae
INFRAORDER Sauropoda SUBORDER Sauropodomorpha
ORDER Saurischia
TIME Late Jurassic PLACE Argentina
DESCRIPTION Large four–legged plant–eater with long neck and tail and pillarlike legs. Less than half as large as *Patagosaurus* and with more primitive spinal bones. Named after a paleontologist.

Vulcanodon "volcano tooth" FAMILY Vulcanodontidae
INFRAORDER Sauropoda SUBORDER Sauropodomorpha
ORDER Saurischia
TIME Early Jurassic PLACE Zimbabwe
DESCRIPTION Four–legged plant–eater perhaps 20ft (6.5m) long, with small head, long neck and tail, bulky body and pillarlike legs. Bones had some prosauropod and some sauropod features.

Vulcanodontids The family Vulcanodontidae INFRAORDER Sauropoda SUBORDER Sauropodomorpha ORDER Saurischia
TIME Early to Mid Jurassic PLACE Zimbabwe? and China
DESCRIPTION Four–legged plant–eaters with small heads, long necks and tails, and bulky bodies; the most primitive sauropods known, with tail bones including features found in prosauropods. The family included *Vulcanodon* and possibly the "cetiosaurid" *Bellusaurus*.

Walgettosuchus "Walgett crocodile" Perhaps *Rapator*.
Walkeria "Walker's" FAMILY Herrerasauridae?
INFRAORDER ? SUBORDER ? ORDER Herrerasauria

Vectisaurus

Velociraptor

Volkheimeria

Vulcanodon

©DIAGRAM

Walkeria

Wannanosaurus – Yangchuanosaurus

Wuerhosaurus

TIME Late Triassic PLACE Andhra Pradesh, India
DESCRIPTION Small lightweight bipedal predator perhaps 4ft (1.2m) long, with a long low head, large pointed and unserrated teeth, muscular legs, and long tail. Some think it was a coelophysid or halticosaurid. Named in 1987 in honor of a paleontologist.
Wannanosaurus "Wannan lizard" FAMILY Homalocephalidae
SUBORDER Pachycephalosauria ORDER Ornithischia
TIME Late Cretaceous PLACE Anhui, China
DESCRIPTION Tiny two-legged plant-eater about 2ft (61cm) long; a bone-headed dinosaur with a thick but evidently low-domed skull.
Wuerhosaurus "Wuerho lizard" FAMILY Stegosauridae
SUBORDER Stegosauria ORDER Ornithischia
TIME Early Cretaceous PLACE Wuerho region in Xinjiang, China
DESCRIPTION Four-legged plant-eater perhaps 20ft (6m) long, with small low head, high back, two rows of long low bony plates down neck, back, and upper tail, and probably four lower-tail spikes.

Xenotarsosaurus "strange-ankle lizard" FAMILY Abelisauridae
INFRAORDER Carnosauria SUBORDER Theropoda ORDER Saurischia
TIME Late Cretaceous PLACE Chubut, Argentina
DESCRIPTION Large two-legged flesh-eater known only from two spinal bones and some hindlimb bones with fused ankle bones, an unusual feature in large predatory dinosaurs. Named in 1986.
Xiaosaurus "little lizard" FAMILY Fabrosauridae?
SUBORDER uncertain ORDER Ornithischia
TIME Middle Jurassic PLACE Sichuan, China
DESCRIPTION Slim two-legged plant-eater about 5ft (1.5m) long, with deep head, leaflike cheek teeth, short arms, long shins and ankles, and long stiffened tail. Named in 1983 by a Chinese paleontologist who later claimed it was *Yandusaurus*.

Xuanhanosaurus

Xuanhanosaurus "Xuanhan lizard" FAMILY Torvosauridae?
INFRAORDER Carnosauria SUBORDER Theropoda ORDER Saurischia
TIME Middle Jurassic PLACE Xuanhan in Sichuan, China
DESCRIPTION Flesh-eating dinosaur about 20ft (6m) long, with powerful arms and strong short hands with robust claws. Described in 1984 by a scientist who argued that it walked on all fours.
Xuanhuasaurus "Xuanhua lizard" FAMILY Chaoyoungosauridae
SUBORDER Pachycephalosauria ORDER Ornithischia
TIME Late Jurassic PLACE Xuanhua in ?Hebei, China
DESCRIPTION Small two-legged plant-eater with canine-type teeth in the front upper jaw, cheek teeth of primitive design, and cheek bones foreshadowing *Psittacosaurus*'s. Named in 1986.

Yandusaurus

Yaleosaurus "Yale lizard" A former name of *Anchisaurus*.
Yandusaurus "Yandu lizard" FAMILY Hypsilophodontidae
SUBORDER Ornithopoda ORDER Ornithischia
TIME Middle Jurassic PLACE Sichuan, China
DESCRIPTION Slim two-legged plant-eater about 5ft (1.5m) long, with deep head, leaflike cheek teeth, short arms, long legs with long shins and ankles, and long stiff tail. See also *Yubasaurus*.
Yangchuanosaurus "Yangchuan lizard" FAMILY Ceratosauridae
INFRAORDER Carnosauria SUBORDER Theropoda ORDER Saurischia

Yangchuanosaurus

0   80ft (24m)

TIME Late Jurassic PLACE Yangchuan Country in Sichuan, China
DESCRIPTION Two-legged flesh-eater up to 33ft (10m) long, with
ridges and hornlets on a skull 3ft 7in (1.1m) long, with vast jaws
armed with curved saw-edged daggerlike fangs. It had fairly short
arms with clawed three-fingered hands, powerful legs with large
toe claws, and a long heavy tail balancing head, neck, and trunk.
Possibly a low skin fin ran down the back.

Yaverlandia

Yaverlandia "from Yaverland" FAMILY Pachycephalosauridae
SUBORDER Pachycephalosauria ORDER Ornithischia
TIME Early Cretaceous PLACE Yaverland (Isle of Wight) England
DESCRIPTION Two-legged plant-eater only about 3ft (90cm) long
with two thick bony areas capping its skull. The earliest known
bone-head, or just possibly an ankylosaur.

Yaxartosaurus See *Jaxartosaurus*.

Yingshanosaurus "?Mt. Ying lizard" FAMILY Stegosauridae
SUBORDER Stegosauria ORDER Ornithischia
TIME Jurassic PLACE Sichuan, China
DESCRIPTION Four-legged plant-eating dinosaur seemingly with
rows of plates or spines down the back, plus tail and shoulder
spikes. Perhaps *Tuojiangosaurus*.

Yingshanosaurus

Yubasaurus "Yuba lizard" Perhaps the dinosaur later named
Yandusaurus. If so, *Yubasaurus* is its rightful name.

Yunnanosaurids The family Yunnanosauridae
INFRAORDER Prosauropoda SUBORDER Sauropodomorpha
ORDER Saurischia
TIME Early Jurassic PLACE Yunnan, China
DESCRIPTION Early plant-eating dinosaurs with distinctive chisel-
shaped teeth. Only one member known. See *Yunnanosaurus*.

Yunnanosaurus

Yunnanosaurus "Yunnan lizard" FAMILY Yunnanosauridae
INFRAORDER Prosauropoda SUBORDER Sauropodomorpha
ORDER Saurischia
TIME Early Jurassic PLACE Yunnan, China
DESCRIPTION Bipedal/quadrupedal plant-eater perhaps 7ft (2.1m)
long, with small head, long neck, bulky body, longer hind limbs
than fore limbs, and long tail. This was the only known
prosauropod with chisel-shaped self-sharpening teeth.

Zapsalis Evidently *Paronychodon*.

Zephyrosaurus "west wind lizard" FAMILY Hypsilophodontidae
SUBORDER Ornithopoda ORDER Ornithischia
TIME Early Cretaceous PLACE Montana, USA
DESCRIPTION Lightweight bipedal plant-eater about 6ft (1.8m) long,
with ridged teeth for chewing plant food.

Zephyrosaurus

Zigongosaurus "Zigong lizard" Probably *Omeisaurus*.

Zizhongosaurus "Zizhong lizard" FAMILY Cetiosauridae
INFRAORDER Sauropoda SUBORDER Sauropodomorpha
ORDER Saurischia
TIME Early Jurassic PLACE Zizhong County in Sichuan, China
DESCRIPTION Four-legged plant-eater about 30ft (9) long, with small
head, long neck, bulky body, long forelimbs, and long tail: a
primitive sauropod, somewhat like *Barapasaurus*. Named in 1983.

Zizhongosaurus

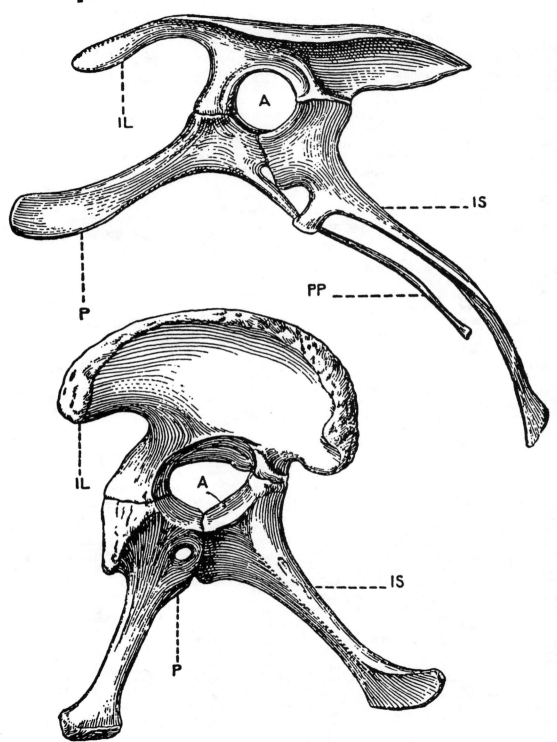

DINOSAURS CLASSIFIED

This chapter describes both major groups of dinosaurs. Then brief accounts of their chief subdivisions precede one-page entries on families, mainly the better known. Each family is described with a pictured example (plus mouse, cat, dog, or human to show scale), time line, distribution map, and list of genera. Certain genera are of doubtful identity, and a few pictured animals must be partly guesswork (shown in outline).

Our main groupings follow established practice, with a few amendments – all liable to change as research makes relationships clearer. We also introduce more complex classifications based on cladistics (see page 21). Its close study of anatomical similarities is regrouping dinosaurs, but work is incomplete and some diagnoses differ.

Drawings from an article by the Franco-Belgian paleontologist Louis Dollo show differences in hip design between both main dinosaur groups.
Above: Hip girdle of an ornithischian, *Iguanodon*.
Below: Hip girdle of a saurischian, *Diplodocus*. Labeled bones are ilium (IL), ischium (IS) and pubis (P and PP); in Iguanodon P is an extension of the pubis. The acetabulum (A) is a socket for the hip bone.

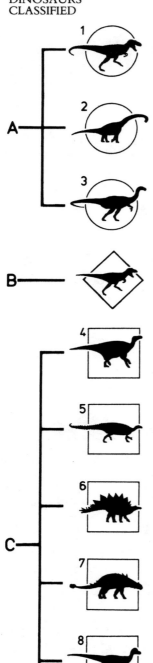

Two great groups

Paleontologists (scientists studying ancient prehistoric life) group dinosaurs and every other animal according to a scheme based on relationships. Traditionally dinosaurs form two orders, subdivided into successively lesser groupings – suborders, infraorders, families, genera, and species. Each group bears a scientific name at least partly formed from Greek or Latin words. Scientists worldwide use the same scientific names for these to prevent confusion in meetings and scientific writings.

The order Saurischia ("lizard hipped") held dinosaurs with large holes reducing the skull's weight, teeth (in most) set in the outer rim of the jaws, and (in most) a forward-pointing pubis – the front hip bone. There were three saurischian suborders: the two-legged flesh-eating theropods (pages 110–135), mainly four-legged plant-eating sauropodomorphs (pages 136–146), and segnosaurs (pages 136–137 and 147).

The order Ornithischia ("bird hipped") held plant-eating dinosaurs whose hip bones had a backward-pointing pubis as in birds and some advanced saurischians. Ornithischians also had a horny beak, an extra bone at the lower jaw tip, and leaf-shaped tooth crowns. Many lacked front teeth but had powerful cheek teeth, cheek pouches, and bony tendons stiffening the spine. Ornithischians appear on pages 148–171.

As time passed ornithischians outnumbered saurischians, and in both groups, old species, genera, and families gave way to new ones better fitted for getting food, escaping enemies, or surviving harsh climatic change.

Differences between saurischians and ornithischians long persuaded scientists that each group sprang from a different archosaur ancestor. Strictly, that would mean there was no single group of animals called dinosaurs. But paleontologists have found similarities in key joints of both groups, and many experts now think ornithischians and saurischians both evolved from earlier dinosaurs (herrerasaurs). In 1974 Robert Bakker and Peter Galton argued that ornithischians, saurischians, and birds formed subclasses of the Dinosauria – a class equal to but unlike ordinary reptiles, the class Reptilia. Bakker later claimed that the Dinosauria included pterosaurs and lagosuchids, and that ornithischians and sauropodomorphs – both with double breastbone – formed a single major group, the Phytodinosauria: "plant dinosaurs." Debates are likely to go on.

Two groups (*left*)
Letters and numbered symbols correspond to orders and suborders named on the right-hand page.

Hip bones (*right*)
1 Saurischian hip bones with forward-angled pubis (**a**).
2 Ornithischian hip bones with backward-angled pubis (**a**).

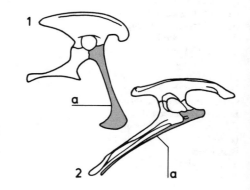

Order	Suborder	Infraorder	Family

A
Saurischia

1 Theropoda

Coelurosauria
- Coelophysidae
- Halticosauridae
- Coeluridae
- Noasauridae
- Compsognathidae
- Archaeopterygidae

Carnosauria
- Megalosauridae
- Eustreptospondylidae?
- Torvosauridae
- Allosauridae
- Abelisauridae
- Ceratosauridae

Deinonychosauria
- Dromaeosauridae
- Therizinosauridae?
- Troodontidae
- Baryonychidae
- Spinosauridae
- Dryptosauridae
- Tyrannosauridae
- Aublysodontidae

Ornithomimosauria
- Ornithomimidae
- Garudimimidae
- Deinocheiridae
- Itemiridae

Oviraptorosauria
- Avimimidae
- Caenagnathidae
- Oviraptoridae
- Ingeniidae

2 Sauropodomorpha

Prosauropoda
- Anchisauridae
- Plateosauridae
- Blikanasauridae
- Melanorosauridae
- Yunnanosauridae

Sauropoda
- Vulcanodontidae
- Cetiosauridae
- Barapasauridae
- Brachiosauridae
- Chubutisauridae?
- Camarasauridae
- Titanosauridae
- Diplodocidae
- Euhelopodidae
- Dicraeosauridae

3 Segnosauria
- Segnosauridae
- Enigmosauridae

B
Herrerasauria
- Staurikosauridae
- Herrerasauridae

C
Ornithischia

? Fabrosauridae
- Hypsilophodontidae
- Dryosauridae
- Thescelosauridae
- Camptosauridae
- Iguanodontidae
- Hadrosauridae
- Lambeosauridae
- Heterodontosauridae

4 Ornithopoda

5 Scelidosauria
- Scutellosauridae
- Scelidosauridae

6 Stegosauria
- Huayangosauridae
- Stegosauridae

7 Ankylosauria
- Nodosauridae
- Ankylosauridae

8 Pachycephalosauria
- Chaoyoungosauridae
- Pachycephalosauridae
- Homalocephalidae

9 Ceratopsia
- Psittacosauridae
- Protoceratopsidae
- Ceratopsidae

©DIAGRAM

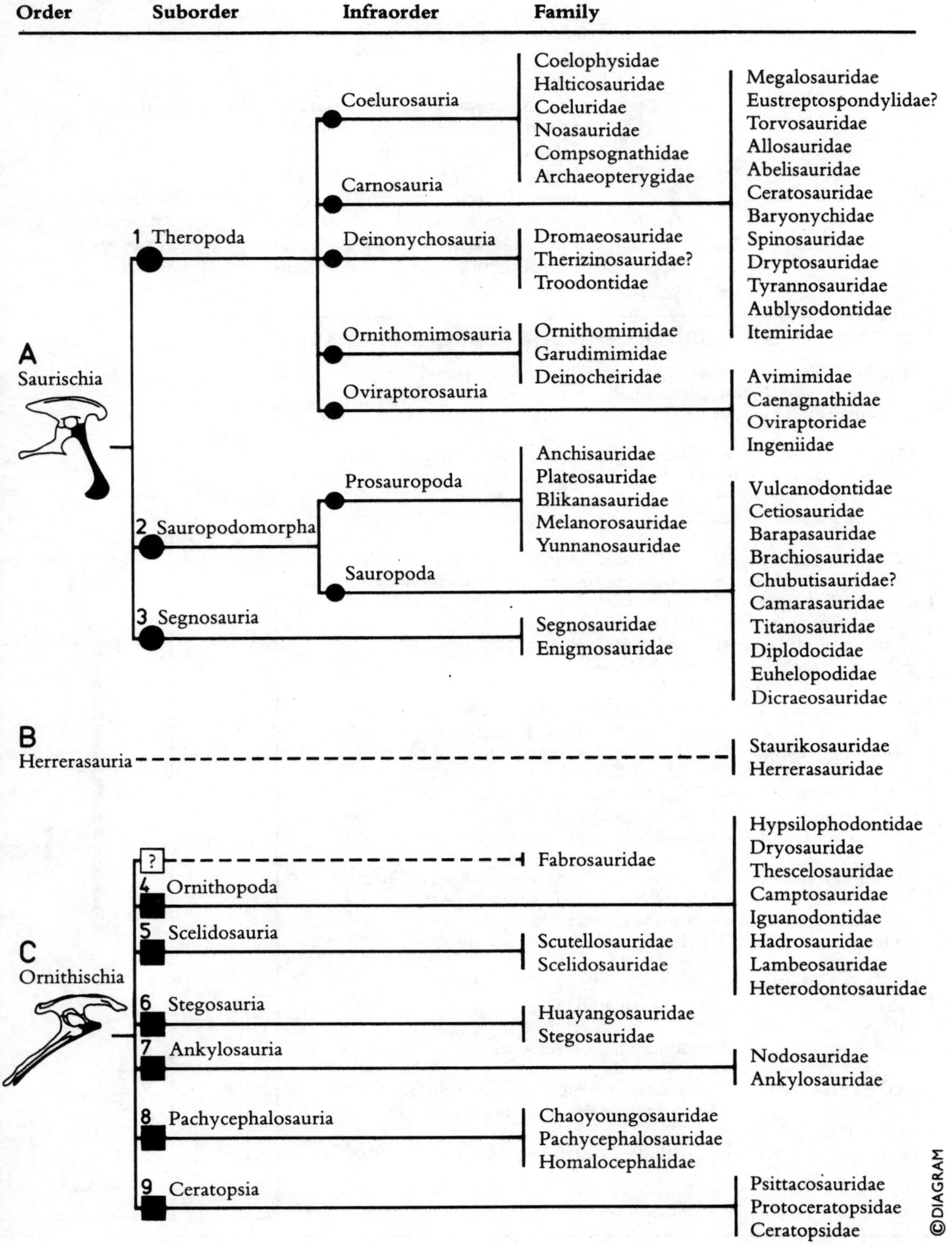

Saurischians 1: theropods (with Herrerasaurs)

The first known predatory dinosaurs belonged to the **Herrerasauria**, possibly the stock that gave rise to all other dinosaurs.

The saurischian suborder **Theropoda** ("beast feet") held most predatory dinosaurs. These bipeds had a broadly birdlike body plan, but most had sharp teeth, and all had a long bony tail core, arms with clawed fingers, and scales not feathers. Only the "bird–dinosaur" *Archaeopteryx* left undoubted fossil feather impressions, though some small theropods might have had feathers, too. From early, lightly-built small-game chasers no bigger than a chicken came big-game hunters as heavy as an elephant. Some forms evolved with reduced fingers, and horny beaks instead of teeth.

THEROPOD INFRAORDERS AND THE HERRERASAURIA

Numbered items depict the Herrerasauria and five theropod infraorders named in this book. Small letters indicate families. (Some groupings are artificial and **j** may be **i**.)

1 Herrerasauria ("Herrera lizards") Small to medium early predatory dinosaurs; the only dinosaurs with only two spinal bones above the hips – so not true theropods at all. Families: pages 112-113.
a Staurikosauridae **b** Herrerasauridae

2 Coelurosauria ("hollow-tail lizards") A largely artificial grouping of small predatory dinosaurs. Coelurosaurs were lightly built with long slim jaws, small sharp teeth, long legs, fairly long arms, and sharp claws. Selected families: pages 114–117 and 121.
c Coelophysidae **d** Halticosauridae **e** Coeluridae **f** Noasauridae
g Compsognathidae **h** Archaeopterygidae

3 Carnosauria ("flesh lizards") A largely artificial grouping of the big flesh-eating dinosaurs. Carnosaurs had strong jaws, sharp fangs, and formidable claws on toes and fingers. Some were the largest-ever land predators. Selected families: pages 128-135.
i Megalosauridae **j** Eustreptospondylidae **k** Torvosauridae **l** Allosauridae
m Abelisauridae **n** Ceratosauridae **o** Baryonychidae **p** Spinosauridae
q Dryptosauridae **r** Tyrannosauridae **s** Aublysodontidae **t** Itemiridae

4 Deinonychosauria ("terrible-claw lizards") Formidable lightweight Cretaceous predators with a stiffened tail and large-clawed second toe flicked forward for attack. Families: pages 125-127.
u Dromaeosauridae **v** Therizinosauridae **w** Troodontidae

5 Ornithomimosauria ("bird mimic lizards") Speedy ostrich-like theropods (mainly Late Cretaceous) with long legs, fairly long arms, and a narrow toothless beak. Families: pages 122-124.
x Ornithomimidae **y** Garudimimidae **z** Deinocheiridae

6 Oviraptorosauria ("egg-thief lizards") Lightly-built birdlike Late Cretaceous theropods with short deep heads and toothless beaks. Best-known families: pages 118-120.
aa Avimimidae **bb** Caenagnathidae **cc** Oviraptoridae **dd** Ingeniidae

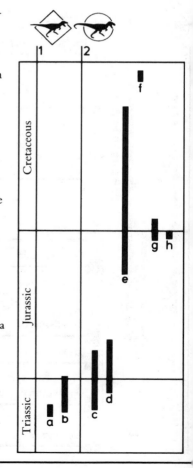

Theropod families are traditionally grouped as (small) coelurosaurs and (large) carnosaurs. We now know that some natural groups held both large and small creatures, but research is still under way, with experts producing rival classifications. Ours undoubtedly still lumps together some beasts that will end in other camps – for instance ceratosaurid "carnosaurs" and coelophysid "coelurosaurs" arguably belong together in the Ceratosauria and most other theropods arguably belong in the so-called Tetanurae. Page numbers here refer to entries on the best-known theropod families. Shorter entries on other families appear in Chapter 2.

CHAPTER 3

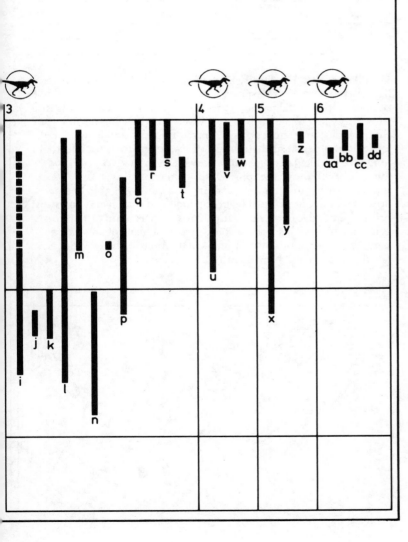

Paul's theropods
In 1988 US paleontologist Gregory Paul suggested grouping predatory dinosaurs in superorders of increasingly birdlike forms: items **1–4** in this simplified diagram.
1 Paleodinosaurs (eg *Staurikosaurus*): the first predatory dinosaurs, with four-toed feet and no long birdlike ilium (a hip bone).
2 Herreravians (eg *Herrerasaurus*): with four-toed feet but also some birdlike features.
3 Theropods, with long ilium and three-toed birdlike feet, and subdivided into:
a Paleotheropods (eg *Coelophysis*): birdlike but with old-fashioned features. **b,c** Avetheropods: two sister groups of advanced theropods, with double-jointed lower jaw, birdlike rib cage, and other innovations. **b** included *Tyrannosaurus*. **c** comprised "protobirds" such as *Ornithomimus*.
4 Birds: arguably a superorder of dinosaurs.
A Triassic Period
B Jurassic Period
C Cretaceous Period

©DIAGRAM

111

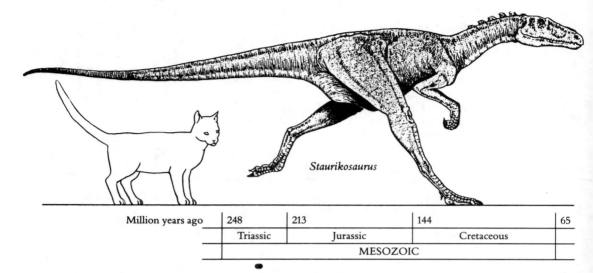

Staurikosaurus

Million years ago	248	213	144	65
	Triassic	Jurassic	Cretaceous	
		MESOZOIC		

**Genera
(some doubtful)**
"Chindesaurus"
Frenguellisaurus
Staurikosaurus

Staurikosaurids The family Staurikosauridae ("Southern Cross lizards") ORDER Herrerasauria
DESCRIPTION Bipedal predators ranging from as heavy as a big dog to as heavy as a man. Probably all had a relatively big head, large sharp teeth, fairly short arms with five-fingered hands, long agile legs with longer shins than thighs, five-toed or four-toed feet, and long tail. Unlike later dinosaurs they had a mere two vertebrae to join the backbone to the hips. Despite their small size, staurikosaurids might have been the first dinosaurs able to run down and kill big game. The group included the earliest and most primitive of all known dinosaurs. Most experts think them too primitive to have been theropods, or saurischians of any other kind. LENGTH 6ft 6in–10ft (2–3m) TIME Mid to Late Triassic PLACE South America and North America.

Where they lived
Major areas of fossil finds

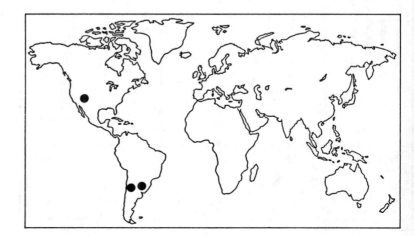

Herrerasaurids

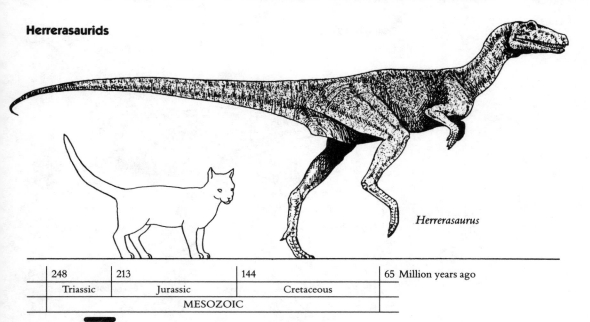

Herrerasaurus

248	213	144	65 Million years ago
Triassic	Jurassic	Cretaceous	
MESOZOIC			

Herrerasaurids The family Herrerasauridae ("Herrera lizards")
ORDER Herrerasauria
DESCRIPTION Early bipedal flesh–eating kin of staurikosaurids. Like
these, herrerasaurids had curved, pointed teeth, but a shorter neck,
longer arms, distinctive hip and leg bones, and thighs longer than
shins. The hips' pubic bones sloped back much like an
ornithischian's yet ended in a "boot" – an advanced theropod
design. Shin bones show some similarities to sauropods', so
herrerasaurids just might have been their ancestors. Yet they had
birdlike features, too, especially hip joint, backward–angled pubic
bone, and straplike shoulder blade. If *Aliwalia* were a herrerasaurid
some kinds grew as big as *Allosaurus*. LENGTH 7–10ft or even 36ft
(2–3m or even 11m) TIME Late Triassic to Early Jurassic PLACE
South America, China, India, and maybe Africa.

Genera
Herrerasaurus
Ischisaurus
Sinosaurus
Walkeria

Where they lived
Major areas of fossil finds

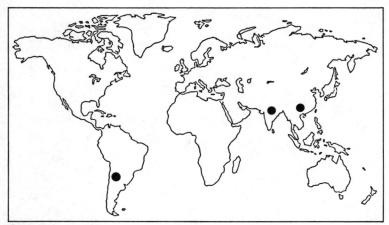

©DIAGRAM

Coelophysids

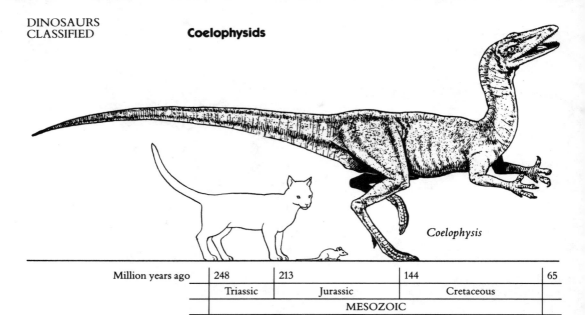

Coelophysis

Million years ago	248	213	144	65
	Triassic	Jurassic	Cretaceous	
	MESOZOIC			

**Genera
(some doubtful)**
Avipes
Coelophysis
Longosaurus
Lukousaurus
Podokesaurus
Procompsognathus
Pterospondylus
Saltopus
Segisaurus
Syntarsus
Velocipes

Coelophysids The family Coelophysidae ("hollow forms")
INFRAORDER Coelurosauria SUBORDER Theropoda ORDER Saurischia
DESCRIPTION Early, lightweight, bipedal hunting dinosaurs that
chased, seized, and ate big insects, lizards, and even their own
young. Coelophysids had a long, low, head with a sharp, narrow
snout, long flexible neck, long forearms, large sharp–clawed hands,
long sprinters' legs, slim body, and long tail held aloft for balancing
the forepart of the body. At least some had conical front teeth for
seizing prey; other teeth were shaped as slashing blades. Some
coelophysids showed a tendency to grow head crests. In
certain kinds, stronger and weaker individuals might represent
males and females, and fossilized groups suggest that coelophysids
roamed in packs. LENGTH 2–10ft (60cm–3m) TIME Late Triassic to
Early Jurassic PLACE North America, Europe, Africa, China.

Where they lived
Major areas of fossil finds

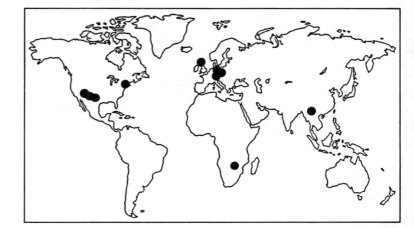

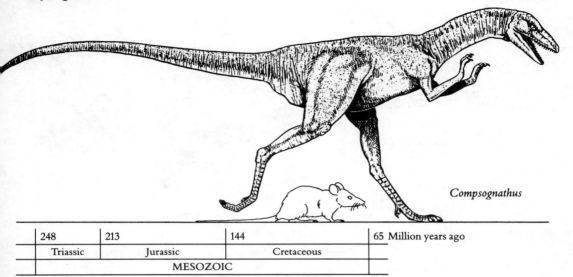

Compsognathus

248	213		144		65 Million years ago
Triassic	Jurassic		Cretaceous		
MESOZOIC					

Compsognathids The family Compsognathidae ("pretty jaws")
INFRAORDER Coelurosauria SUBORDER Theropoda ORDER Saurischia
DESCRIPTION Tiny bipedal predators known only from
Compsognathus, a beast no bigger than a cat. Compsognathids had a
long narrow head with small sharp teeth, a long curved neck, slim
body, short arms with clawed, two-fingered hands (some scientists
claim extra fingers), long legs with shins longer than the thighs,
and clawed, three-toed feet. The tail was very long indeed. Ribs,
shoulder blades, and wrist bones suggest that compsognathids
were in some ways more advanced and birdlike than the
coelophysids. *Compsognathus* sprinted after lizards on the small dry
islands where it lived (one *Compsognathus* fossil had a swallowed
lizard in its belly). LENGTH 2–3ft (60-91cm) TIME Late Jurassic to
Early Cretaceous PLACE Europe (West Germany and France).

Genera
Compsognathus

Where they lived
Major areas of fossil finds

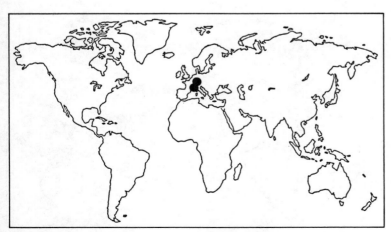

©DIAGRAM

115

Coelurids

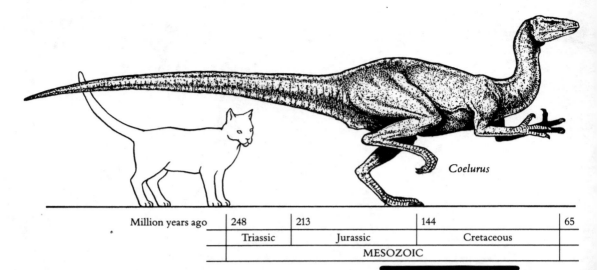

Coelurus

Million years ago	248	213	144	65
	Triassic	Jurassic	Cretaceous	
		MESOZOIC		

**Genera
(some doubtful)**
Calamospondylus
Chuandongocoelurus
Coeluroides
Coelurus
Inosaurus
Jubbulpuria
Kakuru
Ngexisaurus
Nuthetes
Ornitholestes
Ornithomimoides
Sinocoelurus
Teinurosaurus
Thecocoelurus
Tugulusaurus

Coelurids The family Coeluridae ("hollow tails")
INFRAORDER Coelurosauria SUBORDER Theropoda ORDER Saurischia
DESCRIPTION Small lightweight bipedal predators. They had a low,
narrow head with sharp-toothed jaws. Some might have sprouted a
low nasal horn. Neck, arms, legs, and tail were long. Each foot had
three main toes and each hand had three fingers with strongly
curved claws. The coelurids' pubic hip bone ended in a "boot," a
more advanced design than that of compsognathids. Most were
little longer and much lighter than a man. These were speedy
hunters capable of chasing and seizing small birds, lizards,
pterosaurs, and mammals. Perhaps some also scavenged meat from
the kills of larger predators, as jackals and hyenas do today.
LENGTH 4–8ft (1.2–2.4m) TIME Late Jurassic to Late Cretaceous
PLACE North America, Europe, Africa, Asia, and maybe Australia.

Where they lived
Major areas of fossil finds

116

Noasaurids

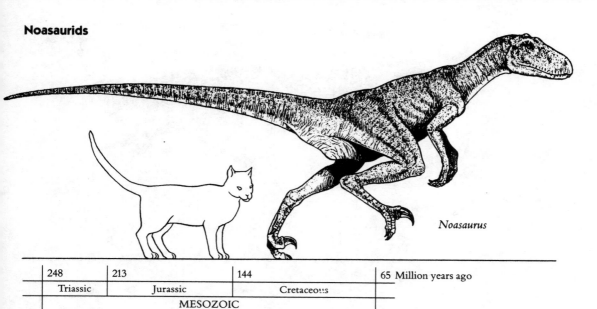

Noasaurus

248	213		144		65 Million years ago
Triassic	Jurassic		Cretaceous		
MESOZOIC					

Noasaurids The family Noasauridae ("NW Argentina lizards")
INFRAORDER Coelurosauria SUBORDER Theropoda ORDER Saurischia
DESCRIPTION Small lightly built bipedal predators. Like
dromaeosaurids they had a large, sharp, curved second-toe claw
that they could pull back for walking and switch forward to attack
an enemy. Yet the tendon that pulled the claw back slotted into a
depression low down on the claw; it was not anchored to a jutting
bit of bone like a dromaeosaurid's retractor tendon. Also, the
neck bones, fairly deep head, and lightly built jaws recall an
abelisaurid's. The arms remain unknown. We are unsure how
noasaurids used these in a fight, but a pack of noasaurids could
probably bring down and eat a half-grown sauropod. Perhaps
noasaurids were late survivals of a group of theropods designed
largely on old-fashioned lines. LENGTH 8ft (2.4m) TIME Late
Cretaceous PLACE northwest Argentina.

Genera
Noasaurus

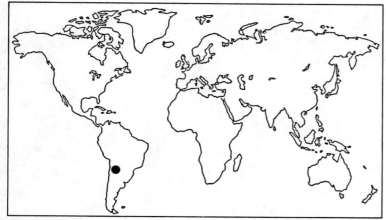

©DIAGRAM

Oviraptorids

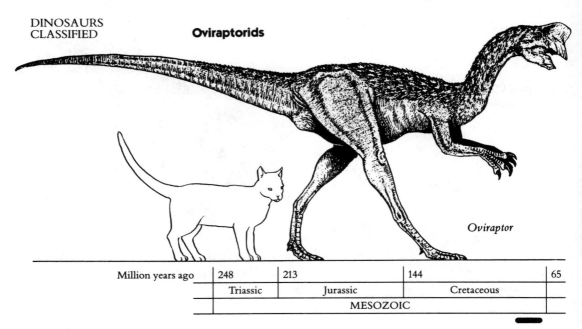

Oviraptor

Million years ago	248	213	144	65
	Triassic	Jurassic	Cretaceous	
		MESOZOIC		

Genera
Conchoraptor
Ingenia
Oviraptor

Oviraptorids The family Oviraptoridae ("egg thieves")
INFRAORDER Oviraptorosauria SUBORDER Theropoda ORDER
Saurischia
DESCRIPTION Small two-legged birdlike predators with a bizarrely
deep short head. One skull bears a nasal bump, another is crested
like a cassowary's, maybe for display. Its powerful toothless beak
looked somewhat like a parrot's but there were two small, strong
pointed teeth set in the mouth roof. *Oviraptor* had a birdlike wrist
and wishbone, and hips with birdlike and theropod features. There
were big strong arms and shoulders, and hands with three long
fingers tipped with strong curved claws. Legs were evidently long
with effectively three-toed feet, and the tail was deep and short.
Oviraptorids could have crunched up mollusks and used their teeth
to crack open dinosaur eggs. LENGTH 6ft (1.8m) TIME Late
Cretaceous PLACE Mongolia.

Where they lived
Major areas of fossil finds

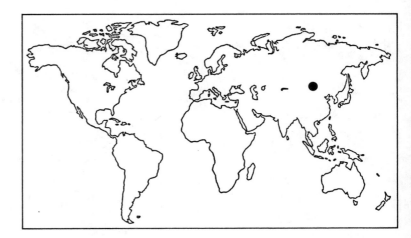

Caenagnathids

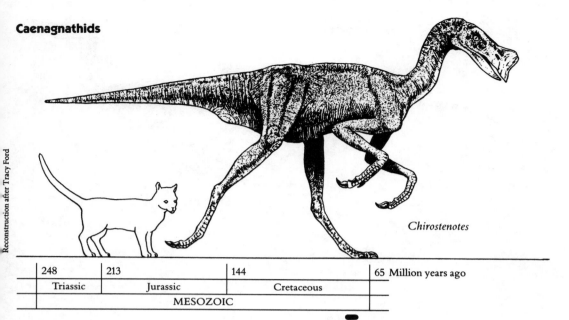

Chirostenotes

248	213		144		65 Million years ago
Triassic	Jurassic		Cretaceous		
MESOZOIC					

Caenagnathids The family Caenagnathidae ("recent jawless")
INFRAORDER Oviraptorosauria SUBORDER Theropoda ORDER
Saurischia

DESCRIPTION Small two–legged predatory dinosaurs sometimes
placed with oviraptorids in a single family. They include dinosaurs
once grouped as elmisaurids. Caenagnathids are known mainly
from bits of skeleton behind the skull. Each hand had three long,
clawed slender fingers, and effectively three long birdlike toes. As
in birds, some kinds had certain foot bones fused together. Hip
bones and finger claws resemble *Oviraptor*'s, though the feet and
long thumbs resemble those of early ostrich mimics. Bits of skull
perhaps from caenagnathids hint at a long, deep toothless beak,
with an upward bulging jaw joint. Robust and slightly built forms
of *Chirostenotes* might have been males and females. LENGTH 7ft
(2m) TIME Late Cretaceous PLACE North America and Asia.

**Genera
(some doubtful)**
Caenagnathus
Chirostenotes
Elmisaurus
Laevisuchus
Macrophalangia
Microvenator

Where they lived
Major areas of fossil finds

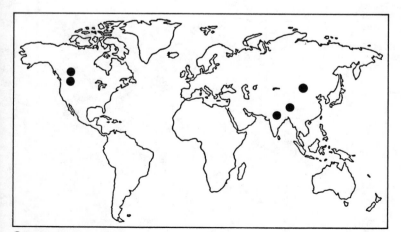

©DIAGRAM

Avimimids

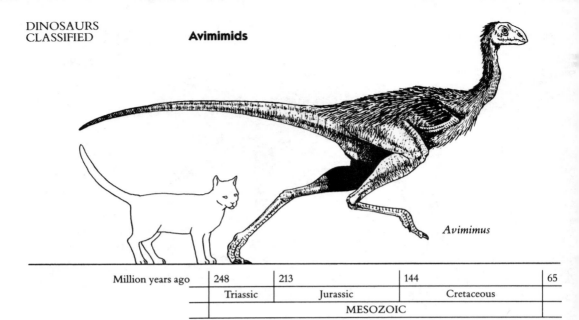

Avimimus

Million years ago	248	213	144	65
	Triassic	Jurassic	Cretaceous	
	MESOZOIC			

Genera
Avimimus

Avimimids The family Avimimidae ("bird mimics")
INFRAORDER Oviraptorosauria SUBORDER Theropoda ORDER
Saurischia
DESCRIPTION Extremely birdlike dinosaurs with a small, short, deep
head, toothless beak, long slim legs and three-toed feet with
narrow pointed claws. There were fused wrist bones, and probably
clawed fingers on the "wings" – short, feathered arms that could be
folded like a bird's. Little tail is known, but hip design suggests the
tail was long. The eyes and brain were relatively large, and a saw
edge served the upper beak like teeth. Avimimids seemingly
roamed open plains, sprinting to catch small prey and escape
predators. They could not fly or even flutter off the ground like
chickens, though possibly evolved from animals that did. The
only known avimimid is *Avimimus*. LENGTH 5ft (1.5m) TIME Late
Cretaceous PLACE Mongolia.

Where they lived
Major areas of fossil finds

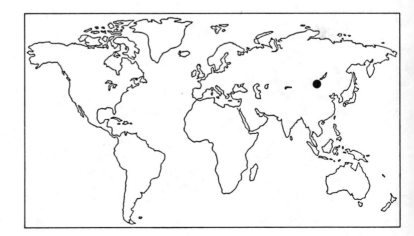

Archaeopterygids

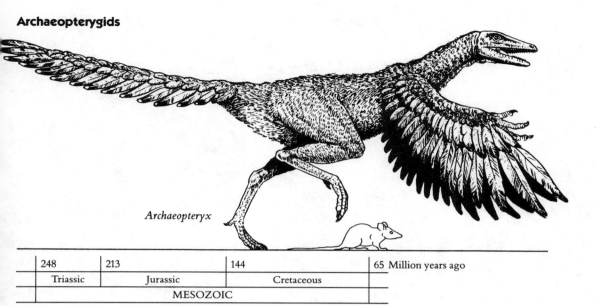

Archaeopteryx

248	213		144		65 Million years ago
Triassic	Jurassic		Cretaceous		
MESOZOIC					

●

Archaeopterygids The family Archaeopterygidae ("ancient wings")

INFRAORDER Coelurosauria SUBORDER Theropoda ORDER Saurischia
DESCRIPTION The first known birds, a subgroup of predatory dinosaurs, perhaps related to the dromaeosaurids. Like many small theropods archaeopterygids had sharp little teeth in long slim jaws, a thin flexible neck, (three) long clawed fingers, a short body, long legs with stiff ankle joints, (four) long clawed toes, and a bony tail core. Like dromaeosaurids, they could have walked (or maybe climbed) with the second toe raised. They were feathered like most birds, with wings, wishbone, and shoulder girdle designed for flight. They could climb, run, leap, and swim. The only known kind lived on low scrubby tropical islands, perhaps plucking fish from lagoons or scavenging along the shore. LENGTH 3ft (about 1m) TIME Late Jurassic PLACE Bavaria, West Germany.

Genera
Archaeopteryx

Where they lived
Major areas of fossil finds

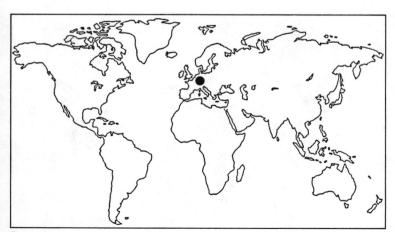

©DIAGRAM

121

Ornithomimids

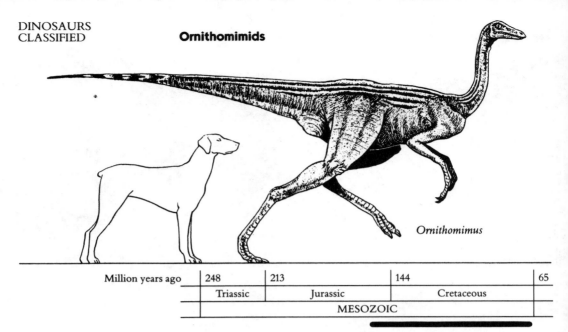

Ornithomimus

Million years ago	248	213		144		65
	Triassic	Jurassic		Cretaceous		
			MESOZOIC			

**Genera
(some doubtful)**
Anserimimus
Archaeornithomimus
"*Arkansaurus*"
Betasuchus
Dromiceiomimus
Elaphrosaurus
Gallimimus
Ornithomimus
"*Sanchusaurus*"
Struthiomimus

Ornithomimids The family Ornithomimidae ("bird mimics")
INFRAORDER Ornithomimosauria SUBORDER Theropoda ORDER
Saurischia
DESCRIPTION Ostrich-like dinosaurs with small, light head,
relatively big brain, large eyes, and long narrow toothless beak.
They had a long, slim, curved, mobile neck, compact body, and
fairly long arms with grasping, clawed, three-fingered hands.
There were long, strong legs, with longer shins than thighs, and
long feet each with three toes tipped with claws. The stiffly held
tapered tail held level with the back balanced the forepart of the
body when they ran. Ornithomimids ate low-growing plants and
maybe insects and small reptiles. They might have kicked enemies
but their chief defense was a speedy getaway. LENGTH 11ft 6in–19ft
8in (3.5–6m) TIME Late Jurassic to Late Cretaceous PLACE North
America, maybe Africa, Asia, and maybe Europe.

Where they lived
Major areas of fossil finds

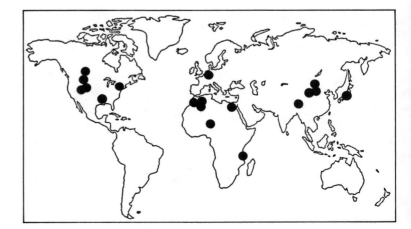

Garudimimids

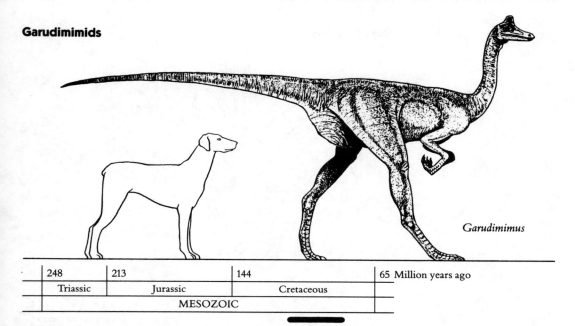

Garudimimus

248	213	144	65 Million years ago
Triassic	Jurassic	Cretaceous	
MESOZOIC			

Garudimimids The family Garudimimidae ("Garuda mimics")
INFRAORDER Ornithomimosauria SUBORDER Theropoda ORDER
Saurischia
DESCRIPTION Ostrich-like dinosaurs closely related to
ornithomimids. Garudimimids resembled large, long-legged
flightless birds, though with arms not wings, a long bony tail, and
scaly skin. They differed from and were more primitive than
ornithomimids. Thus *Garudimimus* had a brow hornlet and its
toothless beak ended in a rounded tip, while *Harpymimus*'s lower
beak tip had 10 or more tiny teeth – the only teeth known from an
ostrich dinosaur. Both had "old-fashioned" bones in the feet, and
Garudimimus preserved an inner toe, which ornithomimids had
lost. They probably ate plants, though *Harpymimus* also perhaps ate
insects and small backboned animals. LENGTH about 11ft 6in
(3.5m) TIME Mid to Late Cretaceous PLACE Mongolia.

Genera
Garudimimus
Harpymimus

Where they lived
Major areas of fossil finds

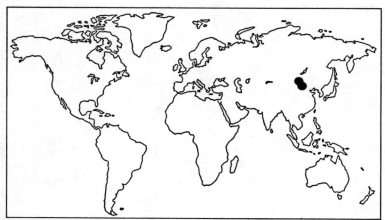

Deinocheirids

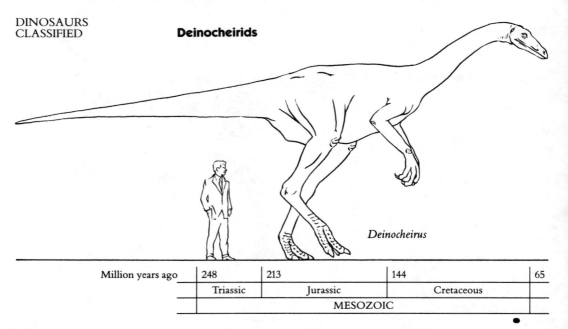

Deinocheirus

Million years ago	248	213		144		65
	Triassic	Jurassic		Cretaceous		
			MESOZOIC			

Genera
Deinocheirus

Deinocheirids The family Deinocheiridae ("terrible hands")
INFRAORDER Ornithomimosauria SUBORDER Theropoda ORDER
Saurischia

DESCRIPTION Dinosaurs known only from an enigmatic pair of
enormous arms and three-fingered hands tipped with long curved
claws. Each arm with its hand is longer than the tallest normal
man. Bone for bone, the arms resemble those of ornithomimids,
but the claws are stronger and more noticeably curved. Their
owner could have been a giant long-armed ostrich dinosaur as
heavy as one or even two elephants. Some experts have suggested
deinocheirids were big-game hunters capable of ripping open a
sauropod's belly with their claws. Others think the claws too blunt
for that. Either way, deinocheirids had longer arms than any known
creatures except the equally mysterious therizinosaurids. LENGTH
uncertain TIME Late Cretaceous PLACE Mongolia.

Where they lived
Major areas of fossil finds

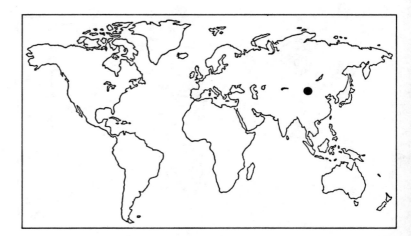

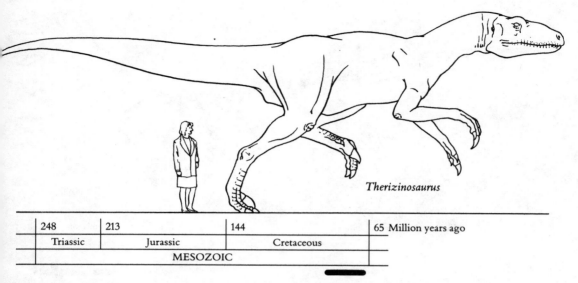

Therizinosaurus

248	213		144		65 Million years ago
Triassic	Jurassic		Cretaceous		
MESOZOIC					

Therizinosaurids The family Therizinosauridae ("scythe lizards") · INFRAORDER Deinonychosauria? SUBORDER Theropoda? ORDER Saurischia?
DESCRIPTION Very large two-legged predatory dinosaurs with powerfully muscled arms, each longer than a man. Each hand evidently had three fingers tipped with great claws curved like sickle blades. One bony claw core measured 28in (70cm) around the outer curve, and its long-lost horny sheath would have been still larger. Robust forelimbs, partial hindlimbs, and a tooth suggest therizinosaurids were more powerfully built than the slender-armed deinocheirids. They could have used their claws for anything from attacking hadrosaurs and armored dinosaurs to ripping open ants' nests. One scientist suspects that these strange dinosaurs were not theropods but segnosaurs. LENGTH 35ft (10.7m) TIME Late Cretaceous PLACE Asia.

Genera
Therizinosaurus

Where they lived
Major areas of fossil finds

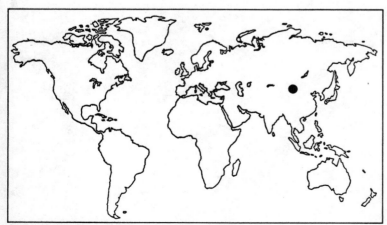

© DIAGRAM

Dromaeosaurids

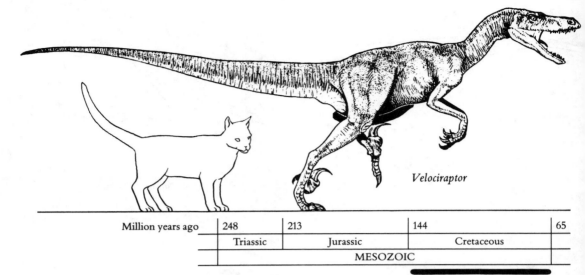

Velociraptor

Million years ago	248	213		144		65
	Triassic	Jurassic		Cretaceous		
	MESOZOIC					

**Genera
(some doubtful)**
Adasaurus
Bradycneme
Deinonychus
Dromaeosaurus
Hulsanpes
Koreanosaurus
Phaedrolosaurus
Saurornitholestes
Velociraptor

Dromaeosaurids The family Dromaeosauridae ("running lizards")
INFRAORDER Deinonychosauria SUBORDER Theropoda ORDER
Saurischia
DESCRIPTION Two-legged flesh-eaters, possibly among the fastest,
fiercest predators of any kind. Dromaeosaurids had a long head
with relatively big brain, keen eyes, and sharp curved fangs. Each
long arm had a hand with three grasping fingers tipped with sharp,
curved claws. Dromaeosaurids ran and leapt on long legs bearing
weight effectively on just the third and fourth toes. The retracted
second toe bore a savage "switchblade" claw flicked forward for
attack. Thin bony rods stiffened the tail to aid balance as
dromaeosaurids ran or stood on one leg to deliver slashing kicks
that cut through victims' hides. A pack could have run down a
large *Tenontosaurus*. LENGTH 6–13ft (1.8–4m) TIME Early to Late
Cretaceous PLACE North America, Europe, and Asia.

Where they lived
Major areas of fossil finds

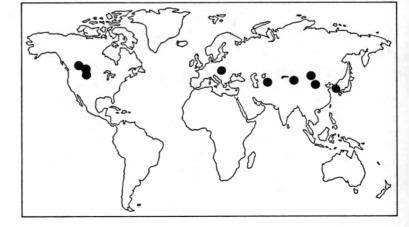

Troodontids

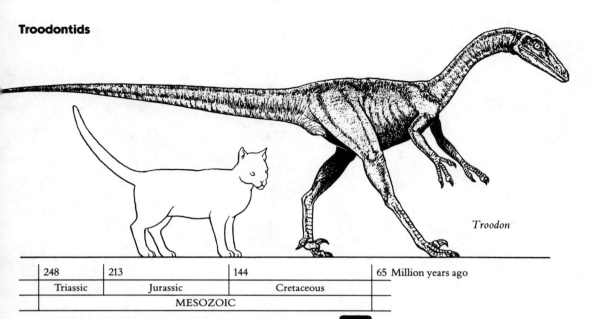

Troodon

248	213		144		65 Million years ago
Triassic	Jurassic		Cretaceous		
MESOZOIC					

Troodontids The family Troodontidae ("wounding teeth")
INFRAORDER Deinonychosauria SUBORDER Theropoda ORDER
Saurischia
DESCRIPTION Two-legged flesh-eaters once called saurornithoidids.
Some of these man-length predators had relatively bigger brains
than any other dinosaurs, and big, keen, wide-set eyes perhaps
capable of seeing prey in twilight. Their light skulls held a capsule
similar to that in ostrich dinosaurs, but their long jaws contained
sharp bladelike teeth. Like dromaeosaurids, troodontids had long
arms and probably tail-stiffeners formed by bony rods growing
back from the tail bones. They also had a retractable second toe,
but this was weaker than the dromaeosaurids' and with a smaller
claw. Troodontids were arguably the equivalent of those slender
big cats, cheetahs. LENGTH 6ft 6in (2m) TIME Late Cretaceous
PLACE North America, Europe, and Asia.

**Genera
(some doubtful)**
Borogovia
Heptasteornis
Paronychodon
Saurornithoides
Troodon

Where they lived
Major areas of fossil finds

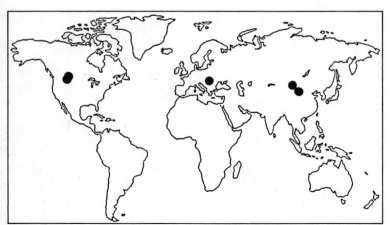

© DIAGRAM

127

Megalosaurids

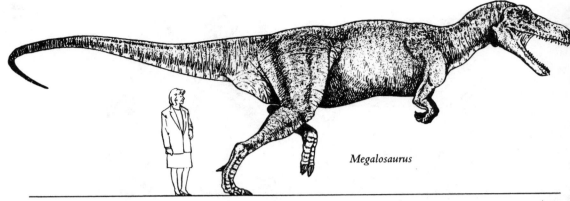

Megalosaurus

Million years ago	248	213		144		65
	Triassic	Jurassic		Cretaceous		
	MESOZOIC					

**Genera
(some doubtful)**

Altispinax
Embasaurus
Erectopus
Eustreptospondylus
Gasosaurus
Iliosuchus
Jiangjunmiaosaurus
"*Kagasaurus*"
Kaijiangosaurus
Kelmayisaurus
Megalosaurus
Metriacanthosaurus
"*Mifunesaurus*"
Orthogoniosaurus
Piveteausaurus
Poekilopleuron

Megalosaurids The family Megalosauridae ("great lizards")
INFRAORDER Carnosauria SUBORDER Theropoda ORDER Saurischia
DESCRIPTION Great two-legged flesh-eaters, some poorly known
and possibly from other families. Megalosaurids had a large high
narrow head with blade-like serrated teeth, a strong, curved flexible
neck, strong short arms with three clawed fingers, huge powerful
legs with three large clawed toes and a tiny backward-directed big
toe, and a large tail flattened from side to side. The hips probably
featured short broad pubic bones not ending in large expanded
"boots." Megalosaurids might have seized prey in their clawed
hands and feet while taking mighty bites, or rushed large victims,
open jawed. LENGTH 23–30ft (7-9m) TIME Early Jurassic to Late
Cretaceous PLACE Europe, Asia, and maybe Africa.

Where they lived
Major areas of fossil finds

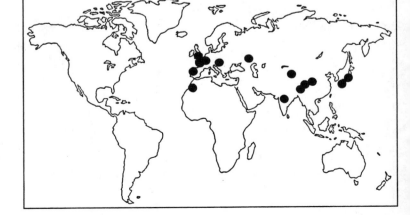

Abelisaurids

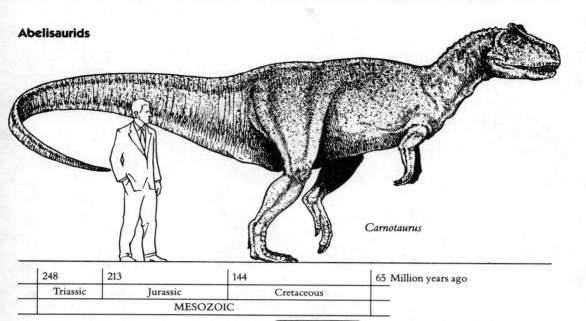

Carnotaurus

248	213		144		65 Million years ago
Triassic	Jurassic			Cretaceous	
MESOZOIC					

Abelisaurids The family Abelisauridae ("Abel's lizards")
INFRAORDER Carnosauria SUBORDER Theropoda ORDER Saurischia
DESCRIPTION Big two-legged flesh-eaters with unusual skulls and
fused ankle bones. *Carnotaurus*, the best-known kind, had a short,
deep head with flat horns jutting out above the eyes like little wings
and a crest across the back of the braincase anchoring jaw and neck
muscles. The lower jaw was slightly built, with slender teeth.
Abelisaurids' deep snouts and partly shut-off eye sockets
recall tyrannosaurs, but more old-fashioned features suggest to
some that these were late-surviving megalosaurs. Abelisaurids
evidently had a slim body, short arms, and long slender legs. Finds
suggest they evolved in the southern supercontinent Gondwana.
LENGTH up to 36ft (11m) TIME Early to Late Cretaceous PLACE
South America, India, **Madagascar**, and maybe Africa and Europe.

**Genera
(some doubtful)**
Abelisaurus
Carnotaurus
Indosaurus
Indosuchus
Majungasaurus
Xenotarsosaurus

Where they lived
Major areas of fossil finds

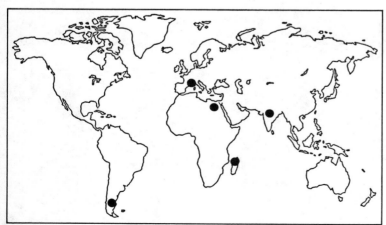

©DIAGRAM

129

Allosaurids

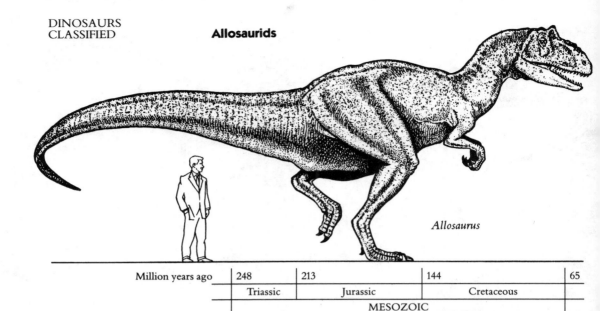

Allosaurus

Million years ago	248	213	144	65
	Triassic	Jurassic	Cretaceous	
		MESOZOIC		

**Genera
(some doubtful)**

Acrocanthosaurus
Allosaurus
Antrodemus
Chilantaisaurus
Compsosuchus
Piatnitzkysaurus
Stokesosaurus
Szechuanosaurus

Allosaurids The family Allosauridae ("different lizards")
INFRAORDER Carnosauria SUBORDER Theropoda ORDER Saurischia
DESCRIPTION Two-legged flesh-eaters as long as a bus. The large,
lightly built head had bony ridges and hornlets, and curved,
serrated fangs rimmed the great jaws. There was an S-shaped
"bulldog" neck and deep, narrow body. Each powerful arm had
three clawed fingers. The great legs effectively bore three-toed feet.
A long stiffly held tail counterbalanced the forepart of the body
when allosaurids walked or ran, head low and back held horizontal.
Called the tigers of their age, allosaurids more likely roamed in
packs that brought down sauropods as hunting dogs combine to
fell a wildebeeste or zebra far larger than themselves. LENGTH 33–
42ft (10-12.8m) TIME mainly Late Jurassic PLACE North and South
America, Asia, Africa, Australia, and maybe Europe.

Where they lived
Major areas of fossil finds

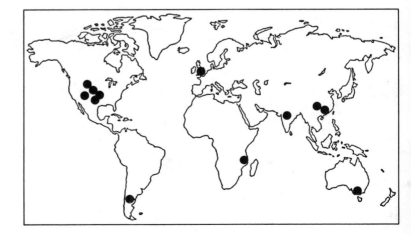

Ceratosaurids

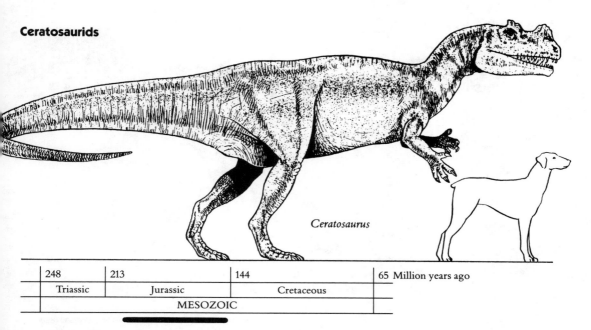

Ceratosaurus

248	213		144		65 Million years ago
Triassic	Jurassic		Cretaceous		
MESOZOIC					

Ceratosaurids The family Ceratosauridae ("horned lizards")
INFRAORDER Carnosauria SUBORDER Theropoda ORDER Saurischia
DESCRIPTION Large two-legged flesh-eaters best known for
Ceratosaurus's evidently bladelike nasal horn and the low horns
above its eyes. Ceratosaurids had a large, deep head with a lightly
built skull, and huge curved bladelike teeth. The neck was fairly
straight, the chest narrow, and small bony plates ran down a low
ridge on the middle of the back. There were strong arms, small,
four-fingered hands, powerful legs with three-toed feet, and a deep
broad tail. Four-fingered hands are among primitive features also
found in coelophysids, but fused hip and foot bones figure in birds,
while the thigh and ankle bones foreshadow later trends in
theropod design. LENGTH 11ft 6in–20ft (3.5–6m) TIME Early to Late
Jurassic PLACE North America, Europe, Asia, and Africa.

Genera
Ceratosaurus
Sarcosaurus?
Yangchuanosaurus

Where they lived
Major areas of fossil finds

Tyrannosaurids

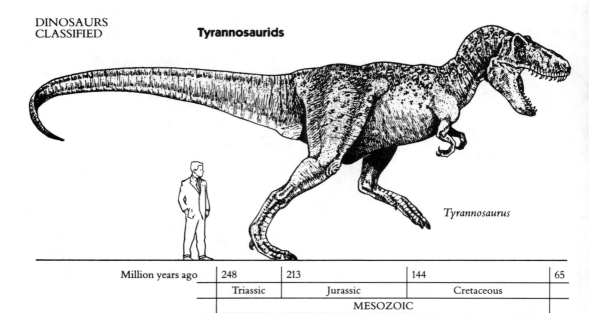

Tyrannosaurus

Million years ago	248	213	144	65
	Triassic	Jurassic	Cretaceous	
		MESOZOIC		

Genera (some doubtful)

Albertosaurus
Alectrosaurus
Alioramus
Chingkankousaurus
Daspletosaurus
Gorgosaurus
Nanotyrannus
Prodeinodon
Tarbosaurus
Tyrannosaurus

Tyrannosaurids The family Tyrannosauridae ("tyrant lizards") INFRAORDER Carnosauria SUBORDER Theropoda ORDER Saurischia DESCRIPTION Large bipedal flesh-eaters including the most massive theropods of all. Tyrannosaurids had a huge head, with semi-forward-facing eyes in some, and long, curved, saw-edged fangs in jaws big enough to swallow animals as big as humans. There was a thick, short, muscular neck and short, deep, broad-chested and narrow-hipped body. The tail was fairly short and slim. Each great muscular leg bore three forward-pointing toes with short, rounded claws, but arms were tiny with just two fingers on each "hand." Tyrannosaurids probably ran fast, chasing horned and duck-billed dinosaurs and lunging with their heads to take deep "scoop bites" from their victims' bodies. LENGTH 16–39ft (5–39m) TIME Late Cretaceous PLACE North America and Asia.

Where they lived
Major areas of fossil finds

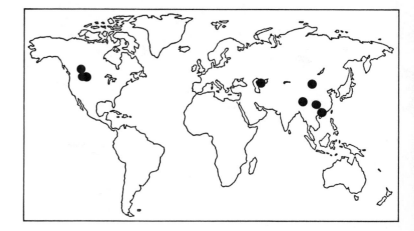

Dryptosaurids

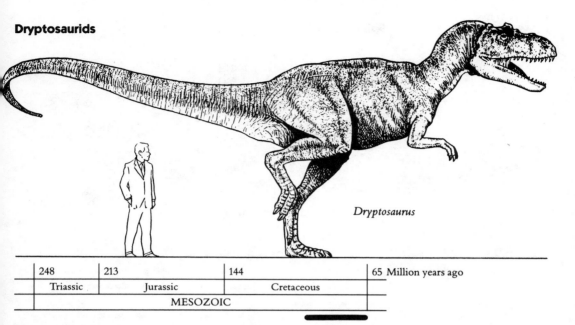

Dryptosaurus

248	213		144		65 Million years ago
Triassic	Jurassic		Cretaceous		
MESOZOIC					

Dryptosaurids The family Dryptosauridae ("wounding lizards")
INFRAORDER Carnosauria SUBORDER Theropoda ORDER Saurischia
DESCRIPTION Big bipedal lightly built flesh-eaters once thought to
be megalosaurids or tyrannosaurids but seemingly different from
both. *Dryptosaurus*, the only dryptosaurid known with certainty,
had curved teeth and claws resembling *Megalosaurus*'s, yet its thigh
bone was a bit like *Iguanodon*'s. There were strong arms with very
large claws, and big muscular legs with an "advanced" ankle unlike
that of any other theropod. *Dryptosaurus*'s discoverer believed the
monster leapt upon its enemies and named it *Laelaps* from a
mythological Greek dog turned to stone while leaping.
Dryptosaurids probably attacked and killed the large duck-billed
dinosaurs. LENGTH more than 20ft (6m) TIME Late Cretaceous
PLACE North America (and maybe Africa and even Asia).

Genera
Diplotomodon?
Dryptosaurus

Where they lived
Major areas of fossil finds

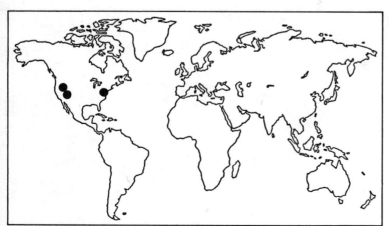

© DIAGRAM

Spinosaurids

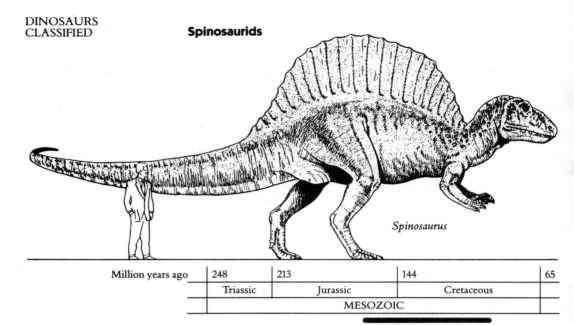

Spinosaurus

Million years ago	248	213		144		65
	Triassic	Jurassic		Cretaceous		
	MESOZOIC					

Genera
Siamosaurus
Spinosaurus

Spinosaurids The family Spinosauridae ("thorn lizards")
INFRAORDER Carnosauria SUBORDER Theropoda ORDER Saurischia
DESCRIPTION Immense two-legged predators known from
Spinosaurus, perhaps the longest but not heaviest of all theropods.
Spinosaurids had a crocodile-like lower jaw and **non-serrated,
straight, rounded, crocodile-type teeth.** Seemingly the neck was
fairly straight. Tall spines on the vertebrae bore the tallest skin sail
known from any theropod – used perhaps in threat display or as a
radiator controlling body temperature. The limbs are little known.
Although weighing maybe 4.4 tons (4 metric tons), *Spinosaurus*
was lightly built. It might have hunted large and small game, even
fish. Other tall–spined "spinosaurids" were probably allosaurids or
megalosaurids. LENGTH 50ft (15m) TIME Late Jurassic through Late
Cretaceous PLACE Africa and Asia.

Where they lived
Major areas of fossil finds

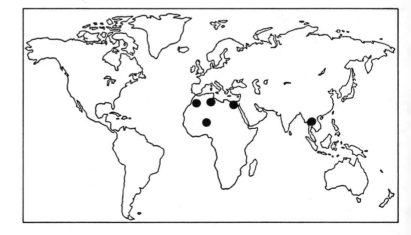

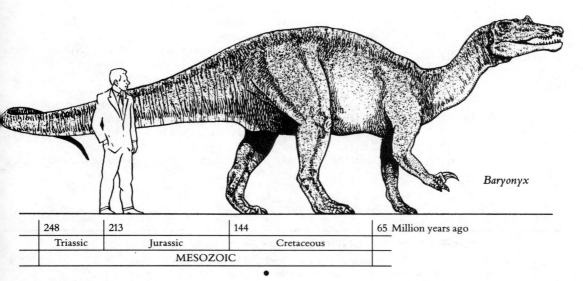

Baryonyx

248	213		144		65 Million years ago
Triassic	Jurassic		Cretaceous		
MESOZOIC					

Baryonychids The family Baryonychidae ("heavy claws")
INFRAORDER Carnosauria SUBORDER Theropoda ORDER Saurischia
DESCRIPTION Large bipedal or bipedal/quadrupedal predators
known from *Baryonyx*. Its long, low crocodile-like head had slim
"fish–eater's" jaws and twice as many (crocodile-like) teeth as most
theropods. The neck was long and fairly straight, and the long
arms evidently bore three-fingered hands, with a great claw on the
thumb (the largest finger). Baryonychids might have fished like
brown bears, hooking big fish with their claws; or they might have
seized fish in their jaws. They almost certainly ate fish, for partly
digested fish scales lay inside a *Baryonyx* rib cage. Although jaws
and teeth resembled those of *Spinosaurus*, teeth, snout, and nostrils
(placed far back) recall those of *Dilophosaurus*. LENGTH 30ft (9m)
TIME Early Cretaceous PLACE Europe and maybe Africa.

Genera
Baryonyx

Where they lived
Major areas of fossil finds

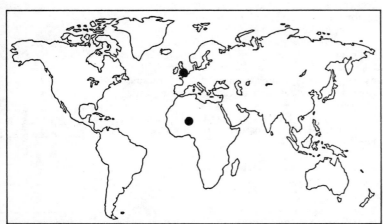

Saurischians 2: sauropodomorphs and segnosaurs

The saurischian suborder **Sauropodomorpha** ("lizard-feet forms") included two infraorders: the prosauropods and their immense presumed descendants sauropods – the largest animals that ever walked on land. Sauropodomorphs tended to have a small head, long neck, bulky body, pillar-like limbs, and long tail. Their teeth were shaped for cropping leaves not chewing them. Plant food was probably ground up by swallowed gizzard stones and chemically broken down by bacteria living in the gut. Dinosaur counterparts of today's gerenuk antelopes and giraffes, sauropodomorphs reared or craned their necks to browse on shrubs and trees.

Small early bipedal prosauropods probably gave rise to bulky

SAUROPODOMORPH INFRAORDERS AND SEGNOSAURS

Numbered items depict both sauropodomorph infraorders named in this book, and the Segnosauria. Small letters indicate families. (Some groupings are doubtful.)

1 Prosauropoda ("before sauropods") Small to large bipedal, bipedal/quadrupedal, and quadrupedal plant-eating dinosaurs. Prosauropods mainly had a small head, fairly long neck, bulky body, long tail, massive hind limbs with five-toed feet and shorter, slimmer fore limbs with five-fingered hands and enormous curved thumb claws used perhaps for hooking down leafy branches. Most had spoon-shaped teeth with ridged edges. Prosauropods ranged in size from little longer than a man to longer than a tennis court is wide. The smaller, lighter forms reared to feed and maybe run; others ambled on all fours, weighed down by the digestive system in their bulky body. All date from Triassic or Early Jurassic times. Best-known families: pages 138–140
a Anchisauridae **b** Plateosauridae **c** Blikanasauridae **d** Melanorosauridae **e** Yunnanosauridae

2 Sauropoda ("lizard feet") Very large to immense quadrupedal plant-eaters, some as long as several buses and as heavy as several elephants. Many had a brain no bigger than a cat's and peg- or spoon-shaped teeth in a head no bigger than a horse's at one end of a long, boom-like neck with light, interlocking bones. The backbone was often light and deeply hollowed out; the tail long and balancing the neck. Propping up the great deep body were four elephantine limbs, anchored to a massive hip girdle and to broad flat shoulder blades. Each "hand" and foot had five digits set in a fleshy pad. In many, large claws sprouted from the thumbs and first three toes. Sauropods lived from Early Jurassic to Late Cretaceous times. Main families: pages 141–146
f Vulcanodontidae **g** Cetiosauridae **h** Barapasauridae **i** Brachiosauridae **j** Chubutisauridae **k** Camarasauridae **l** Titanosauridae **m** Diplodocidae **n** Euhelopodidae **o** Dicraeosauridae

3 Segnosauria ("slow lizards") Best-known family: page 147.
p Segnosauridae **q** Enigmosauridae

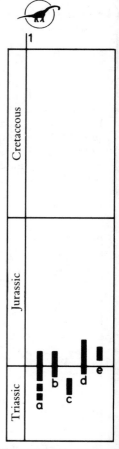

136

quadrupedal prosauropods during the Triassic Period. By the end
of the Jurassic Period the tendency toward increasing size reached
its climax in colossal sauropods. Their seeming subsequent decline
– especially in northern continents – probably owed much to
competition from the ornithischians and the spread of plants that
sauropods proved ill-equipped to eat. Page numbers here refer to
entries on the best-known sauropodomorph families. Others are
described in Chapter 2.

The suborder **Segnosauria** ("slow lizards") held Late Cretaceous
dinosaurs combining saurischian and ornithischian features. They
included the segnosaurids described on page 147. See also
Chapter 2 on segnosaurs, enigmosaurids, and *Nanshiungosaurus*.

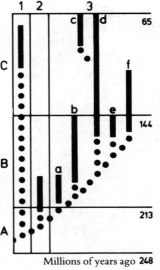

Millions of years ago **248**

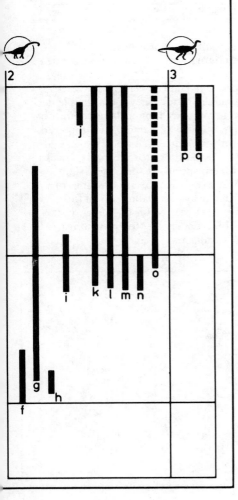

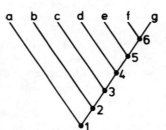

Prosauropod cladogram
This is based on a scheme
proposed by Peter Galton.
Nodes 2-6 mark anatomical
innovations in
prosauropods.
1 Ancestral
sauropodomorph
2 Bipedal prosauropods
3 Bipedal-quadrupedal
4 Broad-footed
5 Jaw hinged below lower
tooth row
6 Quadrupedal
a Sauropods
b *Thecodontosaurus*
c *Anchisaurus*
d *Yunnanosaurus*
e *Plateosaurus*
f *Melanorosaurus*
g *Blikanasaurus*

**Sauropodomorph
cladogram**
Based on an evolutionary
tree compiled by Michael
Benton, this cladogram
shows relationships
between one genus (-*us*) and
selected families (-idae) of
sauropodomorphs, plus the
strange segnosaurs.
1 Segnosauria
2 "Prosauropods"
3 Sauropodomorpha
a *Barapasaurus*
b Cetiosauridae
c Titanosauridae
d Diplodocidae
e Camarasauridae
f Brachiosauridae
A Triassic Period
B Jurassic Period
C Cretaceous Period

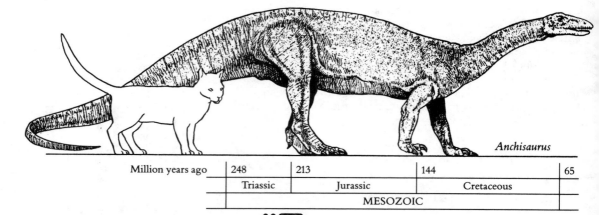

Anchisaurus

Million years ago	248	213		144		65
	Triassic	Jurassic		Cretaceous		
			MESOZOIC			

**Genera
(some doubtful)**
Agrosaurus
Anchisaurus
Nyasasaurus
Sellosaurus
Tawasaurus

Anchisaurids The family Anchisauridae ("near lizards")
INFRAORDER Prosauropoda SUBORDER Sauropodomorpha ORDER
Saurischia
DESCRIPTION Early bipedal/quadrupedal plant-eating dinosaurs
lighter than a man. They had a small head, fairly long flexible neck,
long back, and long tail. Hind limbs were longer than front limbs,
and, unlike plateosaurids, anchisaurids had narrow five-fingered
hands and five-toed feet. Thumbs bore great curved claws, used
perhaps as weapons of defense. As in other prosauropods, cheeks
held leaves bitten off by the ridged, spoon-shaped teeth. The
swallowed leaves were probably ground up by small stones in a
gizzard. Anchisaurids were front-heavy so walked on all fours, but
reared to reach high leafy twigs. LENGTH 7-10ft (2.1-3m) TIME
perhaps Mid Triassic to Early Jurassic PLACE North America,
Europe, Africa, and maybe Australia and Asia.

Where they lived
Major areas of fossil finds

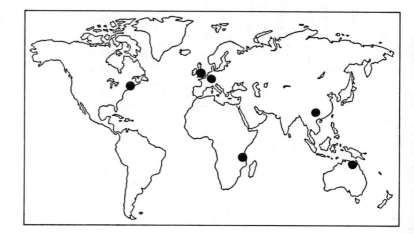

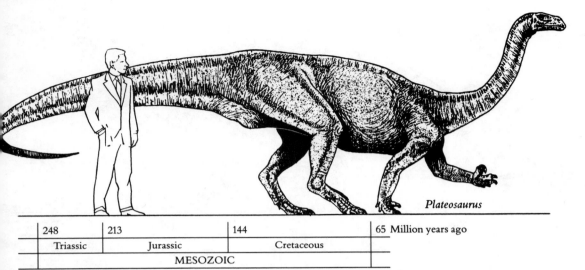

Plateosaurus

248	213		144		65 Million years ago
Triassic	Jurassic		Cretaceous		
MESOZOIC					

Plateosaurids The family Plateosauridae ("flat lizards")
INFRAORDER Prosauropoda SUBORDER Sauropodomorpha ORDER
Saurischia
DESCRIPTION Small to quite large bipedal/quadrupedal plant-eating
dinosaurs with relatively small head, long neck, long and fairly
bulky body, and long tail. Their high, ridged, spoon-shaped teeth
were shaped for shredding not grinding vegetation. Plateosaurids
were built much like anchisaurids, yet tended to be larger and had
broader feet and hands, a bigger, stronger skull, and, in most, a jaw
hinge set below the level of the teeth, which gave a more effective
bite. Several possibly belong in other families, for instance
Massospondylus, with a more old-fashioned jaw joint and a lower
jaw that might have ended in a horny beak. LENGTH 5–26ft
(1.5–8m) TIME Late Triassic to Early Jurassic PLACE North and
South America, Europe, Africa, and Asia.

**Genera
(some doubtful)**
Ammosaurus
Coloradisaurus
Euskelosaurus
Lufengosaurus
Massospondylus
Mussaurus
Plateosaurus

Where they lived
Major areas of fossil finds

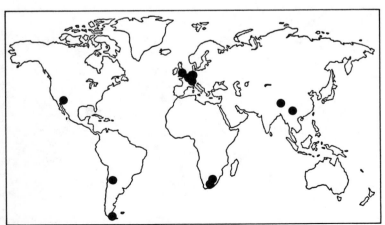

Melanorosaurids

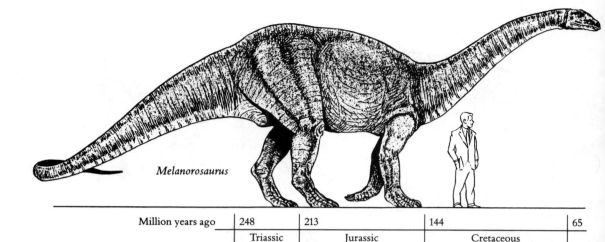

Melanorosaurus

Million years ago	248	213		144		65
	Triassic	Jurassic		Cretaceous		
			MESOZOIC			

Genera (some doubtful)

Camelotia
Chinshakiangosaurus
Likhoelesaurus
Melanorosaurus
Riojasaurus
Thotobolosaurus

Melanorosaurids The family Melanorosauridae ("black mountain lizards") INFRAORDER Prosauropoda SUBORDER Sauropodomorpha ORDER Saurischia
DESCRIPTION Large early quadrupedal plant–eating dinosaurs. Like most prosauropods they had a fairly long neck and tail, and a small head with serrated, spoon–shaped teeth. (Sharp, curved teeth found near their bones had come from predators.) But they were bigger and more ponderous than other prosauropods, with long, bulky bodies, more massive limbs and distinctively straight thigh bones as seen from front to back. Unlike anchisaurids and plateosaurids, melanorosaurids could not have reared to hurry on their hind limbs. Scientists once thought melanorosaurids had given rise to sauropods, but a difference in ankle-bone design makes this unlikely. LENGTH 19-40ft (6-12m) TIME Late Triassic to Early Jurassic PLACE Europe, South America, Asia, and Africa.

Where they lived
Major areas of fossil finds

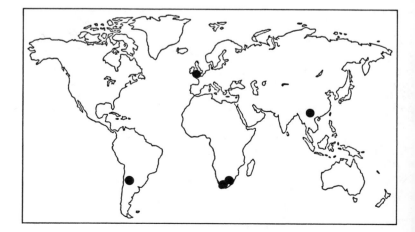

Cetiosaurids

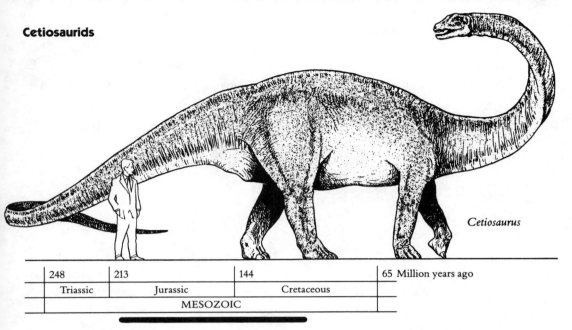

Cetiosaurus

248	213		144	65 Million years ago
Triassic	Jurassic		Cretaceous	
		MESOZOIC		

Cetiosaurids The family Cetiosauridae ("whale lizards") INFRAORDER Sauropoda SUBORDER Sauropodomorpha ORDER Saurischia

DESCRIPTION Very large four-legged plant-eaters with short, blunt head, long neck, long back, bulky body, pillar-like limbs with front limbs shorter than hind limbs, and fairly short tail (*Shunosaurus*'s had a bony club and four short spikes). Teeth shaped like thick flattish spoons cropped vegetation. Mainly early, primitive sauropods perhaps ancestral to later groups, cetiosaurids had spinal bones with almost solid centers, not forked at the top or hollowed out for lightness. One expert has argued that *Lapparentosaurus* and *Volkheimeria* had a more primitive type of backbone than cetiosaurids such as *Cetiosaurus* and *Barapasaurus*. LENGTH 30–60ft (9–18m) TIME Early Jurassic to Mid Cretaceous PLACE The Americas, Europe, Africa, Asia and Australia.

Genera (some doubtful)
Amygdalodon
Austrosaurus
Barapasaurus
Bellusaurus
Cetiosaurus
Dachongosaurus
Datousaurus
Dystrophaeus
Haplocanthosaurus
Kunmingosaurus
Lapparentosaurus
Ohmdenosaurus
Oshanosaurus
Patagosaurus
Protognathus
Rhoetosaurus
Shunosaurus
Volkheimeria
Zizhongosaurus

Where they lived
Major areas of fossil finds

© DIAGRAM

Brachiosaurids

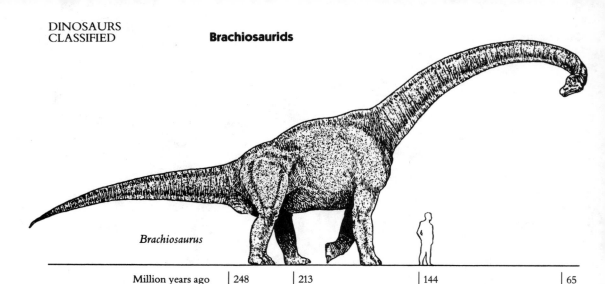

Brachiosaurus

Million years ago	248	213		144		65
	Triassic	Jurassic		Cretaceous		
	MESOZOIC					

**Genera
(some doubtful)**
Astrodon
Bothriospondylus
Brachiosaurus
Damalasaurus
Dinodocus
Dystylosaurus
Giraffatitan (subgenus)
"Hughenden sauropod"
Lancangjianosaurus
Pelorosaurus
Pleurocoelus
Rebbachisaurus
Ultrasaurus
"Ultrasaurus"

Where they lived
Major areas of fossil finds

Brachiosaurids The family Brachiosauridae ("arm lizards")
INFRAORDER Sauropoda SUBORDER Sauropodomorpha ORDER
Saurischia
DESCRIPTION Immense four-legged plant-eaters including probably
the largest-ever land animals. Like monstrous giraffes, they had a
very long neck, deep body sloping down from shoulders to tail,
elephantine limbs (arms as long as or longer than legs), and a
relatively short, thickset tail. Hollows lightened the backbone, and
bony struts the skull. Large nostrils opened high on the head above
eye-level, hinting at a keen sense of smell, or at a skin lining that
shed heat to cool the brain, or, just maybe, at the base of a trunk.
Wear on the big chisel-like teeth suggests these cropped tough
leaves. Brachiosaurids could have browsed on the treetops.
LENGTH 33–82ft (10–25m) TIME Mid–Late Jurassic to Early
Cretaceous PLACE North America, Europe, Africa, Asia, and
perhaps Australia.

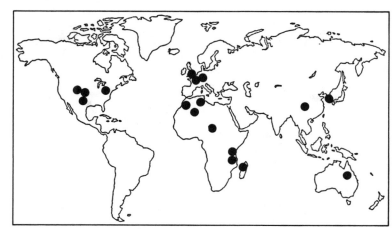

142

Camarasaurids

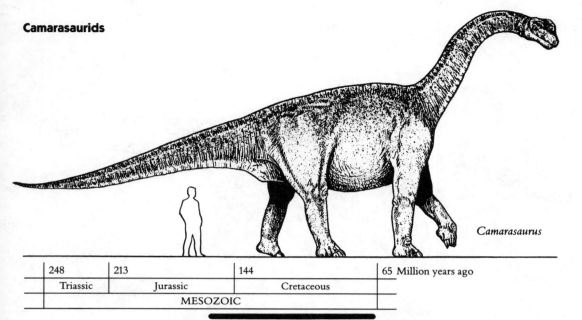

Camarasaurus

248	213		144	65 Million years ago
Triassic	Jurassic		Cretaceous	
	MESOZOIC			

Camarasaurids The family Camarasauridae ("chambered lizards")
INFRAORDER Sauropoda SUBORDER Sauropodomorpha ORDER
Saurischia
DESCRIPTION Very large four-legged plant-eaters named from the
hollow chambers in their spinal bones. The body was deep but
relatively short. Limbs were pillarlike with hind limbs slightly
longer than front limbs and the back was level, or, in some, highest
at the shoulders. Each foot's short splayed digits helped to bear
enormous weight. As in other sauropods, the inner toe bore a long
pointed claw. The head tended to be deep and short but relatively
large, with strong jaws rimmed by chisel-like teeth. Large nostrils
opened ahead of and above the eyes. Camarasaurids' tails and necks
were relatively shorter than those of many sauropods. LENGTH
40–60ft (12–18m) TIME Late Jurassic to Late Cretaceous PLACE
North America, Europe, Africa and Asia.

**Genera
(some doubtful)**
Algoasaurus
Aragosaurus
Asiatosaurus
Camarasaurus
Cathetosaurus
Chiayuesaurus
Opisthocoelicaudia
Parrosaurus

Where they lived
Major areas of fossil finds

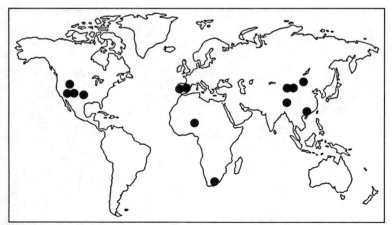

143

Euhelopodids

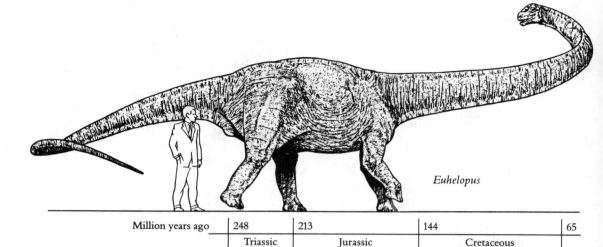

Euhelopus

Million years ago	248	213		144		65
	Triassic	Jurassic		Cretaceous		
			MESOZOIC			

Genera
Euhelopus
Mamenchisaurus
"Moshisaurus"
Omeisaurus
Tienshanosaurus

Euhelopodids The family Euhelopodidae ("good marsh feet")
INFRAORDER Sauropoda SUBORDER Sauropodomorpha ORDER
Saurischia
DESCRIPTION Very large four-legged plant-eaters only known from
China, and sometimes grouped with the camarasaurids. Like those,
euhelopodids had chisel-shaped (or spoon-shaped) teeth and
apparently a tall blunt snout, though a head of *Omeisaurus* (or
perhaps *Zigongosaurus*) has been confusingly described as long and
low. Then, too, "split" projections and "skids" seen on certain
vertebrae resemble features found in diplodocids, yet the relative
lengths of *Euhelopus*'s upper limb bones recall the brachiosaurids.
At least some euhelopodids had amazingly long necks with 17 and
even 19 vertebrae. At up to maybe 49ft (15m), *Mamenchisaurus*'s
neck was probably the longest of any creature ever. LENGTH
33–?89ft (10–?27m) TIME Late Jurassic PLACE Asia.

Where they lived
Major areas of fossil finds

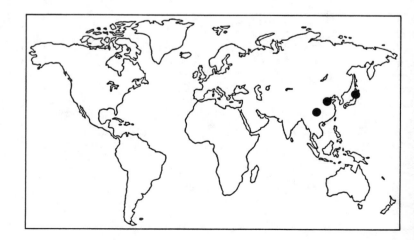

Titanosaurids

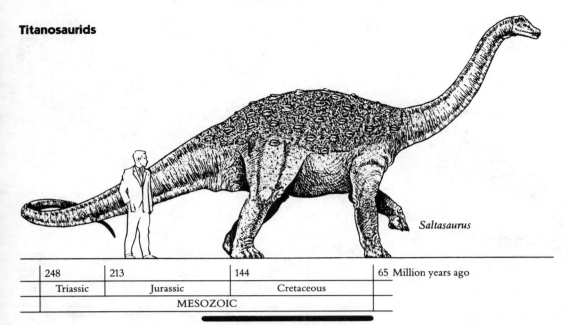

Saltasaurus

248	213		144		65	Million years ago
Triassic	Jurassic		Cretaceous			
MESOZOIC						

Titanosaurids The family Titanosauridae ("titanic lizards")
INFRAORDER Sauropoda SUBORDER Sauropodomorpha ORDER
Saurischia
DESCRIPTION Small to very large sauropods. They were four-legged
plant–eaters, and are known mostly from rather scrappy remains.
Titanosaurids seemingly had a broad head, steep face, and peg-
shaped teeth. There was a fairly long neck and long slim tail,
perhaps used to lash enemies. Pillar-like hind limbs and front limbs
three-quarters their length supported the bulky body.
Titanosaurids lacked the deeply hollowed-out spinal bones of most
other late sauropods, but at least some were novel, with fist-sized
bony plates (perhaps supporting horny spikes) and small bony
studs set in their thick skin to guard back and flanks. LENGTH
30–70ft (9–21m) TIME Late Jurassic to Late Cretaceous PLACE
North and South America, Europe, Africa, and Asia.

**Genera
(some doubtful)**
Aegyptosaurus
Aepisaurus
Alamosaurus
Antarctosaurus
Argyrosaurus
Campylodoniscus
Chondrosteosaurus
Hypselosaurus
Lametasaurus
Laplatasaurus
Loricosaurus
Macrurosaurus
Microcoelus
Saltasaurus
Titanosaurus

Where they lived
Major areas of fossil finds

Diplodocids

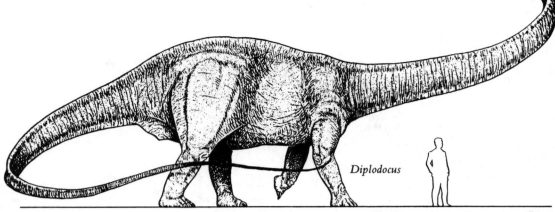

Diplodocus

Million years ago	248	213		144		65
	Triassic	Jurassic		Cretaceous		
			MESOZOIC			

**Genera
(some doubtful)**
Amphicoelias
Apatosaurus
Atlantosaurus
Barosaurus
Cetiosauriscus
Diplodocus
"Hisanohamasaurus"
Megacervixosaurus
Microdontosaurus
Mongolosaurus
Nemegtosaurus
Quaesitosaurus
"Seismosaurus"
Supersaurus
Tornieria

Where they lived
Major areas of fossil finds

Diplodocids The family Diplodocidae ("double beams")
INFRAORDER Sauropoda SUBORDER Sauropodomorpha ORDER
Saurischia
DESCRIPTION Very large four-legged plant-eaters including some of
the longest of all dinosaurs. They were relatively lightly built
thanks largely to deep, weight-reducing hollows in the backbone.
The head was small, low, and sloping, with eyes far back, nostrils
set above the eyes, a broad snout, and peg-like teeth only at the
front of the jaws. Diplodocids also had a long, slim neck and very
long, slim, tapered tail. They stood highest at the hips, bearing
weight upon their elephantine limbs with short broad "hands" and
feet. Their name comes from the middle tail bones' fore-and-aft
skids, maybe shielding blood vessels when the tail dragged on the
ground. LENGTH 54–90ft (16.6–27m) TIME Late Jurassic to Late
Cretaceous PLACE North America, Europe, Africa, and Asia.

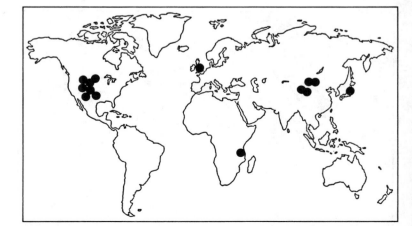

Segnosaurids

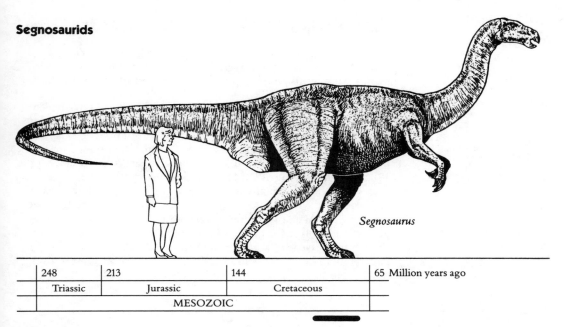

Segnosaurus

248	213		144		65 Million years ago
Triassic	Jurassic		Cretaceous		
MESOZOIC					

Segnosaurids The family Segnosauridae ("slow lizards")
SUBORDER Segnosauria ORDER Saurischia?
DESCRIPTION Strange dinosaurs with features found in saurischian
and ornithischian dinosaurs, and perhaps more primitive than both.
They had lightly built bodies with a narrow toothless beak, small
sharp cheek teeth, cheeks, and short arms each with three fingers
tipped by sharp claws. The long legs had feet with four toes armed
with long claws. All toes faced forward, and maybe they were
webbed – prints left by webbed four-toed feet have been
discovered. In the hips, the pubis lay back parallel to the ischium as
in ornithischian dinosaurs, not jutting forward as in most
saurischians. Certain scientists suggest that segnosaurids swam and
hunted fish, yet slippery creatures could have wriggled from their
captors' toothless beaks. LENGTH 16–30ft (5–9m) TIME Late
Cretaceous PLACE Asia and North America (Alberta).

Genera
Erlikosaurus
Segnosaurus

Where they lived
Major areas of fossil finds

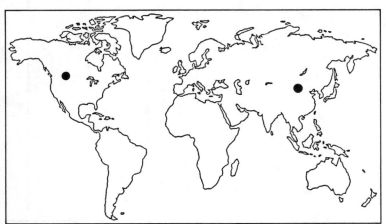

©DIAGRAM

Ornithischians 1: ornithopods

The ornithischian suborder **Ornithopoda** ("bird feet") comprised
bipedal and bipedal/quadrupedal families of small to very large
plant-eating dinosaurs. Despite their name, ornithopods did not
have particularly birdlike feet. Superficially many resembled the
predatory theropods. But they had cheeks, teeth with leaf-shaped
crowns, jaws ending in a horny beak, hip bones aligned like those
of birds, and bony tendons stiffening the tail. All this they shared
with most other ornithischians. Walking and running on their long
hind limbs once seemed to set ornithopods apart from these. Yet in
1986 US paleontologist Paul Sereno defined ornithopods more
precisely as ornithischians with no hole in the outside of the lower
jaw, and (in the hips) a pubic bone jutting farther forward than the
ilium. Once called ornithopods, fabrosaurids now appear to have
been too primitive for that, and even the heterodontosaurids were
arguably just close relatives of the true ornithopods. Here, though,
pages 150–157 include them in eight families of ornithopods: the
heterodontosaurids, hypsilophodontids, dryosaurids,

ORNITHOPOD FAMILIES

In this diagram, small
letters indicate the
Fabrosauridae and eight
families of ornithopods.

a Fabrosauridae
b Heterodontosauridae
c Hypsilophodontidae
d Dryosauridae
e Thescelosauridae
f Camptosauridae
g Iguanodontidae
h Hadrosauridae
i Lambeosauridae

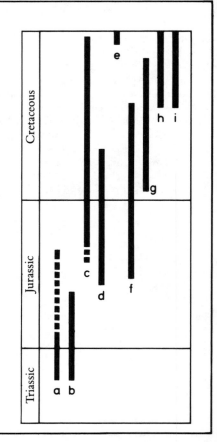

thescelosaurids, camptosaurids, iguanodontids, hadrosaurids, and lambeosaurids.

All these had longer legs than arms. Small early ornithopods were agile sprinters. Large later forms probably walked on all fours but reared to browse high up or to hurry away from an enemy. Walking or running, ornithopods held their long stiff tails off the ground to balance the forepart of the body. As evolution produced bigger ornithopods the head grew relatively large but lost front teeth. Behind the cropping beak evolved batteries of self-sharpening cheek teeth superbly made for pulping leaves stored conveniently in cheek pouches. In larger ornithopods, claws evolved into broad hoof-like nails, and the fifth toes and fingers shrank or disappeared.

True ornithopods appeared in Mid Jurassic times. Members of this group spread worldwide, and in Late Cretaceous western North America hadrosaurid and lambeosaurid ornithopods were among the most abundant dinosaurs of all.

Ornithopod cladogram
This simplified cladogram shows groupings proposed by Paul Sereno in 1986 for ornithopods and their close kin in the Euornithopoda. (For its relationship to other ornithischians see page 159.) Each numbered node marks anatomical innovations not seen in ornithischians lower down in the diagram. Sereno divided the Ornithopoda into two infraorders, one with a complex of progressively subordinate subgroups from gigafamily to family.

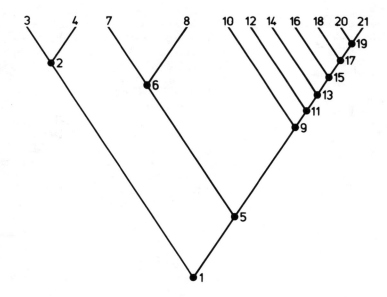

1 Hypoorder
   Euornithopoda
2 Suborder
   Heterodontosauria
3 Genus *Abrictosaurus*
4 Family "Xiphosauridae"
   eg *Heterodontosaurus*
5 Suborder Ornithopoda
6 Infraorder
   Hypsilophodontia
7 Genus *Thescelosaurus*

8 Family
   Hypsilophodontidae
9 Infraorder Iguanodontia
10 Genus *Tenontosaurus*
11 Gigafamily
   Dryomorpha
12 Genus *Dryosaurus*
13 Megafamily
   Ankylopollexia
14 Genus *Camptosaurus*

15 Grandfamily
   Styracosterna
16 Genus *Probactrosaurus*
17 Hyperfamily
   Iguanodontoidea
18 Genus *Iguanodon*
19 Superfamily
   Hadrosauroidea
20 Genus *Ouranosaurus*
21 Family Hadrosauridae

Heterodontosaurids

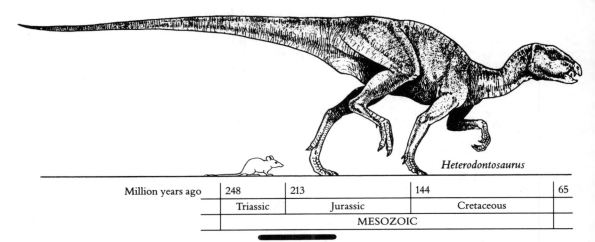

Heterodontosaurus

Million years ago	248	213	144	65
	Triassic	Jurassic	Cretaceous	
		MESOZOIC		

**Genera
(some doubtful)**
Abrictosaurus
Dianchungosaurus
Geranosaurus
Heterodontosaurus
Lanasaurus
Lycorhinus
Pisanosaurus

Heterodontosaurids The family Heterodontosauridae ("different-teeth lizards") SUBORDER Ornithopoda ORDER Ornithischia DESCRIPTION Small, lightly built, bipedal/quadrupedal plant-eaters unusual for three kinds of teeth: cutting incisors in the front upper jaw, ridged to leaflike grinding or shredding cheek teeth, and in between (in males at least), paired stabbing tusks fitting into sockets, much as in some bone-headed dinosaurs. The sturdy arms bore flexible wrists and long, slim, five-fingered hands with claws. There were long lower legs each with three long, forward- facing, clawed toes. Bony rods stiffened the back, hips, and tapered tail. Heterodontosaurids could have walked on all fours and sprinted on their hind limbs to escape danger. LENGTH most about 4ft (1.2m) TIME Late Triassic through Early Jurassic PLACE Argentina(?), southern Africa, and maybe China

Where they lived
Major areas of fossil finds

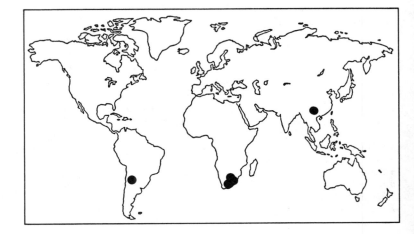

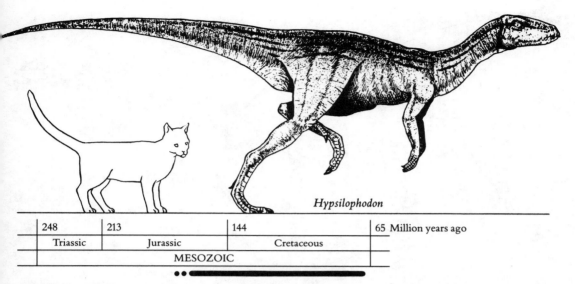

Hypsilophodon

248	213		144		65 Million years ago
Triassic	Jurassic		Cretaceous		
MESOZOIC					

Hypsilophodontids The family Hypsilophodontidae ("high ridge teeth") SUBORDER Ornithopoda ORDER Ornithischia DESCRIPTION Long-lived group of mainly small bipedal plant–eaters. They had a small head with large eyes, a horny cropping beak with upper teeth, self–sharpening cheek teeth replaced by new ones as they wore out, cheek pouches, and strong jaws. These new improved techniques for eating plants doubtless helped hypsilophodontids supersede the fabrosaurids and heterodontosaurids. Hypsilophodontid arms were short, but long shins and feet imply an ability to sprint that earns this family its nickname "dinosaur gazelles." A long stiffened tail served as a balancer. There were five-fingered hands and four-toed feet, all tipped with claws. LENGTH 3-8ft (90cm-2.4m) TIME Mid Jurassic to Late Cretaceous PLACE North America, Europe, **Asia**, Australia, and Antarctica.

Genera (some doubtful)
Atlascopcosaurus
Fulgurotherium
Hypsilophodon
Laosaurus
Leaellynosaura
Orodromeus
Othnielia
Parksosaurus
Phyllodon
Rhabdodon
Tenontosaurus
Yandusaurus
Zephyrosaurus

Where they lived
Major areas of fossil finds

Dryosaurids

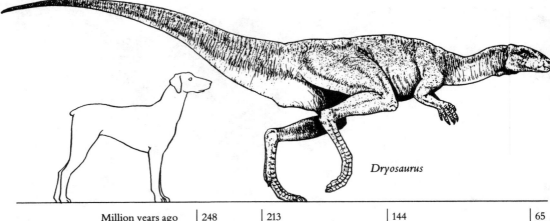

Dryosaurus

Million years ago	248	213		144		65
	Triassic	Jurassic		Cretaceous		
			MESOZOIC			

Genera
Dryosaurus
Kangnasaurus
Valdosaurus

Dryosaurids The family Dryosauridae ("oak lizards")
SUBORDER Ornithopoda ORDER Ornithischia
DESCRIPTION Bipedal and bipedal/quadrupedal plant–eaters with a
cropping beak, self-sharpening cheek teeth, much longer legs than
arms, and a long stiffened tail. They were much like but larger than
the hypsilophodontids. Indeed *Dryosaurus* and *Valdosaurus* were
once thought to have been big hypsilophodontids, though
Kangnasaurus had been lumped with iguanodontids. Unlike
Hypsilophodon, *Dryosaurus* had a toothless front upper jaw,
distinctive hip bones, and three-toed, not four-toed feet.
Tenontosaurus, the biggest, bulkiest hypsilophodontid (or maybe
iguanodontid) was also once grouped with the dryosaurids.
LENGTH 9–21ft (2.7-6.5m) TIME Middle Jurassic to Early
Cretaceous PLACE North America, Europe, and Africa, and maybe
New Zealand.

Where they lived
Major areas of fossil finds

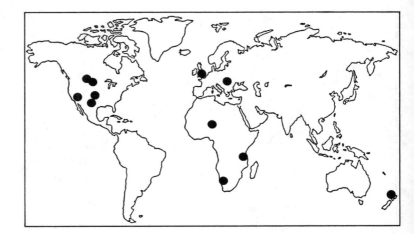

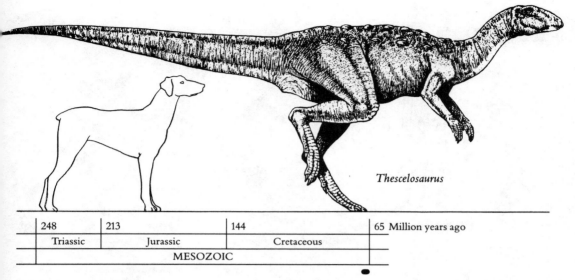

Thescelosaurus

248	213		144		65 Million years ago
Triassic		Jurassic		Cretaceous	
MESOZOIC					

Thescelosaurids The family Thescelosauridae ("wonderful lizards") SUBORDER Ornithopoda ORDER Ornithischia DESCRIPTION Bipedal/quadrupedal plant-eaters known from several skulls and partial skeletons all evidently from a single genus. Thescelosaurids seemingly had a small head, front teeth (enameled on both sides), cheek teeth, a plump body perhaps with rows of bony studs down the back, five-fingered hands, thigh bones longer than the shins (so more like *Iguanodon* than *Hypsilophodon*), four-toed feet with hooflike claws, and a long stiffened tail. Some experts consider *Thescelosaurus* just a bulky hypsilophodontid, others an iguanodontid. Either group might have given rise to the thescelosaurids, which were among the latest dinosaurs of all. LENGTH 11ft (3.4m) TIME latest Late Cretaceous PLACE Canada (Alberta, Saskatchewan) and USA (Montana, Wyoming).

Genera
Thescelosaurus

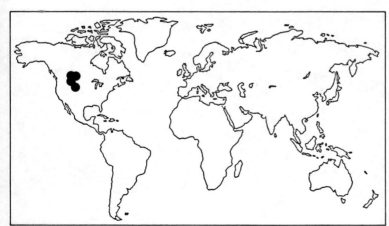

Where they lived
Major areas of fossil finds

©DIAGRAM

Camptosaurids

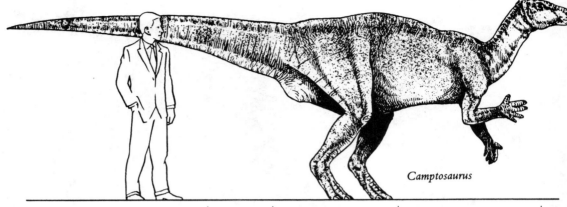

Camptosaurus

Million years ago	248	213	144	65
	Triassic	Jurassic	Cretaceous	
	MESOZOIC			

**Genera
(some doubtful)**
Callovosaurus
Camptosaurus
Muttaburrasaurus

Camptosaurids The family Camptosauridae ("bent lizards")
SUBORDER Ornithopoda ORDER Ornithischia
DESCRIPTION Medium to large bipedal/quadrupedal plant-eaters
built more heavily than their likely ancestors the
hypsilophodontids. Some experts think camptosaurids were really
iguanodontids. The head was long and low with a sharp, horny,
toothless beak and tightly packed ridged cheek teeth.
Camptosaurids had a bulky body, short but sturdy arms, and
five-fingered hands. Hind limbs were long and strong with longer
thighs than shins, and four-toed feet. Toes and fingers bore small
hooflike claws, but some camptosaurids evidently had a spiky
thumb claw. Camptosaurids walked on all fours to browse on low
vegetation, and rose on hind limbs to run, balanced by a long
stiffened tail. LENGTH 4–23ft (1.2–7m) TIME Mid Jurassic to
Mid-Late Cretaceous PLACE North America, Europe, Australia.

Where they lived
Major areas of fossil finds

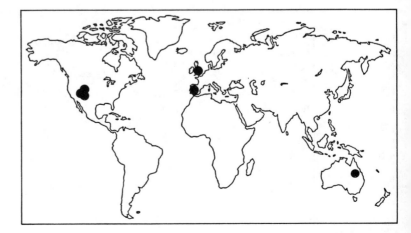

Iguanodontids

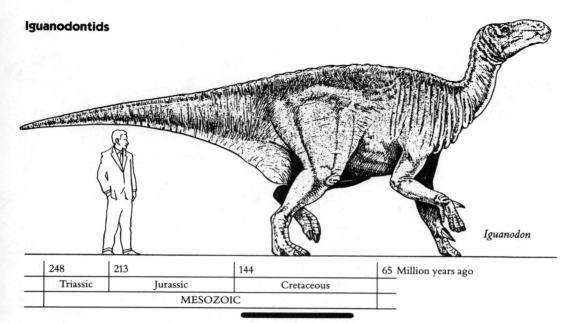

Iguanodon

248	213		144		65 Million years ago
	Triassic	Jurassic		Cretaceous	
			MESOZOIC		

Iguanodontids The family Iguanodontidae ("iguana teeth")
SUBORDER Ornithopoda ORDER Ornithischia
DESCRIPTION Medium to big, heavily built bipedal/quadrupedal
plant-eaters with more teeth and relatively bigger arms and
straighter thigh bones than the otherwise largely similar
camptosaurids. They had a fairly large head, long snout, toothless
beak, tightly packed ridged cheek teeth, and possibly a long
prehensile tongue. Large powerful hindlimbs with broad three-
toed feet supported the bulky body, though iguanodontids often
walked on all fours: their shoulders, arms, and sturdy fingers
tipped with hooflike claws could bear considerable weight. Big
thumb spikes were capable of stabbing rivals or large aggressive
theropods. LENGTH 13ft 6in–29ft 6in (4–9m); weight up to 5 US
tons (4.5 metric tons) TIME Early to Late Cretaceous PLACE North
America, Europe, Africa, and Asia.

**Genera
(some doubtful)**
Anoplosaurus
Craspedodon
Iguanodon
Ouranosaurus
Probactrosaurus
Vectisaurus

Where they lived
Major areas of fossil finds

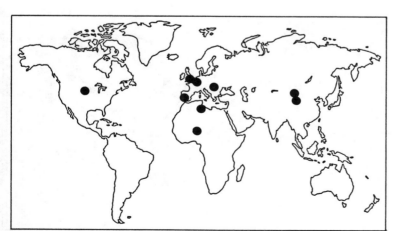

©DIAGRAM

155

Hadrosaurids

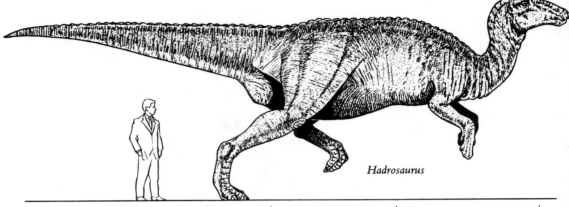

Hadrosaurus

Million years ago	248	213		144		65
	Triassic	Jurassic		Cretaceous		
	MESOZOIC					

**Genera
(some doubtful)**
"Anatotitan"
Aralosaurus
Arstanosaurus
Brachylophosaurus
Cionodon
Claosaurus
Diclonius
Edmontosaurus
Gilmoreosaurus
Gryposaurus
Hadrosaurus
"Hironosaurus"
Kritosaurus
Lophorhothon
Maiasaura
Mandschurosaurus
Microhadrosaurus
Orthomerus
Prosaurolophus
Saurolophus
Secernosaurus
Shantungosaurus
Tanius
Telmatosaurus
Thespesius
Trachodon
Tsintaosaurus

Hadrosaurids The family Hadrosauridae ("big lizards")
SUBORDER Ornithopoda ORDER Ornithischia
DESCRIPTION Medium to huge, heavily built bipedal/quadrupedal
plant-eaters; among the last and largest of all bird-footed,
bird-hipped dinosaurs. There were two such families of hadrosaurs
or duck-bills, so nicknamed from their broad, flat toothless beaks.
Both groups had powerful jaws and pavements of self-sharpening
cheek teeth chewing leaves and twigs stored in roomy cheeks.
Most were big and heavy, with longer limbs and deeper tails than
their iguanodontid forebears, and each hand had only four fingers,
cushioned in a padded paw. Unlike other hadrosaurs, hadrosaurids
had a flat skull or one with crests or bumps of solid bone, and a
relatively longer lower jaw and longer, slimmer limbs. LENGTH
12-49ft (3.7-15m) TIME Late Cretaceous PLACE North and South
America, Europe, and Asia.

Where they lived
Major areas of fossil finds

156

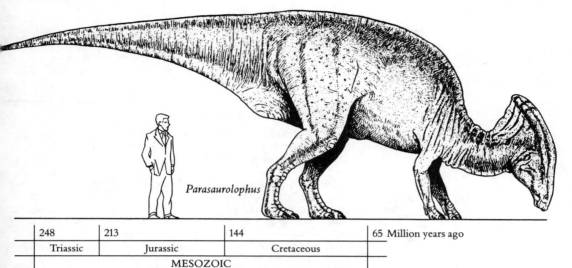

Parasaurolophus

248	213		144		65 Million years ago
Triassic	Jurassic		Cretaceous		
MESOZOIC					

Lambeosaurids The family Lambeosauridae ("Lambe's lizards")
SUBORDER Ornithopoda ORDER Ornithischia
DESCRIPTION Medium to huge, heavily built bipedal/quadrupedal
plant-eaters. Lambeosaurids were built much like those other
hadrosaurs the hadrosaurids, but with relatively shorter lower jaws
and limbs, and a variety of high, hollow, bony head crests that
served at mating time as visual recognition signals and vocal
resonators. Males had larger crests than young and females of their
own species. Lambeosaurids and hadrosaurids browsed largely on
all fours, relying on keen senses of sight, smell, and hearing to
warn of danger. Lacking powerful defense, scared hadrosaurs ran
off on their powerful hind limbs, head and back held low with the
tail held stiffly out behind balancing the forepart of the body.
LENGTH 13–49ft (4–15m) TIME Late Cretaceous PLACE North
America and Asia.

**Genera
(some doubtful)**
Bactrosaurus
Barsboldia
Corythosaurus
Hypacrosaurus
Jaxartosaurus
Lambeosaurus
Nipponosaurus
Parasaurolophus
Pteropelyx

Where they lived
Major areas of fossil finds

©DIAGRAM

Ornithischians 2: five suborders

Like ornithopods, the ornithischians described on these two
pages had horny beaks and birdlike hip bones, and they ate plants.
But most were armored, too. Pachycephalosaurs (bone- heads) and
ceratopsians (horned dinosaurs) developed armored heads.
Scelidosaurs had bony studs down the back. Maybe these gave rise

FIVE SUBORDERS OF ORNITHISCHIANS

Numbered items depict five ornithischian suborders recognized in this
book. Small letters indicate their families. (Some groupings are
provisional.) For fabrosaurids see page 160.

1 Scelidosauria ("limb lizards") A possible suborder of bipedal and
bipedal/quadrupedal plant-eaters with rows of bony studs running down
the back – precursors of the big bony plates, shields, or spikes seen in the
scelidosaurs' close kin stegosaurs and ankylosaurs. All three groups
perhaps evolved from primitive forms like *Scutellosaurus*. Scelidosaurs
flourished in Jurassic times across the Northern Hemisphere, and evidently
later gave way to their better armored relatives. Families: pages 163–164
a Scelidosauridae **b** Scutellosauridae

2 Stegosauria ("roof lizards") The plated dinosaurs: four-legged plant-
eaters with two rows of tall plates or spines embedded in thick skin and
jutting from neck, back, and tail. Probably all stegosaurs had long bony
shoulder spikes and paired spikes jutting from the tail. The head was small
and low, the neck short, the body bulky, the tail fairly long. Hind limbs far
longer than front limbs made the body highest at the hips. (Some people
think that stegosaurs could rear to browse.) Stegosaurs had lost big toes
and the bony tendons that stiffened the tails of other ornithischians. They
lived from Mid Jurassic through Late Cretaceous times. Fossils come from
northern continents, Africa, and India. Families: pages 165–166.
c Huayangosauridae **d** Stegosauridae

3 Ankylosauria ("fused lizards") The armored dinosaurs: four-legged
plant-eaters with broad, low, uniquely solid skulls, barrel-shaped bodies,
short but massive limbs, and sturdy tails. A flexible armor of fused bony
plates and studs and spikes sheathed with horn reinforced the tough skin of
back and flanks, and slabs of bone encased the head. Ankylosaurs lived
from Mid Jurassic through Late Cretaceous times. Most seemingly
inhabited northern continents, though fossil finds have also come from the
Antarctic and Australia. Families: pages 167–168.
e Nodosauridae **f** Ankylosauridae

4 Pachycephalosauria ("thick-headed lizards") Bipedal and bipedal/
quadrupedal plant-eaters. Their skulls were rigid and often thick roofed
and partly rimmed by rows of bony knobs. Many had canine-type front
teeth and a gap between these and the cheek teeth. Pachycephalosaurs
tended to have long legs, short arms, and interwoven bony tendons
stiffening the tail down to its tip. The group lived from Late Jurassic
through Late Cretaceous time. Most fossil finds come from northern
continents. Families: pages 161–162 (for Chaoyoungosaurids see Chapter 2).
g Chaoyoungosauridae **h** Pachycephalosauridae **i** Homalocephalidae

to the jutting back plates and tail and shoulder spikes of stegosaurs (plated dinosaurs) and the bony armor encasing ankylosaurs (armored dinosaurs). All these and the ornithopods probably evolved from speedy bipeds such as fabrosaurids – more primitive than all the rest.

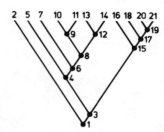

5 Ceratopsia ("horned faces") The horned dinosaurs: bipedal and four-legged plant-eaters with a tall narrow snout like a parrot's beak, and a triangular skull seen from above, with a bony frill at the back. Many were built rather like a rhinoceros, with a huge head, bony nose horn, two horns above the eyes, and a great bony frill covering the neck. Most lived (perhaps in herds) in Late Cretaceous northern continents. Ceratopsians perhaps evolved from early pachycephalosaurs. Families: pages 169–171.
j Psittacosauridae **k** Protoceratopsidae **l** Ceratopsidae

Ornithischian cladogram
This simplified cladogram shows many major and lesser ornithischian branches proposed in 1986 by Paul Sereno. Each numbered node marks anatomical innovations absent lower in the diagram. All subgroups above a node belong to the group that represents.
  1 Order Ornithischia
  2 Genus *Lesothosaurus*
  3 Parvorder Genasauria
  4 Nanorder Thyreophora
  5 Genus *Scutellosaurus*
  6 Hypoorder
     Thyreophoroidea
  7 Genus *Scelidosaurus*
  8 Minorder Eurypoda
  9 Suborder Stegosauria
 10 Genus *Huayangosaurus*
 11 Family Stegosauridae
 12 Suborder Ankylosauria
 13 Family Nodosauridae
 14 Family Ankylosauridae
 15 Nanorder Cerapoda
 16 Hypoorder
    Euornithopoda
 17 Hypoorder
    Marginocephalia
 18 Suborder
    Pachycephalosauria
 19 Suborder Ceratopsia
 20 Genus *Psittacosaurus*
 21 Family Ceratopsidae

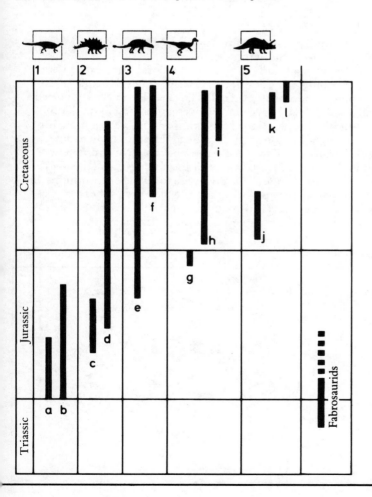

Fabrosaurids

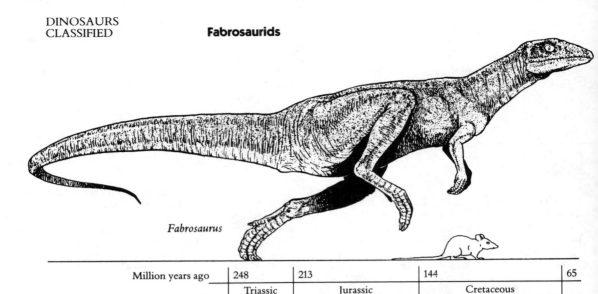

Fabrosaurus

Million years ago	248	213	144	65
	Triassic	Jurassic	Cretaceous	
		MESOZOIC		

**Genera
(some doubtful)**
Alocodon
Fabrosaurus
Gongbusaurus
Lesothosaurus
Lufengocephalus
Nanosaurus
Technosaurus
Xiaosaurus

Fabrosaurids The family Fabrosauridae ("Fabre's lizards")
SUBORDER Uncertain ORDER Ornithischia
DESCRIPTION Small, early, lightly built bipedal plant–eaters with
long legs, four–toed feet, short arms, five–fingered hands, and a
long, bony-tendon-stiffened tail. The fairly long neck supported a
small head with large eyes and a lower jaw ending in toothless
horn-sheathed bone. Ridged teeth rimmed the jaws, leaving no
space for well-developed cheek pouches like those where other
ornithischians stored food for future chewing. More differences
seemingly involved the jaw joint, hips and thighs. All this suggests
that fabrosaurids might have given rise to all the other ornithischian
dinosaurs. If so, they probably deserve their own suborder.
LENGTH about 3ft 4in (1m) TIME Early Late Triassic to Early
Jurassic PLACE North America, Europe, Africa, and Asia.

Where they lived
Major areas of fossil finds

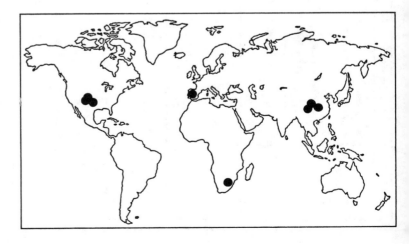

Pachycephalosaurids

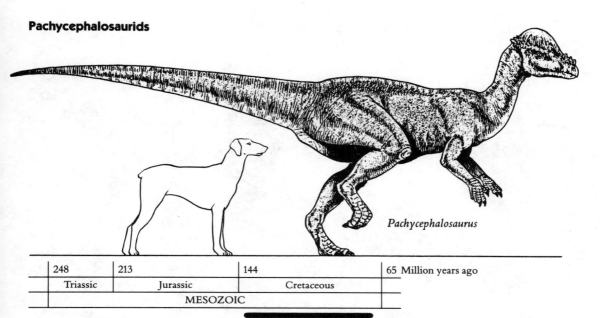

Pachycephalosaurus

248	213		144		65 Million years ago
Triassic	Jurassic		Cretaceous		
		MESOZOIC			

Pachycephalosaurids The family Pachycephalosauridae ("thick-headed lizards") SUBORDER Pachycephalosauria ORDER Ornithischia

DESCRIPTION Bipedal plant–eaters with thick domed skulls, a bony bar and bony bumps or spikes behind each eye. Like their flat-headed kin, these domed bone-heads had short arms, strong hips and legs, and interwoven bony tendons stiffening the tail. They walked with level back, and were not designed for running fast. Pachycephalosaurids ate leaves, fruits, seeds, and perhaps insects; and detected danger with sharp eyes and a keen sense of smell. Males probably had especially high-domed skulls and fought head–butting contests, the winners mating with and ruling herds of females. Chaoyoungosaurids could have been their ancestors. LENGTH 3–15ft (90cm–4.6m) TIME Early to Late Cretaceous PLACE North America, Europe, Madagascar, Mongolia, and China.

Genera (some doubtful)
Gravitholus
Majungatholus
Ornatotholus
Pachycephalosaurus
Prenocephale
Stegoceras
Stygimoloch
Tylocephale
Yaverlandia

Where they lived
Major areas of fossil finds

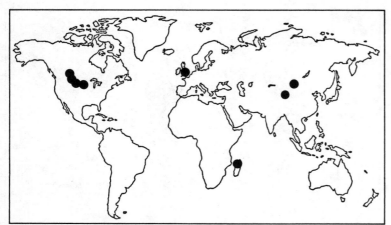

© DIAGRAM

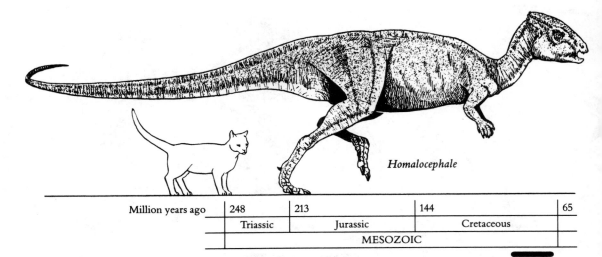

Homalocephale

Million years ago	248	213		144		65
	Triassic	Jurassic		Cretaceous		
	MESOZOIC					

Genera
Goyocephale
Homalocephale
Micropachycephalosaurus
Wannanosaurus

Homalocephalids The family Homalocephalidae ("even–heads")
SUBORDER Pachycephalosauria ORDER Ornithischia
DESCRIPTION Bipedal plant–eaters with thick flat skulls, some
bearing pits and knobs. These flat-headed bone-heads were built
and doubtless lived much like the pachycephalosaurids, though
rival males probably pushed against each other with their heads like
marine iguanas rather than bashing heads like bighorn sheep. The
most primitive homalocephalid was tiny *Wannanosaurus*, the only
one without a broadened bar and row of bony bumps behind each
eye. Others could have branched off one by one from the line
leading to the domed bone-headed dinosaurs. Accordingly at least
one expert thinks that the homalocephalids formed not a single
family but a sequence of increasingly advanced design. LENGTH
20in–10ft (51cm–3m) TIME Late Cretaceous PLACE China and
Mongolia.

Where they lived
Major areas of fossil finds

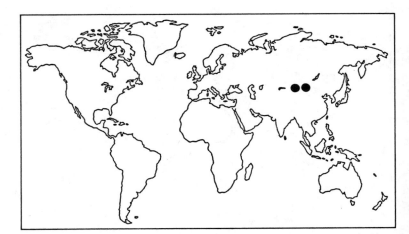

Scutellosaurids

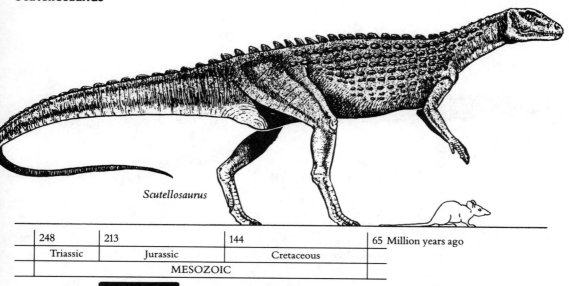

Scutellosaurus

248	213		144		65 Million years ago
Triassic	Jurassic			Cretaceous	
MESOZOIC					

Scutellosaurids The family Scutellosauridae ("small–shield lizards") SUBORDER Scelidosauria or Ankylosauria ORDER Ornithischia DESCRIPTION Small semi-armored bipedal and bipedal/quadrupedal plant–eaters with serrated leaflike teeth and small cheeks. The best-known form, *Scutellosaurus*, bore body armor comprising rows of little bony plates – some flat, some ridged like tiny roofs – all maybe with a covering of leathery or horny scales. A long tail helped counterbalance the armor's extra weight, and long arms suggest that such little dinosaurs often walked on all fours to help support their relatively heavy bodies. Seemingly related to but more primitive than scelidosaurids, scutellosaurids may be the scelidosaur family closest to the origins of the stegosaurs and ankylosaurs. LENGTH 2–4ft (60cm–1.2m) TIME Early to Late Jurassic PLACE North America, Europe, and Asia.

Genera
Echinodon?
Scutellosaurus
Tatisaurus
Trimucrodon

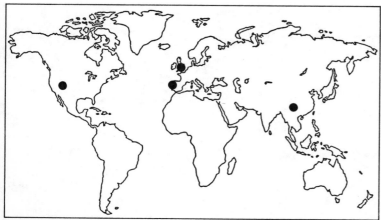

Where they lived
Major areas of fossil finds

©DIAGRAM

163

Scelidosaurids

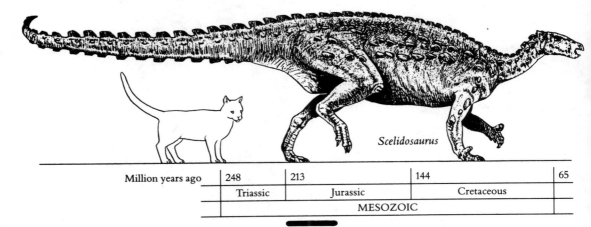

Scelidosaurus

Million years ago	248	213		144		65
	Triassic	Jurassic		Cretaceous		
	MESOZOIC					

Genera
Lusitanosaurus
Scelidosaurus

Scelidosaurids The family Scelidosauridae ("limb lizards")
SUBORDER Scelidosauria ORDER Ornithischia
DESCRIPTION Four-legged plant-eating ornithischians highest at the
hips, with rows of low bony studs that formed protective armor
plating embedded in the skin. This also had a covering of low,
rounded scales. Scelidosaurids walked with pillar-like limbs. They
had four-toed feet, and a long tail partly counterbalancing the
forepart of the body. The neck was fairly short and the head was
small with bony reinforcements, small leaf-shaped teeth, and
probably a bony beak. Scelidosaurids seem to have been slow
movers, relying on their body armor for **defense**. Skull similarities
suggest that members of this group's suborder might have been the
ancestors of stegosaurs and ankylosaurs. LENGTH about 13ft (4m)
TIME Early Jurassic PLACE USA, England, Portugal, and Tibet.

Where they lived
Major areas of fossil finds

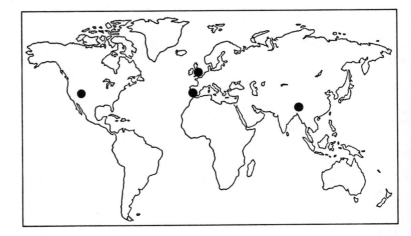

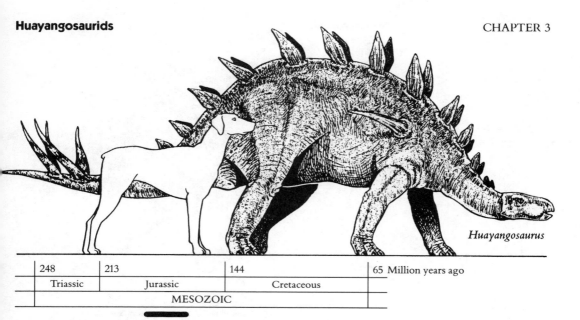

Huayangosaurus

248	213		144		65 Million years ago
Triassic	Jurassic		Cretaceous		
MESOZOIC					

Huayangosaurids The family Huayangosauridae ("Huayang lizards") SUBORDER Stegosauria ORDER Ornithischia DESCRIPTION Four-legged plant-eating dinosaurs with a bulky body highest at the hips, and two rows of narrow, pointed bony plates jutting upward from the neck and back. Long, defensive, bony spikes projected from the tail and shoulders. Held low, the head was small, deep, and short-snouted and the front upper jaw had teeth, absent in the later plated dinosaurs whose jaw tips formed a toothless beak for cropping leaves. Their front teeth, relatively square head, and distinctive bones in other parts of the skeleton suggest that huayangosaurids formed a primitive group of plated dinosaurs. Described from the sole known genus, these creatures underpin the notion that plated dinosaurs first appeared in China or nearby. LENGTH 13ft (4m) TIME Middle Jurassic PLACE China

Genera
Huayangosaurus

Where they lived
Major areas of fossil finds

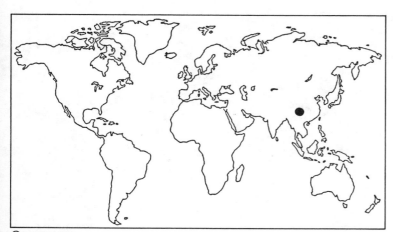

Stegosaurids

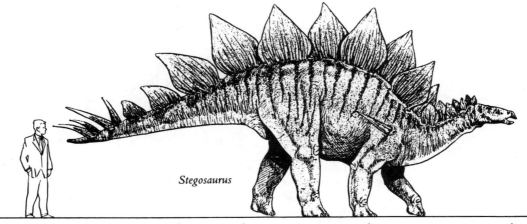

Stegosaurus

Million years ago	248	213		144		65
	Triassic	Jurassic		Cretaceous		
	MESOZOIC					

**Genera
(some doubtful)**
Changdusaurus
Chialingosaurus
Chungkingosaurus
Craterosaurus
Dacentrurus
Diracodon
Dravidosaurus
Kentrosaurus
Lexovisaurus
Monkonosaurus
Paranthodon
Stegosaurus
Tuojiangosaurus
Wuerhosaurus
Yingshanosaurus

Where they lived
Major areas of fossil finds

Stegosaurids The family Stegosauridae ("roof lizards")
SUBORDER Stegosauria ORDER Ornithischia
DESCRIPTION Four-legged plant-eating dinosaurs with a bulky body
highest at the hips, two rows of bony plates and/or spikes jutting
up from neck, back, and tail, and long defensive spikes projecting
from the tail and shoulders. The largest plates might have served as
heat-loss fins, giving off convected heat to prevent the body
overheating in hot weather. They had a small, low head, a brain no
bigger than a dog's, and small cheek teeth set in jaws that ended
in a toothless beak. Stegosaurids probably cropped low-growing
plants but they also might have reared to browse on taller
vegetation. These ornithischians lacked big toes and spine-
stiffening bony tendons. LENGTH 10–30ft (3–9m) TIME Mid Jurassic
to Late Cretaceous PLACE North America, Europe, Africa, and
Asia.

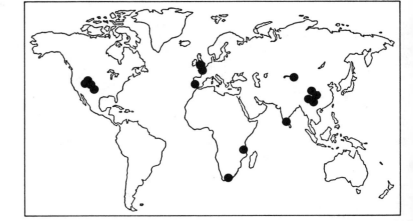

166

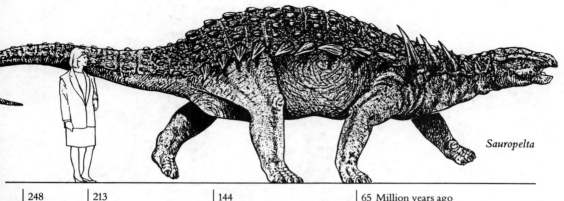

Sauropelta

248	213		144	65 Million years ago
Triassic	Jurassic		Cretaceous	
		MESOZOIC		

Nodosaurids The family Nodosauridae ("node lizards") SUBORDER Ankylosauria ORDER Ornithischia DESCRIPTION Four-legged plant–eaters with a heavy armored body. Many had short and relatively slim limbs, a short neck, a fairly narrow head with pointed snout, a skull hole behind the eye, and massive jaws with small leaf-shaped teeth and a horny toothless beak. Bands of bony plates, spines, and nodules "floating" in the skin protected back and hips, and in at least some nodosaurids bony spines longer than they were broad projected sideways from the flanks. The long heavy tail lacked a tail club. Nodosaurids browsed on low-growing plants. Some think they might have held their bodies higher than ankylosaurids when they walked. If a carnosaur attacked, they could have crouched to guard their bellies. LENGTH 6–25ft (1.8–7.6m) TIME Mid Jurassic to Late Cretaceous PLACE North America, Europe, Asia, Australia.

Genera (some doubtful)
Acanthopholis
Brachypodosaurus
Chassternbergia
Crataeomus
Cryptodraco
Danubiosaurus
Denversaurus
Dracopelta
Edmontonia
Hoplitosaurus
Hylaeosaurus
Minmi
Panoplosaurus
Polacanthoides
Polacanthus
Priconodon
Priodontognathus
Sarcolestes
Sauropelta
Silvisaurus
Struthiosaurus
"*Vectensia*"

Where they lived
Major areas of fossil finds

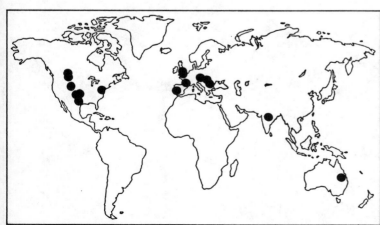

©DIAGRAM

167

Ankylosaurids

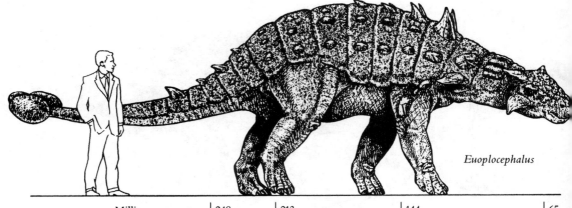

Euoplocephalus

Million years ago	248	213		144		65
	Triassic	Jurassic		Cretaceous		
			MESOZOIC			

**Genera
(some doubtful)**
Amtosaurus
Ankylosaurus
Dyoplosaurus
Euoplocephalus
Heishansaurus
Maleevus
Peishansaurus
Pinacosaurus
Saichania
Sauroplites
Shamosaurus
Stegosaurides
Tarchia
Tenchisaurus

Ankylosaurids The family Ankylosauria ("fused lizards")
SUBORDER Ankylosauria ORDER Ornithischia
DESCRIPTION Four-legged plant-eaters with a heavy armored body.
Like nodosaurids, they had short necks, sturdy limbs held
underneath the body, a long tail, and bony and horny armor
plating in the skin. Combining armor with mobility, at least some
had bands of hollow-based armor plates across the back and tail,
and horn-sheathed bony plates jutting up from back and shoulders.
The reinforced skull was at least as broad as long (with bony horns
and broad toothless beak). Ankylosaurids lacked some
nodosaurids' long flank spines but the tail (stiffened near its tip by
bony tendons) ended in a bony club. S-shaped nasal passages linked
to hollows in the skull perhaps filtered, warmed, and moistened
breathed-in air. LENGTH 18-35ft (5.5-10.7m) TIME Early to Late
Cretaceous PLACE North America, Asia, Antarctica.

Where they lived
Major areas of fossil finds

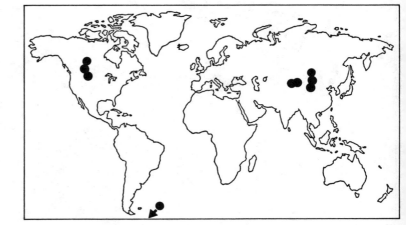

Psittacosaurids

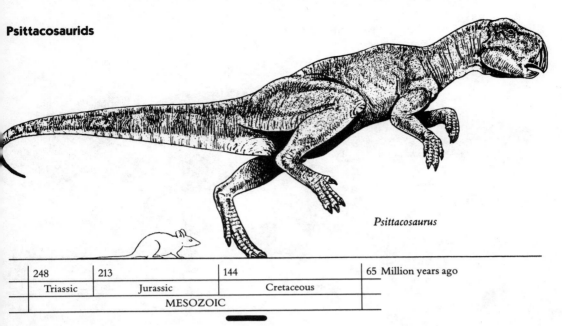

Psittacosaurus

248	213		144		65 Million years ago
Triassic	Jurassic			Cretaceous	
MESOZOIC					

Psittacosaurids The family Psittacosauridae ("parrot lizards") SUBORDER Ceratopsia ORDER Ornithischia DESCRIPTION Small mainly bipedal plant-eaters once considered ornithopods but now known to be related to horned dinosaurs. Like these they had a deep parrotlike beak (perhaps for cropping new kinds of tough-leaved plants) and cheek bones forming little horns. Eyes and nostrils were located high up in the head. Psittacosaurs had long hindlimbs, and strong short forelimbs with blunt claws suitable for walking on or grasping leaves. The long tail counterbalanced the forepart of the body when psittacosaurids walked or ran. By the end of the 1980s scientists had identified one genus with five species (others turned out to be be young or males and females of species already known). LENGTH 6ft 6in (2m) TIME Early Cretaceous PLACE Mongolia, China, Siberia, and Europe.

Genera
Psittacosaurus
Stenopelix?

Where they lived
Major areas of fossil finds

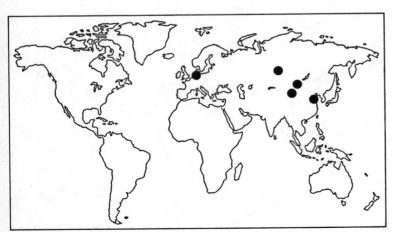

Protoceratopsids

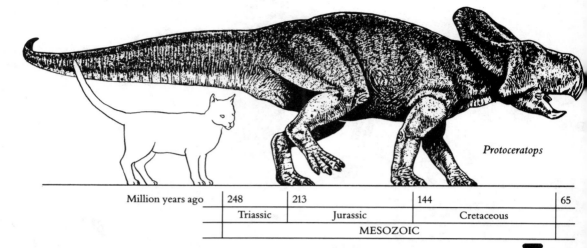

Protoceratops

Million years ago	248	213		144		65
	Triassic		Jurassic		Cretaceous	
			MESOZOIC			

**Genera
(some doubtful)**
Bagaceratops
Leptoceratops
Microceratops
Montanoceratops
Notoceratops
Protoceratops

Protoceratopsids The family Protoceratopsidae ("first horned faces") SUBORDER Ceratopsia ORDER Ornithischia DESCRIPTION Small quadrupedal and bipedal/quadrupedal plant-eaters with a deep parrotlike beak and a battery of shearing cheek teeth worked by powerful muscles tethered to a bony neck frill. Protoceratopsids are often thought more primitive than any of the large horned dinosaurs. Some indeed had clawed rather than hooflike toes, relatively small heads, and bumps instead of well developed horns. Yet a bony neck frill, cheek hornlets, and three fused neck bones figure in both groups, so some scientists lump protoceratopsids with the ceratopsid dinosaurs. Male protoceratopsids seem to have had larger frills and taller snouts than females. LENGTH 3ft 3in–10ft (1–3m) TIME Late Cretaceous PLACE North and South America, and East Asia.

Where they lived
Major areas of fossil finds

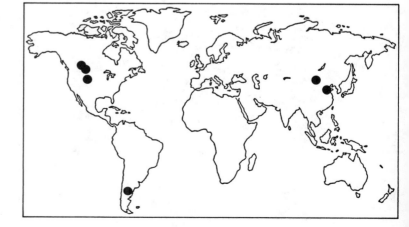

Ceratopsids

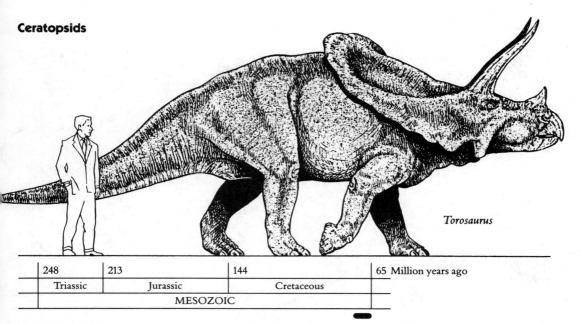

Torosaurus

248	213		144		65 Million years ago
Triassic	Jurassic			Cretaceous	
		MESOZOIC			

Ceratopsids The family Ceratopsidae ("horned faces")
SUBORDER Ceratopsia ORDER Ornithischia
DESCRIPTION The rhinoceroses of their day: horned quadrupedal
plant-eaters with huge heads, bulky bodies, and pillarlike limbs
with hooflike claws. Most had two long brow horns and a short
nose horn, or vice versa. The head was deep and massive with a
narrow, parrotlike beak, batteries of shearing cheek teeth, and
powerful jaws. Jaw muscles were anchored to a backswept bony
skull frill shielding the back of the neck, and serving in sexual
display. Scientists often subdivide ceratopsids into two groups
based on length of frill or length of the bone that forms each side of
the frill. Ceratopsids arguably roamed in herds, browsing on
low-growing vegetation. Threatened individuals very likely
charged their enemies. LENGTH about 6-30ft (1.8-9m) TIME Late
Cretaceous PLACE North America.

Genera (some doubtful)

Agathaumas
Anchiceratops
Arrhinoceratops
Avaceratops
Brachyceratops
Ceratops
Chasmosaurus
Dysganus
Eoceratops
Eucentrosaurus
Monoclonius
Pachyrhinosaurus
Pentaceratops
Styracosaurus
Torosaurus
Triceratops
Ugrosaurus

Where they lived
Major areas of fossil finds

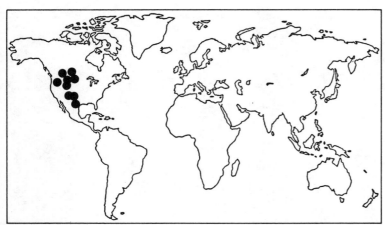

Chapter 4

DINOSAUR LIFE

How dinosaurs were built, how their bodies worked, and how they lived are the themes of these pages. We explore the dinosaurs' bony framework; muscles operating limbs; heart–lung system; brain and senses; digestive system; and heads, necks, limbs, tails, skin and scales. After a look at how dinosaurs kept their bodies warm we pass on to how they moved, fed, fought, and bred. The chapter ends with life expectancy and death. Much of what we say and show is not proved fact, just plausibly inferred.

Two lively views of dinosaur life from Gerhard Heilmann's perceptive *The Origin of Birds* (1925).
Above: The small theropod *Compsognathus* sprinting, with neck and head outstretched and balanced by the stiffly held tail.
Below: Ostrich dinosaurs shown as harmless fruit-eaters. Scientists still speculate about the likely diet of these toothless dinosaurs.

Bony scaffolding

A dinosaur's skeleton supported the body, formed levers that enabled it to move, guarded vital organs, and stored blood-forming bone marrow. Thick, solid limb bones propped up heavy dinosaurs, though lighter kinds had thin-walled hollow bones, and in large theropods and sauropods holes and hollows lightened skull or vertebrae. The spine ran the length of the body, reinforcing neck, back, and tail, and supporting skull and ribs – shields for the brain, heart and lungs. Vertebrae fused to the pelvic (hip) bones linked spine to bones of thighs, legs, and feet. Shoulder blades supported arm and hand bones. All bones met at joints – immovable in many skulls, or movable, as in the limbs where fibrous cartilage buffered hinge or ball-and-socket joints, held in place by strong flexible bands called ligaments.

Giant femur
A man beside a sauropod femur (*left*) shows its colossal size. Such pillarlike thigh bones transmitted body weight from hips to lower legs. Experts once wrongly thought even such massive bones could only hold up the largest dinosaurs if they were buoyed up by water.

Tyrannosaur skeleton
Labels indicate main bones or groups of bones in a big predatory dinosaur.
a Skull
b Cervical vertebrae
c Dorsal vertebrae
d Sacral vertebrae

e Caudal vertebrae
f Ribs
g Gastralia (belly ribs)
h Scapula (shoulder blade)
i Humerus (upper arm bone)
j Radius/ulna (forearm)
k Carpus (wrist)

l Phalanges (digit bones)
m Pelvis (hip region)
n Femur (thigh bone)
o Tibia (main shin bone)
p Fibula
q Tarsus (ankle)
r Metatarsal bones

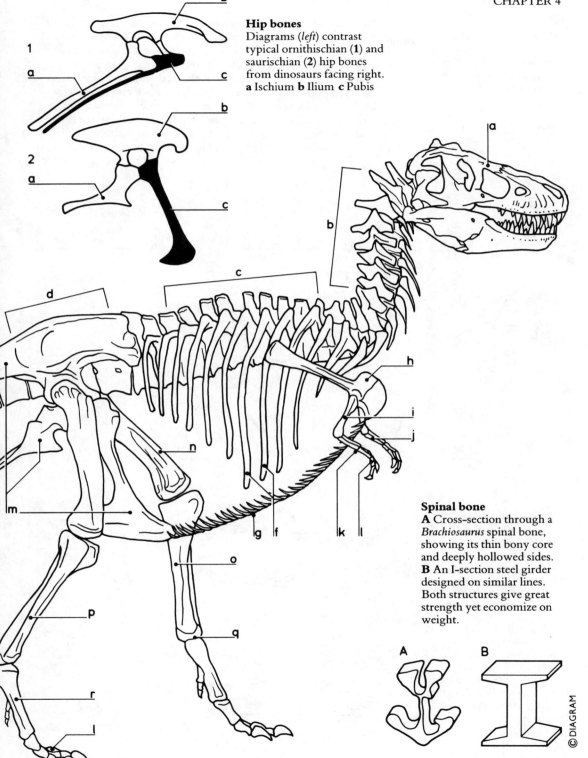

Hip bones
Diagrams (*left*) contrast typical ornithischian (**1**) and saurischian (**2**) hip bones from dinosaurs facing right.
a Ischium **b** Ilium **c** Pubis

Spinal bone
A Cross-section through a *Brachiosaurus* spinal bone, showing its thin bony core and deeply hollowed sides.
B An I-section steel girder designed on similar lines. Both structures give great strength yet economize on weight.

© DIAGRAM

Muscles

Levers

Body movements involved joints that worked as levers of three main types. In each, muscular effort (E) moved a load (L) about a fulcrum (F).

1 Nodding the head: a first-class lever (LFE).

2 Walking foot action: a second-class lever (FLE).

3 Bending the elbow: a third-class lever (LEF).

The muscles of a dinosaur held its bones together, gave its body shape, and made it move. Muscles are elastic fibers grouped in sheets and bundles contracting and relaxing under orders from the nervous system. Nerve signals shortening muscles operated a dinosaur's jaws, head, neck, limbs, and tail; pumped blood through its heart; and pushed food through its gut. Each end of each long skeletal muscle joined a separate bone (at some ends via a tough flexible tendon). When the muscle contracted usually one bone moved. By alternating paired flexor and extensor muscles a dinosaur could bend and straighten joints to operate its limbs.

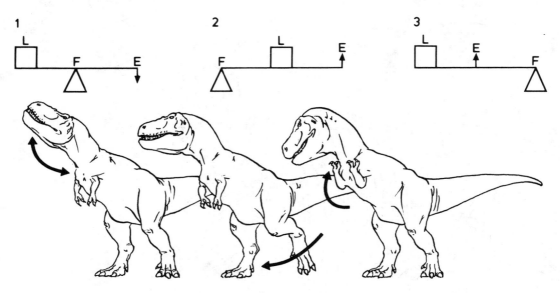

To and fro (*right*)

Alternate action of paired muscles in the human arm indicates how dinosaurs bent and straightened limbs. Muscles causing active movement are prime movers; those opposing them are antagonists.

1 Extending the elbow. The triceps muscle (**b**) contracts and the biceps muscle (**a**) relaxes.

2 Bending the elbow. The biceps muscle (**a**) contracts and the triceps muscle (**b**) relaxes.

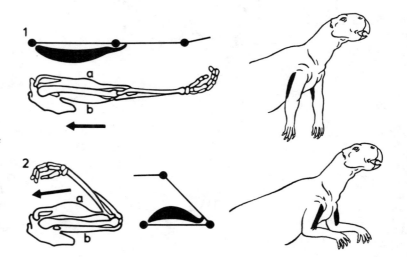

Jaws

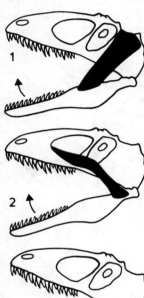

Shoulders

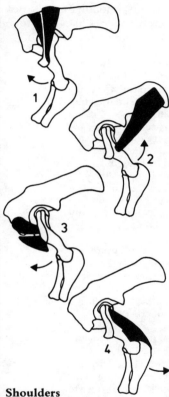

Hips

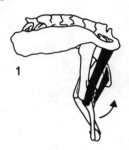

Jaw muscles

These diagrams indicate three muscles operating the jaws of the predatory dinosaur *Deinonychus*. Each muscle had one end fixed to the mandible (the lower jaw).

1 Adductor mandibularis: the big strong muscle that powerfully shut jaws when these were almost closed.

2 Pterygoideus: the muscle that smartly snapped shut wide-open jaws.

3 Depressor mandibulae: a small muscle at the back of the skull, used to pull the jaws wide open.

Shoulders

These four diagrams show shoulder muscles of armored *Euoplocephalus* or *Dyoplosaurus*. The arms served as weight-bearing forelimbs, not for grasping as in theropods.

1 Supracoracoideus and scapulo-humeralis anterior: raised the arm.

2 Teres: pulled the arm back.

3 Coraco-brachialis and pectoralis: pulled the arm forward.

4 Triceps: straightened the arm.

Hips

These two diagrams illustrate the muscles that joined legs to hips in the same armored dinosaur whose shoulder muscles also figure on this page.

1 Flexor tibialis anterior and ilio–fibularis: the muscles between the ilium (top hip bone) and lower leg bones, contracting to bend the leg.

2 Ilio-tibialis muscles that joined the ilium to the main shin bone and contracted to straighten the leg.

Fresh blood (oxygenated blood)

Used blood (deoxygenated blood)

Heart-lung system

Dinosaurs' hearts pumped nutrient-rich blood around their bodies, building and repairing cells, and washing wastes away. Meanwhile lungs breathed in air containing oxygen that "burned" carbon in the blood, releasing energy for growth and movement. The chemical reaction gave off carbon dioxide gas as breathed-out waste. Because dinosaurs stood and walked erect like elephants and ostriches, some scientists believe they had big, efficient hearts and lungs as birds and mammals do. Certainly some dinosaurs had rib cages roomy enough for large hearts and lungs, and hollow bones perhaps for air sacs like those found in living birds.

Three types of heart

1 A lizard's heart lacks a wall separating fresh blood from lungs and used blood from the body.

2 A crocodile's heart, with a valve in a dividing wall, sometimes separates fresh blood from used.

3 A bird's heart always separates fresh blood from used, providing body tissues with a rich supply of oxygen for active movement.

4 Some people think dinosaurs had efficient birdlike hearts. Maybe some had birdlike hearts, while others' were like those of crocodiles.

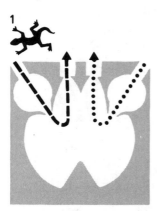

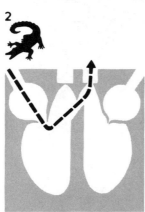

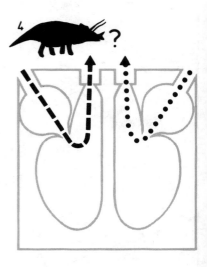

Blood pressures (*right*)
Bars show likely heart-level blood pressure for two dinosaurs and known blood pressure for four living animals. High pressure produced by efficient hearts is needed to pump blood to the brain in beasts with heads relatively high above their hearts, so arguably *Apatosaurus* had a heart designed like those of birds and mammals.

a Alligator
b *Triceratops*
c Man
d Duck
e Giraffe
f *Apatosaurus*

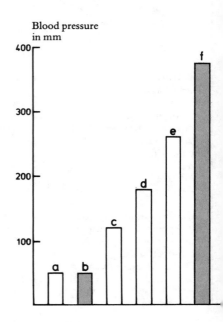

Blood pressure in mm

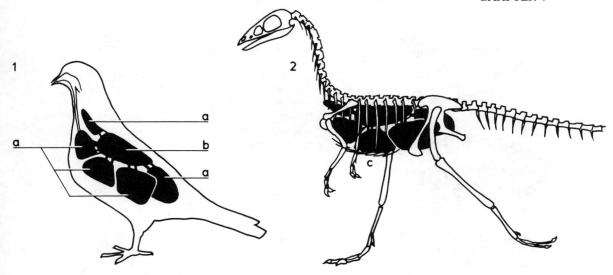

Air sacs (*above*)
1 Inside a bird air sacs (**a**) assure a steady one-way flow of fresh air through the lungs (**b**).
2 Inside a birdlike theropod dinosaur, belly ribs (**c**) might have squeezed similar air sacs so that they filled and emptied like bellows.

Lungs and hearts (*below*)
Cross-sections (not to scale) through two living animals hint at the likely size of lungs and heart in a sauropod dinosaur.
1 Crocodile. Ribs (**a**) enclose a shallow chest cavity with small heart (**b**) and lungs (**c**).

2 Horse. Its deep chest cavity holds large powerful heart and lungs.
3 *Apatosaurus*. Its deep chest cavity suggests heart and lungs more like a horse's than a crocodile's.

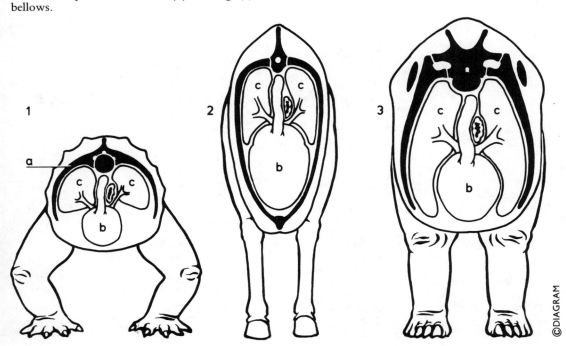

©DIAGRAM

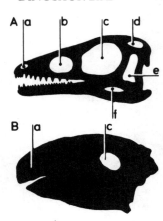

Heads

Horned dinosaurs and big flesh-eaters had huge heads with powerful jaws. Yet sauropods the size of several elephants had heads no larger than a horse's. Small theropods and most ornithischians had moderately sized heads and jaws. Beneath the skin, the skulls' sides were pierced by "windows" as in other archosaurs. In certain sauropods and theropods gigantic holes meant skulls were little more than jaws and braincase linked by bony struts. Besides lightening the skull, certain holes left extra room for muscles closing jaws. In ankylosaurs, though, solid bony armor had overgrown the windows in the skull.

Hollow and solid
Above: Windows in the skull as in the theropod *Compsognathus* (**A**) became closed in the armored skulls of such dinosaurs as *Panoplosaurus* (**B**).
a Nasal opening
b Antorbital opening
c Orbit (for eye)
d Upper temporal opening
e Lower temporal opening
f Mandibular opening

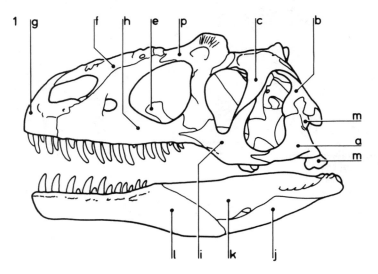

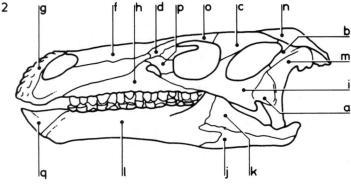

Skull bones
Dinosaur skulls, like other vertebrates' skulls, formed a mosaic of bones. Bone shapes and proportions and joint rigidity varied within both major groups of dinosaurs, and some had certain skull bones fused together. The main difference between both groups is the predentary bone of ornithischians.
1 Skull of *Allosaurus*, a saurischian dinosaur.
2 Skull of *Camptosaurus*, an ornithischian dinosaur.

a Quadratojugal	**j** Angular
b Squamosal	**k** Surangular
c Postorbital	**l** Dentary
d Prefrontal	**m** Quadrate
e Parasphenoid	**n** Parietal
f Nasal	**o** Frontal
g Premaxilla	**p** Lacrimal
h Maxilla	**q** Predentary
i Jugal	

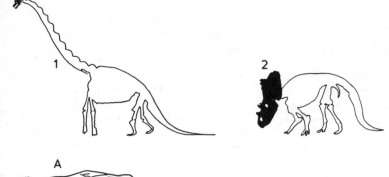

Head sizes (*top left*)

1 *Brachiosaurus*, one of the largest of all dinosaurs, had a relatively tiny head. Most dinosaur heads were small for body size.

2 *Torosaurus*, a horned dinosaur, had the largest head of any animal that ever lived on land.

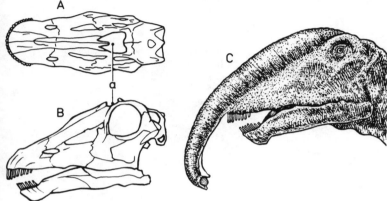

Hint of a trunk (*left*)

Top and side views (**A**, **B**) of a *Diplodocus* skull show nostril openings (**a**) above the eyes. High nostril openings in mammals such as elephants go with a trunk. Perhaps some sauropods had trunks as well. If so, *Diplodocus* might have had a head like this (**C**). Most scientists doubt this, however.

Head shapes

Dinosaurs' head shapes came in a remarkable variety that reflected different modes of feeding, fighting, or communication.

1 A duck-bill's head with a hollow resonating tube that amplified its calls.

2 A horned dinosaur's head with parrotlike beak, brow horns, and bony frill.

3 A big theropod's head with huge powerful jaws.

4 The domed head of a bone-headed dinosaur that used its thick skull in combat.

5 A lightweight predator's long narrow head and jaws.

6 The strange short head of birdlike *Oviraptor*, possibly an egg-eater. Its crest helped individuals to identify their own kind.

©DIAGRAM

Brains and intelligence

People think of dinosaurs as small-brained, stupid creatures. Was this really true? No dinosaur brains survive. But we can judge their size and weight from fossil skulls. A skull includes the bony, hollow braincase, sometimes filled with sediment that formed a mold of brain-shaped rock.

Such molds reveal some dinosaurs had very tiny brains indeed. *Stegosaurus* had a brain no bigger than a dog's. Sauropods, with a head as big as a horse's, had a brain no larger than a cat's.

Small brains need not imply stupidity. One famous writer had a tiny brain. Brain size in relation to body size is a better guide to mental ability. Weight for weight, most dinosaurs had smaller,

Brain/body weights
Some backboned creatures' brain weights appear here as percentages of their body weights. On this scale man and monkeys contrast strongly with *Apatosaurus*, a dinosaur with a brain 100,000 times lighter than its body.

A *Apatosaurus* 0.001%
B Whale 0.003%
C Elephant 0.2%
D Rat 0.48%
E Dog 0.85%
F Man 2.5%
G Sparrow 4.2%
H Spider monkey 4.8%

Brains compared (*right*)
Tyrannosaurus's brain (**A**) was larger than a human brain (**B**). But the "thinking part," the cerebrum (**a**), was small. Other parts largely helped it see, hear, smell, and coordinate its limbs.

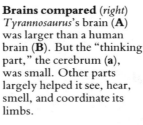

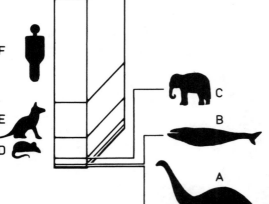

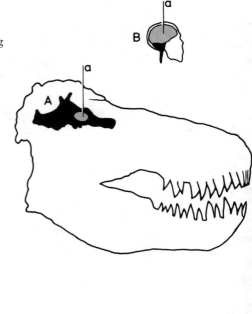

lighter brains than birds or mammals. But a huge python with a relatively smaller brain than a small snake need be no stupider than that. Relative brain size plus brain complexity give a truer guide to a creature's levels of behavior and activity.

Dinosaurs' relative brain weights and sizes matched owners' lifestyles. The great plant-eating, plodding sauropods had relatively smaller, lighter brains than any other backboned animal. A sauropod brain weighed a mere one hundred thousandth as much as its colossal body. (Your own brain is one fortieth your body's weight.) Slow-moving armored and plated dinosaurs had the next smallest brains. Then came the seemingly more active, agile horned dinosaurs. Big ornithopods had relatively larger, better-developed brains, linked with high abilities to interact, sense enemies, and run from danger on two legs. Yet a duck-billed dinosaur's brain was a mere one twenty thousandth of its body weight.

The brainiest dinosaurs were theropods – bipedal hunters with forelimbs freed for grasping. Yet *Tyrannosaurus's* brain mainly handled sight, smell, and limb coordination – the cerebrum containing the brain's "thinking part" was far tinier than ours. Easily the best developed brains belonged to speedy, agile, keen-eyed coelurosaurs such as *Troodon*. This creature's brain was at least one thousandth as heavy as its body, and its well-developed forebrain gave fine hand-eye coordination.

Only small hunting dinosaurs like this had brains relatively as big and complex as those of some birds and certain mammals. All other dinosaurs were probably no more intelligent than modern reptiles.

Relative brainpower
This diagram plots the range of brain sizes of dinosaurs against that of their living relatives the crocodiles. Encephalization quotient (EQ) numbers take account of body size. The higher the EQ the greater the assumed brainpower.
A Sauropods
B Ankylosaurs
C Stegosaurs
D Ceratopsians
E Ornithopods
F Crocodiles
G Carnosaurs
H Coelurosaurs

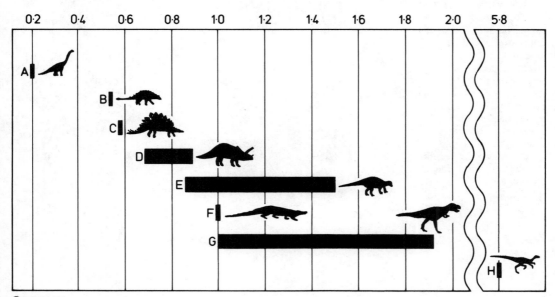

Sight, smell, and hearing

Day-active as most were, dinosaurs relied especially on sight for sensing food, friends, and enemies. Ostrich dinosaurs and troodontids had big, keen eyes; and predators with forward-facing eyes judged distance with precision. Large-snouted dinosaurs had a well-developed sense of smell, and diplodocids' high nasal

Coordination center

Tyrannosaurus brain based on a skull endocast. Labels show areas of brain receiving signals from the nose, eyes, and ears.
a Olfactory bulb, the brain's smell center
b Optic nerve, handling visual signals
c Auditory nerve, handling sound signals

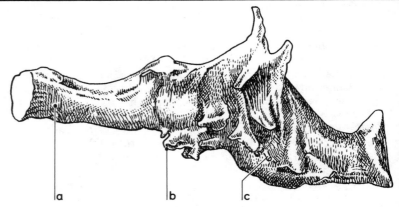

Sight

As with mammals, what dinosaurs saw depended largely on the positions of the eyes within the skull. (Like living reptiles, but unlike most mammals, dinosaurs probably saw their world in color.) Predatory *Troodon* (**1**) had large forward-facing eyes somewhat like a cat's (**2**). Like a cat it would have judged distance well, an important aid in stalking and seizing prey.

An ostrich dinosaur (**3**) had eyes on the sides of its head, somewhat like a horse (**4**). Creatures with eyes in this position can see danger approaching from behind, so enemies seldom catch them unaware.

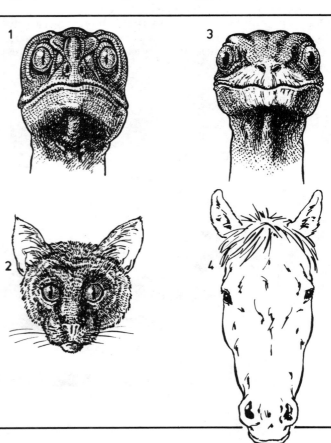

openings hint at a long, sensitive trunk. Dinosaurs lacked external ears, yet skulls and brain casts suggest an acute sense of hearing in hadrosaurs and their tyrannosaurid enemies. Doubtless dinosaurs had voices too, and bellowings arose from hadrosaurs with ballooning facial flaps or hollow head crests.

Hearing and voice
Supposed vocal structures hint at keen hearing in the duck-billed dinosaurs. *Saurolophus* (**1A**) had a solid bony crest jutting from the back of the head. This probably supported a skin balloon, inflated (**1B**) when the creature called, amplifying its voice and giving that distinctive resonance.

Sense of smell
The large snout of a big predatory dinosaur (**2**) and the large nasal openings (**a**) in such dinosaurs as *Brachiosaurus* (**3**) suggest these dinosaurs had a keen sense of smell. Yet ostrich dinosaurs lacked a sharp sense of smell and even large-snouted dinosaurs perhaps did not detect faint scents as well as dogs do.

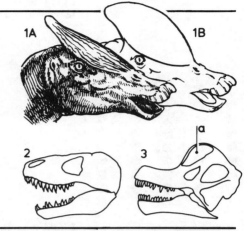

Pupil shapes and sizes
1 Day-active gecko with rounded pupils.
2 Nocturnal gecko with slit-shaped pupils giving good nocturnal vision. (Pupils open up at night.)
3 *Troodon* seemingly had large eyes, perhaps with good light-gathering ability. If it hunted at dusk it might have had slit-shaped pupils like a nocturnal gecko's.

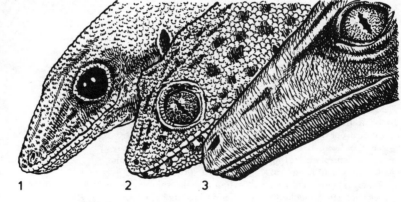

Bony eye rings
Skulls of a chicken (**A**) and the dinosaur *Hypsilophodon* (**B**) each show a bony ring inside a large eye socket. Bony eye rings occur in many fossil dinosaurs and living birds and reptiles. Such rings help to support the eyes and maybe help them focus. Like living birds and reptiles, dinosaurs were certainly sharp sighted.

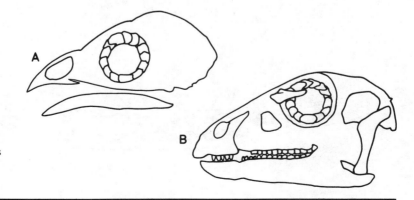

Necks

Dinosaurs' necks joined heads to bodies in ways that matched their heads and lifestyles. Short necks were long enough for the low-browsing horned and armored dinosaurs, and horned dinosaurs' necks received protection from a backswept bony skull frill. Necks curved like those of bisons probably fitted hadrosaurs for feeding near the ground. A sauropod's long, lightweight neck operated like a crane's boom, raising the head to browse on treetop leaves or dropping it to drink from pools and streams. A theropod's birdlike neck formed an S-shaped curve like a spring ready to uncoil as – jaws agape – the head struck out at prey.

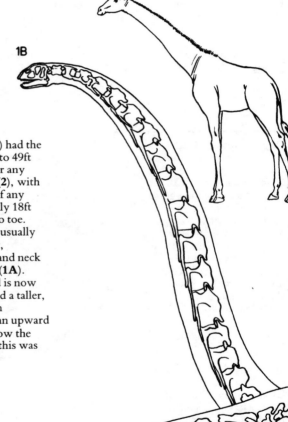

Neck bones (*above*)
Units are numbers of neck bones in two mammals (**AB**) and three dinosaurs (**C, D, E**).
A Man
B Giraffe
C *Psittacosaurus*
D Most theropods
E *Mamenchisaurus*
Most mammals have the same number of cervical vertebrae. Long-necked mammals simply have longer neck bones. But long-necked dinosaurs had more bones than short-necked dinosaurs.

Longest neck
Mamenchisaurus (**1**) had the longest neck – up to 49ft (15m) – known for any animal. A giraffe (**2**), with the longest neck of any animal alive, is only 18ft (5.5m) from top to toe. *Mamenchisaurus* is usually shown with a low, diplodocid head, and neck held horizontally (**1A**). But that sauropod is now known to have had a taller, blunter snout than diplodocids, and an upward bend in joints below the neck implies that this was held aloft (**1B**).

Neck curvatures
Diagrams (after Paul)
contrast neck bones of
a thecodont, predatory
dinosaur, and diving bird.
1 The thecodont *Euparkeria*
had a fairly straight neck,
like most reptiles and
mammals.
2 *Velociraptor* and other
theropods had neck bones
forming an S-shaped curve.
3 Loons have even more
strongly curved necks.
In all three, ribs made the
neck strong and supple.

Two necks compared
Similarity between spinal
curves in an American
bison (**1**) and a hadrosaur
(**2**) sheds light on the duck-
bill's likely feeding habits.
Scientists noted that in
both the backbone bends
down sharply at the
shoulders. This bend keeps
a bison's head low down,
for grazing. Hadrosaurs
were also evidently built for
feeding on low-growing
vegetation. Even when a
hadrosaur raised its head as
high as possible (**3**), its
mouth was still below the
level of its back unless the
creature reared.

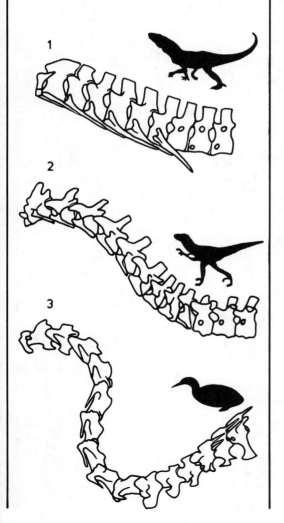

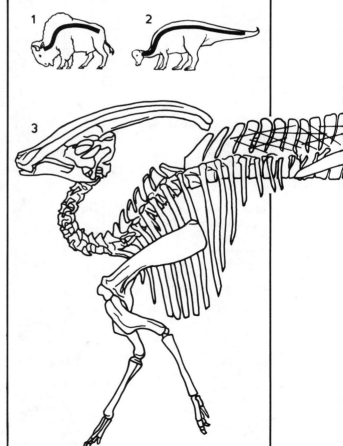

Arms and hands

Theropods and ornithopods mainly had far shorter arms than legs and some had grasping hands that seized the animals or plants they ate. Theropods' hands bore from two to five fingers tipped with sharp curved claws. Ornithopods' four- to five-fingered hands ended in hooflike nails. Sauropods, most prosauropods, and plated, horned and armored dinosaurs stood and walked with the front part of the body borne on long forelimbs with the elbows held tucked in. These creatures' "hands" were broad fleshy pads, with stubby hooflike nails. However, sauropods, prosauropods, and iguanodontids had spiky thumb claws designed as weapons of defense.

An ornithischian hand
The wrist bones (*above*) and specialized phalanges (digit bones) in *Iguanodon*'s hand.
a Fused wrist bones
b Digit 1: thumb spike
c, d, e Digits 2-4 with hooflike nails, designed for bearing weight when *Iguanodon* walked or rested on all fours.
f Digit 5: a flexible little finger, perhaps used for hooking leafy twigs to *Iguanodon*'s mouth.

Saurischian hands
Saurischian hands (*right*) varied in number of digits and design. Here four sets of digits contrast the hand bones of two predators (**A,B**) and two plant-eating sauropodomorphs (**C,D**).
A Bones of *Albertosaurus*'s two-fingered hand.
B Bones and sharply curved claws of *Deinonychus*'s three-fingered hand.
C Bones and thumb claw of the five-fingered weight-bearing "hand" of the sauropod *Diplodocus*.
D Bones and thumb claw of the five-fingered hand of a prosauropod, *Plateosaurus*.

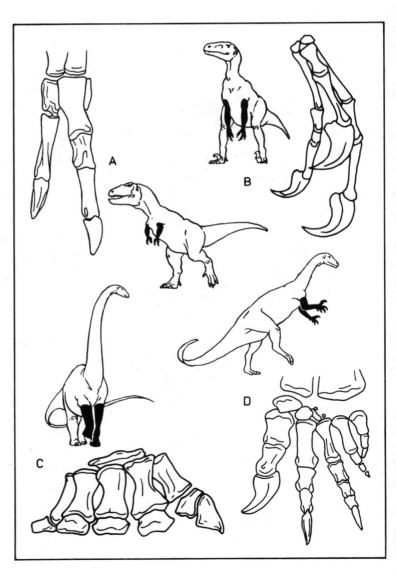

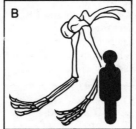

Arms small and large
A For its size, *Tarbosaurus* had the smallest arms and hands of any predatory dinosaur. **B** For its size, the unknown theropod *Deinocheirus* might have had the longest arms and hands of all.

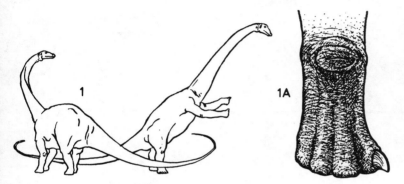

Elephantine pads
1 Sauropods could rear to feed or fight, but walked on all fours. A sauropod hand (**1A**) resembled an elephant's front foot, but with a sharp thumb claw and hooflike nails or (in some) block–like bones encased within a fleshy pad.

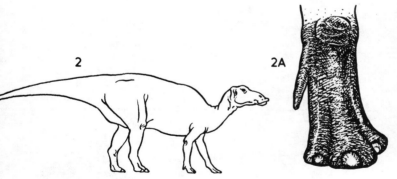

Duck-bills' hands
2 Hadrosaurs walked on all fours. Each forepaw (**2A**) left a smooth curved print. Fleshy pads probably cushioned the digits and spread when pressed on the ground. Flattened pads in mummified hadrosaurs once made people think the creatures had webbed fingers.

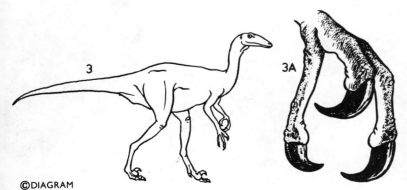

Grasping hands
3 *Troodon* has been pictured with sharp-clawed digits opposable (**3A**) for grasping prey. Yet in many predatory dinosaurs extending the fingers made the thumb claw turn away from these to form a vicious weapon. Some such birdlike theropods had a wrist-elbow system for folding arms much as birds fold wings.

©DIAGRAM

Digestive systems

Sauropods' spoon-shaped or peg-shaped teeth cropped leaves, that were then ground to pulp by gizzard stones. Ornithischians and certain prosauropods had horny beaks for cropping leaves, stored in cheek pouches until chopped up or sliced by cheek teeth (some self-sharpening). Many theropods had blade-like teeth for biting

Dinosaur teeth

Like living reptiles, most dinosaurs had teeth all one shape. But the plant-eaters had very different teeth from the meat-eaters, and large dinosaurs tended to have bigger teeth than small dinosaurs. New teeth were always growing and replaced old worn teeth as these dropped out.

Flesh-eaters' teeth

Jaws (1) and tooth (2) (not to scale) of a large theropod. Such a curved, blade-like tooth with "steak-knife" serrations (a, enlarged), sliced through tough flesh as if it were soft butter.

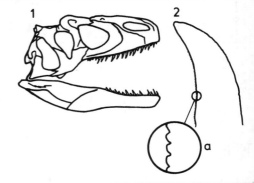

Predators' jaws

Loose skull construction helped *Allosaurus* bite and swallow.
1 Jaws in normal position (a) and (b) pulling back upper jaw to slice flesh gripped by the lower jaw.
2 Schematic head-on view shows jaws moving outward to bolt down a big mouthful of meat.

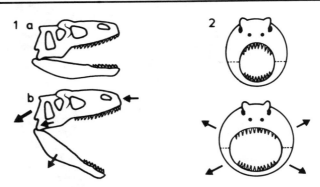

Digestive organs

Digestive organs and hip girdles influenced the body bulk and posture of some groups of dinosaurs.
1 Primitive dinosaur: a bipedal predator with a small digestive system in front of the pubic bone.
2 Sauropod: a plant-eater whose bulky digestive system in front of the pubic bone helped force it to bear it's body's weight on all fours. Some of its weight lay in swallowed gizzard stones (2a), polished as they ground up food inside the creature's gut.

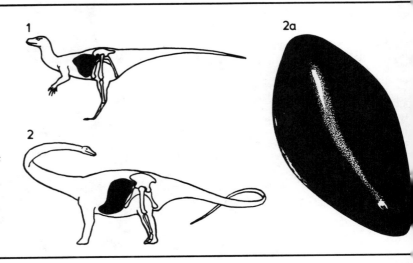

flesh from prey, and *Tyrannosaurus* took huge mouthfuls with front teeth that formed a monstrous "cookie cutter." Meat is easily digested, so theropods had a relatively short, simple gut as cats do. Leaves and twigs are harder to digest, so the plant-eating dinosaurs needed longer and larger digestive systems.

Plant–eaters' teeth
1 *Iguanodon* had an ornithischian's toothless cropping beak (**a**), gap between beak and teeth (**b**), and cheek teeth (**c**).
2 Leaf-shaped tooth of *Thecodontosaurus*, with little upward pointing ridges (**a**).
3 Spoon-shaped tooth of *Amygdalodon* ("almond tooth"), a sauropod.

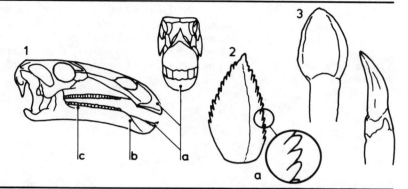

Plant–eaters' jaws
1 The duck-billed dinosaur *Corythosaurus*
a Skull
b Lower jaw, revealing a pavement of self-sharpening teeth.
2 Cross-section through *Iguanodon*'s jaws. Closing the jaws pushed apart the upper jaws, so top teeth slid across bottom teeth with a grinding action.

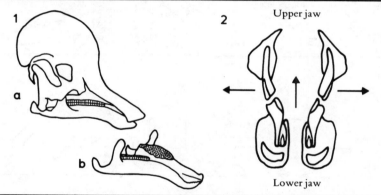

Upper jaw

Lower jaw

3 Ornithopod: a bipedal plant-eater with a bulky digestive system slung beneath a backward-angled pubic bone, and so kept below the creature's center of gravity.
4 Sauropod's hip bones.
5 Ornithopod's hip bones, with a backward-angled main stem to the pubis.
a Pubis
b Ischium
c Ilium

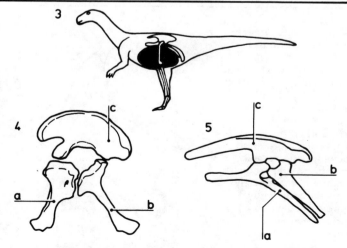

Hips, legs, and feet

Stance and gait
Three tetrapods (four-legged animals) with different types of stance appear above simplified cross-sections through their limbs and bodies.
1 Lizard: sprawling stance.
2 Crocodile: semi-improved gait (hurrying with body held above the ground).
3 Horse: fully improved stance and gait, as in the dinosaurs.
a Body
b Thigh
c Leg
d Foot

Dinosaurs' legs supported the body from directly underneath thanks to straight thigh bones with turned-in tops that fitted in deep sockets in the hip bones. Legs were long in fast running theropods and ornithopods, and the fastest sprinters seemingly had longer shins than thighs. Pillarlike legs supported the heavy four-legged dinosaurs. All dinosaurs had high ankles with a simple hinge joint, and long foot bones. Most walked upon their toes, like dogs, not flat-footedly, like bears. Theropod feet were birdlike, usually with three forward-pointing toes armed with large sharp claws, and one small claw turned back. Fleshy "heels" supported sauropods' broad toe pads, with three claws or more. Ornithischians had three to four toes with hooflike claws.

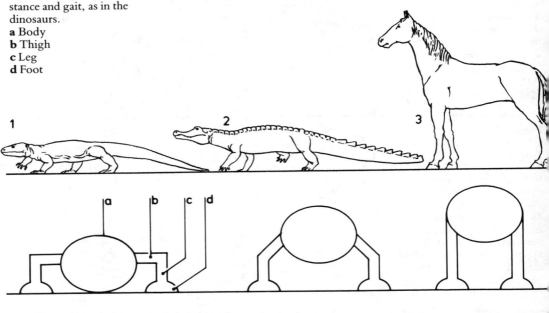

Hip joints
Two diagrams contrast hip joints of a semi-improved reptile and a dinosaur.
A Semi-improved hip joint
B Dinosaur hip joint
a Femur (thigh bone)
b Head of femur
c Pelvic (hip) bones
d Hip socket
e Supra-acetabular crest
Their hip design enabled dinosaurs to support their weight with legs directly below the body. Fully improved gait increased the efficiency with which these creatures walked and ran.

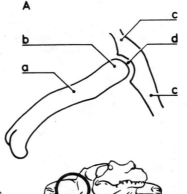

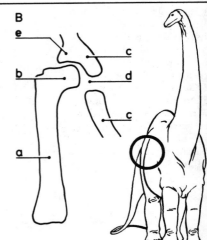

192

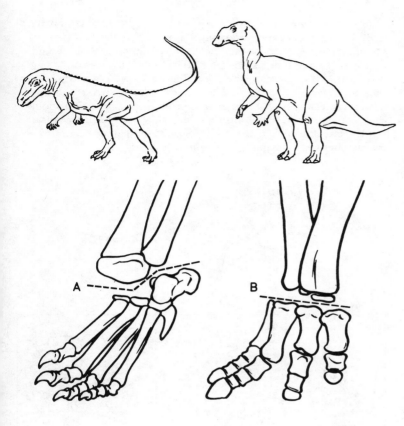

Ankle joints
A Bent hinge line seen in crocodilians and thecodonts.
B Straight hinge line as seen in dinosaurs, pterosaurs, and birds. Distinctive ankle joints help to identify fossil dinosaurs. In life these simple hinges were good enough to let dinosaurs move fast on rough ground. Such ankles also let the dinosaurs' descendants birds climb trees.

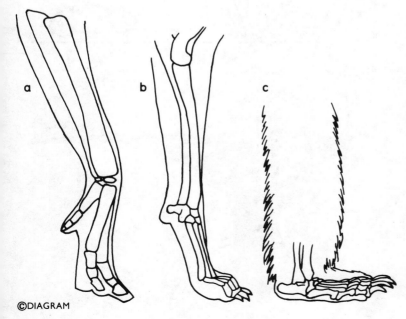

Feet compared
Three diagrams compare the foot bones of a dinosaur with those of two living mammals representing two kinds of foot design.
a Dinosaur foot, with high ankle and weight supported on long toes – the kind of foot known as digitigrade.
b Dog's foot, also of digitigrade design. Fast-running mammals tend to be long limbed and bear their weight upon their toes.
c Bear's foot resting flat on the ground, the kind of foot called plantigrade.

©DIAGRAM

Tails

Dinosaur tails were lizardlike with bony cores, though largely held aloft, not dragged along the ground. Long, stiffened tails counterbalanced the necks and heads of running ornithopods and theropods. Long tails also balanced the elongated necks of prosauropods and sauropods. Thick, short, heavy tails sufficed for the short-necked, four-legged horned dinosaurs. Strong tails might have served as props for stegosaurs, prosauropods and sauropods that reared to browse. Swimming dinosaurs waggled their tails, but less effectively than crocodiles. Some four-legged dinosaurs fought enemies by using tails as whips or clubs.

Stiffened tails
Ornithischians had bony tendons reinforcing the backbone and stiffening the tail. This bony corset was best developed among big ornithopods.
1 Skeleton of a duck-billed dinosaur.
a Spinal region reinforced by tendons.
b Enlarged detail of spine with criss-crossed solid bony tendons (**c**) fixed by ligaments to spines (**d**) rising from the vertebrae.

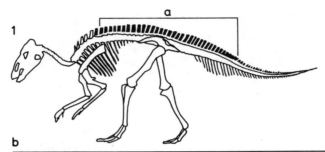

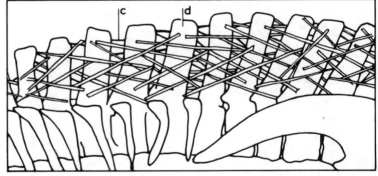

Balancers
Theropods like this ostrich dinosaur (**2**) held their tails aloft as balancers. The tails swung from side to side as they walked, but theropod tails moved more readily up and down than sideways. The tail's mass might have helped to stabilize a theropod that made tight turns. Long bony prongs stiffened the tail tips of ostrich dinosaurs, and dromaeosaurids had most of the tail stiffened by bony rods growing backward from the vertebrae.

©DIAGRAM

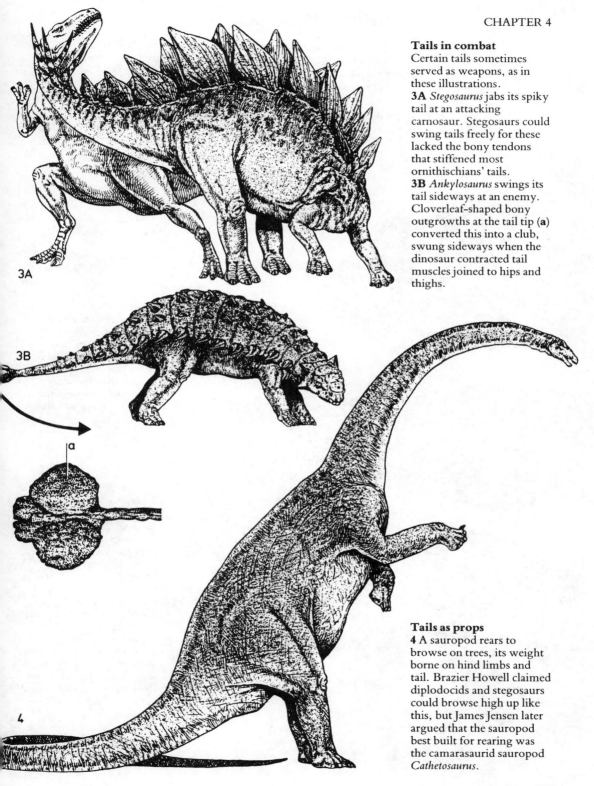

Tails in combat
Certain tails sometimes
served as weapons, as in
these illustrations.
3A *Stegosaurus* jabs its spiky
tail at an attacking
carnosaur. Stegosaurs could
swing tails freely for these
lacked the bony tendons
that stiffened most
ornithischians' tails.
3B *Ankylosaurus* swings its
tail sideways at an enemy.
Cloverleaf-shaped bony
outgrowths at the tail tip (**a**)
converted this into a club,
swung sideways when the
dinosaur contracted tail
muscles joined to hips and
thighs.

3A

3B

a

4

Tails as props
4 A sauropod rears to
browse on trees, its weight
borne on hind limbs and
tail. Brazier Howell claimed
diplodocids and stegosaurs
could browse high up like
this, but James Jensen later
argued that the sauropod
best built for rearing was
the camarasaurid sauropod
Cathetosaurus.

195

Skin and scales

Dinosaurs had thick, tough, scaly skin. Instead of overlapping like a fish's scales, dinosaur scales were round or many-sided bumps called tubercles. Large flat tubercles covered the belly, and in some ceratopsians and hadrosaurs formed rows or clusters on the back. Big theropods seemingly had big scales on the head, and bipeds had large leg scales like a bird's. Certain theropods and hadrosaurs probably sported frills or wattles, and small theropods might have had a covering of feathers as did their bird–dinosaur descendant *Archaeopteryx*. Bony plates floated in the armored skin of ankylosaurs and titanosaurid sauropods.

Two kinds of scales
Two lizards illustrate two types of horny scales found as body covering in living and prehistoric reptiles.
1 Spiny lizard, a reptile with scales that overlap like the tiles on a roof.
2 Gila monster, a reptile with scales consisting of non-overlapping horny tubercles set in the skin. Fossil skin impressions suggest that dinosaurs' scales were designed more like a Gila monster's than a spiny lizard's.

Tyrannosaurid scales
A museum restoration suggests that the scaly head of *Tyrannosaurus* might have looked like this. The scales are guesswork, though, and might have varied more in size and shape. *Carnotaurus*'s skin impressions, the best from any theropod, reveal that that dinosaur's head scales were mainly small tubercles but with rows of big raised scales forming patterns on the upper snout and around the eyes. Quite possibly *Tyrannosaurus* also had "display" scales around the eyes and nostrils and in other prominent positions.

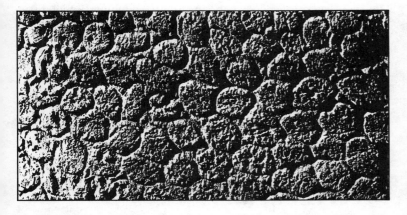

Skin impressions
Some dinosaur skins left
their impressions in fine-
grained sediments that later
hardened into rocks.
Top left: Impression left
by a duck-billed dinosaur's
leathery skin with horny
tubercles that formed a
raised pebbled pattern.
Hadrosaur skin impressions
include clustered larger
bumps that might have had
distinctive colors. Some
hadrosaurs had rows of big
bumps on the hips and
belly.
Left: Feather impressions
from the wings
of the bird dinosaur
Archaeopteryx survive in
fine-grained limestone long
quarried for making
lithographic plates. In the
1980s museum scientists
disproved a claim that the
feather impressions had
been fraudulently added to
the fossil bones.

Feathered dinosaurs?
Below: The small theropod
Syntarsus is sometimes
shown with feathered head
crest and short feathers
covering the body. Some
scientists think all small
theropods had an insulating
covering of feathers. Were
they warm-blooded,
feathers would have helped
them keep an even body
temperature. Yet no
feathered dinosaur is
known apart from
Archaeopteryx, usually
thought of as a bird.

© DIAGRAM

197

Color and camouflage

Dinosaurs were most likely colored or patterned much as living reptiles, birds, and mammals are. Small agile dinosaurs might have been as colorful as parrots, and, in the breeding season, large males might have shown off brightly colored heads, crests, or frills; some lizards do. But many dinosaurs were doubtless camouflaged to hide

Spotted like a leopard
A leopard's spots break up its outline so it blends with the light and shade beneath trees. A spotted pattern similarly could have camouflaged dinosaurs that lived in areas of broken light and shade.

Countershading
Dark back and pale belly make an antelope more difficult to see in sunlit open countryside. Countershading similarly might have helped to camouflage those dinosaurs living outside shady forests.

them from their enemies. Spotted babies and striped or spotted adults could have stood unseen in dappled glades until they moved. But the largest dinosaurs were probably the same drab grays you see in elephants and crocodiles.

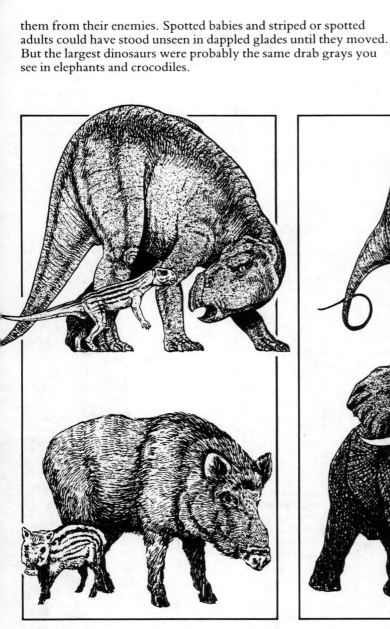

Stripy young
Pale and dark stripes conceal vulnerable wild boar piglets in the broken light of woodlands. Stripes similarly might have helped conceal this *Psittacosaurus* baby if it lived in sun-splashed glades.

Drab giants
The African elephant relies for protection more on tusks and bulk than camouflage. Sauropods were also probably drab gray. Like elephants, though, even such giants could be hard to see under shady trees.

Keeping warm

To stay active, dinosaurs needed to keep comfortably warm. If they were cold-blooded like lizards they controlled body temperature by moving in or out of sun or shade. If they were warm-blooded like birds and mammals their bodies' tissues "burned" food to heat and energize their bodies, and a thermostat in the brain prevented overheating. This way small theropods quite likely kept warm day and night, so always had the energy for chasing or escaping enemies. But sheer size would have kept big dinosaurs warm even had they been cold-blooded. Warmed by sunshine, their huge bodies would have stored heat through the night, and most lived where cold winters were unknown.

Body temperatures
Left: Plotted on this thermometer are the known normal/ideal body temperatures of a bird, mammal, and living reptile and likely normal/ideal temperatures of two types of dinosaur.
1 Ostrich 102.6°F (39.2°C)
2 Man 98.6°F (37.0°C)
3 Crocodile 78.1°F (25.6°C)
4 Ostrich dinosaur
5 Sauropod
Items **4–5** assume that birdlike theropods were warm-blooded with a high rate of energy expenditure like birds, while sauropods were cold-blooded creatures like crocodiles.

Warming and cooling
Right: Three temperature lines show the effects of body size on change in body temperature among cold blooded animals between a hot day and a cool night.
A Small alligator.
B Medium-sized alligator.
C Big dinosaur if it were a cold-blooded reptile like an alligator. The dinosaur shows the most constant body temperature, because its surface area is the smallest compared to body volume. Small creatures with a large surface area quickly warm up and cool down all through.

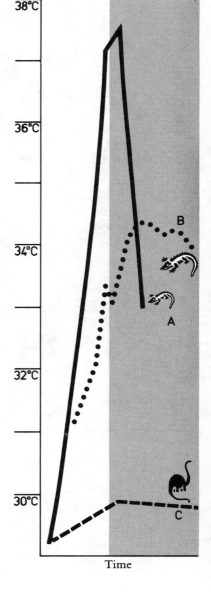

1

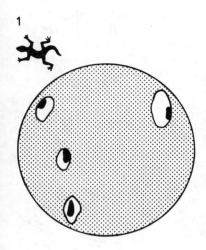

Blood and bone
Left: Three creatures with enlarged sections through a piece of bone from each.
1 Living reptile
2 Dinosaur
3 Mammal
2 and **3** feature rings of bony tissue surrounding blood vessels. Such so-called Haversian systems are numerous in living warm-blooded animals. Because the rings also occur in dinosaur bone some scientists say these must have been warm-blooded. Yet cold-blooded animals contain several bone types also seen in dinosaurs.

2

Basking (*above right*)
A This lizard warms up by basking in sunshine.
B To avoid overheating the warmed lizard moves into the shade. If dinosaurs were cold-blooded animals they might have moved between sun and shade to keep their bodies comfortably warm.

3

Heat exchangers?
Right: Sails or flat plates jutting up from their backs probably helped some dinosaurs to warm up and cool down.
C If *Spinosaurus* stood sideways to the Sun many rays warmed the blood coursing from its skin sail through its body.
D If *Spinosaurus* stood with its back to the Sun, few rays warmed its sail, so its blood did not heat up.

A

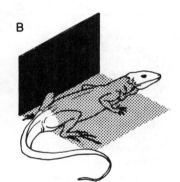

B

C

D

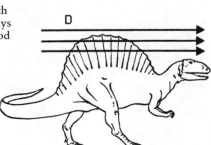

Moving around

Fossil tracks prove conclusively that dinosaurs stood, walked, and ran with limbs held underneath the body. Tracks also reveal where, when, and how sauropods, theropods, hadrosaurs and others moved and rested on the muddy rims of lakes. Big herbivores including sauropods evidently often walked in herds, with tails

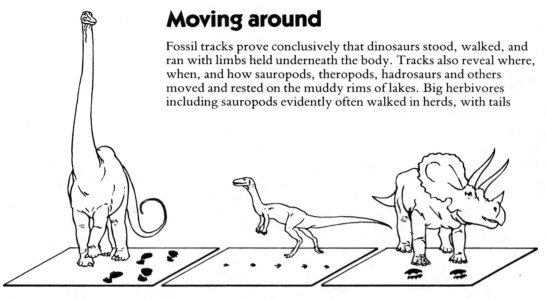

Sauropod tracks

Washtub-sized depressions left by elephantine feet in mud now hardened into rock show where sauropods once roamed. Finds from Texas and elsewhere hint that sauropods and other herbivores had trudged in herds, some seemingly on seasonal migration.

Theropod tracks

Predatory dinosaurs large and small left birdlike tracks on muddy shores of lakes and rivers in the Connecticut Valley and elsewhere in the world. Probably some scavenged corpses washed ashore and others ambushed herbivores that came to take a drink.

Clues to stance

The left and right feet of horned dinosaurs and others left parallel tracks close together. Matched with fossil skeletons, these tracks confirm the supposition that dinosaurs stood and walked with limbs held below the body, not sprawling as in lizards.

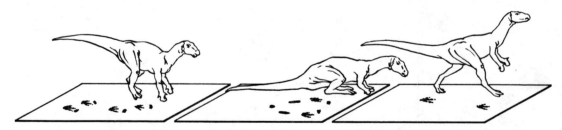

Tails aloft

Tracks left by ornithopods, some sauropods, and other dinosaurs often show no groove left by a dragging tail. These creatures held the tail aloft to balance the body and prevent the tail being trodden on by other members of the herd.

Sitting down

Besides footprints, dinosaurs left other marks as clues to their behavior. Some hint at where a dinosaur sat down to rest or doze or roll in mud to rid its hide of parasites, or where a theropod once lay in wait for prey.

Walking

Tracks with short distances between footprints indicate dinosaurs at slow speeds. By no means every theropod moved leisurely, but all the traces left by sauropods suggest these monsters always ambled and were never in a hurry.

aloft. Running dinosaurs left footprints far apart: the faster the dinosaur, the greater the gaps. One such set of tracks suggests that large theropods could run at 25mph (40kph). Proofs that sauropods and theropods could swim are fossil tracks where a limb served as a punter's pole to push off from a lake bed.

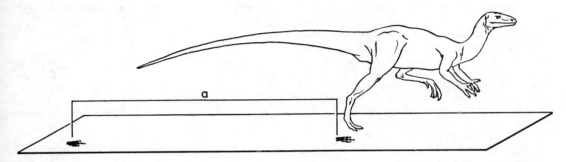

Running
Trackways help scientists to calculate the sizes and the speeds of running dinosaurs. Small prints usually indicate small animals, and the greater the stride length (**a**) the faster an animal was moving. Measuring an Early Jurassic trackway found in Arizona revealed that an ornithopod or theropod no heavier than a whippet had sprinted as quickly as a horse can gallop. Some dinosaurologists believe even the tyrannosaurids attained such speeds as they ran to the attack.

Swimming
Incomplete footprints suggest that dinosaurs sometimes swam.
A The theropod *Dilophosaurus* left birdlike footprints on land, but claw-tip prints seem to show where this dinosaur touched bottom as it swam across a pool. Swimming theropods probably waggled the tail and kicked back with the legs.
B Forefeet tracks show where a swimming sauropod's hind end was buoyed up by water as it poled its way across a lake. A hindfoot print marks where the big herbivore kicked off to change direction.

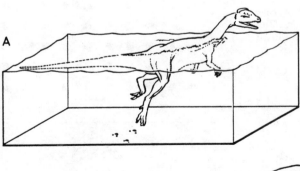

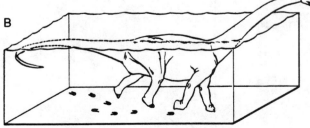

©DIAGRAM

Feeding

Sauropods and ornithischians browsed high or low according to neck length or ability to rear, or both. High-feeding sauropods maybe cropped all leaves and twigs in reach, cutting a distinctive browse-line through the trees. Broad-muzzled herbivores were unfussy eaters; narrow-mouthed beasts ate more choosily. All beat

Food chains

Any animal community has food chains of eaters and eaten. Interlinked chains form a food web. This diagram shows who ate whom or what in Late Cretaceous western North America. Arrows point to food items. Top predators were the tyrannosaurids, but all dinosaurs depended in the end on plants.

a Tyrannosaurids
b Dromaeosaurids
c Ornithomimids
d Hadrosaurs
e Ceratopsians
f Ankylosaurs
g Pachycephalosaurs
h Lizards
i Insects
j Plants

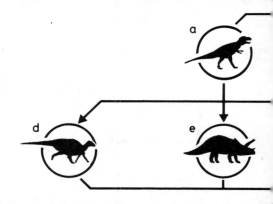

Food pyramid

Percentages of flesh-eating and plant-eating dinosaurs in Late Cretaceous Alberta. Flesh-eaters in any animal community form a pyramid top supported by a broad base of plant-eaters. A tiny top can mean flesh-eaters are warm-blooded. But our diagram draws on fossil finds that might give a false impression.

○ Carnivores
● Herbivores

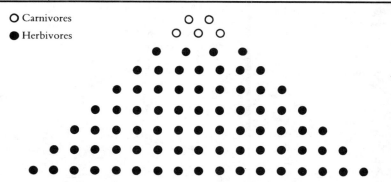

Feeding high and low

A A sauropod – a long-necked dinosaur – rears to crop leafy twigs high above the ground. Most big herbivores were high browsers in Late Jurassic times.

B A horned dinosaur – a short-necked herbivore – eats fronds no higher than its head. Big herbivores were mainly low browsers by Late Cretaceous times.

©DIAGRAM

paths through forests, creating clearings where small dinosaurs could feed. The big herbivores formed food for large theropods. Small theropods ate smaller plant-eaters, also birds and lizards. Each dinosaur's droppings spread or fertilized plant seeds. So new plants grew and kept the dinosaurs' food cycle going.

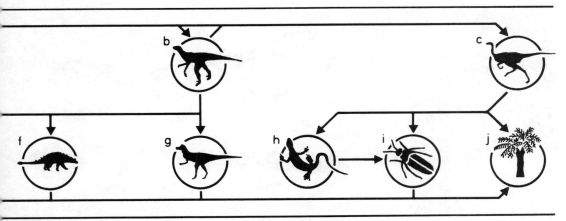

Food requirements

The diagram shows how long different carnivorous beasts take to eat their own weight in food. All but the lizard (**a**) are warm-blooded.

a Komodo dragon
b Cheetah
c Lion
d Wild dog

If they were cold-blooded, flesh-eating dinosaurs had an appetite like **a**, if warm-blooded, like **b**, **c**, or **d**.

a | 60 days

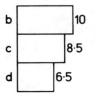

b | 10
c | 8·5
d | 6·5

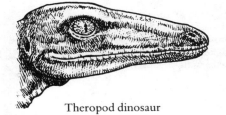

Theropod dinosaur

Wide and narrow mouths

Broad-beaked dinosaurs like *Edmontosaurus* (**1**) and *Euoplocephalus* (**2**) bit off mixed mouthfuls of plants while narrow-beaked dinosaurs like *Anicheratops* (**3**) cropped more choosily. Low-feeding dinosaurs might have helped fast-growing flowering plants to spread at the expense of older forms of vegetation.

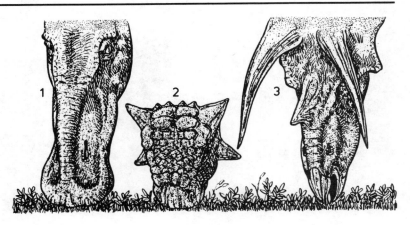

Attack

Theropods had methods of attack that varied with their size, agility, and victims. Small predators chased lizards, seized them in sharp-clawed hands, and swallowed them head first. Hunters from *Deinonychus* up to *Allosaurus* and even *Tyrannosaurus* probably roamed in packs, creeping up on big plant-eaters then killing with a

High-speed chase
Compsognathus and other lightweight theropods chased small game at speed. Each agile hunter grabbed prey with its clawed hands or thrust out its long neck and snapped up lizards, birds, and mammals with its narrow, sharp-toothed jaws.

Slashing claws
Members of a *Deinonychus* pack could have brought down dinosaurs much larger than themselves, just as wild dogs topple zebras. As some grappled with the victim's tail to slow it down, others could have kicked out, savaging its belly with their claws.

Counterattack
A *Triceratops* at full tilt could have driven off *Tyrannosaurus* as today a charging rhino might deter a lion. Counterattack could well have served as a deterrent for other ceratopsians: some as heavy as an elephant, most with two long brow horns or one long horn jutting from the snout.

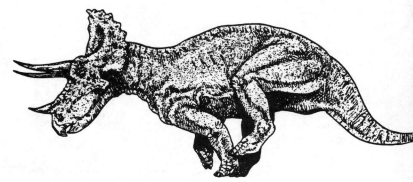

sudden rush. Theropods struck mainly with their fangs, but sharp toe and finger claws could grip or slash at prey. *Baryonyx* might have seized fish in its crocodile-like jaws, but toothless theropods seem ill equipped for catching anything but insects or digging up and eating eggs of other dinosaurs.

Crushing bite
Strange, short-headed *Oviraptor* ("egg thief") lacked teeth for biting prey. Yet two sharp teeth pointed down from the roof of its mouth. These might have crushed the shells of other dinosaurs' eggs, as a sharp bone in the neck helps an egg-eating snake to crush the birds' eggs that it swallows.

Sudden snatch
Baryonyx's crocodile-like head, and fish scales found lying where one specimen's stomach would have been suggest this dinosaur fished like storks or bears. It could have stood in ambush, then seized fish in its sharp-toothed jaws or scooped them up with its claws.

Headlong charge
Immense jaws gaping wide, *Tyrannosaurus* could have run at hadrosaurs head on. Powerful muscles slammed its jaws shut and fangs took out a massive chunk of flesh from the victims' vulnerable necks. These creatures then quickly weakened and collapsed.

©DIAGRAM

Defense

Each group of dinosaurs had some way of coping with flesh-eating enemies. Sheer bulk and traveling in herds helped protect those big plant-eaters the sauropods and horned and duck-billed dinosaurs. Ostrich dinosaurs and hypsilophodontids relied upon a speedy getaway. Scelidosaurs, stegosaurs, armored dinosaurs and titanosaurid sauropods relied on tough skins reinforced by tooth-

Body armor
Four-legged ornithischians evolved increasingly effective body armor.
A Scelidosaurs: rows of bony studs down the back.
B Stegosaurs: bony spines or plates on back; tail and shoulder spines.
C Ankylosaurs: bands of horn-sheathed bony plates. Nodosaurids had long flank spines as in the head-on view of one below.
D Ceratopsians: nose and brow horns and bony frill covering the neck.

Speed
This skeleton and restoration of an ostrich dinosaur stress limb design giving a rapid escape from enemies.
A Relative lengths of hind limb bones suggest ability to sprint.
a Short femur
b Long shin bones
c Long metatarsal bones
d Long phalanges
B An ostrich dinosaur at high speed. Besides running fast its muscular legs could have delivered deadly kicks.

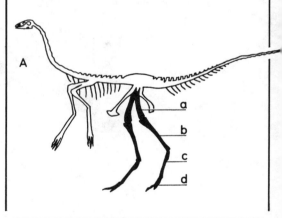

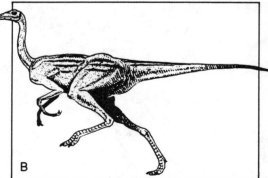

snapping bony studs and plates. Some plant-eaters even counter-attacked. *Triceratops* charged like a rhinoceros. *Iguanodon* stabbed with its spiky thumb claws. Diplodocids used their tails as whips. *Shunosaurus* and ankylosaurids wielded heavy tail clubs, and stegosaurs swung tails as spiky as a medieval mace.

Toe and thumb claws
Sauropods might have used the large claws on their thumbs and big toes as defensive weapons.
A *Camarasaurus* toe bones show the long claw on the big toe. A backward kick with the hind foot might have gored a marauder.
B A rearing *Diplodocus* brandishes its pointed thumb claws at a threatening *Allosaurus*. If *Diplodocus* lunged it might have stabbed and crushed the predator.

Tails
Areas shown in gray are weapons furnished by three types of tail.
A Bony club – a feature first seen in the sauropod *Shunosaurus* but best developed in ankylosaurid ornithischians. Here bones embedded in skin fused with tail vertebrae as in the ankylosaurid below.
B Bony tail spikes – seen in stegosaurids.
C Whiplash – the tapered tail of diplodocid and titanosaurid sauropods.

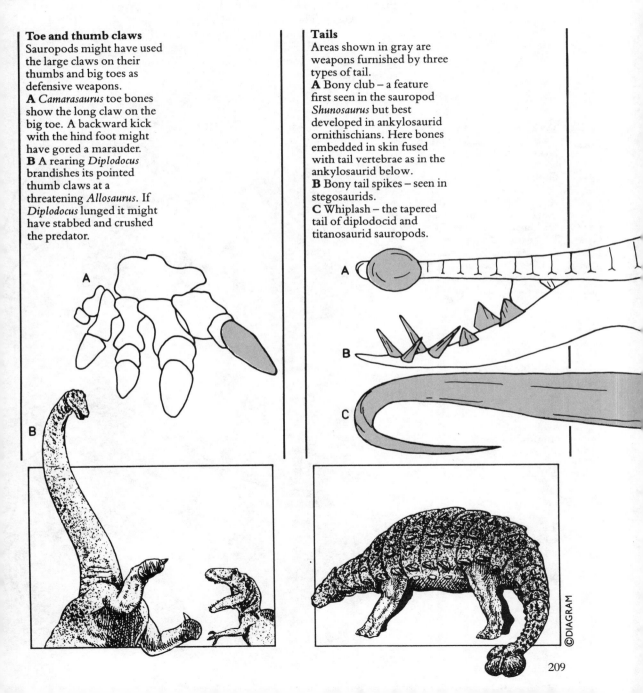

©DIAGRAM

Winning a mate

Male birds, mammals, and even fish and reptiles win mates by attracting females and repelling rival males. So it must have been with dinosaurs. Many males were very likely larger and more showy than females of their kind. The biggest lambeosaurid crests and carnosaur hornlets probably belonged to males. Tuskless *Abrictosaurus* was arguably a female *Heterodontosaurus*, and some say high-domed bone-heads were all males while low-domed forms were females. The males' horns and crests probably intimidated rivals, but sometimes duels decided which male mated with and ruled a herd of females. Bone-heads butted one another, dromaeosaurids could have sparred with toe claws, and ceratopsians locked horns.

Tusks and no tusks
Two pairs of heads hint that tusks marked a difference between sexes in some dinosaurs as well as in some living mammals.
A Male (**a**) and female (**b**) musk deer. The male alone has long curved tusks.
B The tusked dinosaur *Heterodontosaurus* (**a**) and tuskless *Abrictosaurus* (**b**) might have been a male and female of the same genus.

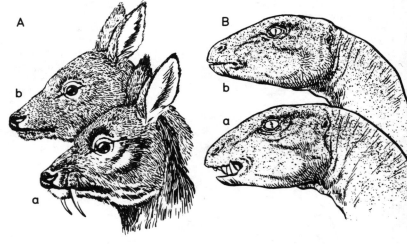

Flamboyant headgear
Two more pairs of heads suggest that showy outgrowths marked a difference between sexes in certain dinosaurs as well as in some living mammals.
C Red deer stag (**a**) and (**b**) hind. Only the stag grows antlers.
D *Lambeosaurus* male (**a**) and female (**b**). Both had a crest but the male's was much more prominent than the female's.

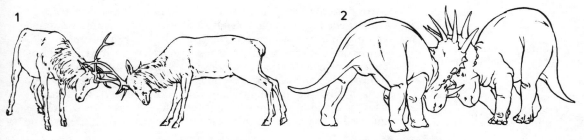

Locking horns
Similar scenes of combat
(1–2) hint that some male
dinosaurs might have
fought like stags to win
mastery over females.

1 Red-deer stags lock
antlers, twist heads, and
shove against each other.
Whichever pushes harder
tends to win the fight and
dominate the herd.

2 *Styracosaurus* males
perhaps clashed the horns
projecting from their bony
frills or merely brandished
these to scare off would-be
rivals.

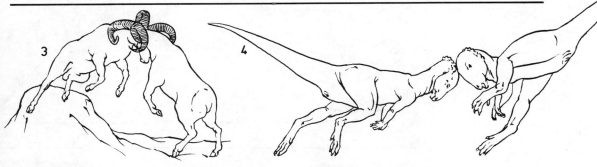

Banging heads
Two more combat scenes
(3–4) suggest a different
kind of duel in which male
mammals could have had a
dinosaur counterpart.

3 Male bighorn rams run at
one another, rear, and bash
their heads together.
Reinforced skulls prevent
these savage impacts
damaging their brains.

4 Male bone-headed
dinosaurs also evidently
used their heads as battering
rams to win a herd of
females. Thick skulls
minimized injury.

Clawing contests
A third pair of duels (5–6)
depicts a type of contest
where male birds probably
still fight as lightweight
theropods did.

5 Fighting gamecocks leap
at one another, stabbing
viciously with the long
sharp claws called spurs (in
cockfights sheathed in bone
or metal).

6 Male dromaeosaurids
very likely also fought like
that. Swinging its second
toe claws forward each
could strike slashing blows
at a rival.

©DIAGRAM

Eggs

Most dinosaurs evidently hatched from rounded or elongated hard-shelled eggs weighing up to 15lb 7oz (7kg) – any larger and an egg might break or suffocate the young inside. Prosauropod, sauropod, ornithopod, or ceratopsian eggs have come from almost every continent. Different species laid on bare ground, in sandy hollows they then covered with sand, and in nests with raised mud rims. There were nesting colonies of hadrosaurs in Alberta and Montana, and of *Protoceratops* in Mongolia. Mothers very likely guarded eggs until the Sun's heat hatched them.

Safety in numbers
Maiasaura mothers built their giant nests each 7ft (2m) across, almost in pecking distance of one another. Such guarded colonies were safe from almost any predator.

Largest egg
A Life-size sauropod egg, probably *Hypselosaurus*'s: length 1ft (30cm); diameter 10in (25cm); capacity 5.8pt (3.3l). No egg much larger could have hatched.
B Life-size chicken's egg shown for comparison.

A

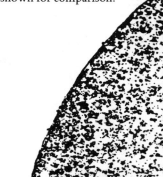

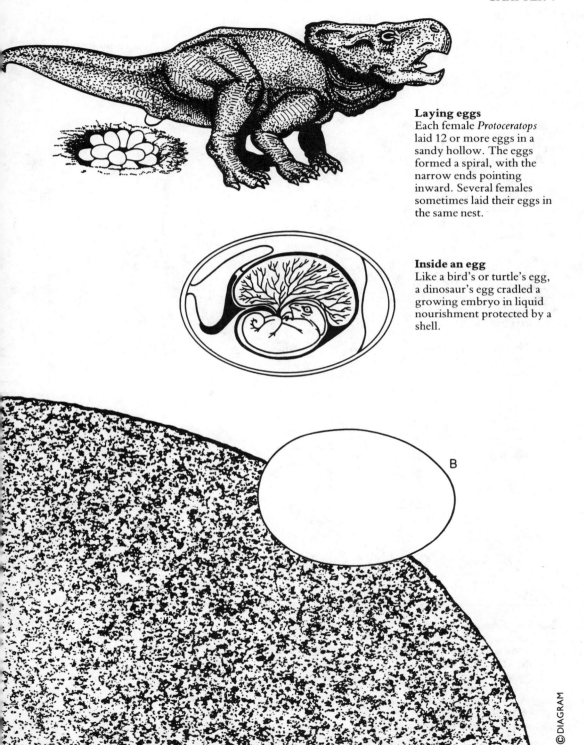

Laying eggs
Each female *Protoceratops* laid 12 or more eggs in a sandy hollow. The eggs formed a spiral, with the narrow ends pointing inward. Several females sometimes laid their eggs in the same nest.

Inside an egg
Like a bird's or turtle's egg, a dinosaur's egg cradled a growing embryo in liquid nourishment protected by a shell.

B

©DIAGRAM

Young dinosaurs

Fossil embryos, hatchlings, and adolescents tell us much about how dinosaurs grew up. Hatchlings were quite tiny – as little as one-sixteen-thousandth their mothers' size. Hatchling hadrosaurs had legs too weak to forage, and mothers evidently fed them in the nest. But well-developed limb bones suggest that even baby

Egg and infant
A prosauropod egg and baby from Argentina reveal that some kinds of dinosaur began life very small indeed.
A Egg (shown actual size) found in a nest with the remains of tiny dinosaurs.
B *Mussaurus* skeleton, one of five or six from the same nest as the egg. None was longer than 8in (20cm) – no larger than a thrush. Puppylike outsize eyes, knees, and feet prove these creatures had died still in infancy. Their parents might have been as much as 10ft (3m) long.

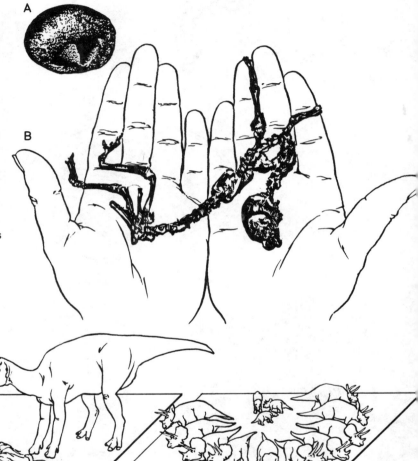

Feeding young
A *Maiasaura* mother brings plant food to her young. Scientists think this could have happened because they found young hadrosaurs' skeletons at a nest. About 3ft 3in (1m) long, these individuals showed signs of tooth wear yet their limb bones were not strong enough for foraging. Very likely, then, their mother had been feeding them before they left the nest as most birds feed their chicks before these fly.

Protecting young
Horned dinosaurs (not shown to the same scale as the adult *Maiasaura*) could have formed an outward-facing ring to shield their young from marauding theropods, as musk-oxen face out to deter wolves.

hypsilophodontids fed themselves. Baby dinosaurs had relatively bigger heads and eyes than adults, although relatively shorter limbs, necks, tails, crests, horns, frills, or plates. At least some parents guarded their young, and seemingly all juveniles grew fast. Despite that few of them survived to reach full size.

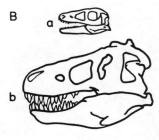

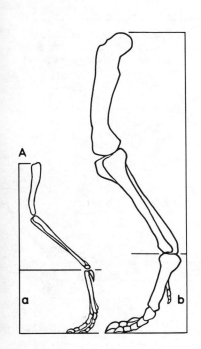

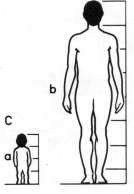

Changing proportions

Certain bodily proportions changed with age in dinosaurs as others do in man.

A Changes in the hind limb of tyrannosaurids.

a Young, with relatively long ankle region.

b Adult, with relatively short ankle region

B Changes in tyrannosaurids' skulls.

a Young, with relatively big round eye socket, and slim snout and jaws.

b Adult, with relatively smaller eye socket, and deep snout and jaws.

C Changes in proportions of a human head and body.

a Newborn baby, with head one-quarter total length.

b Adult, with head one-eighth total length.

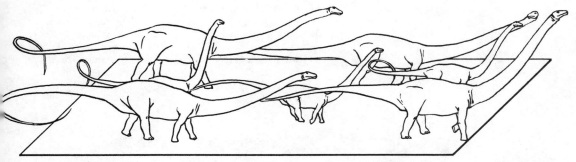

On the march

Sauropods evidently marched in herds like elephants, with adults guarding vulnerable young. Evidence includes the distribution of large and small footprints in a trackway found in Texas.

How and when young joined a herd remains in doubt. Some experts think they were born on the march. Others argue that they came from eggs laid in the ground, but surely these would have hatched after the herd had moved on.

Life expectancy

How long a dinosaur could live is guesswork. Growth rings in certain bones and teeth suggest at least 120 years. If dinosaurs were warm-blooded, big sauropods might have reached that age; if cold-blooded, 200 years or more. But injury or disease killed most before extreme old age. Many fossils show bones broken by a

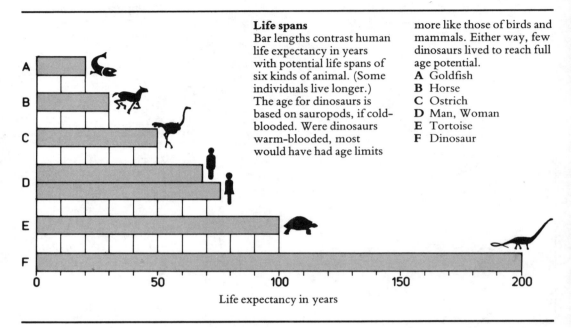

Life spans
Bar lengths contrast human life expectancy in years with potential life spans of six kinds of animal. (Some individuals live longer.) The age for dinosaurs is based on sauropods, if cold-blooded. Were dinosaurs warm-blooded, most would have had age limits more like those of birds and mammals. Either way, few dinosaurs lived to reach full age potential.
A Goldfish
B Horse
C Ostrich
D Man, Woman
E Tortoise
F Dinosaur

Life expectancy in years

Diseased bones
Diplodocus tail bones seen below show signs of damage by ankylosing spondylitis.
a Normal joint between two tail bones.
b Joints fused by bony overgrowth.

Restricting movement of affected joints, fusion made this tail useless as a defensive whip and laid its owner open to attack. So even non-fatal diseases could indirectly kill.

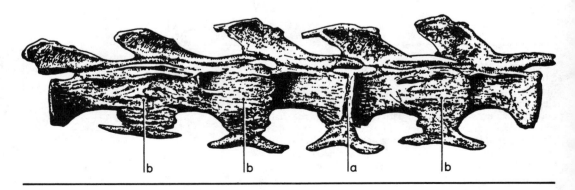

fall or fighting, or damaged by infections, tumors, or arthritis. Twisted skeletons hint at sauropods that died of thirst and dried up in droughts. Fossil–hunters have found horned and armored dinosaurs smothered by windblown sands, and herds of horned and duck–billed dinosaurs drowned by river floods.

Duel to the death
This restoration based on the positions of two skeletons reminds us that death often came to dinosaurs with violence. A flesh-eating *Velociraptor* (**a**) died gripping the head shield of a plant-eating *Protoceratops* (**b**) and kicking out with savage toe claws. Meanwhile the *Protoceratops* had evidently used its armored head to smash through the *Velociraptor*'s chest. Both creatures then perished locked in combat.

Death by drought?
Contorted neck and tail bones indicate this ostrich dinosaur dried out after death, so that ligaments and muscles shrank, pulling on its spine. Many dinosaurs are found like this, including even sauropods. Some scientists think all died in droughts severe enough to kill off scavengers that would have smashed and jumbled up the bones.

Chapter 5

DINOSAURS WORLDWIDE

This global look at dinosaurs starts with how their fossils formed and can be found; how paleontologists dig up fossils and describe them; and how museum experts clean bones, preserve them, and connect them to rebuild whole skeletons. Remaining pages survey the world's fossil dinosaurs continent by continent and nation by nation, with lists of dinosaur discoveries and details of dinosaur collections. Experts from scores of museums around the world have helped us make this section up to date.

Opinions differ, so a few listed distributions may differ slightly from those elsewhere in this book. Note, too, some museum exhibits are casts, some bear invalid names, and not all listed items are on show.

Above: A nineteenth-century visitor to Amherst College's "Appleton Cabinet" inspects track-imprinted stone slabs from the Connecticut Valley. Amherst, Massachusetts, still boasts one of the best of all collections of dinosaur footprints.
Below: Chinese marvel at the *Mamenchisaurus* skeleton in Beijing's Museum of Natural History.

How dinosaurs were fossilized

Proof that dinosaurs once roamed the world comes from **fossils** – remains of long-dead living things preserved in rocks. Maybe only one in a million dinosaurs became a fossil; the rest entirely vanished soon after death, gobbled up by other dinosaurs or decomposed by billions of bacteria.

Most dinosaur fossils come from individuals that died in or near a river, lake, or sea. (Some come from creatures that fell in fissures or were overwhelmed by desert sands.) Often, a drowned dinosaur settled on the bed of a lake or sea or drifted downstream until it lodged against a sandbank. Either way, the soft parts – skin and muscles – quickly rotted, but sometimes sand or mud had time to cover and protect the hard parts: teeth and bones. This kept out oxygen needed by the bacteria that bring about decay. Yet water full of dissolved minerals could penetrate the tiny pores in bone, and holes left by rotted collagen. As the saturated water shed its mineral load, the hollow bones gained a hard, heavy filling of calcite, iron sulfide, or silica. This **permineralization** process reinforced the bones, and made them able to resist the great weight of mud or sand slowly building up above. Sometimes minerals replaced the bone itself until the bone was turned to stone or

Fossil factory
Numbered diagrams show processes that formed and exposed a fossil dinosaur.
1 A dead dinosaur lies on an underwater sandbank.
2 Flesh decays revealing the bony skeleton.
3 River mud buries the bones, preventing decay.
4 Mud layers accumulate above the bones and water seeping from above deposits minerals that harden them. Around this fossil mud becomes rock.
5 Raised by a shift in the Earth's crust, the rocks are worn away by weather that lays bare the fossil.

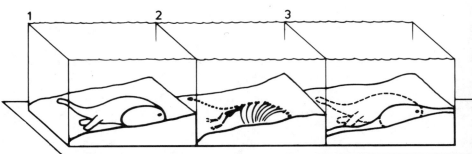

Four fossil clues
Small letters indicate four kinds of fossil evidence of dinosaurs.
a Ichnites: fossil footprints, formed in soft wet mud that hardened before water washed the prints away. Ichnogenera are fossil creatures named from distinctive ichnites.
b Coprolites: fossilized droppings. Some hint at the size of dinosaurs' intestines.
c Fossilized scaly skin or skin impressions, formed in dry conditions.
d Ooliths: fossil eggs. Eggs of various dinosaurs occur worldwide.

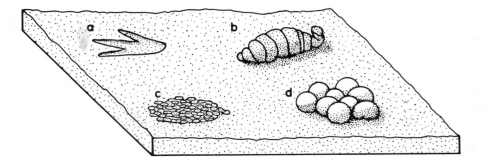

petrified. Teeth – the hardest parts of all – often tended to survive with little change at all.

Certain minerals dissolved some bones but left bone-shaped hollows. Hollow fossils of this kind are **molds**. A mold that was later filled by other minerals became a **cast**. Some molds or casts even show a dinosaur's scaly skin.

Besides bones, teeth, and skin impressions, dinosaurs left other traces. These **trace fossils** include **fossil footprints** left in lakeside mud that dried out in the sun. Fossil trackways can show where dinosaurs walked on two or four limbs, trudged or sprinted, and traveled singly or in herds. Then, too, certain creatures' **coprolites** (fossil droppings) are molds that show the shape of the intestines.

For millions of years, thick beds of sand or mud piled up above fossils dating from the Age of Dinosaurs. Beds pressing down on those beneath squeezed these into thinner layers, hardened into rock by natural cements. In time the Earth's crust heaved slowly, crumpling and shoving up as mountains rock layers laid down under water. Rain, sun, and frost at once began to gnaw down the mountains, slowly laying bare their cores. So, bit by bit, weather shows up ancient rock beds and their fossil treasures.

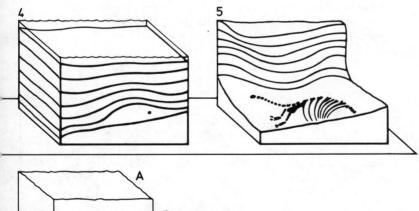

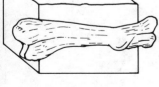

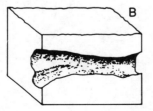

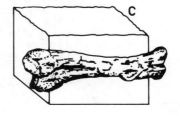

Mold and cast
In some conditions rock contains a dinosaur bone (**A**) that dissolves and leaves a bone-shaped hole or mold (**B**). If minerals then fill the mold the product is a bone-shaped cast (**C**).

©DIAGRAM

221

Discovery and excavation

Fossil dinosaurs have now been found in every continent, but only certain lands are rich in their remains. These areas have four ingredients. First, their rocks were formed from sediments – they did not well up molten from the Earth's interior, and heat and pressure have not melted or crushed their fossils. Second, the sedimentary rocks are of the right kinds, for instance sandstone, mudstone, or limestone laid down in deserts, or in swamps, lakes, deltas, or shallow coastal seas where the corpses of land animals could drift before they sank. Third, the rocks date from about 230 to 65 million years ago, within the Mesozoic Era. Fourth, the rocks lie exposed. That rules out rocks hidden under other rocks or under plants, soil, ice, or water; rocks rotted by hot, humid climates; and rocks that have been completely worn away.

Most finds occur where unusually severe erosion lays bare Mesozoic sediments. Sea cliffs can prove fruitful hunting grounds, and fossil hunters scour likely quarries, and road and railroad cuttings, holes dug for building foundations, and waste from certain coalmines. But the richest hunting grounds are the deserts and semideserts of North and South America, Central and East Asia, and North Africa.

Sometimes, people stumble on a dinosaur boneyard by chance. The first finds are often due to stockmen or road or railroad engineers. Amateur fossil hunters have also made spectacular discoveries. Meanwhile, paleontologists armed with geological maps systematically scour likely rock exposures.

Mesozoic rocks
Black areas on this world map are rocks dating from the Age of Dinosaurs. But not all areas of Mesozoic rock bear fossil dinosaurs and some that do are too small to appear here.

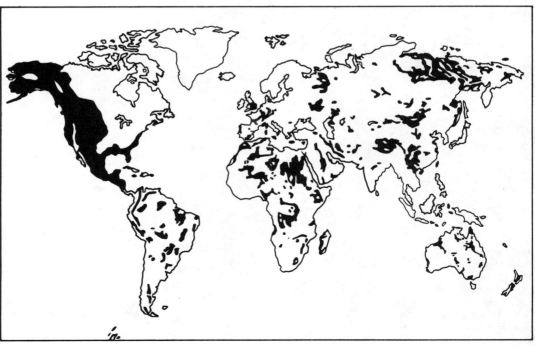

©DIAGRAM

Experienced hunters scan slopes and gullies for fossils washed down from above. Their first find is often an isolated fossil no bigger than your thumb – a bit of bone that most of us would think was just a shiny or spongy-looking stone. Identifying dinosaurs from scraps like this is difficult, and even scientists have made mistakes. For instance they mistook fossil mollusk borings for the jawbone of a "dinosaur" they called *Succinodon*. Unfortunately many a dinosaur is never known by more than fragments, for scavengers or floods have scattered or destroyed its other bones.

Sometimes, though, the slope above the first find yields much of a skeleton still stuck in rock. A paleontologist tries to dig around the bones to judge the fossil's state and size; but freeing a large dinosaur from its rocky tomb may require the services of a team of experts and their workers. Power hammers, bulldozers, and explosives help them strip away hard overlying rock. Picks and shovels will remove soft and crumbly rock. (You can simply brush away the sand covering some Saharan Desert dinosaurs.) Careful scraping and chiseling begin as a team homes in on brittle bones.

Scientists number and photograph the bared bones, and plot exactly where they lie. Then they spray resin or paint glue on fragile bones to harden them. Plastic foam cushions big bones or bones in lumps of rock, or these are jacketed in sackcloth soaked in plaster. Now the frail trophies are ready to withstand a bumpy truck ride across rough tracks to a museum.

Fossil hunters' tools
1 Rucksack
2 Geological hammer
3 Bolster
4 Cold chisel
5 Geological map
6 Notebook
7 Marking pen
8 Punch
9 Trowel
10 Compass
11 Rule
12 Hand lens
13 Sticky tape
14 Pick
15 Plastic bags
16 Kitchen knife
17 Toothbrush
18 Shovel
19 Newspapers
20 Boxes
21 Paper tissues

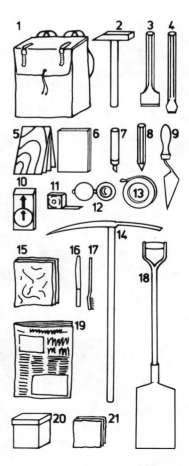

Fossil hunters' tools
This toolkit (*right*) features items that a paleontologist might use to recover, measure, record, and transport small fossil finds. Hard rock and large, fragile fossil bones call for extra gear.

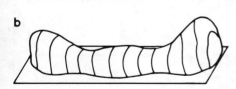
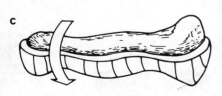
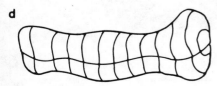

Recovering a big bone
a More than half of one side of a big dinosaur femur is freed from rock.
b Sackcloth bandages soaked in plaster of Paris cover wet paper packed around the exposed half.
c The hardening plaster forms a protective case, then all the bone is freed from rock and turned over.
d Next the other half is bandaged.

223

Dating fossil dinosaurs

Dinosaurs roamed the world for about 160 million years. All through that time new groups evolved and old ones disappeared. To understand which lived when, scientists must date the rocks formed when each group of creatures was alive.

Comparative dating tells us whether one kind of dinosaur lived before or after others. This method depends upon **stratigraphy** – studying exposed strata (layers) of sedimentary rocks such as mudstone and sandstone. Many a cliff or quarry is like a layer cake of rocks that formed from sediments laid down on top of one another over many million years. Each layer's fossil creatures lived when that layer was laid down, so a dinosaur found in the bottom of a cliff is likely to have lived much earlier than one found in the top. The snag is that most rock exposures show dinosaurs dating only from one time. Finding similar dinosaurs in two exposures far apart suggests the same age for both exposures; thus we know *Barosaurus* lived in North America and East Africa in Late Jurassic times. Scientists can also correlate (match) the relative ages of two whole sets of widely separated rock layers provided one layer in one set matches a layer in the other set. (The matching may be by rock type or a variety of fossil animals or plants, including fossil pollen.) Correlating strata like this helps paleontologists piece together the worldwide puzzle of which dinosaurs lived before or after others. Tantalizingly, the puzzle has many missing pieces.

Comparative dating involves examining rock layers in particular **formations** – mappable rock units given place names, for instance the Kayenta Formation of Early Jurassic rocks named for Kayenta in Arizona. Formations can be subdivided into smaller areas called **members** and **beds**; the latter are the smallest of all rock units.

Comparative dating
Similar dinosaurs from different regions help show relative ages of their rocks. In North America *Barosaurus* lies in Morrison Formation rocks (**1**), lower and older than the Lakota Sandstone (**2**) containing *Hypsilophodon*. This indirectly shows that Europe's Wealden rocks (**3**) are younger than rocks at Tendaguru (**4**) in East Africa.

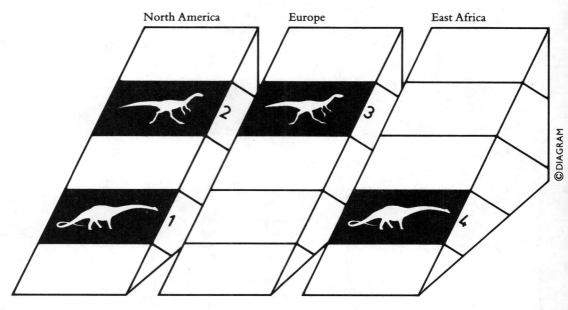

North America   Europe   East Africa

©DIAGRAM

Formations are also grouped in successively larger units called **subgroups**, **groups**, and **supergroups** (the Newark Supergroup of eastern North America is one dating from the Age of Dinosaurs).

Comparative dating merely tells us the relative ages of various dinosaurs, but **chronometric dating** attempts to show us how long ago they lived. **Radiometric dating** of certain rocks is the chronometric method used for dating fossils as ancient as the dinosaurs. Radiometric dating depends upon the regular rate of decay of a radioactive element into others. Half an element's substance decays into another element in one half-life, a time that varies with the kind of element. In potassium-argon dating, for example, half the potassium-40 isotope decays into a measurable amount of argon-40 in 1310 million years. Thus measuring the proportions of radioactive elements in rocks helps scientists calculate their age. This system works best with lava in which the geological clock began "ticking" from the time the molten lava cooled and set. Potassium-argon dating is also used for sedimentary rocks containing the mineral glauconite.

Working out a dinosaur's age can mean combining radiometric measurements of rare lava samples with comparative dating of the fossil-bearing beds between.

Radiometric dating
Potassium-argon dating depends on the steady radioactive decay of potassium-40.
A Amount of potassium-40 in newly formed rock.
B Amount after 1310 million years (one half-life).
C After 2620 million years (two half-lives)
D After 3930 million years (three half-lives).
E After 5240 million years (four half-lives).

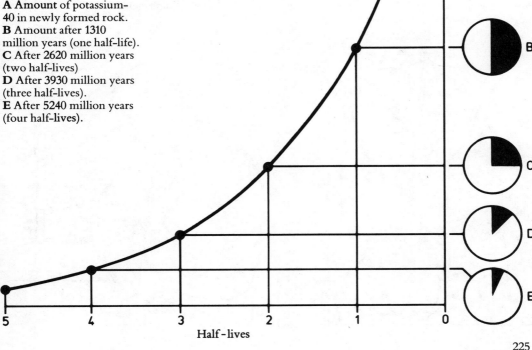

Half-lives

Preparing fossils

When fossil dinosaurs arrive at a museum, the work of studying their skeletons begins.

First somewhere must be found to house the bones – no easy task when a successful expedition brings back hundreds of colossal specimens.

Next, laboratory technicians known as **preparators** tackle the often tricky job of teasing out those fossil bones still stuck in chunks of rock. This process can take many months. Often it begins with soaking, sawing, and slicing off the hardened plaster jackets that saved specimens from damage on their journey from the place where they were found. Next, chemical solutions harden weak areas of exposed bone. Cushioning the rocky chunks against damage, preparators may then bring to bear an arsenal of power tools to free fossils from unwanted rock. They chip away with small pneumatic chisels, "sandblast" with abrasive powder fired by jets of gas, wield dental drills with diamond cutting wheels, or attack with vibropens whose fast-vibrating tips eat away hard rock as if it were soft cheese. Sewing needles, though, are often best for cleaning out small, fragile skulls.

Certain kinds of rock are best removed by soaking in dilute acetic acid. Over several months, acid baths dissolve away the rock but leave the fossil bones intact.

Some fossil dinosaurs are difficult to tackle in these ways – for instance embryos in stony, fossil eggs; skulls filled with solid stone;

Removing packing
A technician cuts away the plaster jacket that has protected a bone on its trip from excavation site to museum laboratory.

Removing rock
Powerful magnification helps this preparator wield a power tool with precision to free fragile bones from rock.

and skeletons buried deep in rocks almost too hard to excavate. Now, though, new techniques mean we can "see" these fossil objects without the need to touch or cut away their rocky cores or coverings. Devices used for taking human brainscans can scan a stone-filled dinosaur braincase, and indicate how well that animal could see, hear, smell, and think. X rays and CAT (computerized axial tomography) scans can also show unhatched baby dinosaurs inside their eggs. A special "radar" scanner from New Mexico's Los Alamos National Laboratories probed the hard rock tomb of **"Seismosaurus"**, seemingly detecting a monstrous skeleton still hidden underground.

Back in the laboratory, preparators do more than clean up fossils. They may need to guard them from decay. Exposed to humid air, some fossil bones soon crack and crumble to dust. This problem once threatened Belgium's famous herd of *Iguanodon*. The fossil bones contained "fool's gold" (iron pyrites). Early hardening treatment trapped moisture, prolonging damage done as hard iron pyrites slowly turned to powdery iron sulfate. Modern preparators treat "pyrite disease" with ethanolamine thioglycolate which neutralizes and removes the decay products.

Acid bath
Wearing protective mask and gloves, a preparator hauls a tray of bones from an acid bath. This has dissolved away the block of rock in which the bones had been embedded.

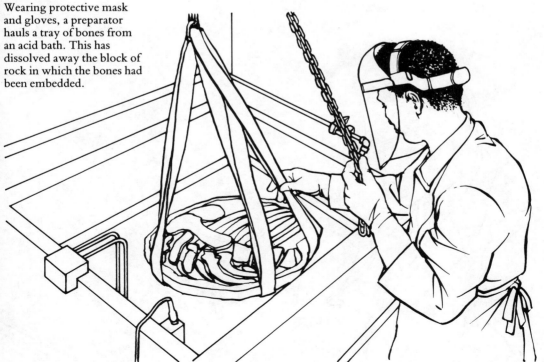

Understanding fossils

Cleaned, and maybe mended with a special glue, distinctive bones enable scientists to identify a dinosaur. Understanding how the bones had joined makes it possible to reconstruct the skeleton.

Study of a new kind of dinosaur means producing an illustrated article. First the scientist measures and describes the bones. Technical terms help the scientist name each bone and locate special features – ridges or hollows for example. Photographs and/or detailed drawings show key bones from several aspects – dorsal (from above), ventral (from below), medial (from the inside), lateral (from the outside), proximal (closest to the point of attachment to the body), and distal (farthest from the point of attachment to the body). How the bones resemble or differ from bones of other dinosaurs suggests to which group of dinosaurs the animal belonged.

Fossils not only show how a dinosaur was built; they hint at how it lived. Braincase, eye sockets, teeth, backbone, limbs, muscle scars, and bony ridges that had anchored muscles are clues to sight, hearing, and level of intelligence; how its jaws worked; what it ate; and, not least, how it walked or ran.

The paleontologist sums up such findings and gives the dinosaur a scientific name allotted to no other animal. Then he or she submits the written paper to a scientific journal. Independent experts approve the article before it is published.

Keeping up to date with new discoveries published in obscure journals and unfamiliar languages is difficult. Then, too, even

Studying a dinosaur
Careful study of even a few bones can help a scientist to work out the shape and size of the skeleton they came from.
1 Using calipers to make key measurements of individual bones.
2 Extrapolating bones from fragments, and plotting their relationships to one another. (Damaged bones can be repaired and missing bones may be replaced by casts.)

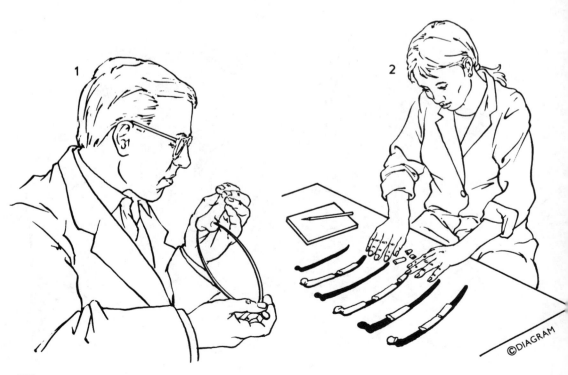

writers of scientific articles make mistakes. Experts therefore do their best to visit museum collections worldwide, to study and compare specimens at first hand. This work has produced "new" kinds of dinosaurs from dusty storerooms where scores of bones had lodged for decades, misdescribed or nameless. Comparative dinosaur studies can also profit from computers. Already some paleontologists can produce and transmit computer images of a fossil bone as seen from different angles.

If most of a skeleton has been recovered and described, preparators can rebuild the skeleton in standing pose, replacing missing bits with glass-fiber substitutes. Hip girdle, skull, ribs, limb bones, breastbone, and vertebrae (the bones of neck, back, and tail) may go up in a special sequence. If the skeleton is large, strong scaffolding is needed to hold heavy bones in place. Then metal rods or tubes are bent to fit and are clipped onto the jointed bones. After maybe months of work, people can remove the heavy scaffolding, leaving almost all the skeleton on view.

A museum can make lifesize replicas of its famous dinosaur skeletons. First, technicians produce silicone rubber molds of individual bones, then they fill the molds with glass-fiber casts. The museum can then sell its glass-fiber skeletons or swap these with other museums for casts of beasts to add to its collection.

Reconstructed real or imitation skeletons enable artists and sculptors to produce lifelike restorations of long vanished creatures' bodies. (see also Chapter 7).

Rebuilding a dinosaur
3 Mounting sauropod bones to reconstruct the entire skeleton in a lifelike standing pose. Metal rods and tubes give support as unobtrusively as possible.
4 Modeling a lifelike restoration from the reconstructed skeleton. Comparing its size and posture with those of living animals gives the sculptor an idea of body bulk and muscle distribution. Also bumps and ridges on limb bones show where powerful muscles were attached.

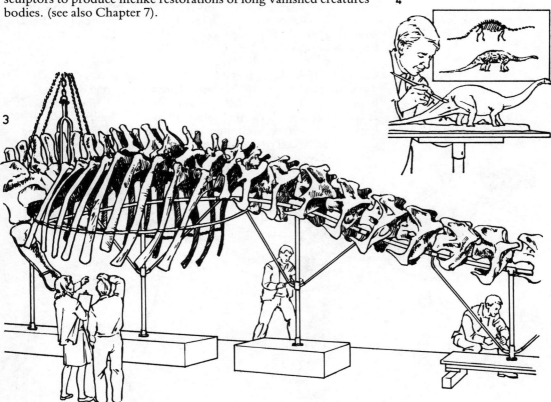

3

4

North American dinosaurs 1

Famous dinosaur localities
1 Red Deer River, Alberta
2 Hell Creek, Montana
3 Como Bluff, Wyoming
4 Connecticut Valley
5 Canyon City, Colorado
6 Ghost Ranch,
  New Mexico
7 Dinosaur National
  Monument, Utah and
  Colorado

Dinosaurs inhabited North America from Early Late Triassic time right through the Age of Dinosaurs. Great numbers roamed Late Jurassic riversides, and lowlands west of the seaway that bisected Late Cretaceous North America from north to south. Dinosaur fossils teem in rocks of western US states and the Canadian province of Alberta. Discoveries of evolving kinds suggest North America lost touch with Europe and South America, but gained a land link to East Asia near the end of the Mesozoic time.

CANADA

Canada's earliest known dinosaurs come from Nova Scotia's Late Triassic rocks beside the Bay of Fundy. Here lived prosauropods and theropods, and 225 million years ago an early ornithischian left the fossil footprints known as *Atreipus*.

Most Canadian dinosaur discoveries come from much later and much farther west – from Late Cretaceous rocks where barren hills and valleys flank southern Alberta's Red Deer River. Here, 76–65 million years ago, theropods as heavy as an elephant hunted herds of horned and duck-billed dinosaurs roaming what was then a swampy plain between the rising Rockies and the inland sea.

Dinosaur discovery in Alberta began in the 1880s with pioneers including **Joseph Tyrrell**. Exploration speeded up in 1910 when **Barnum Brown** began collecting for the American Museum of Natural History; he pried bones from Red Deer River cliffs, piling them aboard a large flat-bottomed barge. There was competition from **Charles Sternberg** with his sons and **Lawrence Lambe**, all collecting for the Canadian Geological Survey. This dinosaur harvest continued until 1917.

Canadian dinosaur discovery gained new life as the century grew old. In the 1970s **Dale Russell** shed fresh light on ornithomimid dinosaurs, and by the 1980s **Philip Currie** and other dinosaur hunters were finding hordes of fossil dinosaurs in Alberta's heavily eroded badlands. Rocks bristling with fossils of hadrosaurs and horned *Eucentrosaurus* (*Centrosaurus*) suggest that floods drowned herds up to 10,000 strong – prehistoric versions of the bison that darkened North American prairies a century ago. By the late 1980s

Deinonychus

Alberta's Dinosaur Provincial Park had yielded 500 skeletons of 50 dinosaur species – a whole community of Late Cretaceous theropods, horned dinosaurs, hadrosaurs, and others. Optimists hoped for even more spectacular Canadian discoveries – Early Cretaceous dinosaurs pickled whole like leaves said to have been found in the oily tar sands of Alberta.

By the late 1980s, Canada's 49 genera placed that nation fourth (ahead of the United Kingdom) in the dinosaur league table. Canadian dinosaurs included about a dozen theropods, 1 doubtful prosauropod (*Arctosaurus*), 1 hypsilophodontid (*Parksosaurus*), the only known thescelosaurid (*Thescelosaurus*), 11 hadrosaurs, 4 bone-heads, 6 armored dinosaurs, and 11 horned dinosaurs.

HONDURAS
A few ornithopod (hypsilophodont?) bones are Central America's only known dinosaurs.

MEXICO
Mexico has been credited with the theropods *Albertosaurus* and *Labocania*, the sauropod *Apatosaurus*, hadrosaurs *Hypacrosaurus*, *Kritosaurus*, and *Lambeosaurus*, and horned *Monoclonius*.

UNITED STATES OF AMERICA
Until the early 1990s the US headed the world league of dinosaur discoveries with about 110 genera (though China seemed set soon to overtake that total). US beasts included 31 theropods, 3 prosauropods, 18 sauropods, 2 fabrosaurids, 6 hypsilophodontids, *Thescelosaurus*, *Camptosaurus*, and *Iguanodon*, 1 dryosaurid, up to 16 duck-bills, 3 bone-heads, 3 scelidosaurs, 9 armored dinosaurs, and 15 horned dinosaurs.

American dinosaur discovery arguably dates from 1818 with a Connecticut find of then unidentified *Anchisaurus* bones. In 1834 **Edward Hitchcock** began collecting fossil "bird" tracks in Massachusetts. Philadelphia anatomist **Joseph Leidy** named three dinosaurs from fossil teeth in 1856, and, in 1858, *Hadrosaurus* – the first American dinosaur described from a partial skeleton.

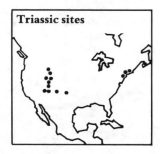

Triassic sites

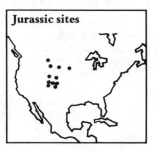

Jurassic sites

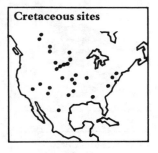

Cretaceous sites

Albertosaurus

©DIAGRAM

North American dinosaurs 2

The US dinosaur rush got under way in the late 1870s when **Othniel Charles Marsh** and **Edward Drinker Cope** competed to unearth and name the most and largest dinosaurs. Collectors such as **O.W. Lucas** and **William H. Reed** teased mighty bones from the Wild West's Late Jurassic rocks – notably near Canyon City and Morrison, Colorado, and at Como Bluff, a rock ridge in south Wyoming. Famous finds included the sauropods *Apatosaurus* (*Brontosaurus*) and *Diplodocus*, the plated dinosaur *Stegosaurus*, and the fearsome carnosaur *Allosaurus*. About 20 dinosaurs still bear Marsh's names, though arguably only 3 of Cope's are valid.

More Late Jurassic dinosaurs emerged in the early 1900s as collectors worked to fill museum halls. The American Museum of Natural History made fresh finds in old sites like Wyoming's Bone Cabin Quarry; and **Earl Douglass**, collecting for Pittsburgh's Carnegie Museum, freed giant bones from the Utah's Carnegie Quarry (now part of Dinosaur National Monument).

Since the 1960s **Peter Galton**, **John Horner**, **James Jensen**, **John Ostrom** and others have shed new light on the Age of Dinosaurs in the USA. It seems theropods, prosauropods, and ornithischians already inhabited the southwest and east by Early Late Triassic times. Yet the Connecticut Valley's supposedly Triassic dinosaurs mostly turn out to have dated from the once poorly known Early Jurassic rocks. *Supersaurus* and other monstrous sauropods have joined the roll of Late Jurassic giants. *Deinonychus* and its switchblade claws could have terrorized Early Cretaceous Montana. The Late Cretaceous West held whole communities of fanged and toothless theropods, and duck-billed, horned, armored, bone- headed and other ornithischians. Two of the most remarkable of all discoveries are that some hadrosaurs built nests and raised their young in colonies, and certain hadrosaurs lived in north Alaska, even then a chilly region inside the Arctic Circle.

Triassic Period
a *Anchisaurus*
b *Coelophysis*

Jurassic Period
a *Allosaurus*
b *Diplodocus*
c *Stegosaurus*

Cretaceous Period
a *Parasaurolophus*
b *Triceratops*
c *Tyrannosaurus*

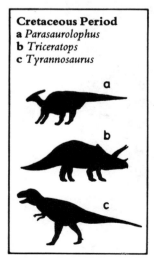

Stegosaurus

NATIONS' NAMED DINOSAURS

CANADA
Albertosaurus
Anchiceratops
Ankylosaurus
Arctosaurus
Arrhinoceratops
Aublysodon
Brachyceratops
Brachylophosaurus
Caenagnathus
Chasmosaurus
Chassternbergia
Chirostenotes
Corythosaurus
Daspletosaurus
Dromaeosaurus
Dromiceiomimus
Dyoplosaurus
Edmontonia
Edmontosaurus
Elmisaurus
Eoceratops
Eucentrosaurus
Euoplocephalus
Gorgosaurus
Gravitholus
Grypsaurus
Hadrosaurus
Hypacrosaurus
Kritosaurus
Lambeosaurus
Leptoceratops
Macrophalangia
Monoclonius
Ornithomimus
Ornatotholus
Pachycephalosaurus

Pachyrhinosaurus
Panoplosaurus
Parasaurolophus
Parksosaurus
Prosaurolophus
Saurolophus
Saurornitholestes
Stegoceras
Struthiomimus
Styracosaurus
Thescelosaurus
Triceratops
Troodon

MEXICO
Albertosaurus
Apatosaurus
Hypacrosaurus
Kritosaurus
Labocania
Lambeosaurus
Monoclonius

UNITED STATES
Acrocanthosaurus
Agathaumas
Alamosaurus
Albertosaurus
Allosaurus
Ammosaurus
Amphicoelias
Anchisaurus
Ankylosaurus
Apatosaurus

Archaeornithomimus
"Arkansaurus"
Astrodon
Atlantosaurus
Aublysodon
Avaceratops
Barosaurus
Brachiosaurus
Brachyceratops
Brachylophosaurus
Camarasaurus
Camptosaurus
Cathetosaurus
Ceratops
Ceratosaurus
Chasmosaurus
Chassternbergia
"Chindesaurus"
Claosaurus
Coelophysis
Coelurus
Deinonychus
Denversaurus
Diclonius
Dilophosaurus
Diplodocus
Diplotomodon
Diracodon
Dryosaurus
Dryptosaurus
Dysganus
Dystrophaeus
Dystylosaurus
Echinodon
Edmontosaurus
Elaphrosaurus
Epanterias

Eucentrosaurus
Hadrosaurus
Haplocanthosaurus
Hoplitosaurus
Hypacrosaurus
Hypsibema
Hypsilophodon
Iguanodon
Kritosaurus
Lambeosaurus
Laosaurus
Leptoceratops
Longosaurus
Lophorhothon
"Madsenius"
Maiasaura
Marshosaurus
Massospondylus
Microvenator
Monoclonius
Montanoceratops
Nanosaurus
Nanotyrannus
Nodosaurus
Ornitholestes
Ornithomimus
Orodromeus
Othnielia
Pachycephalosaurus
Palaeoscincus
Panoplosaurus
Parasaurolophus
Paronychodon
Parrosaurus
Pentaceratops
Pleurocoelus
Podokesaurus

Priconodon
Pteropelyx
Rerueltosaurus
Sauropelta
Scelidosaurus
Scutellosaurus
Segisaurus
"Seismosaurus"
Silvisaurus
Stegoceras
Stegosaurus
Stokesosaurus
Struthiomimus
Stygimoloch
Styracosaurus
Supersaurus
Syntarsus
Technosaurus
Tenontosaurus
Thescelosaurus
Thespesius
Torosaurus
Torvosaurus
Trachodon
Triceratops
Troodon
Tyrannosaurus
Ugrosaurus
"Ultrasaurus"
Zephyrosaurus

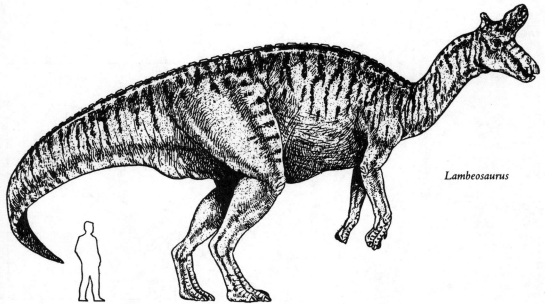

Lambeosaurus

© DIAGRAM

North American museums 1

North America boasts more dinosaur museum exhibits than any
other continent. Dinosaurs figure in national, state, provincial, and
county museums, but some of the finest specimens dominate two
great collections founded by 19th-century philanthropists:
Pittsburgh's Carnegie Museum of Natural History, created by steel
magnate philanthropist **Andrew Carnegie** (whose *Diplodocus* casts
grace several museums around the world), and Yale University's
Peabody Museum, set up by paleontologist **Othniel Marsh** with
funds from his wealthy banker uncle, **George Peabody**.

Map showing locations of
North American museums

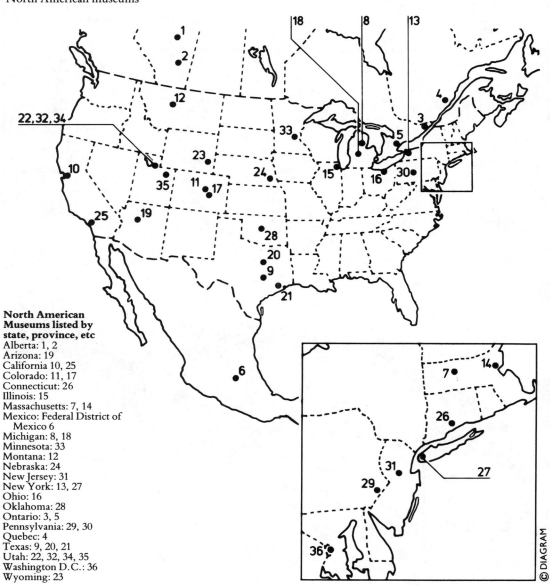

**North American
Museums listed by
state, province, etc**
Alberta: 1, 2
Arizona: 19
California 10, 25
Colorado: 11, 17
Connecticut: 26
Illinois: 15
Massachusetts: 7, 14
Mexico: Federal District of
   Mexico 6
Michigan: 8, 18
Minnesota: 33
Montana: 12
Nebraska: 24
New Jersey: 31
New York: 13, 27
Ohio: 16
Oklahoma: 28
Ontario: 3, 5
Pennsylvania: 29, 30
Quebec: 4
Texas: 9, 20, 21
Utah: 22, 32, 34, 35
Washington D.C.: 36
Wyoming: 23

© DIAGRAM

CANADA

1 Drumheller, Alberta: Tyrrell Museum of Palaeontology A huge hall displays mounted skeletons, mainly of Late Cretaceous dinosaurs of North America. Exhibits include theropods *Allosaurus*, *Albertosaurus*, *Tyrannosaurus*, *Coelophysis*, *Dromaeosaurus*, *Ornitholestes*, and *Struthiomimus*; the sauropod *Camarasaurus*; hadrosaurs *Corythosaurus*, *Hadrosaurus*, *Hypacrosaurus*, *Lambeosaurus*, *Maiasaura*, and *Prosaurolophus*; plated *Stegosaurus*; horned *Triceratops*, *Eucentrosaurus* (*Centrosaurus*), and *Chasmosaurus* plus some restorations.

2 Edmonton, Alberta: Provincial Museum of Alberta This has skeletons of *Lambeosaurus*, *Albertosaurus*, and *Parksosaurus*, four skulls, and lifesize models of the duck-bill *Corythosaurus* and armored *Ankylosaurus*.

3 Ottawa, Ontario: National Museum of Natural Sciences This fine display of dinosaurs from western Canada has superb skeletons of horned dinosaurs *Anchiceratops* and *Styracosaurus*, with *Leptoceratops* in stages of restoration; *Triceratops*; *Thescelosaurus*; duck-bills *Brachylophosaurus*, *Edmontosaurus*, and *Hypacrosaurus*; a *Euoplocephalus* tail club; and theropods *Daspletosaurus* and *Dromiceiomimus* plus a model *Troodon* (*Stenonychosaurus*).

4 Quebec: Redpath Museum Has fragments of North America's *Saurornithoides* (*Troodon?*) and *Zephyrosaurus*, and the Madagascan bonehead *Majungatholus*. None is on display.

5 Toronto, Ontario: Royal Ontario Museum A dinosaur gallery shows 13 skeletons of North American dinosaurs: the theropods *Albertosaurus*, *Allosaurus (2)*, and *Ornithomimus*, and 9 ornithischians. These are *Camptosaurus*; duck-bills *Corythosaurus*, *Edmontosaurus* (*Anatosaurus*), *Kritosaurus*, *Lambeosaurus*, *Parasaurolophus*, and *Prosaurolophus*; the plated dinosaur *Stegosaurus*; and the horned dinosaur *Chasmosaurus*.

MEXICO

6 Mexico City: Natural History Museum Exhibits include a cast of the sauropod *Diplodocus*.

UNITED STATES OF AMERICA

7 Amherst, Massachusetts: Pratt Museum (Amherst College) Here are remains of *Diplodocus*, *Kritosaurus*, *Triceratops*, etc., and the world's largest dinosaur track collection.

8 Ann Arbor, Michigan: University of Michigan Exhibit Museum *Allosaurus*, *Anatosaurus*, and *Stegosaurus* feature here with a *Tyrannosaurus* skull and sauropod bones.

9 Austin, Texas: Texas Memorial Museum This has Mesozoic fossils.

10 Berkeley, California: University of California Museum of Paleontology On show: *Edmontosaurus* skull and casts of *Dilophosaurus*, *Tyrannosaurus* (skull), *Heterodontosaurus*, *Parasaurolophus*, and *Maiasaura*. In store: much more.

11 Boulder, Colorado: University Natural History Museum Jurassic dinosaur remains figure among exhibits.

12 Bozeman, Montana: Museum of the Rockies Features nest-building *Maiasaura* and *Orodromeus* and (from late 1990) an almost complete *Tyrannosaurus* skeleton.

Ornitholestes skeleton similar to that on display in the Tyrrell Museum of Palaeontology, Drumheller.

Exhibits of the horned dinosaur *Triceratops* can be seen at many museums in North America.

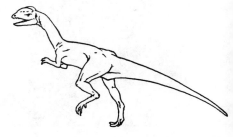

Two Californian museums display *Dilophosaurus* specimens.

North American museums 2

Above: The right foreleg and shoulder blade of *Camarasaurus* on display at the Field Museum of Natural History, Illinois.

Below: Dinosaurs being excavated from Utah's Quarry Visitor Center.

13 Buffalo, New York: Buffalo Museum of Science Features an *Allosaurus* skeleton; some dinosaur bones; casts of *Psittacosaurus* and *Triceratops*; a *Hypselosaurus* egg; and dinosaur gizzard stones, skin impressions, teeth, and tracks.

14 Cambridge, Massachusetts: Museum of Comparative Zoology, Harvard University On display: skeletons of *Deinonychus*, *Plateosaurus*, and *Heterodontosaurus* (cast); six different skulls; and early saurischian tracks.

15 Chicago, Illinois: Field Museum of Natural History On view: *Albertosaurus*, *Apatosaurus*, *Lambeosaurus*, *Protoceratops*, horned dinosaur skulls, and more.

16 Cleveland, Ohio: Natural History Museum Has mounted skeletons of *Haplocanthosaurus* and *Edmontosaurus* (*Anatosaurus*), and skulls or skull casts including *Nanotyrannus*.

17 Denver, Colorado: Denver Museum of Natural History A fine *Stegosaurus* skeleton is on show with *Diplodocus*, *Edmontosaurus* (*Anatosaurus*), *Denversaurus*, a *Tyrannosaurus* cast, and more.

18 East Lansing, Michigan: The Museum, Michigan State University Includes *Allosaurus* and *Stegosaurus* skeletons, also a *Tyrannosaurus* skull in the large Hall of Evolution.

19 Flagstaff, Arizona: Museum of Northern Arizona This has the early theropod *Coelophysis* and the armored ornithopod *Scutellosaurus*.

20 Fort Worth, Texas: Fort Worth Museum of Science Mounted skeletons depict an *Allosaurus* attacking a *Camptosaurus*.

21 Houston, Texas: Houston Museum of Natural Science On show: much of a *Diplodocus* skeleton.

22 Jensen, Utah: Dinosaur National Monument Spectacular canyons and a covered Quarry Visitor Center (formerly Carnegie Quarry) where viewers can see dinosaur bones embedded in Upper Jurassic rock. Finds here included theropods *Allosaurus* and *Ceratosaurus*, sauropods *Apatosaurus*, *Camarasaurus*, and *Diplodocus*; ornithopods *Camptosaurus* and *Dryosaurus*; and plated *Stegosaurus*. On show are a mounted *Allosaurus* and *Camarasaurus* and a replica *Stegosaurus*.

23 Laramie, Wyoming: The Geological Museum Has a mounted *Apatosaurus* skeleton, *Anchiceratops* and *Edmontosaurus* (*Anatosaurus*) skulls, and casts of hadrosaur skulls and *Maiasaura* skeleton.

24 Lincoln, Nebraska: University of Nebraska State Museum Features mounted skeletons of *Allosaurus* and *Stegosaurus* and a partial *Triceratops* skeleton.

25 Los Angeles, California: Los Angeles County Museum of Natural History Here are the theropods *Allosaurus*, *Dilophosaurus*, and a *Tyrannosaurus* skull; ornithopods *Camptosaurus*, *Corythosaurus*, *Edmontosaurus* (*Anatosaurus*), and a *Parasaurolophus* skull; plus a *Stegosaurus* skeleton and large, lifelike model *Allosaurus*.

26 New Haven, Connecticut: Peabody Museum of Natural History, Yale University Many type specimens (first of their kind described) occur here. Skeletons include the theropod *Deinonychus*; sauropods *Apatosaurus* and *Camarasaurus*; ornithopods *Othnielia* (*Laosaurus*), *Tenontosaurus*, *Camptosaurus*, *Claosaurus*, and *Edmontosaurus* (*Anatosaurus*); plated *Stegosaurus*; and horned

Monoclonius. There are skulls of three horned dinosaurs and *Allosaurus* (*Antrodemus*); also casts.

27 New York City, New York: American Museum of Natural History The world's largest dinosaur collection stresses North American skulls and skeletons, also dinosaur eggs, skin impressions, and tracks. Skeletons include theropods *Albertosaurus, Allosaurus, Coelophysis, Ornitholestes, Struthiomimus,* and *Tyrannosaurus;* the prosauropod *Plateosaurus;* the sauropod *Apatosaurus;* ornithopods *Camptosaurus, Corythosaurus, Edmontosaurus* (*Anatosaurus*) *copei, Lambeosaurus,* and *Saurolophus;* plated *Stegosaurus;* armored *Panoplosaurus;* the "parrot lizard" *Psittacosaurus,* and horned *Monoclonius, Montanoceratops, Protoceratops, Styracosaurus,* and *Triceratops.*

28 Norman, Oklahoma: Stovall Museum, University of Oklahoma Remains of the theropod *Acrocanthosaurus* feature here.

29 Philadelphia, Pennsylvania: Academy of Natural Sciences Items include the theropod *Deinonychus;* a *Supersaurus* (*Barosaurus?*) leg; ornithopods *Tenontosaurus, Corythosaurus,* and *Hadrosaurus;* and the horned dinosaurs *Avaceratops* and *Brachyceratops.*

30 Pittsburgh, Pennsylvania: Carnegie Museum of Natural History Fine skeletons of Jurassic and Cretaceous dinosaurs stand in the Mesozoic Hall – the theropods *Allosaurus* and *Tyrannosaurus;* sauropods *Apatosaurus, Camarasaurus,* and *Diplodocus;* ornithopods *Camptosaurus, Corythosaurus,* and *Dryosaurus;* plated *Stegosaurus,* and horned *Protoceratops.* There are also skulls and casts.

31 Princeton, New Jersey: Museum of Natural History, Princeton University Footprints, *Allosaurus,* and Late Cretaceous dinosaurs figure here (but many items have gone to New Haven).

32 Provo, Utah: Earth Science Museum, Brigham Young University Items kept include remains of *Supersaurus* and "Ultrasaurus" and *Allosaurus* and *Camptosaurus* skeletons.

33 St. Paul, Minnesota: The Science Museum of Minnesota Includes skeletons of *Thescelosaurus, Allosaurus, Camptosaurus* and *Triceratops,* and in preparation, *Diplodocus* and *Haplocanthosaurus.* Technicians are on view preparing sauropod bones.

34 Salt Lake City, Utah: Utah Museum of Natural History, University of Utah Items include the theropod *Allosaurus,* the sauropod *Barosaurus,* ornithopod *Camptosaurus,* and plated *Stegosaurus.* Some exhibits come from the Cleveland-Lloyd Quarry, origin of more than 10,000 dinosaur bones.

35 Vernal, Utah: Utah Natural History State Museum Kept here: a *Diplodocus* skeleton and cast.

36 Washington, D.C.: National Museum of Natural History, Smithsonian Institution A major national collection, with theropods *Albertosaurus, Allosaurus, Ceratosaurus* and *Tyrannosaurus* skull; sauropods *Camarasaurus* and *Diplodocus;* ornithopods *Camptosaurus, Corythosaurus, Edmontosaurus, Heterodontosaurus, Maiasaura,* and *Thescelosaurus;* plated *Stegosaurus;* and horned *Brachyceratops, Monoclonius,* and *Triceratops.* Some items are casts.

The National Museum of Natural Sciences (Ottawa) and the American Museum of Natural History (New York) both have skeletons of the horned dinosaur *Styracosaurus.*

©DIAGRAM

237

European dinosaurs 1

European Triassic sites
1 Bristol, England
2 Halberstadt,
  East Germany
3 Heroldsberg,
  West Germany
4 Pfaffenhofen,
  West Germany
5 Trössingen,
  West Germany

West Germany is a rich source of Triassic dinosaurs. Europe's Jurassic dinosaurs come largely from France, Portugal, the United Kingdom, and West Germany. Early Cretaceous dinosaurs abounded on a delta stretching from southern England through northern France and Belgium. In Late Cretaceous times, dinosaurs inhabited a chain of islands from Spain through southern France to Austria and Romania. However, a sea that isolated Europe from Asia would have kept out many of the later Asian dinosaurs.

AUSTRIA

This was a Late Cretaceous home of those likely island dwellers the small armored dinosaurs *Crataeomus* and *Struthiosaurus*.

BELGIUM

Europe's most famous dinosaur discovery came at Bernissart in 1878 when coalminers 1,056ft (322m) down found remains of 39 *Iguanodon*, many of them whole skeletons. The bodies had piled up one by one in what was once a marshy depression. Belgium has also yielded teeth of *Craspedodon*, another iguanodontid.

FRANCE

The 20 or so genera range from north to south and from Late Triassic through Late Cretaceous time. They include theropods *Compsognathus*, *Erectopus*, *Eustreptospondylus*, *Halticosaurus*, *Megalosaurus*, *Piveteausaurus*, *Poekilopleuron*, and deinonychosaur teeth; sauropods *Aepisaurus*, *Bothriospondylus*, *Hypselosaurus*, and *Titanosaurus*; ornithopods *Iguanodon*, *Rhabdodon*, and *Telmatosaurus*; the stegosaur *Lexovisaurus*; and the ankylosaur *Struthiosaurus*. There are also trackways and, near Aix-en-Provence, many eggs attributed to *Hypselosaurus*.

GERMANY, EAST

This had at least two small theropods.

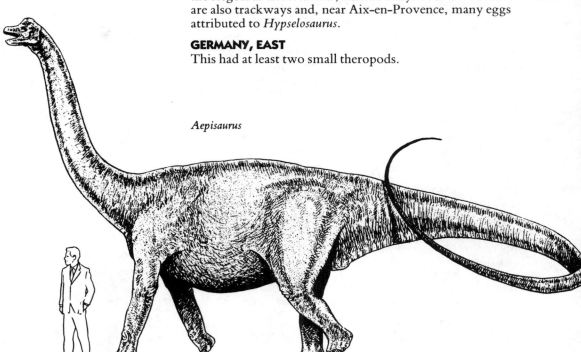

Aepisaurus

GERMANY, WEST
The tally includes 8 theropods, 2 prosauropods, 2 sauropods, and 2 ornithischians. **Hermann von Meyer**, **Friedrich von Huene** and others revealed a wealth of early dinosaurs in southwest Germany, where a Trössingen quarry produced thousands of *Plateosaurus* bones, once mistakenly considered relics of a herd that perished in a Triassic desert. Solnhofen's fine-grained Late Jurassic rocks are the source of the "bird dinosaur" *Archaeopteryx*.

NETHERLANDS
Bones arguably represent the sauropod *Pelorosaurus*, the hadrosaur *Orthomerus*, and the supposed ostrich dinosaur, *Betasuchus*.

NORWAY
Paleontologists found fossil iguanodontid tracks on the Arctic archipelago Spitsbergen.

POLAND
Prosauropods are known but not described.

PORTUGAL
Portugal's Jurassic dinosaurs include 1 alleged fabrosaurid, 2 hypsilophodontids, 1 camptosaurid, 1 iguanodontid, 2 scelidosaurs, 1 stegosaur, and an armored dinosaur. Portugal probably also held the Early Cretaceous sauropod *Astrodon*.

ROMANIA
Here lived the theropods *Bradycneme* and *Heptasteornis*; possibly the sauropod *Titanosaurus*; ornithopods including *Dryosaurus* and *Iguanodon*; and small, armored *Crataeomus* and *Struthiosaurus*.

SPAIN
Finds include a theropod, several sauropods (*Aragosaurus* is only known from Spain), a dryosaurid, and a hypsilophodontid.

SWEDEN
Prosauropod bones are known from the south.

SWITZERLAND
The Late Triassic prosauropod *Plateosaurus* lived here and sauropod remains come from the Jura Mountains.

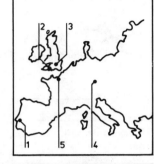

European Jurassic sites
1 West-central Portugal
2 Charmouth, England
3 Oxfordshire, England
4 Solnhofen, West Germany
5 Caen and Dives, France

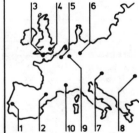

European Cretaceous sites
1 West-central Portugal
2 North-eastern Spain
3 Isle of Wight, England
4 Weald, England
5 Bernissart, Belgium
6 Bückeberg, West Germany
7 Eastern Austria
8 Transylvanian Romania
9 Maastricht, Netherlands
10 Provence, France

Struthiosaurus

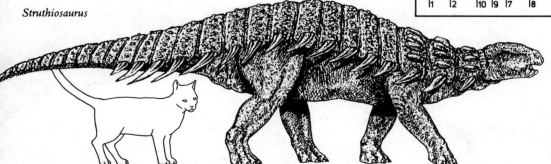

©DIAGRAM

European dinosaurs 2

UNITED KINGDOM

With 47 genera, the United Kingdom is ranked as the world's fifth-largest source of dinosaurs. They include 11 theropods, 3 prosauropods, 9 sauropods, 8 ornithopods, 2 scelidosaurs, 3 stegosaurs, and maybe 8 armored dinosaurs. The early theropod *Saltopus* lived in Scotland, and prosauropods roamed parts of Wales, but most other dinosaurs come from southern England's Jurassic and Cretaceous rocks. More kinds of Early Cretaceous dinosaur are known from the Isle of Wight and the Weald of southeast England than from anywhere on Earth. In the marshy delta that then stretched to Belgium and France, *Baryonyx* seized fish in its crocodile-like jaws, and powerful *Megalosaurus* perhaps stalked the sauropod *Pelorosaurus*, or the ornithischians *Iguanodon*, *Hypsilophodon*, *Hylaeosaurus*, and *Yaverlandia* – perhaps the oldest known bone-headed dinosaur.

Scientific dinosaur discovery first emerged in England. In the 1820s **William Buckland** named *Megalosaurus* and **Gideon Mantell** described *Iguanodon* (although other people had collected bones of both before). Dinosaurs "came of age" in Britain in 1841 when **Richard Owen** gave them the collective name Dinosauria.

USSR

Apart from a possible hadrosaur and supposed theropod most finds have come from Asian regions of the USSR (see **Asian dinosaurs 1**). One reason for this is the shallow sea that drowned huge tracts of Russia for much of Mesozoic time.

Triassic Period
a *Plateosaurus*
b *Procompsognathus*
c *Saltopus*

Jurassic Period
a *Cetiosaurus*
b *Compsognathus*
c *Scelidosaurus*

Cretaceous Period
a *Hypsilophodon*
b *Iguanodon*
c *Hypselosaurus*

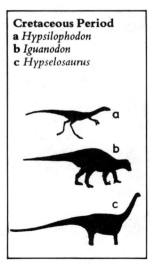

Saltopus

NATIONS' NAMED DINOSAURS

AUSTRIA
Crataeomus
Rhabdodon
Struthiosaurus

BELGIUM
Craspedodon
Iguanodon

FRANCE
Aepisaurus
Bothriospondylus
Cetiosaurus
Compsognathus
Dacentrurus
Erectopus
Eustreptospondylus
Halticosaurus
Hypselosaurus
Iguanodon
Lexovisaurus
Megalosaurus
Piveteausaurus
Poekilopleuron
Rhabdodon
Struthiosaurus
Teinurosaurus
Telmatosaurus
Titanosaurus

**GERMANY,
EAST**
Avipes
Pterospondylus

**GERMANY,
WEST**
Archaeopteryx
Cetiosaurus

Compsognathus
Dolichosuchus
Halticosaurus
Iguanodon
Liliensternus
Megalosaurus
  (*Altispinax?*)
Ohmdenosaurus
Plateosaurus
Procompsognathus
Sellosaurus
Stenopelix
Velocipes

NETHERLANDS
Betasuchus
Orthomerus
Pelorosaurus

POLAND
Thecodontosaurus

PORTUGAL
Alocodon
Camptosaurus
Dacentrurus
Dracopelta
Hypsilophodon
Iguanodon
Lusitanosaurus
Phyllodon
Trimucrodon

ROMANIA
Bradycneme
Crataeomus
Dryosaurus
Heptasteornis
Iguanodon

Rhabdodon
Struthiosaurus
Telmatosaurus
Titanosaurus

SPAIN
Aragosaurus
Hypselosaurus
Hypsilophodon
Telmatosaurus
Valdosaurus

SWITZERLAND
Ornithopsis
Plateosaurus

**UNITED
KINGDOM**
Acanthopholis
Altispinax
Anoplosaurus
Astrodon
Baryonyx
Bothriospondylus
Calamospondylus
Callovosaurus
Camelotia
Camptosaurus
Cetiosauriscus
Cetiosaurus
Chondrosteosaurus
Craterosaurus
Cryptodraco
Dacentrurus
Dinodocus
Dryosaurus
Echinodon
Eustreptospondylus
Hylaeosaurus
Hypsilophodon

Iguanodon
Iliosuchus
Lexovisaurus
Macrurosaurus
Megalosaurus
Metriacanthosaurus
Nuthetes
Pelorosaurus
Plateosaurus
Polacanthoides
Polacanthus
Priodontognathus
Proceratosaurus
Regnosaurus
Saltopus
Sarcolestes
Sarcosaurus
Scelidosaurus
Thecodontosaurus
Thecospondylus
Titanosaurus
Valdosaurus
"*Vectensia*"
Vectisaurus
Yaverlandia

**USSR
(European)**
Macrodontophion
Orthomerus

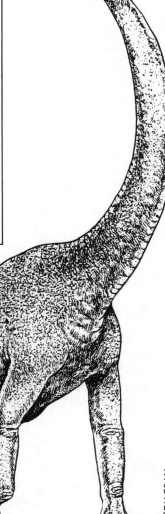

Pelorosaurus

European museums 1

Belgium, West Germany, and the United Kingdom respectively show skeletons of *Iguanodon*, *Plateosaurus*, and *Eustreptospondylus*; and East Germany and the United Kingdom have fine fossils of the "bird dinosaur" *Archaeopteryx*. But many European dinosaurs left only scraps of bone. The best museum exhibits include imported skeletons or casts from Africa, Mongolia, and North America.

European museums (See other maps for France, Germany and the United Kingdom.)

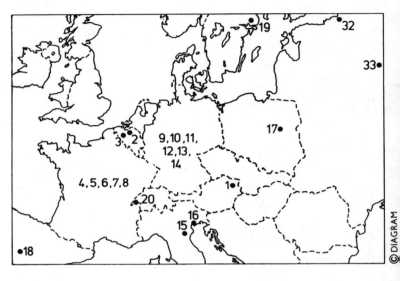

AUSTRIA

1 Vienna: Natural History Museum Small, armored *Struthiosaurus* and the sail-backed African iguanodont *Ouranosaurus* are represented.

BELGIUM

2 Bernissart, Hainaut: Bernissart Museum Includes *Iguanodon* fossils from the famous local coalmine.

3 Brussels: Royal Institute of Natural Sciences Displays the world's largest group of *Iguanodon* skeletons. Eleven are mounted, 20 remain embedded in rock. *Megalosaurus* is represented, too.

FRANCE

4 Aix en Provence: Natural History Museum This shows locally discovered eggs attributed to the sauropod *Hypselosaurus*.

5 Le Havre: Natural History Museum Here are a partial skeleton of the stegosaur *Lexovisaurus* and dinosaur eggs from Provence.

6 Nancy: Museum of Earth Sciences The collection includes a fossil *Iguanodon*.

7 Nantes: Natural History Museum A major museum, with a dinosaur egg from Provence and fossil dinosaur footprints.

8 Paris: National Museum of Natural History Dinosaur fossils or casts from Africa, Asia, Europe, and North America figure here. Items include the theropods *Allosaurus*, *Compsognathus*,

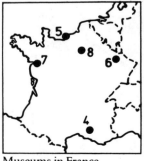

Museums in France

Tyrannosaurus, and *Tarbosaurus*; the prosauropod *Massospondylus*, sauropods *Bothriospondylus*, *Diplodocus*, and *Rebbachisaurus*; ornithopods *Rhabdodon (Mochlodon)*, *Iguanodon*, *Ouranosaurus*, and *Anatosaurus*; the stegosaurid *Lexovisaurus* and the horned dinosaur *Triceratops*. There are fossil eggs of *Hypselosaurus* and *Protoceratops*.

GERMANY, EAST

9 East Berlin: Natural History Museum, Humboldt University
This has splendid Late Jurassic skeletons from Tanzania: the ostrich dinosaur *Elaphrosaurus*; sauropods *Dicraeosaurus* and – the largest mounted dinosaur skeleton anywhere – *Brachiosaurus* (*Giraffatitan*); the ornithopod *Dryosaurus*; and the plated dinosaur *Kentrosaurus*. European items are a *Plateosaurus* and an *Archaeopteryx*, arguably the most important natural history specimen of all.

GERMANY, WEST

10 Frankfurt am Main: Senckenberg Nature Museum Fossils or casts of dinosaurs from Africa, Asia, Europe, and North America are on show. Items include a *Tyrannosaurus* cast; skeletons of the prosauropod *Plateosaurus*; *Diplodocus* and *Brachiosaurus* remains; a mummified *Edmontosaurus* (*Anatosaurus*); *Iguanodon* and *Stegosaurus* skeleton casts; *Triceratops* skulls; and a skull cast of *Protoceratops*.

11 Munich: Bavarian State Institute for Paleontology and Historical Geology Here are a *Compsognathus* skeleton, *Triceratops* skull, *Diplodocus* bones, and *Monoclonius* cast.

12 Münster: Geological and Paleontological Museum Has an *Iguanodon* skeleton and *Tyrannosaurus* skull cast.

13 Stuttgart: State Museum for Natural History The collection displays bones or casts of early German dinosaurs including four skeletons of the prosauropod *Plateosaurus* and partial skeletons of *Sellosaurus* and *Procompsognathus*. Also kept: bones or casts of *Halticosaurus*, *Coelophysis*, *Thecodontosaurus*, *Iguanodon*, *Tornieria*, "*Brontosaurus*" and *Hypsilophodon*.

14 Tübingen: Institute and Museum for Geology and Paleontology, University of Tübingen Displayed here are skeletons of *Plateosaurus* and *Kentrosaurus*; remains of *Diplodocus* and *Protoceratops*; and whole or partial casts of *Coelophysis*, *Tyrannosaurus*, *Iguanodon*, and *Hypsilophodon*.

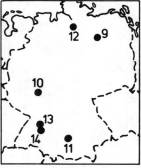

Museums in Germany

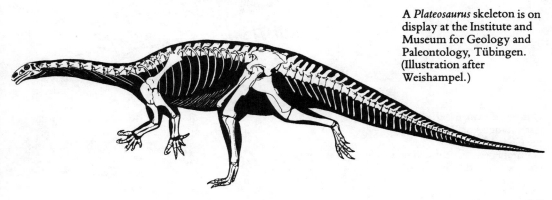

A *Plateosaurus* skeleton is on display at the Institute and Museum for Geology and Paleontology, Tübingen. (Illustration after Weishampel.)

European museums 2

ITALY
15 Bologna: G. Capellini Museum Has a *Diplodocus* cast.
16 Venice: Civic Museum of Natural History Exhibits include the African sailbacked iguanodont *Ouranosaurus*.

POLAND
17 Warsaw: Paleobiology Institute, Academy of Sciences This displays (mainly casts of) remarkable Mongolian dinosaurs: the theropods *Deinocheirus*, *Gallimimus*, and *Tarbosaurus*; the sauropod *Opisthocoelicaudia*; hadrosaurs *Barsboldia* and *Saurolophus*; bone-headed *Homalocephale* and *Prenocephale*; armored *Saichania*; and horned *Protoceratops* and *Bagaceratops*; plus eggs. Bones of eight other Mongolian dinosaurs are held in store.

SPAIN
18 Madrid: Natural Science Museum Has a *Diplodocus* cast, skull casts of *Tyrannosaurus*, *Carnotaurus*, *Anatosaurus*, and *Protoceratops*, and fragments of dinosaurs from Spain.

SWEDEN
19 Uppsala: Paleontological Museum, Uppsala University Items from China or North America depict the theropod *Tyrannosaurus*, sauropods *Euhelopus* and *Alamosaurus*, hadrosaurs *Tanius* and *Parasaurolophus*, horned *Pentaceratops*, and an ankylosaur.

20 SWITZERLAND
Geneva: Natural History Museum Has a cast of *Camptosaurus* and an *Allosaurus* that is part cast, part fossil.

Casts of the arms of the theropod *Deinocheirus mirificus* mounted at the Warsaw Institute of Paleobiology.

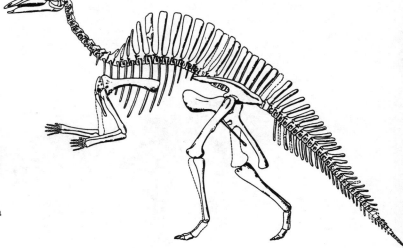

Ouranosaurus nigeriensis (after Taquet) on display at the Civic Museum of Natural History, Venice. (For a restoration of this dinosaur, see page 261.)

UNITED KINGDOM

21 Birmingham: Birmingham Museum Contains a full-size *Tyrannosaurus* model and a *Triceratops* skull.

22 Cambridge: Sedgwick Museum, Cambridge University Fragments of several British dinosaurs including *Iguanodon* are here.

23 Dorchester: The Dinosaur Museum Exhibits include *Megalosaurus*, *Tyrannosaurus*, *Hypsilophodon*, *Iguanodon*, *Anatosaurus*, *Protoceratops*, and models of *Tyrannosaurus*, *Stegosaurus*, *Triceratops*, and *Corythosaurus*.

24 Edinburgh: Royal Museum of Scotland Features *Allosaurus* and *Triceratops* casts, and dinosaur footprints and stores a postcranial *Allosaurus* skeleton.

25 Glasgow: Hunterian Museum Has a *Triceratops* skull and *Iguanodon* footprints.

26 Ipswich: Ipswich Museum Features some dinosaur bones, teeth, and footprints.

27 Leicester: Leicestershire Museum A mounted skeleton (part replica) of the sauropod *Cetiosaurus* stands here.

28 London: The Natural History Museum Here are African, European, Asian, and North American dinosaur fossils and/or casts. English items include the strange theropod *Baryonyx* and ornithopods *Hypsilophodon* and *Iguanodon*. Overseas items include the fossil skin of a *Euoplocephalus* (*Scolosaurus*); a camarasaurid limb bone and vertebrae; and casts of *Gallimimus*, *Diplodocus*, *Triceratops*, and *Protoceratops* eggs. One of the world's great collections of fossil dinosaurs is held in store.

29 Maidstone: Maidstone Museum *Iguanodon* bones and model.

30 Oxford: University Museum This has the large theropods *Megalosaurus*, *Metriacanthosaurus*, and (remarkably preserved) *Eustreptospondylus*; the sauropod *Cetiosaurus*; England's only known and Europe's best-preserved *Camptosaurus*; an *Iguanodon* cast; and the plated dinosaur *Lexovisaurus*.

31 Sandown: Museum of Isle of Wight Geology Displays remains of *Hypsilophodon*, *Iguanodon*, the early bone-head *Yaverlandia*, and megalosaurid and ornithopod footprints.

USSR

32 Leningrad: Central Geological and Prospecting Museum Here are the Chinese hadrosaur *Mandschurosaurus* and a *Diplodocus* cast.

33 Moscow: Paleontological Institute A fine dinosaur collection includes theropods *Avimimus* and *Tarbosaurus*; ornithopods *Bactrosaurus*, *Iguanodon*, *Probactrosaurus*, and *Saurolophus*; ceratopsians *Psittacosaurus*, *Bagaceratops*, and *Protoceratops*; and armored *Talarurus*.

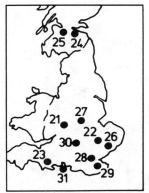

Museums in the United Kingdom

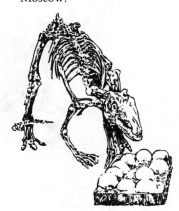

Probactrosaurus mongoliensis skeleton (with eggs) displayed at the Paleontological Institute in Moscow.

Asian dinosaurs 1

Mongolian Sites
1 Dzergen Basin
2 Orog Nur
3 Oshi-Nur
4 Ologoi-Ulan-Tsab
5 Bayn-Shire
6 Khara-Khutul-Ula
7 Ergil-Obo
8 Bayn-Dzak
9 Shiregin-Jashun
10 Nemegt Basin
11 Beger-Nur

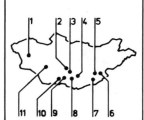

Rich bonebeds lie in the deserts of Mongolia; southern Mongolia's
Nemegt Basin alone holds a great graveyard of Late Cretaceous
theropods, sauropods, and duck-billed, armored, and other
dinosaurs – all evidently drowned by floods. Duck-billed
Saurolophus and the great flesh-eater *Tarbosaurus* had close kin in
Canada, showing that Asia and North America were linked by
land. Far fewer dinosaurs are known from West Asia and the Soviet
Union, but East Siberian discoveries may change all that.

AFGHANISTAN
Scientists have found what appeared to be sauropod footprints in
northwest Afghanistan.

IRAN
Finds include Early Jurassic theropod tracks from several areas.

ISRAEL
Elaphrosaurus tracks are reported. Hundreds of footprints of Early
Late Cretaceous theropods, maybe ornithomimids, occur in rocks
near Jerusalem.

MONGOLIA
By 1990 Mongolia had yielded hundreds of dinosaurs of more
kinds than in any nation outside the United States and China. The
more than four dozen genera of mainly Late Cretaceous beasts
included 24 theropods, 3 segnosaurs, at least 4 sauropods, at least 5
ornithopods, 4 bone-headed dinosaurs, 7 armored dinosaurs, 1
"parrot lizard," and 4 protoceratopsids. Remarkable discoveries
included the first known dinosaur nests and eggs (of *Protoceratops*),
birdlike *Avimimus*, strange *Erlikosaurus* and *Segnosaurus*, the weird
beaked theropod *Oviraptor*, and the great clawed arms of
Deinocheirus and *Therizinosaurus*.

Discovery began in the 1920s with motorized US expeditions
led by **Roy Chapman Andrews** for the American Museum of
Natural History. Later finds were made by paleontologists
including the Russians **Ivan Efremov** and **Sergei Kurzanov**, the
Poles **Zofia Kielan-Jaworowska** and **Halszka Osmólska**, and the
Mongolians **Altangerel Perle** and **Rinchen Barsbold**. (See also
Asian museums 1.)

Segnosaurus

SAUDI ARABIA
Titanosaurid bones have been discovered.

SYRIA
The shin bone of a big Late Cretaceous theropod came from southwest Syria.

USSR
By 1990 the world's largest nation had produced only about a dozen named dinosaur genera, mostly Late Cretaceous dinosaurs: the theropods *Coeluroides, Velociraptor, Embasaurus, Alectrosaurus,* and *Itemirus;* the sauropod *Antarctosaurus;* 5 hadrosaurs (*Aralosaurus, Arstanosaurus, Bactrosaurus, Jaxartosaurus, Orthomerus*), and the "parrot lizard" *Psittacosaurus.* Most came from Central Asia, along with trackways and thousands of egg fragments. Farther east, in 1988 scientists announced abundant Late Jurassic carnosaur, sauropod, and stegosaur fossils from East Siberia's Yakut region, and Late Cretaceous carnosaurs and hadrosaurs along the Amur River. (For museums of the USSR see **European Museums** 2.)

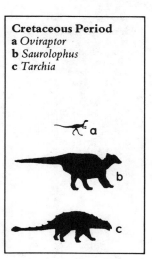

Cretaceous Period
a *Oviraptor*
b *Saurolophus*
c *Tarchia*

NATIONS' NAMED DINOSAURS

ISRAEL	Conchoraptor	Maleevus	Saurolophus	Aralosaurus
Elaphrosaurus	Deinocheirus	Mandschurosaurus	Saurornithoides	Arstanosaurus
	Elmisaurus	Microceratops	Segnosaurus	Bactrosaurus
	Enigmosaurus	Mongolosaurus	Shamosaurus	Coeluroides
MONGOLIA	Erlikosaurus	Nemegtosaurus	Talarurus	Embasaurus
Adasaurus	Gallimimus	Opisthocoelicaudia	Tarbosaurus	Itemirus
Alectrosaurus	Garudimimus	Oviraptor	Tarchia	Jaxartosaurus
Alioramus	Goyocephale	Pinacosaurus	Therizinosaurus	Psittacosaurus
Amtosaurus	Harpymimus	Prenocephale	Tylocephale	Therizinosaurus
Anserimimus	Homalocephale	Probactrosaurus	Velociraptor	Velociraptor
Asiatosaurus	Hulsanpes	Prodeinodon		
Avimimus	Iguanodon	Protoceratops		
Bagaceratops	Ingenia	Psittacosaurus	**USSR (Asian)**	
Barsboldia	Leptoceratops	Quaesitosaurus	Alectrosaurus	
Borogovia	"Maleevosaurus"	Saichania	Antarctosaurus	

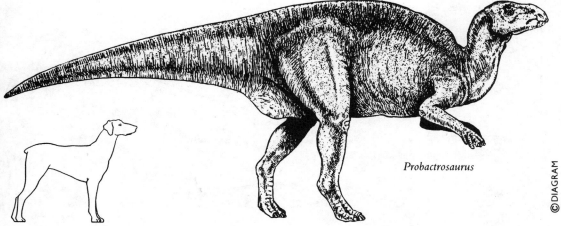

Probactrosaurus

©DIAGRAM

Asian dinosaurs 2

China has revealed a wealth of dinosaurs that roamed far harsher lands than the lush lowlands inhabited by most North American dinosaurs. Mesozoic China featured mountain ranges enclosing dry inland drainage basins liable to sudden floods that seemingly drowned countless dinosaurs. Coniferous upland forests gave way lower down to scrub and semidesert flanking shallow, often salty, lakes. About 80 million years ago transarctic migration probably linked dinosaurs of China and North America.

CHINA

Chinese dinosaur discovery began with Russian excavation of the duck-bill *Mandschurosaurus* in the early 1900s, and gained momentum under **Friedrich von Huene**'s former student **Young Chung Chien**, and later under **Dong Zhiming**. By 1989 all Chinese provinces but one had yielded dinosaurs. Hundreds emerged from amazing bone beds in Sichuan, and roadbuilders even struck dinosaur bones 13,800 ft (4200 m) above sea level in Tibet. In the Gobi Desert in the late 1980s a long-term Canadian-Chinese project located Asia's longest-ever sauropod, a fine skeleton of 26-feet-long flesh-eating *Yangchuanosaurus*, a herd of young *Pinacosaurus*, a wealth of tracks and eggshells, and much besides.

Chinese dinosaurs spanned Early Jurassic through Late Cretaceous time (*Lufengosaurus* and other once supposedly "Triassic" Chinese dinosaurs now bear a later date). Their 95 genera and the many kinds of eggs, including nests, outnumbered those from any other nation except the United States. The 25 theropods ranged from small, agile hunters like *Velociraptor* to the terrifying monster *Tyrannosaurus*. There were 5 prosauropods, and 20 sauropods including *Mamenchisaurus* with the longest neck of any animal on Earth and *Shunosaurus* – the first known sauropod with a tail that ended in a bony club. But more than 40 Chinese dinosaurs were ornithischians: 3 fabrosaurids, 1 heterodontosaurid, 2 hypsilophodontids, 1 iguanodontid, 9 hadrosaurs, 2 scelidosaurs, 3 bone-headed dinosaurs, 8 plated dinosaurs (more than half the world's known total), 8 armored dinosaurs, 1 "parrot lizard," 2 chaoyoungosaurids, and at least 2 protoceratopsids.

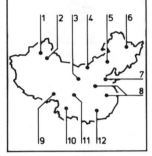

Chinese dinosaur-rich regions
1 Junggar Basin
2 Turpan Basin
3 Ordos Basin
4 The Gobi of inner Mongolia
5 Hebei-Liaoning area
6 South Bank of the Heilongjiang river
7 Shandong Peninsula
8 The provinces of Henan and Anhui
9 Oamdo Basin (Tibet)
10 Lufeng Basin
11 Sichuan Basin
12 Nanxiong Basin

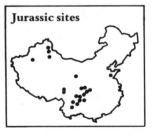

Jurassic sites

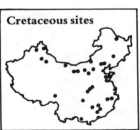

Cretaceous sites

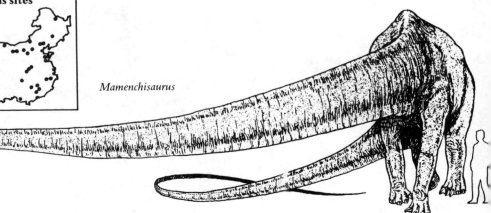

Mamenchisaurus

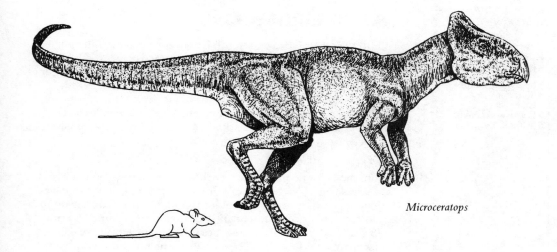

Microceratops

LAOS
Fragmentary sauropod remains have been ascribed to the duck–bill *Mandschurosaurus* and the sauropod *Titanosaurus*.

THAILAND
Discoveries include remains of an unnamed sauropod, and Jurassic teeth attributed to a spinosaurid theropod, *Siamosaurus*.

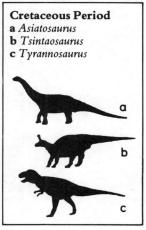

Jurassic Period
a *Mamenchisaurus*
b *Tuojiangosaurus*
c *Yangchuanosaurus*

Cretaceous Period
a *Asiatosaurus*
b *Tsintaosaurus*
c *Tyrannosaurus*

NATIONS' NAMED DINOSAURS

CHINA (including Tibet)
Alectrosaurus
Anchisaurus
Archaeornithomimus
Asiatosaurus
Aublysodon
Avimimus
Bactrosaurus
Bellusaurus
Changdusaurus ★
Chaoyoungosaurus
Chialingosaurus
Chiayuesaurus
Chilantaisaurus
Chingkankousaurus
Chinshakiangosaurus
Chuandongocoelurus
Chungkingosaurus
Dachongosaurus
Damalasaurus ★
Datousaurus
Dianchungosaurus
Euhelopus
Euoplocephalus
Gasosaurus
Gilmoreosaurus
Gongbusaurus
Heishansaurus
Huayangosaurus
Jaxartosaurus
Jiangjunmiaosaurus
("*Monolophosaurus*")
Kaijiangosaurus
Kelmayisaurus
Kunmingosaurus
Lancangjiangosaurus ★

Lufengocephalus
Lufengosaurus
Lukousaurus
Mamenchisaurus
Mandschurosaurus
Megacervixosaurus ★
Microceratops
Microdontosaurus ★
Microhadrosaurus
Micropachycephalosaurus
Microvenator
Monkonosaurus
Nanshiungosaurus
Nemegtosaurus
Ngexisaurus ★
Omeisaurus
Ornithomimus
Oshanosaurus ★
Peishansaurus
Phaedrolosaurus
Pinacosaurus
Probactrosaurus
Prodeinodon
Protoceratops
Protognathus
Psittacosaurus
Sangonghesaurus ★
Sanpasaurus
Saurolophus
Sauroplites
Scelidosaurus
Segnosaurus
Shanshanosaurus
Shantungosaurus
Shunosaurus
Sinocoelurus

Sinosaurus
Stegoceras
Stegosaurides
Szechuanosaurus
Tanius
Tatisaurus
Tawasaurus
Tenchisaurus ★
Tienshanosaurus
Tsintaosaurus
Tugulusaurus
Tuojiangosaurus
Tyrannosaurus
Velociraptor
Wannanosaurus
Wuerhosaurus
Xiaosaurus ★
Xuanhanosaurus
Xuanhuasaurus
Yandusaurus
Yangchuanosaurus
Yingshanosaurus ★
Yubasaurus
Yunnanosaurus
Zizhongosaurus

LAOS
Mandschurosaurus
Titanosaurus

THAILAND
Siamosaurus

★Not formally described

©DIAGRAM

249

Asian dinosaurs 3

Until the 1970s Japan and South Korea appeared completely blank on maps of dinosaur discoveries. No more. Korean and Japanese scientists examining their countries' Mesozoic rocks have begun detecting fossil bones and tracks that confirm the worldwide distribution of the dinosaurs. Finds so far come from the Cretaceous period. Dinosaurs evidently colonized at least two of Japan's largest islands while these still formed part of mainland Asia as recently as Late Cretaceous times.

JAPAN

Until the 1970s no dinosaurs were known from the string of islands now making up Japan. Japan's only dinosaur to bear a name was *Nipponosaurus*, a young hadrosaur found down a coalmine upon Sakhalin which was subsequently occupied and claimed by the USSR. Yet by 1989 Professor **Yoshikazu Hasegawa** of Yokohama National University had studied fossils possibly attributed to 9 genera of Early and Late Cretaceous dinosaurs from within his nation's present boundaries. These finds came from seven localities in six prefectures that ranged from Iwate in northeast Honshu to Kumamoto on Kyushu Island in the southwest.

By 1990 the items were still only known by chironyms (handy unofficial names) ending in –*ryu* ("dragon"), the Japanese equivalent of -*saurus*. Substituting -*saurus* endings gives 6 theropods nicknamed "Futabasaurus," "Kagasaurus," "Katsuyamasaurus," "Kitadanisaurus," "Mifunesaurus," and "Sanchusaurus"; 3 sauropods, known as "Hisanohamasaurus," "Moshisaurus," plus "Sugiyamasaurus" known only from somewhat spoon-shaped teeth; the iguanodontid "Fukuisaurus," and the hadrosaur "Hironosaurus." Most of these beasts survived only as teeth or single bones of dubious identity, so some are probably the same as dinosaurs already known from China or Mongolia. For instance, "Moshisaurus" might well be *Mamenchisaurus* and "Sanchusaurus" could be *Gallimimus*.

Besides these fossils, scientists have found theropod and ornithopod footprints in the Cretaceous rocks of central and east–central Honshu.

JAPAN'S NAMED DINOSAURS

"Fukuisaurus"
"Futabasaurus"
"Hironosaurus"
"Hisanohamasaurus"
"Kagasaurus"
"Katsuyamasaurus"
"Kitadanisaurus"
"Mifunesaurus"
"Moshisaurus"
 Nipponosaurus
"Sanchusaurus"
"Sugiyamasaurus"

"Hironosaurus"

SOUTH KOREA

In and since the 1970s Korean scientists have found Cretaceous
sauropod and other bones and dinosaur trackways in the country's
southeast quarter. In 1982 **Seong Young Yang** reported 7 types of
footprints from 13 south-coast sites near Deogmyeongri. In 1979
Haang Mook Kim named *Koreanosaurus* (probably a theropod). In
1983 he named *Ultrasaurus*, a sauropod first thought to be larger
than *Supersaurus* but evidently smaller. The Korean *Ultrasaurus* was
also smaller than an identically named US sauropod. (Because the
Korean dinosaur was named first in a scientific publication, only
that *Ultrasaurus* has a scientifically valid name.)

South Korean sites
1 Tabri, North
   Gyeongsang-do
2 Eoyang Village, South
   Gyeongsang-do
3 Deogmyeongri, South
   Gyeongsang-do

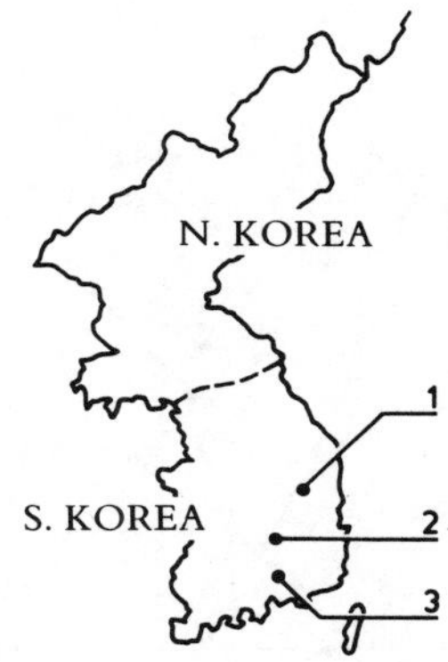

N. KOREA

S. KOREA

1
2
3

SOUTH KOREA'S NAMED DINOSAURS

Koreanosaurus
Ultrasaurus

Ultrasaurus

©DIAGRAM

Asian dinosaurs 4

While the Age of Dinosaurs was young the Indian subcontinent began splitting from the supercontinent Pangaea. Later, India became an island drifting north before crashing into Asia, evidently after dinosaurs became extinct. Some scientists have blamed the worldwide death of dinosaurs on effects of massive lava flows welling up in Late Cretaceous India. Undoubtedly the lava buried much dinosaur-bearing rock, some since exposed by river valleys cutting down through the lava sheets.

INDIA

The subcontinent's significant discoveries all come from what is now its largest nation. European palaeontologists began finding dinosaurs in India in 1860, when India lay under British rule. (Most Indian dinosaurs, though, bear names coined by the German scientist **Friedrich von Huene**.) Since independence, Indian paleontologists such as **Sohan Jain**, **Sankar Chatterjee**, and **P. Yadagiri** have helped add fresh discoveries. By 1990 central and southern India had yielded 18 mainly Late Cretaceous genera. Ten were theropods large and small (*Coeluroides, Compsosuchus, Dryptosauroides, Indosaurus, Indosuchus, Jubbulpuria, Laevisuchus,*

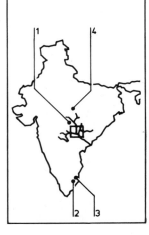

Indian localities
1 Pisdura
2 Tiruchirapalli
3 Ariyalur
4 Jabalpur

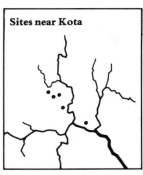

Sites near Kota

INDIA'S NAMED DINOSAURS

Antarctosaurus
Barapasaurus
Brachypodosaurus
Coeluroides
Compsosuchus
Dravidosaurus
Dryptosauroides
Indosaurus
Indosuchus
Jubbulpuria
Kotasaurus
Laevisuchus
Lametasaurus
Laplatasaurus
Ornithomimoides
Orthogoniosaurus
Titanosaurus
Walkeria

Barapasaurus

Ornithomimoides, and *Orthogoniosaurus*. There were also six sauropods (*Antarctosaurus*, *Barapasaurus*, *Kotasaurus*, *Lametasaurus*, *Laplatasaurus*, and *Titanosaurus*), a plated dinosaur (*Dravidosaurus*), an armored dinosaur (*Brachypodosaurus*), eggshells, nests, and droppings.

Early and late dinosaurs brought some surprises. East–central Indian Triassic fossils including Asia's earliest known dinosaur *Walkeria* implied links with northern continents; this challenges established notions that India had formed part of Gondwana, the southern supercontinent created when Pangaea split. Early Jurassic rocks from Kota in Central India produced large numbers of strange, primitive *Barapasaurus*, among the first of those largest of all land herbivores, the sauropods. Plainly, sauropods had reached (or evolved in) India before it split off as an island. Late Cretaceous rocks from southern India revealed *Dravidosaurus*, a plated dinosaur seemingly persisting after all its relatives outside India had petered out. Perhaps the island continent of India never gained theropods capable of wiping out these "old–fashioned" ornithischians.

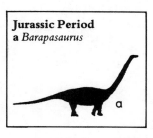

Jurassic Period
a *Barapasaurus*

Cretaceous Period
a *Antarctosaurus*
b *Indosuchus*
c *Jubbulpuria*

Laevisuchus

©DIAGRAM

Asian museums 1

This list is only representative. Many Chinese city museums display Chinese dinosaurs. Chinese dinosaur exhibitions have toured the world, and packaged tours of Chinese museums and sites were under way before 1989's disturbances. Numerous Japanese cities show casts or models of dinosaurs from North America and Asia. For museums in India see **Asian dinosaurs 4**.

Museums in China and Mongolia

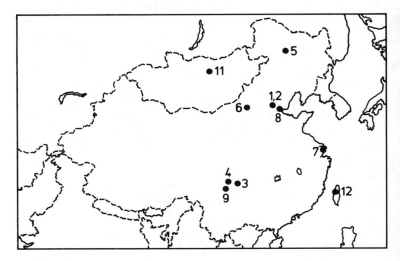

CHINA

1 Beijing (Peking): Beijing Natural History Museum This impressive collection has mounted skeletons or casts of the theropod *Gasosaurus*, the sauropod *Mamenchisaurus*, the hadrosaurs *Shantungosaurus* and *Tsintaosaurus*, and the "parrot lizard" *Psittacosaurus*.

2 Beijing (Peking): Museum of the Institute of Vertebrate Paleontology and Paleoanthropology A major collection of mounted skeletons of Chinese dinosaurs including the theropod *Gasosaurus*; the prosauropod *Lufengosaurus*; sauropods *Bellusaurus*, *Datousaurus*, *Mamenchisaurus*, and *Shunosaurus*; the hadrosaur *Tsintaosaurus*; the "parrot lizard" *Psittacosaurus*, and the horned dinosaur *Protoceratops*.

3 Beipei (Pei-p'ei), Sichuan: Beipei Museum This has skeletons of the theropod *Yangchuanosaurus*, the sauropod *Omeisaurus*, and the stegosaurs *Huayangosaurus* and *Tuojiangosaurus*.

4 Chengdu (Ch'eng-tu), Sichuan: Museum of Chengdu College of Geology Its many dinosaurs include theropods *Chuandongocoelurus* and *Kaijiangosaurus*, sauropods *Mamenchisaurus* and *Omeisaurus*, and the ornithopod *Yandusaurus*.

5 Harbin: Heilongjiang Museum This contains two skeletons of the hadrosaur *Mandschurosaurus*.

6 Hohhot, Inner Mongolia: Inner Mongolia Museum Here are the theropod *Archaeornithomimus*, the "parrot lizard" *Psittacosaurus*, and horned *Protoceratops*.

7 Shanghai: Shanghai Museum Casts depict *Mamenchisaurus*, *Tsintaosaurus*, and *Tuojiangosaurus*.

8 Tianjin (Tientsin): Tianjin Museum of Natural History Shows *Lufengosaurus*, *Omeisaurus*, and *Tuojiangosaurus*.

9 Zigong, Sichuan: Zigong Dinosaur Museum Asia's first dinosaur museum opened in 1987. Its Burial Hall stands over exposed rock beds rich in bones of 180–million-year-old dinosaurs, and the museum's fine array of mounted skeletons feature Middle Jurassic beasts including the theropod *Gasosaurus*; the sauropods *Datousaurus*, *Omeisaurus*, and *Shunosaurus*; the small ornithopods *Xiaosaurus* and *Yandusaurus*; and the plated dinosaur *Huayangosaurus*.

INDIA
10 Calcutta:

Geology Museum, Indian Statistical Institute The chief exhibit is the world's only mounted skeleton of the Early Jurassic sauropod *Barapasaurus*. Other items include remains of *Lametasaurus*, perhaps partly a titanosaurid sauropod.

MONGOLIA
11 Ulan-Bator: Academy of Sciences This remarkable collection of Gobi Desert dinosaurs contains the theropods *Tarbosaurus* (*Tyrannosaurus*?), *Velociraptor*, *Saurornithoides* (*Troodon*?), *Gallimimus*, *Garudimimus*, *Anserimimus*, *Therizinosaurus*, and *Deinocheirus*; enigmatic saurischians *Enigmosaurus*, *Erlikosaurus*, and *Segnosaurus*; sauropods *Nemegtosaurus* and *Opisthocoelicaudia*; the hadrosaur *Saurolophus*; the "parrot lizard" *Psittacosaurus*; and horned *Bagaceratops* and *Protoceratops*.

TAIWAN
12 Taichung: National Museum of Natural Science Displays include casts of *Camarasaurus* and *Stegosaurus*, and full-size lifelike models of *Euoplocephalus* (*Scolosaurus*), *Gallimimus*, and a robotic *Corythosaurus* with a juvenile.

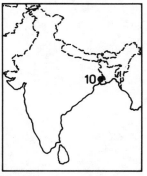

Geology Museum, Calcutta

©DIAGRAM

Burial Hall of the Zigong Dinosaur Museum, Sichuan.

Asian museums 2

Museums in Japan

JAPAN

1 Iwaki, Fukushima: Iwaki City Museum of Coal and Fossils
Figures an imposing cast of the skeleton of the long-necked Chinese sauropod *Mamenchisaurus*.

2 Kagoshima, Kagoshima: Kagoshima Prefectural Museum
Shows the theropod *Allosaurus* and the ornithopod *Camptosaurus*.

3 Kitakyushu, Fukuoka: Kitakyushu Museum of Natural History
Here are casts of the theropod *Allosaurus*, the sauropod *Camarasaurus*, the Asian iguanodontid *Probactrosaurus* (next to a lifesize model), the hadrosaur *Saurolophus*, plated *Stegosaurus*, and ceratopsians *Protoceratops* and *Triceratops*.

4 Kyoto: Kyoto Municipal Science Center for Youth Replica skeletons represent the theropod *Tarbosaurus*, the hadrosaur *Saurolophus*, and the ceratopsian *Protoceratops*.

5 Maebashi, Gunma: Gunma Prefectural Museum of History
Has a cast of the toothless theropod *Gallimimus*.

6 Niigata, Niigata: Niigata Prefectural Natural Science Museum Shows a cast of the horned dinosaur *Triceratops*.

7 Osaka: Osaka Museum of Natural History This has casts of the theropods *Allosaurus*, *Coelophysis*, and *Ornitholestes*, and the plated dinosaur *Stegosaurus*.

Mamenchisaurus cast, Iwaki City Museum of Coal and Fossils.

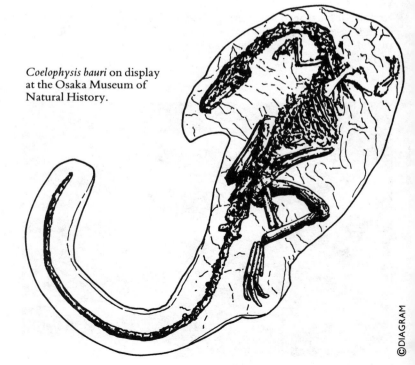

Coelophysis bauri on display at the Osaka Museum of Natural History.

©DIAGRAM

8 Sapporo, Hokkaido: Historical Museum of Hokkaido Includes a cast of the theropod *Allosaurus*.

9 Sendai, Miyagi: Saito Ho-on Kai Museum of Natural History Contains a cast of *Allosaurus*.

10 Shimizu, Shizuoka: Tokai University, Natural History Museum Has casts of *Tarbosaurus* and *Probactrosaurus*.

11 Takikawa, Hokkaido: Takikawa Museum of Art and Natural History Has casts of the skeletons of *Tyrannosaurus* and *Protoceratops*.

12 Tokyo: National Science Museum An *Allosaurus* skeleton is on show, with casts of *Tarbosaurus* and *Coelophysis*, the ornithopod *Camptosaurus*, and the ceratopsian *Protoceratops*.

13 Toyohashi, Aichi: Toyohashi Museum of Natural History Features the hadrosaur *Edmontosaurus* (*Anatosaurus*), casts of the theropod *Allosaurus*, and the stegosaur *Stegosaurus*, and life-size models of *Iguanodon*, *Ankylosaurus*, and *Triceratops*.

14 Utsunomiya, Tochigi: Tochigi Prefectural Museum Has casts of *Allosaurus* and *Stegosaurus*.

Tarbosaurus skeleton on view at the Kyoto Municipal Science Center for Youth.

Skeleton and model reconstruction of *Probactrosaurus gobiensis* at the Kitakyushu Museum of Natural History.

South American dinosaurs

Dinosaurs left traces from Colombia in the north to Argentina and Chile in the south. None come from Amazonia's deeply rotted rocks and only a few fossil tracks and bones have turned up in the high Andes of the west. Easily the richest bone beds lie in the dry grasslands and semideserts of the southeast. By 1990 these had yielded more than three dozen named genera from four nations. All genera but one occurred in Argentina. Discoveries prove that South America was linked to northern lands early and late in the Age of Dinosaurs. Remarkable finds include likely ancestors of dinosaurs, some of the world's oldest dinosaurs, a strange bull-headed theropod, prosauropod babies no bigger than a sparrow, and sauropods with armored hides.

ARGENTINA

Fossil dinosaurs represent all three Mesozoic periods. *Pisanosaurus* ranked among the world's earliest ornithischians. The carnosaur *Piatnitzkysaurus*, and the sauropods *Patagosaurus* and *Volkheimeria* lived in Late Jurassic times. In the Late Cretaceous, sauropods and other dinosaurs roamed a low, hot land, with rivers where lungfish, crocodiles, and turtles swam. Outstanding Argentinian finds include the bull-headed abelisaurid *Carnotaurus*, the noasaurid *Noasaurus*, the armored titanosaurid *Saltasaurus*, tiny young of the prosauropod *Mussaurus*, the hadrosaurids *Kritosaurus* and *Secernosaurus*, and a possible protoceratopsid, *Notoceratops*. These last three hint at migration from North America before South America became, and long remained, an island.

Dinosaur discoveries began in Argentina in 1882. They gained momentum under **Carlos** and **Florentino Ameghino**. By the 1980s systematic excavations went on apace under experienced paleontologists such as **José Bonaparte**. Most fossils have come from the west and south, especially the great southern tract of grassland and semidesert, Patagonia.

**South American
dinosaur localities**
1 Laguna Umayo, Peru
2 Bauru Formation, Brazil
3 Santa Maria Formation,
  Brazil
4 Andean Basin, Argentina
5 Ischigualasto
6 Neuquen Basin,
  Argentina
7 Chubut Province,
  Argentina
8 Chubut Province,
  Argentina

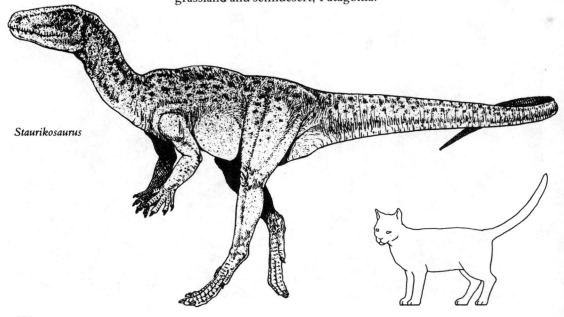

Staurikosaurus

BRAZIL

Southern Brazil has yielded some of the oldest dinosaur fossils found anywhere. In the 1920s the German scientist **Friedrich von Huene** unearthed alleged prosauropod fossils from gullies in Triassic rocks near Santa Maria. Later, the same area produced the undoubted Mid Triassic prosauropod *Staurikosaurus*. From Bauru in the south-east state of São Paulo came Late Cretaceous sauropod remains, discovered by a Brazilian geological survey official, **Llewellyn Price**. Brazilian sauropods included the titanosaurid *Antarctosaurus*.

CHILE

This has yielded the sauropod *Antarctosaurus* and a theropod.

COLOMBIA

Sauropod bones and theropod teeth have been found.

PERU

Dinosaur remains have come from near an Andean mountain lake, Laguna Umayo, in southern Peru.

URUGUAY

Discoveries include the Late Cretaceous titanosaurid sauropods *Antarctosaurus*, *Argyrosaurus*, and *Titanosaurus*.

Triassic Period
a *Pisanosaurus*
b *Staurikosaurus*

Jurassic Period
a *Amygdalodon*
b *Piatnitzkysaurus*

NATIONS' NAMED DINOSAURS

ARGENTINA			BRAZIL
Abelisaurus	*Genyodectes*	*Piatnitzkysaurus*	*Antarctosaurus*
Aeolosaurus	*Herrerasaurus*	*Pisanosaurus*	*Staurikosaurus*
Amargasaurus	*Ischisaurus*	*Plateosaurus*	*Titanosaurus*
Amygdalodon	*Kritosaurus*	*Riojasaurus*	
Antarctosaurus	*Laplatasaurus*	*Saltasaurus*	
Argyrosaurus	*Lapparentosaurus*	*Secernosaurus*	**CHILE**
Campylodoniscus	*Loncosaurus*	*Titanosaurus*	*Antarctosaurus*
Carnotaurus	*Loricosaurus*	*Unquillosaurus*	
Chubutisaurus	*Microcoelus*	*Volkheimeria*	
Clasmodosaurus	*Mussaurus*	*Xenotarsosaurus*	**URUGUAY**
Coloradisaurus	"*Neuquensaurus*"		*Antarctosaurus*
"*Epachtosaurus*"	*Noasaurus*		*Argyrosaurus*
Frenguellisaurus	*Notoceratops*		*Titanosaurus*
	Patagosaurus		

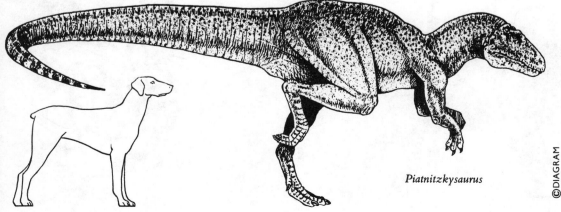

Cretaceous Period
a *Noasaurus*
b *Saltasaurus*
c *Secernosaurus*

Piatnitzkysaurus

©DIAGRAM

Museums in South America

South American museums

The lion's share of South America's dinosaur collections is in Argentina, where most South American dinosaurs were dug up. Argentina's dinosaur displays had their origins in the fossil collection built up in and after the 1880s by **Florentino Ameghino** for the La Plata Museum. Recent finds are mainly in the Museum of Natural Sciences, Buenos Aires.

ARGENTINA

1 Buenos Aires: Argentine Museum of Natural Sciences
This can now claim the richest store of dinosaur discoveries in South America. Recently discovered genera figure among the bones or casts on show. Specimens include the theropods *Piatnitzkysaurus* (Mid Jurassic), and *Carnotaurus* (Late Cretaceous), the sauropod *Patagosaurus* (Mid Jurassic), and the Patagonian hadrosaur *Kritosaurus australis* (Latest Cretaceous).

2 La Plata: Museum of La Plata University Most dinosaur remains held here were found in Argentina, but North America is represented by a cast of the sauropod *Diplodocus* and a skull of *Centrosaurus*, a horned dinosaur.

3 San Miguel de Tucumán: Museum This includes a mounted skeleton of the prosauropod *Riojasaurus*.

4 BRAZIL

Rio de Janeiro National Museum The collection includes remains of various sauropods.

Saltasaurus, an Argentinian dinosaur had bony plates (**a**) and bony studs (**b**) guarding its back and sides.

Bony studs are shown here actual size. Illustration after Bonaparte.

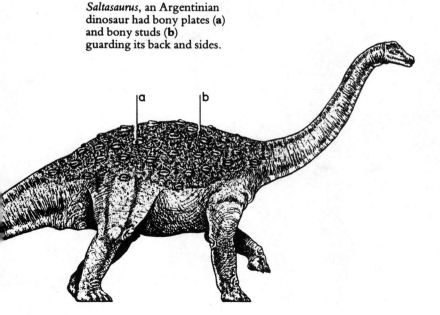

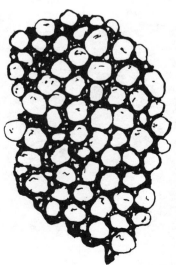

African dinosaurs

Dinosaurs from Triassic through Early Cretaceous time include close kin of North American contemporaries. Key finds have come from the Atlas Mountains, Sahara Desert, Madagascar, and eastern and southern Africa; Niger's and Tanzania's famous boneyards formed where river mud preserved skeletons drowned by ancient floods. Discoverers have included Germany's **Werner Janensch** and **Ernst Stromer**, France's **Albert de Lapparent** and **Philippe Taquet**, and Great Britain's **Robert Broom** and **Alan Charig**.

ALGERIA
Late Jurassic/Early Cretaceous finds including teeth and tracks reveal theropods and hint at the great sauropod *Brachiosaurus*.

CAMEROON
This has theropod, sauropod, and ornithopod remains.

CHAD
Bones of a small theropod were found here.

EGYPT
Early and Late Cretaceous rocks have yielded sail-backed *Spinosaurus*, other theropods and the sauropod *Aegyptosaurus*.

African nations with dinosaurs
1. Morocco (mainly in the Atlas Mountains)
2. Algeria (in the Atlas Mountains and Sahara Desert)
3. Tunisia (Sahara Desert)
4. Egypt (Sahara Desert)
5. Kenya
6. Tanzania
7. Madagascar
8. Malawi
9. Zimbabwe
10. Lesotho (Stormberg Formation)
11. South Africa (Stormberg and other formations)
12. Cameroon
13. Chad
14. Nigeria
15. Niger (Sahara Desert)
16. Mali

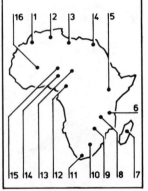

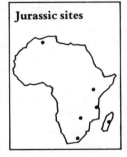

Triassic sites

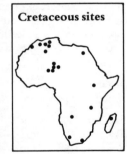

Jurassic sites

Cretaceous sites

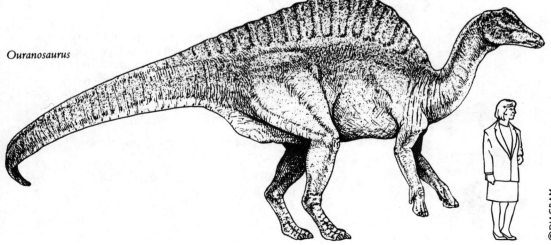

Ouranosaurus

©DIAGRAM

African dinosaurs 2

Triassic Period
a *Sellosaurus*
b *Lesothosaurus*
c *Syntarsus*

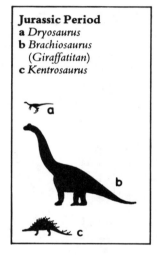

Jurassic Period
a *Dryosaurus*
b *Brachiosaurus*
  (*Giraffatitan*)
c *Kentrosaurus*

Cretaceous Period
a *Aegyptosaurus*
b *Ouranosaurus*
c *Spinosaurus*

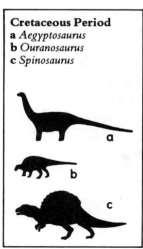

KENYA
Cretaceous sauropod remains lie west of Lake Turkana.

LESOTHO
Early dinosaurs include prosauropods, fabrosaurids, a heterodontosaurid, and a wealth of trackways.

MADAGASCAR
The north west yielded a Late Cretaceous theropod, a titanosaurid sauropod, and the first Southern pachycephalosaur.

MALAWI
Dinosaur beds of northern Malawi have yielded Early Cretaceous ornithischians, sauropods, and theropods, to be described.

MALI
This has the sauropod *Rebbachisaurus*.

MOROCCO
The High Atlas Mountains yielded Mid-Triassic and Early Jurassic dinosaurs. Major Moroccan items include the early prosauropod *Azendohsaurus*, the brachiosaurid *Rebbachisaurus*, a huge *Cetiosaurus* skeleton, and *Breviparopus*, a huge sauropod known by tracks.

NIGER
Saharan Desert expeditions have found Cretaceous spinosaurid and smaller theropods, camarasaurid and other sauropods, iguanodontids including sailbacked *Ouranosaurus*, and dinosaur footprints. Many bones lie exposed where wind erodes the sandy surface.

NIGERIA
The sauropod *Laplatasaurus* reportedly lived here.

SOUTH AFRICA
By 1990, 11 genera of early dinosaurs had come from Jurassic and Triassic rocks. Four were prosauropods, five heterodontosaurids and one a theropod. Later beasts included a sauropod, ornithopod, and a plated dinosaur.

TANZANIA
Mid-Triassic rocks revealed the early prosauropod *Nyasasaurus*. Exacavating Tendaguru Hill, **Werner Janensch** unlocked a treasury of (Late Jurassic) dinosaurs including the theropod *Ceratosaurus*; sauropods *Barosaurus*, *Dicraeosaurus*, *Brachiosaurus* (*Giraffatitan*), and *Tornieria*; the ornithopod *Dryosaurus*; and plated *Kentrosaurus*.

TUNISIA
Ornithopod and sauropod remains come from southern Tunisia.

ZIMBABWE
This was home to the early theropod *Syntarsus*, the early sauropod *Vulcanodon*, and Tanzanian-type Jurassic dinosaurs.

NATIONS' NAMED DINOSAURS

ALGERIA
Bahariasaurus
Brachiosaurus (Giraffatitan?)
Carcharodontosaurus
Elaphrosaurus
Rebbachisaurus

EGYPT
Aegyptosaurus
Bahariasaurus
Carcharodontosaurus
Elaphrosaurus
Majungasaurus
Spinosaurus

LESOTHO
Abrictosaurus
Fabrosaurus
Heterodontosaurus
Lesothosaurus
Likhoelesaurus
Thotobolosaurus

MADAGASCAR
Laplatasaurus
Lapparentosaurus
Majungasaurus
Majungatholus

MALAWI
Tornieria

MOROCCO
Azendohsaurus
Carcharodontosaurus
Cetiosaurus
Elaphrosaurus
Rebbachisaurus

NIGER
Aegyptosaurus
Bahariasaurus
Carcharodontosaurus
Elaphrosaurus
Gravisaurus
Inosaurus
Ouranosaurus

Rebbachisaurus
Spinosaurus
Valdosaurus

NIGERIA
Laplatasaurus

SOUTH AFRICA
Abrictosaurus
Algoasaurus
Aliwalia
Blikanasaurus
Euskelosaurus
Geranosaurus
Heterodontosaurus
Kangnasaurus
Lanasaurus
Lycorhinus
Massospondylus
Melanorosaurus
Paranthodon
Syntarsus

TANZANIA
Allosaurus
Barosaurus
Brachiosaurus (Giraffatitan)
Ceratosaurus
Dicraeosaurus
Dryosaurus
Elaphrosaurus
Kentrosaurus
Nyasasaurus
Tornieria

TUNISIA
Carcharodontosaurus
Rebbachisaurus
Iguanodon

ZIMBABWE
Barosaurus
Brachiosaurus
Dicraeosaurus
Syntarsus
Tornieria
Vulcanodon

African museums

By the 1990s five museums displayed significant dinosaur remains. None rivals the most spectacular fossils lost to Africa in the early 1900s when **Werner Janensch** shipped them to Berlin from Tanzania (then part of German East Africa). But since European colonial rule gave way to independence, African nations have begun developing their own museums and national collections.

Museums in Africa

MOROCCO
1 Rabat: Museum of Earth Sciences This young establishment includes fossils of the Moroccan sauropods *Cetiosaurus* and *Rebbachisaurus*.

NIGER
2 Niamey: National Museum of Niger A complete skeleton of the sail-backed iguanodontid *Ouranosaurus* is on display.

SOUTH AFRICA
3 Cape Town: South African Museum Here are some fossils of important early dinosaurs: the prosauropods *Anchisaurus(?)*, *Massospondylus*, and *Melanorosaurus*, and the small ornithopod *Heterodontosaurus*.

4 Johannesburg: Bernard Price Institute of Palaeontology This stores remains of the early prosauropods *Melanorosaurus* and *Massospondylus*, the theropod *Syntarsus*, and ornithischians *Fabrosaurus* and *Lanasaurus*.

5 ZIMBABWE
Harare: National Museum of Zimbabwe Fossils include the early theropod *Syntarsus*, the prosauropod *Massospondylus*, and the primitive sauropod *Vulcanodon*.

Dinosaurs down under

Until the 1980s Australia had yielded few dinosaurs, and none had come from New Zealand or Antarctica. There were several explanations – the right fossil-bearing rocks were hard to find. Level grassland masks and deep weathering destroys many Mesozoic fossils in Australia; volcanic rocks occupy much of New Zealand; and an immense ice sheet smothers most Antarctica. Yet we now know dinosaurs inhabited all three – confirmation that they once formed fragments of the supercontinent, Pangaea.

ANTARCTICA

In 1986 Argentinian scientists found the Southern Hemisphere's first ankylosaurid armored dinosaur. In 1989 British scientists announced a fossil hypsilophodont. Both came from Late Cretaceous rocks of James Ross Island off the Antarctic Peninsula.

AUSTRALIA

By 1990 Australia had yielded nearly a dozen named genera of dinosaurs. These were the prosauropod *Agrosaurus*; theropods *Allosaurus*, *Kakuru*, and *Rapator*; sauropods *Austrosaurus* and *Rhoetosaurus*; hypsilophodontids *Atlascopcosaurus*, *Fulgurotherium*, and *Leaellynosaura*; the camptosaurid *Muttaburrasaurus*; and the nodosaurid ankylosaur *Minmi*. Most date from Early Cretaceous time, though some are earlier or later. The prosauropod implies early links with other continents, but the Early-Mid Cretaceous survival of oldfashioned *Austrosaurus* suggests a barrier emerged, shutting off more advanced competitors likely to have wiped it out. As Australia then lay near the South Pole, that barrier might have been the three-month polar night, interfering with migrations from Antarctica before Australia had broken free. Yet those dinosaur "gazelles" the hypsilophodontids flourished in south-east Australia when that lay within the Antarctic Circle.

After chance early finds of dinosaurs, systematic hunting got under way by 1980. Nearly half of Australia's dinosaurs were named in the 1980s by paleontologists including **Ralph Molnar** and **Thomas Rich**. Dinosaur hunters found most fossils on Queensland's grasslands and in the sea cliffs of Victoria – a source of several hypsilophodontids. People have also discovered dinosaur tracks, notably near Winton in Queensland, and in Western Australia.

Australian "dinosaur states"
1 Queensland
2 New South Wales
3 Victoria
4 South Australia

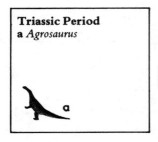

Triassic Period
a *Agrosaurus*

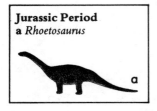

Jurassic Period
a *Rhoetosaurus*

Cretaceous Period
a *Austrosaurus*
b *Minmi*
c *Muttaburrasaurus*

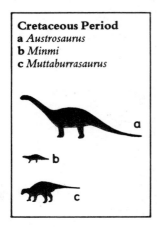

Triassic site	Jurassic site	Cretaceous sites
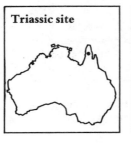	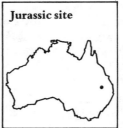	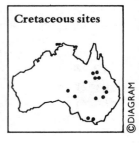

©DIAGRAM

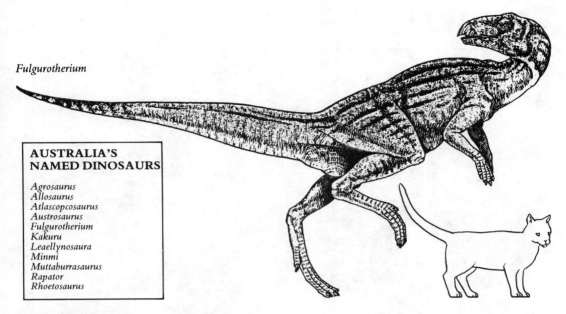

Fulgurotherium

NEW ZEALAND

In 1980 **Ralph Molnar** described the tail bone of New Zealand's first known dinosaur, a theropod from North Island discovered by amateur fossil hunter **Joan Wiffen**. Later island finds included a dryosaurid and an armored dinosaur.

AUSTRALIAN MUSEUMS

1 Adelaide, South Australia: South Australian Museum Has a cast of an *Allosaurus* skeleton.

2 Fortitude Valley, Queensland: Queensland Museum This has remains of sauropods *Rhoetosaurus* and *Austrosaurus*, the nodosaurid *Minmi*, and the large ornithopod *Muttaburrasaurus*.

3 Perth, Western Australia: Western Australian Museum Has a cast of an *Albertosaurus* skeleton.

4 Sydney, New South Wales: Australian Museum The collection includes the North American theropod *Dilophosaurus*, a *Stegosaurus* skeleton and a *Tyrannosaurus* skull cast.

Museums in Australia

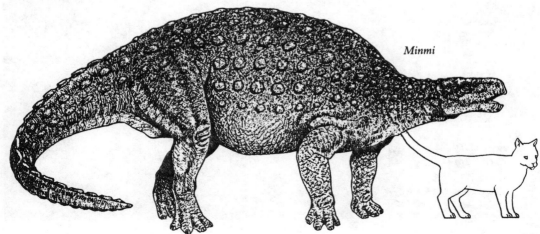

Minmi

Chapter 6

DINOSAUROLOGISTS

Dinosaur finders, namers, describers, and theorists figure on these pages. We name and date their important dinosaur discoveries, but omit achievements unconnected with the dinosaurs. Amateur fossil hunters have made major finds, but we owe most to highly qualified paleontologists (scientists who study fossil life): doctors of philosophy (PhDs) with a degree in paleontology or a related subject. Such experts mainly teach in universities, supervise fossil collections in museums, or work in industry. For many, dinosaurs are only an intriguing sideline.

Above: Roy Chapman Andrews (*right*) and a colleague survey a nest of *Protoceratops* eggs unearthed in the Gobi Desert. Andrews' motorized American team pioneered dinosaur discovery in Mongolia in the 1920s.
Below: Arthur Lakes' naive watercolor done in 1878 shows huge limb bones found at Como Bluff, Wyoming. Such finds revealed rich fossil bonebeds in the then Wild West.

Dinosaurologists

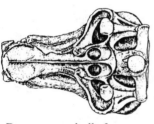

Florentino Ameghino, a pioneer of South American vertebrate paleontology.

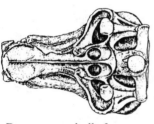

Denversaurus skull after a drawing by Robert Bakker, who named this dinosaur.

Motorized Gobi Desert expedition led by Roy Chapman Andrews.

Alvarez, Luis and **Alvarez, Walter** US father and son scientists who (in 1980) claimed circumstantial proof that organisms including dinosaurs had been wiped out by an asteroid's collision with the Earth.

Ameghino, Florentino (1854-1911) Self-educated Argentinian paleontologist who helped put Argentina's wealth of dinosaurs and prehistoric mammals on the world map. He described more than 6000 fossil species, largely collected by his brother **Carlos** (1865-1936). In the nineteenth century, only fossil finds from the western United States surpassed the Ameghino brothers' South American discoveries. Ameghino was briefly head of paleontology at La Plata Museum where much of his collection ended. He named the dinosaurs *Clasmodosaurus* (1898) and *Loncosaurus* (1898).

Andrews, Roy Chapman (1884-1960) US naturalist and explorer who pioneered dinosaur discoveries in Mongolia's Gobi Desert. Between 1922 and 1925 he led four motorized American Museum of Natural History expeditions to the Gobi. They found fossil *Protoceratops* bones and nests and eggs (the first for any dinosaur), and remains of the hitherto unknown small flesh-eating dinosaurs *Oviraptor*, *Velociraptor*, and *Saurornithoides*, plus a "new" armored dinosaur *Pinacosaurus*.

Attridge, John British paleontologist who showed that *Massospondylus* ground plant food with a gastric mill of swallowed pebbles, and (with **A.W.Crompton** and **F.A. Jenkins**) in 1985 recorded that this prosauropod had lived in North America.

Ayyasami, K Indian paleontologist who with **P. Yadagiri** co-named the Indian plated dinosaur *Dravidosaurus* (1979).

Baird, Donald US "dean of ichnologists" (studiers of fossil tracks), who has published important articles on fossil footprints (in and since the 1950s) and on US East Coast dinosaurs.

Bakker, Robert US paleontologist and anatomical artist who claimed in 1968 that dinosaurs had been "fast, agile, energetic creatures" as warm-blooded as modern mammals are. His drawings show dinosaurs as lively beasts that stood and ran with limbs erect and mostly held their tails up off the ground. In 1971 he argued that sauropods most likely lived on land and browsed on trees like giant giraffes. He rejected **H. G. Seeley**'s long-held views and in 1974, with **Peter Galton**, he argued that birds, ornithischians, and saurischians all belonged to the class Dinosauria – a scheme that he refined in 1986. In 1988 Bakker named the armored dinosaurs *Chassternbergia* and *Denversaurus*, and (with **M. Williams** and **P. J. Currie**) he co-named the small tyrannosaur *Nanotyrannus*.

Baldwin, David US fossil hunter for **O. C. Marsh** and **E. D. Cope**. While collecting for Cope he discovered *Coelophysis* in New Mexico in 1881.

Bannikov, Aleksandr Fedorovich Russian paleontologist who (with **S. M. Kurzanov**) in 1983 co-named *Quaesitosaurus*, a sauropod.

Barsbold, Rinchen Mongolian paleontologist who named the Asian dinosaurs *Adasaurus* (1983), *Anserimimus* (1988), *Conchoraptor* (1986), *Ingenia* (1981), and the dinosaur families Enigmosauridae (1983), Ingeniidae (1986), and Oviraptoridae (1976). With **H. Osmólska** and **E. Roniewicz** he co-named *Gallimimus* (1972); and with **A. Perle** he co-named *Enigmosaurus* (1983), *Harpymimus* and the family Harpymimidae (1984), and the Segnosauria (1980).

Bartholomai, Alan Australian paleontologist who, with **R. Molnar**, in 1981 co-named *Muttaburrasaurus*.

Beckles, Samuel British amateur fossil collector who discovered *Echinodon* (named in 1861).

Béland, Pierre French paleoecologist. With **D. A. Russell**, in 1980 he argued that fossil finds suggesting the ratio of predators to prey may not necessarily imply that dinosaurs had been warm-blooded as birds and mammals are.

Benedetto, Juan Luis Argentinian paleontologist who in 1973 described the primitive dinosaur family Herrerasauridae.

Benton, Michael British paleontologist who argued in 1983 that the dinosaurs did not outcompete their rivals but succeeded them when some unknown factor wiped them out in late Triassic times. He has also contributed to the reclassifying of the dinosaurs.

Berman, David US paleontologist who, with **J. McIntosh**, in 1978 helped to redefine the diplodocid family.

Bird, Roland T. US dinosaur scout for the American Museum of Natural History; he hugely boosted the study of fossil dinosaur footprints by his discoveries in Texas (1938).

Bochatey, Graciela Argentinian co-namer (with **Martínez, Giménez**, and **Rodríguez**) of the carnivorous dinosaur *Xenotarsosaurus* (1986).

Bohlin, Anders Birger Swedish paleontologist who, in 1953, named the following six Chinese dinosaurs: the sauropod *Chiayuesaurus*; the protoceratopsid *Microceratops*; the (arguably) armored trio *Peishansaurus*, *Sauroplites*, and *Stegosaurides*; and the bone-headed or armored dinosaur *Heishansaurus*.

Bonaparte, José F. Argentinian paleontologist whose fossil finds or descriptions of protodinosaurs, a tiny prosauropod, strange theropods, and armored sauropods have spanned the Age of Dinosaurs, adding hugely to our understanding of dinosaurs in South America. He named *Carnotaurus* (1985), *Lapparentosaurus* (1986), *Patagosaurus* (1979), *Piatnitzkysaurus* (1979), *Riojasaurus* (1969), and *Volkheimeria* (1979). He co-named (with **F. E. Novas**) *Abelisaurus* and the Abelisauridae (1985); (with **J. E. Powell**) *Noasaurus* (1980), the Noasauridae (1980), and *Saltasaurus* (1980); and (with **M. Vince**) *Mussaurus* (1979).

Borsuk-Bialynicka, Magdalena Polish paleontologist who named a Mongolian sauropod: *Opisthocoelicaudia* (1977).

Brett-Surman, Michael US paleontologist who, in 1979, named

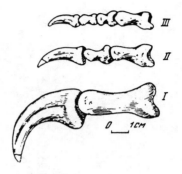

Clawed finger bones of the Mongolian theropod *Ingenia yanshini*, named by Rinchen Barsbold.

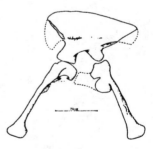

Hip bones of the South American theropod *Piatnitzkysaurus* named by José F. Bonaparte.

©DIAGRAM

Right: Lower jaw of *Megalosaurus*, described by William Buckland (*below*).

Limb bones and inset restoration of *Segisaurus*, named by Charles L. Camp.

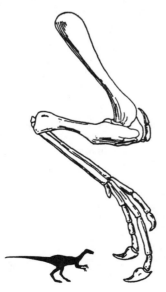

Gilmoreosaurus (an Asian hadrosaur) and *Secernosaurus* (the first-known South American hadrosaur). With **G. S. Paul** in 1985 he co-named the supposed birdlike dinosaur *Avisaurus* (perhaps a bird), and its family, Avisauridae.

Brodkorb, Pierce US specialist in prehistoric birds; in 1978 he reidentified the fossil "owls" *Bradycneme* and *Heptasteornis* as theropod dinosaurs.

Broom, Robert (1866–1951) Scottish paleontologist who named the South African dinosaurs *Algoasaurus* (1904) and *Geranosaurus* (1911). He made significant discoveries about mammal-like reptiles and mammal origins.

Brown, Barnum (1873–1963) American dinosaur hunter. In Montana, in 1902 and 1908, he found the *Tyrannosaurus* skeletons now adorning museums in Pittsburgh and New York City. While collecting for the American Museum of Natural History in 1910, he started the "dinosaur rush" along Alberta's Red Deer River and discovered a number of new ornithischian dinosaurs. He named *Ankylosaurus* (1908) and its armored family Ankylosauridae (1908); the duck-bills *Corythosaurus* (1914), *Hypacrosaurus* (1913), *Kritosaurus* (1910), *Prosaurolophus* (1916), and *Saurolophus* (1912); the protoceratopsid *Leptoceratops* (1914); and the horned dinosaur *Anchiceratops* (1914). Brown also co-named (with **E. M. Schlaikjer**) the bone-head *Pachycephalosaurus* (1943) and the theropod *Dromaeosaurus* (1922).

Buckland, William (1784–1856) British geologist who described *Megalosaurus* (1824), the first dinosaur given a scientific name.

Buffetaut, Eric French paleontologist who, with **R. Ingavat**, in 1986 named *Siamosaurus*, a theropod from Thailand.

Bunzel, Emanuel Austrian paleontologist who named island-dwelling *Danubiosaurus* (1871) and *Struthiosaurus* (1870).

Buscalioni, A. D. Spanish paleontologist who (with **Sanz**, **Casanovas**, and **Santafé**) co-named the camarasaurid sauropod *Aragosaurus* in 1987.

Cabrera, Angel Argentinian paleontologist who named the cetiosaurid sauropod *Amygdalodon* (1947).

Camp, Charles L. US paleontologist who advanced knowledge of early Mesozoic evolution. In 1936 he coined the names *Segisaurus* and Segisauridae for an early Arizona theropod and its family.

Cannon, George Discoverer of horn cores of *Triceratops alticornis* (1887) and the first remains of an ornithomimid dinosaur (1889), both near Denver, Colorado.

Carlin, William E. Union Pacific Railroad agent who, with **W.H. Reed**, in 1877 discovered Wyoming's Como Bluff dinosaur graveyard – among the richest in the world.

Carpenter, Kenneth US paleontologist who has made a study of baby dinosaurs of Late Cretaceous times.

Casamiquela, Rodolfo M. Argentinian paleontologist who named the oldest-known ornithischian dinosaur, *Pisanosaurus* (1967).

Casanovas, M.L. Spanish paleontologist who (with **Sanz**, **Buscalioni**, and **Santafé**) in 1987 named the camarasaurid sauropod *Aragosaurus*.

Chakravarti, Dhirendra K. Indian paleontologist who named *Brachypodosaurus* (1934), possibly an armored dinosaur.

Chang. See **Zhang**.

Chao. See **Zhao**.

Charig. Alan J. British paleontologist who (like **C.B.Cox**, **A.W.Crompton**, and others) has claimed that competition from dinosaurs wiped out rival reptile groups. Charig believed erect limbs held the secret of the dinosaurs' success and, in 1965, worked out that dinosaurs with upright stance and gait evolved from sprawling reptiles via others with a semi-improved gait. He named the early African dinosaurs *Nyasasaurus* (1967) and (with **A.W.Crompton**) co-named *Heterodontosaurus* (1962), and (with **Angela Milner**) the big British theropod *Baryonyx* (1986).

Chatterjee, Sankar Indian paleontologist researching the Triassic reptiles of Texas. He named *Technosaurus* (1984), *Walkeria* (1986), and the likely protodinosaur "Protoavis" (1986). With **S.L. Jain**, **T.S. Kutty**, and **T.K. Roy-Chowdhury**, in 1975 he named the early Indian sauropod *Barapasaurus*.

Chou. See **Zhou**.

Chow.. See **Zhao**.

Chure, Daniel US paleontologist who, with **J. McIntosh**, in 1988 named the horned dinosaur *Eucentrosaurus*.

Cobabe, Emily A. US paleontologist who (with **D. E. Fastovsky**) described the horned dinosaur *Ugrosaurus* in 1987.

Colbert, Edwin H. US vertebrate paleontologist best known for his expertise and books on dinosaurs. In 1955 he suggested that bone-headed dinosaurs' thick skulls could have served as battering rams. He named arguably the earliest of all dinosaurs, *Staurikosaurus* (1970), and the small armored ornithopod *Scutellosaurus* (1981).

Coombs Jr., Walter P. US paleontologist who restudied armored dinosaurs and divided them into two families: the nodosaurids and ankylosaurids. In 1980 he recognized *Psittacosaurus* hatchlings in an old collection of the American Museum of Natural History. Coombs also wrote on sauropods' likely habits and surroundings.

Cooper, Michael R. Zimbabwe-based paleontologist who placed the primitive sauropod *Vulcanodon* in a new family, Vulcanodontidae (1984).

Cope, Edward Drinker (1840-1897) US paleontologist best remembered as **Othniel Marsh**'s great rival in the race to find and name the dinosaurs of North America. From the 1870s Cope or his collectors scoured bone beds of the West – from Colorado and Wyoming to Montana and New Mexico. Cope named more than a thousand species of fossil backboned animals, but often duplicated older finds. Besides *Camarasaurus* (1877), *Coelophysis* (1889), and

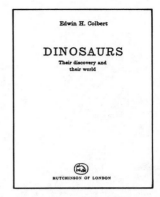

British-edition title page of a dinosaur book by Edwin Colbert.

Edward Cope (*above*), who named dinosaurs including *Agathaumas*, shown (*below*) by bones and inset restoration.

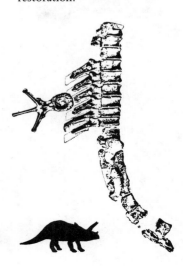

271

Monoclonius (1876), he named other, less well-known dinosaurs. *Agathaumas* (1872), *Amphicoelias* (1877), *Cionodon* (1874), *Diclonius* (1876), *Dysganus* (1876), *Dystrophaeus* (1877), *Hypsibema* (1869), *Paronychodon* (1876), *Pteropelyx* (1889), and *Tichosteus* (1877) include beasts identified from scrappy fossils of uncertain origin. Cope also named the dinosaur families Camarasauridae (1877), Compsognathidae (1875), Hadrosauridae (1869), Iguanodontidae (1869), and Scelidosauridae (1869).

Corro, Guillermo del Argentinian paleontologist who in 1974 named the sauropod *Chubutisaurus* (1974) and placed it in its own family, the Chubutisauridae.

Crompton, Alfred W. South African paleontologist studying mammal-like reptiles and early dinosaurs of southern Africa. With **A.J.Charig**, in 1962 he co-named the early Jurassic ornithischian *Heterodontosaurus*.

Currie, Philip J. Canadian paleontologist who in 1987 showed that the theropod *Stenonychosaurus* was really *Troodon*, and in 1988 (with **R. Bakker** and **M. Williams**) co-named *Nanotyrannus*. He has hunted in the dinosaur bone beds of Alberta and in the late 1980s he took part in Canadian-Chinese expeditions that recovered dozens of dinosaurs from Inner Mongolia.

Cuvier, Baron Georges (1769–1832) French zoologist; founder of comparative anatomy and paleontology. At first Cuvier claimed *Iguanodon* had been a mammal, but **Gideon Mantell**'s evidence soon convinced him of its reptile origin.

Das-Gupta, H. C. Indian paleontologist who named the supposed megalosaurid theropod *Orthogoniosaurus* (1931).

Dodson, Peter Canadian paleontologist who, in 1975, showed that the many supposed species of crested duck-billed dinosaur really represented males, females, and young of just a few species. For instance he reduced 13 species to 2: *Lambeosaurus* and *Parasaurolophus*. In 1986 he named *Avaceratops*, a horned dinosaur.

Dollo, Louis (1857–1931) French-born Belgian paleontologist who provided the first full reconstruction of *Iguanodon*, from the "herd" of skeletons recovered from a Belgian coalmine by **Louis De Pauw**. (See also **Norman, David**). In 1893 Dollo published his law of the irreversibility of evolution, claiming that organisms specialized by evolution cannot re-evolve into unspecialized ones.

Dong Zhiming Major Chinese dinosaurologist who named 19 Chinese dinosaurs between 1973 and the late 1980s. They were the sauropods *Bellusaurus* (1987), *Datousaurus* (1984), *Shunosaurus* (1983), and *Zizhongosaurus* (1983); the theropods *Gasosaurus* (1985), *Kelmayisaurus* (1973), *Shanshanosaurus* (1977), *Tugulusaurus* (1973), *Xuanhanosaurus* (1984), and *Yangchuanosaurus* (1978); the segnosaur *Nanshiungosaurus* (1979); the fabrosaurids *Gongbusaurus* (1983) and *Xiaosaurus* (1983); the duck-billed dinosaur *Microhadrosaurus* (1979); the bone-head *Micropachycephalosaurus* (1978); and the plated dinosaurs *Chungkingosaurus* (1983), *Huayangosaurus* (1982), *Tuojiangosaurus* (1977), and *Wuerhosaurus* (1973). Most came from Sichuan in the south west, and several from north-west China. About half were jointly named by Dong Zhiming and one or more of these Chinese paleontologists: **Li**, **Tang**, **Zhang**, and

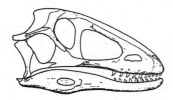

Skull of *Shanshanosaurus*, a theropod named by Chinese paleontologist Dong Zhiming (*below*).

Zhou. In 1978 Dong Zhiming coined the family name
Homalocephalidae for the flat-headed bone-headed dinosaurs.

Douglass, Earl (1862-1931) US dinosaur hunter. In Utah in 1909 he
found the fossil-rich rocks now forming Dinosaur National
Monument. For 13 years Douglass extracted prehistoric skeletons
from the Carnegie Quarry (as it was known at the time), and sent
350 tons of dinosaur and other bones to Andrew Carnegie's
Carnegie Museum of Natural History in Pittsburgh. Douglass's
excavations unearthed well preserved remains of the giant Jurassic
dinosaurs *Allosaurus*, *Apatosaurus*, *Camarasaurus*, *Diplodocus*, and
Stegosaurus, as well as the smaller *Camptosaurus* and *Othnielia*.

Dutuit, Jean M. French paleontologist who in 1972 described one
of the earliest of all dinosaurs – *Azendohsaurus* from Morocco's
Atlas Mountains.

Eaton Jr., Theodore H. US paleontologist who in 1960 described
Silvisaurus, an armored dinosaur from Kansas.

Efremov, Ivan Antonovich Russian paleontologist and novelist who
led three fossil-hunting expeditions to Mongolia in the late 1940s.
His team discovered new dinosaurs and fossil bone beds, and
shipped 120 tons of fossils to Moscow.

Ellenberger, Paul French resident of Lesotho who in 1972 named
two early Lesotho dinosaurs: *Likhoelesaurus* and *Thotobolosaurus*.

Eudes-Deslongchamps, Jacques Amand French paleontologist
who in 1838 described the theropod *Poekilopleuron* from bones
found in a limestone quarry near the town of Caen.

Farlow, James O. US paleobiologist and paleoecologist. In 1975
(with **P. Dodson**) he suggested that horned dinosaurs with
different spikes and horns used these in different ways for fighting
or display. In 1976 (with **C.V.Thompson** and **D.E.Rosner**) he
showed that *Stegosaurus*'s plates lost heat to help their owner stay
comfortably cool. In 1980 he argued that predator/prey biomass
ratios were an unsound basis for inferring that dinosaurs had been
warm blooded as birds and mammals are. In 1981 he calculated that
Texan fossil tracks had been left by theropods running at up to
26mph (42kph).

Fastovsky, David E. US paleontologist who, with **E. A. Cobabe**,
in 1987 named *Ugrosaurus*, a horned dinosaur.

Feduccia, J. Alan US zoologist who helped show in 1979 (with
H.B.Tordoff) that *Archaeopteryx* could fly; and developed theories
about the evolution of birds.

Felch, M.P. US rancher who discovered *Stegosaurus*-rich rocks in
Colorado (1876). While working for **Othniel Marsh**, in
Colorado's Garden Park Quarry he found the first *Ceratosaurus* and

Earl Douglass, the
discoverer of Utah's
Carnegie Quarry dinosaurs.

Archaeopteryx, the bird–
dinosaur restudied by J.
Alan Feduccia.

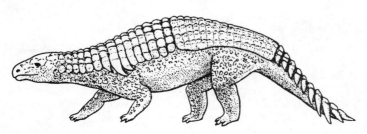

Theodore H. Eaton's
1960 restoration of the
armored dinosaur
Silvisaurus.

©DIAGRAM

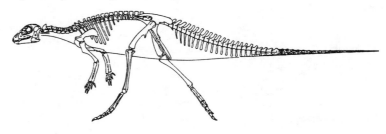

Lower jaw of the theropod *Chirostenotes* named by Charles Gilmore.

excavated an almost complete *Allosaurus* (1883–84).

Foulke, William P. US fellow of the Academy of Natural Sciences who dug up the Americas' first dinosaur skeleton to be described —a *Hadrosaurus* from Haddonfield, New Jersey (1858).

Fox, Rev. William British clergyman who discovered *Polacanthus* (1865) and (by 1878) several *Hypsilophodon* skeletons on the Isle of Wight and named *Calamospondylus*.

Fraas, Eberhard German authority on fossil reptiles whose report on an East African dinosaur graveyard discovered by German mining engineer **W. B. Sattler** in 1907 sparked off **Werner Janensch**'s Tendaguru excavations. Fraas named an early German theropod, *Procompsognathus* (1913).

Galton, Peter M. US-based British paleontologist who has restudied prosauropods, and shown that many ornithischians had cheek pouches; *Hypsilophodon* did not climb trees; hadrosaurs ran with tail and body horizontal; and bone-headed dinosaurs butted their heads. In 1974 with **Robert Bakker** he argued that birds are dinosaurs. Galton named the dinosaurs *Aliwalia* (1985), *Blikanasaurus* (1985, with **J. van Heerden**), *Callovosaurus* (1980), *Camelotia* (1985), *Dracopelta* (1980), *Gravitholus* (1979, with **W. P. Wall**), *Lesothosaurus* (1978), *Ornatotholus* (1983, with **H.-D. Sues**), *Othnielia* (1977), *Stygimoloch* (1983, with **H.-D. Sues**), *Torvosaurus* (1979, with **J. A. Jensen**), *Valdosaurus* (1977), and *Yaverlandia* (1971). He also named the families Blikanasauridae (1985, with **J. van Heerden**), Fabrosauridae (1972), and Staurikosauridae (1977), and the order Herrerasauria (1985).

Gasparini, Zulma B. Argentinian paleontologist who (with **E. Olivero**, **R. Scasso**, and **C. Rinaldi**) in 1988 described the first dinosaur (an ankylosaur) discovered (in 1986) in Antarctica.

Gauthier, Jacques A. US paleontologist whose writings in the 1980s featured an influential reclassification of dinosaurs.

Gervais, F.L. Paul French paleontologist who named *Aepisaurus* (1852), a sauropod from southern France.

Gillette, David Utah state paleontologist who excavated the great sauropod "Seismosaurus" in New Mexico in and after 1985, reportedly the longest ever dinosaur.

Right: Peter Galton's reconstruction of *Hypsilophodon* demolished the old notion (*above*) that it climbed trees.

Gilmore, Charles W. Dinosaur authority at the United States National Museum (1903-45), specializing in North American and Asian dinosaurs. He named *Alamosaurus* (1922), *Alectrosaurus* (1933), *Archaeornithomimus* (1920), *Bactrosaurus* (1933), *Brachyceratops* (1914), *Chirostenotes* (1924), *Mongolosaurus* (1933), *Pinacosaurus* (1933), *Thescelosaurus* (1913), and the family Troodontidae (1924).

Giménez, Olga Argentinian paleontologist who co-named *Xenotarsosaurus* (1986, with **R. Martínez**, **J. Rodríguez**, and **G. Bochatey**).

Ginsburg, Leonard Paleontologist at France's Museum of Natural History. He named *Fabrosaurus* in 1964.

Gow, Chris E. Paleontologist who named the South African heterodontosaurid dinosaur *Lanasaurus* in 1975.

Granger, Walter US geologist who took part in the 1920s expeditions to Mongolia. In 1923, with **W.K. Gregory**, he co-named *Protoceratops* and the family Protoceratopsidae.

Gregory, William K. US paleontologist who co-named *Protoceratops* and the Protoceratopsidae (1923, with **W. Granger**).

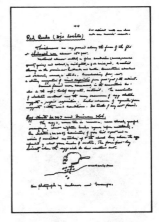

A page about the discovery of *Protoceratops*, from the field notes made by Walter Granger.

Harrison, Colin J. O. British scientist who named the fossil "owls" *Bradycneme* and *Heptasteornis* (1975, with **C. A. Walker**), later redescribed as dinosaurs.

Hasegawa, Yoshikazu Japanese paleontologist studying Japanese dinosaurs reported in the 1980s.

Hatcher, John B. US dinosaur hunter (for **O. C. Marsh**) and authority on horned and other dinosaurs. He discovered the colossal skull of *Torosaurus* and named the sauropod *Haplocanthosaurus* (1903).

Haughton, Sydney H. British paleontologist who named the African dinosaurs *Kangnasaurus* (1915), *Lycorhinus* (1924), and *Melanorosaurus* (1924).

Hay, Oliver P. US paleontologist who reassessed dinosaurs named by **Marsh** and **Cope** and studied skull and brain anatomy.

Hayden, Ferdinand V. US scientific explorer pioneering dinosaur discovery in North America. His 1855 geological reconnaissance of the Upper Missouri produced the first finds of *Troodon*, *Palaeoscincus*, and horned dinosaurs.

He Xinlu Chinese paleontologist who named the dinosaurs *Chuandongocoelurus* (1984), *Kaijiangosaurus* (1984), and *Yandusaurus* (1979).

Heerden, Jacques van South African paleontologist who named the prosauropod *Roccosaurus* (1978) and co-named *Blikanasaurus* and the family Blikanasauridae in 1985, with **P. M. Galton.**

Hennig, Edwin German excavator (with **Werner Janensch**) of Tendaguru in East Africa, 1909-11. He named an African stegosaurid, *Kentrosaurus* (1915).

Hitchcock, Edward B. US clergyman teacher who formed the first great collection of (Connecticut Valley) dinosaur footprints (1835-64). He thought they had been made by birds.

Hoffstetter, Robert Paleontologist who named the French stegosaurid *Lexovisaurus* (1957).

Hopson, James A US anatomist who showed in 1975 that

Fossil dinosaur footprint such as Edward Hitchcock thought had been produced by ancient birds.

©DIAGRAM

lambeosaurids' hollow crests had served as hooters. In 1980 he argued that most dinosaurs had the relative brain sizes of living reptiles, but small theropods had relatively larger brains, like birds. He named the African dinosaur *Abrictosaurus* (1975).

Horner, John R. US paleontologist who (with **R. Makela** and others) excavated Montana nesting grounds of hadrosaurid and hypsilophodontid dinosaurs in and after 1978, after early finds by local rock-shop owners **David** and **Laurie Trexler**. With **D. B. Weishampel** he co-named *Orodromeus* (1988).

Hotton III, Nicholas US paleobiologist who suggested in 1980 that far northern duck-billed dinosaurs migrated south for the winter. He also studied dinosaur locomotion and physiology.

Hou Chinese paleontologist who named bone-headed *Wannanosaurus* (1977).

Howgate, Michael British scientist who in 1985 named a "new" early bird, *Jurapteryx* (probably *Archaeopteryx*).

Hu Chinese paleontologist who named a theropod, *Chilantaisaurus* (1964), and the hadrosaur *Shantungosaurus* (1973).

Huene, Friedrich von German paleontologist: Europe's leading dinosaurologist of the early 20th century. As at 1990 no one else had named so many dinosaurs still known by the names he gave them, though most are theropods identified from scrappy evidence. The list reads *Altispinax* (1922), *Avipes* (1932), *Antarctosaurus* (1929), *Betasuchus* (1932), *Cetiosauriscus* (1927), *Coeluroides* (1932), *Compsosuchus* (1932), *Dolichosuchus* (1932), *Dryptosauroides* (1932), *Erectopus* (1922), *Fulgurotherium* (1932), *Halticosaurus* (1908), *Iliosuchus* (1932), *Indosuchus* (1933), *Jubbulpuria* (1932), *Laevisuchus* (1932), *Laplatasaurus* (1927), *Loricosaurus* (1929), *Magyarosaurus* (1932), *Ornithomimoides* (1932), *Proceratosaurus* (1926), *Rapator* (1932), *Saltopus* (1910), *Sellosaurus* (1908), *Thecocoelurus* (1923), *Velocipes* (1932), *Walgettosuchus* (1932). Von Huene also named the suborder Sauropodomorpha (1932), the infraorder Prosauropoda (1920), and the families Dicraeosauridae (1956), Halticosauridae (1956), Lambeosauridae (1948), Melanorosauridae (1929), Podokesauridae (1914), and Procompsognathidae (1929).

Hulke, J. British namer of the iguanodontid *Vectisaurus* (1879).

Hunt, Adrian P. US scientist who in 1989 named the primitive dinosaur *Revueltosaurus*.

Friedrich von Huene (*above*) and his reconstruction of the sauropod *Cetiosauriscus* (*below*).

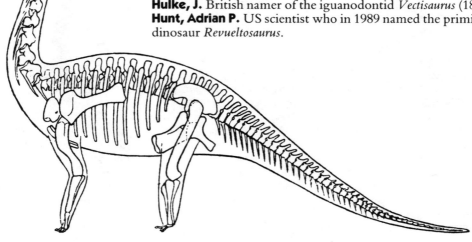

Huxley, Thomas H. (1825-95) British scientist who championed Darwin's theory of evolution and showed similarities between birds and dinosaurs. He named the dinosaurs *Acanthopholis* (1865), *Euskelosaurus* (1866), and *Hypsilophodon* (1869), and the families Archaeopterygidae (1871) and Megalosauridae (1869).

Ingavat, Rucha Thai scientist who co-named the Thai dinosaur *Siamosaurus* (1986, with **Eric Buffetaut**).

Jaekel, O. Scientist who named the theropod *Pterospondylus* (1913).

Jain, Sohan L. Indian paleontologist who co-named the primitive sauropod *Barapasaurus* (1975, with **T. S. Kutty**, **T. K. Roy-Chowdhury**, and **S. Chatterjee**).

Janensch, Werner German Berlin Museum curator who led the (1909-11) Tendaguru excavations in what is now Tanzania, recovering a wealth of Late Jurassic dinosaurs, notably remains of several immense skeletons of *Brachiosaurus*.

Jensen, James A. US paleontologist who discovered the colossal sauropods *Supersaurus* (1972) and "Ultrasaurus" (1979) in west Colorado, and named *Cathetosaurus* (1988), *Dystylosaurus* (1985), *Torvosaurus* (1979, with **P. M.Galton**), and the family Torvosauridae (1985).

Johnston US scientist who named the sauropod *Astrodon* (1859).

Jones, Daniel E. (Eddie) and **Vivian** US fossil hunters who, in Colorado, in and after the 1940s found more new kinds of dinosaur than any other pair of amateurs.

Kermack, Kenneth British scientist who helped demolish the old aquatic sauropod theory by showing that water pressure might have crushed a "snorkeling" sauropod's lungs.

Kim, Haang Mook South Korean scientist who named the Korean dinosaurs *Koreanosaurus* (1979) and *Ultrasaurus* (1983).

Kräusel German scientist whose 1922 discovery of land plants in a mummified hadrosaur's stomach implied that duck-billed dinosaurs lived on land, not in water as commonly supposed.

Kuhn, Oskar German paleontologist who named *Campylodoniscus* (1961) and *Tanystrosuchus* (1963) and the family Heterodontosauridae (1966).

Kurzanov, Sergei Mikhailovich Russian paleontologist who named *Alioramus* (1976), *Amtosaurus* (1978, with **Tumanova**), *Avimimus* (1981), *Itemirus* (1976), and *Quaesitosaurus* (1983 with **A. F. Bannikov**), and the families Avimimidae (1981) and Itemiridae (1976).

Kutty, T.S. Indian paleontologist who co-named the primitive *Barapasaurus* (1975 with **S. L. Jain**, **T. K. Roy-Chowdhury** and **S. Chatterjee**).

Lakes, Arthur British schoolteacher and amateur fossil hunter who helped spark off the US dinosaur rush in 1877 by sending **O. C. Marsh** samples from a rich bone bed near Morrison, Colorado.

Lambe, Lawrence M. Dinosaurologist who fossil hunted in Alberta for the Canadian Geological Survey. Lambe named *Chasmosaurus* (1914), *Edmontosaurus* (1917), *Eoceratops* (1915), *Euoplocephalus*

Shoulder blade of *Supersaurus*, named by James Jensen.

Arthur Lakes, a pioneer of the great American dinosaur rush.

© DIAGRAM

DINOSAUROLOGISTS

Skull reconstruction (after Wann Langston) and whole–body restoration of *Acrocanthosaurus*.

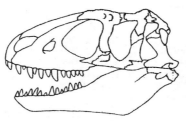

(1910), *Gorgosaurus* (1914), *Gryposaurus* (1914), *Panoplosaurus* (1919), *Stegoceras* (1902), and *Styracosaurus* (1913). Some of these were probably beasts that had already been given other names.

Langston Jr., Wann US paleontologist who co-named *Acrocanthosaurus* (1950, with **J. W. Stovall**) and named *Lophorhothon* (1960).

Lapparent, Albert F. de French paleontologist who named *Inosaurus* (1960) and *Lusitanosaurus* (1957, with **G. Zbyszewski**).

Lavocat, Réné French paleontologist who named *Majungasaurus* (1955) from Madagascar and *Rebbachisaurus* (1954) from Africa.

Leidy, Joseph (1823-91) US anatomist of Philadelphia who gave the first names to dinosaurs discovered in the Americas. In 1856 he named *Deinodon*, *Palaeoscincus*, *Thespesius*, *Trachodon*, and *Troodon* from fossil teeth found by **F. V. Hayden**. In 1858 he described *Hadrosaurus*, the first known duck-billed dinosaur. Leidy's *Antrodemus* (1870) might be the rightful name for *Allosaurus*. He also named *Aublysodon* (1868) and *Diplotomodon* (1868).

Leonardi, Giuseppe Brazil-based Italian scientist who has studied dinosaur footprints in South America.

Li Chinese scientist who co-named the Chinese stegosaur *Tuojiangosaurus* (1977, with **Dong**, **Zhou**, and **Zhang**).

Long, Robert A. US paleontologist who, in the 1980s, helped reveal new insights into the beginning of the age of dinosaurs in what is now Arizona's Petrified Forest National Park.

Longman, Heber A. Scientist who named the Australian dinosaurs *Austrosaurus* (1933) and *Rhoetosaurus* (1925).

Lucas, Frederic A. Scientist who in 1902 named the plated dinosaur *Dacentrurus* and the armored dinosaur *Hoplitosaurus*.

Lucas, O. W. Fremont County schools superintendent who found a rich dinosaur bone bed near Cañon City, Colorado, in 1877 and collected specimens for **E. D. Cope**.

Lull, Richard S. US paleontologist who studied Connecticut Valley dinosaur bones and tracks, and co-named *Anatosaurus* (1942, with **N. E. Wright**).

Lydekker, Richard A leading British paleontologist who described *Argyrosaurus* (1893), *Calamospondylus* (1889), *Cryptodraco* (1889), *Microcoelus* (1893), *Sarcolestes* (1893), *Titanosaurus* (1877), and the dinosaur families Cetiosauridae (1888) and Titanosauridae (1885).

McIntosh, John US authority on sauropods who (with **D. Berman**) helped redefine the diplodocid family in 1978. With **D. Chure** in 1988 he replaced *Centrosaurus*'s (preoccupied?) name by *Eucentrosaurus*.

Madsen Jr., James H. US paleontologist who described the theropods *Marshosaurus* (1976) and *Stokesosaurus* (1974).

Makela, Robert paleontologist who (with **J. R. Horner** and others) excavated Montana nesting grounds of hadrosaurid and

Drawing of vertebrae from *Hadrosaurus*, named by Joseph Leidy.

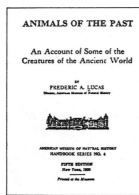

ANIMALS OF THE PAST

An Account of Some of the Creatures of the Ancient World

BY
FREDERIC A. LUCAS
Director, American Museum of Natural History

AMERICAN MUSEUM OF NATURAL HISTORY
HANDBOOK SERIES NO. 4

FIFTH EDITION
New York, 1929

Printed at the Museum

Title page of an edition of *Animals of the Past*, a book on prehistoric beasts by Frederic A. Lucas.

hypsilophodontid dinosaurs in and after 1978.

Maleev, E. A. Russian paleontologist who described *Talarurus* (1952), *Tarbosaurus* (1955), and *Therizinosaurus* (1954), and named its family, the Therizinosauridae.

Mantell, Gideon A. (1790–1852) British physician and fossil hunter who largely pioneered dinosaur discovery. He named *Iguanodon* (1825), *Hylaeosaurus* (1833), and *Pelorosaurus* (1850). *Iguanodon* was the second dinosaur to get a scientific name.

Marsh, Othniel C. (1831–99) Yale-based US paleontologist who named many of today's best-known dinosaurs, and surpassed his rival **E. D. Cope** as his century's greatest dinosaurologist. From 1877, **Hatcher**, **Lakes**, **Mudge**, **Reed**, **Williston** and other collectors working in Western states sent Marsh the wealth of fossil beasts that he described. Marsh named *Allosaurus* (1877), *Ammosaurus* (1890), *Anchisaurus* (1885), *Apatosaurus* (1877), *Atlantosaurus* (1877), *Barosaurus* (1890), *Camptosaurus* (1885), *Ceratops* (1888), *Ceratosaurus* (1884), *Claosaurus* (1890), *Coelurus* (1879), *Creosaurus* (1878), *Diplodocus* (1878), *Diracodon* (1881), *Dryosaurus* (1894), *Dryptosaurus* (1877), *Laosaurus* (1878), *Nanosaurus* (1877), *Nodosaurus* (1889), *Ornithomimus* (1890), *Pleurocoelus* (1888), *Priconodon* (1888), *Stegosaurus* (1877), *Torosaurus* (1891), and *Triceratops* (1889). Between 1870 and 1890 he described four dinosaur suborders (Ceratopsia, Ornithopoda, Stegosauria, and Theropoda); the infraorder Sauropoda; and the families Allosauridae, Anchisauridae, Camptosauridae, Ceratopsidae, Ceratosauridae, Coeluridae, Diplodocidae, Dryptosauridae, Nodosauridae, Ornithomimidae, and Stegosauridae.

Drawing of a tooth of an *Iguanodon*, named by Gideon A. Mantell

Gideon A. Mantell, a pioneer of dinosaur discovery.

Drawing of the skull of *Triceratops*, named by Othniel C. Marsh.

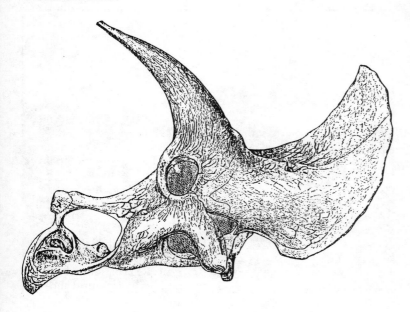

The great American dinosaurologist Othniel C. Marsh.

Claw of *Baryonyx*, described by Alan Charig and Angela Milner.

Vertebra of New Zealand theropod described by Ralph Molnar.

Below: Franz Nopcsa and his restoration of *Struthiosaurus*.

Martínez, Ruben Argentinian co-namer of *Xenotarsosaurus* (1986, with **O. Giménez**, **J. Rodríguez**, and **G. Bochatey**).

Maryańska, T. Polish paleontologist studying Mongolia's armored and bone-headed dinosaurs. She described *Saichania* and *Tarchia* in 1977, and, with **H. Osmólska**, *Bagaceratops* (1975), *Barsboldia* (1981), *Goyocephale* (1982, also with **A. Perle**), *Homalocephale* (1974), *Prenocephale* (1974), *Tylocephale* (1974), and the suborder Pachycephalosauria (1974).

Matheron, Pierre P. E. French paleontologist who named *Hypselosaurus* and *Rhabdodon* in 1869.

Matthew, William D. US paleontologist who named *Dromaeosaurus* (1922, with **B. Brown**).

Meyer, Hermann von German paleontologist who pioneered dinosaur discovery in Germany. He described *Archaeopteryx* (1861), *Plateosaurus* (1837), and *Stenopelix* (1857).

Milner, Angela British paleontologist who co-named *Baryonyx* and the family Baryonychidae (1986, with **A. J. Charig**).

Molnar, Ralph E. Queensland-based US paleontologist who described *Labocania* (1974) and the Australian dinosaurs *Kakuru* (1980, with **N. S. Pledge**), *Minmi* (1980), and *Muttaburrasaurus* (1981, with **A. Bartholomai**). In 1980 he identified New Zealand's first known dinosaur remains, found by a Mr. and Mrs. **Wiffen**.

Mudge, Benjamin One of **O. C. Marsh**'s chief fossil collectors.

Nagao Japanese scientist who named *Nipponosaurus* (1936).

Newman, Barney A. South African scientist whose study of *Tyrannosaurus* (1970) showed that theropods had held their bodies level, not upright like a kangaroo.

Nopcsa, Franz Baron Hungarian nobleman, spy, would–be king of Albania, dinosaurologist, murderer, and suicide victim. He described *Paranthodon* (1929), *Polacanthoides* (1928), *Teinurosaurus* (1928), *Telmatosaurus* (1903), and the family Aublysodontidae (1928).

Norman, David British paleontologist who showed some *Iguanodon* adults walked on all fours.

Novas, Fernando E. Argentinian paleontologist who named *Frenguellisaurus* (1986) and co-named *Abelisaurus* and the Abelisauridae (1985, with **J.F. Bonaparte**) after *Abelisaurus's* discoverer **Roberto Abel**.

Nowinski, A. Polish paleontologist who named the Mongolian sauropod *Nemegtosaurus* (1971).

Oberndorfer German discoverer of *Compsognathus*, in southern Germany in the late 1850s.

Olsen, George US paleontologist who discovered the first *Oviraptor* remains, in Mongolia in 1923.

Osborn, Henry F. Leading US vertebrate paleontologist of the early 1900s who took part in expeditions to Mongolia and helped build the fossil reptile collection of the American Museum of Natural History. He described *Albertosaurus* (1905), *Asiatosaurus* (1924), *Ornitholestes* (1903), *Oviraptor* (1924), *Pentaceratops* (1923), *Prodeinodon* (1924), *Psittacosaurus* (1923), *Saurornithoides* (1924), *Struthiomimus* (1916), *Tyrannosaurus* (1905), and *Velociraptor* (1924). He also named the families Tyrannosauridae and Psittacosauridae and the suborder Ankylosauria.

Osmólska, Halszka Polish paleontologist specializing in Mongolian dinosaurs. She described *Borogovia* (1987), *Elmisaurus* and the family Elmisauridae (1981), and *Hulsanpes* (1982); and, with **T. Maryańska**, *Bagaceratops* (1975), *Barsboldia* (1981), *Goyocephale* (1982, also with **A. Perle**), *Homalocephale* (1974), *Prenocephale* (1974), *Tylocephale* (1974), and the suborder Pachycephalosauria (1974). With **E. Roniewicz** she named *Deinocheirus* and the family Deinocheiridae (1967), and *Gallimimus* (1972, also with **R.Barsbold**).

Ostrom, John H. US paleontologist who in 1969 argued that dinosaurs' erect posture implied a high body temperature. He argued persuasively that birds had evolved from small theropod dinosaurs. With **Grant E. Meyer** and others he discovered *Deinonychus* in 1964 (described 1969), and named *Microvenator* (1970), *Sauropelta* (1970), and *Tenontosaurus* (1970).

Owen, Richard (1804–92) British comparative anatomist who invented the name dinosaur. He considered dinosaurs a unique suborder of huge reptiles which he called Dinosauria (1841). He described *Bothriospondylus* (1875), *Cetiosaurus* (1841), *Chondrosteosaurus* (1876), *Dacentrurus* (1875), *Dinodocus* (1884), *Echinodon* (1861), *Massospondylus* (1854), *Nuthetes* (1854), *Polacanthus* (1867), and *Scelidosaurus* (1859).

Velociraptor skull after the reconstruction by Henry Osborn.

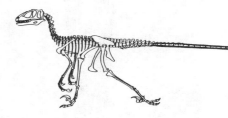

Deinonychus skeleton as reconstructed by John Ostrom.

Richard Owen (*above*), and a title page from one of his books (*below*).

©DIAGRAM

Euoplocephalus tail club, after William Parks.

Huge thigh bone of *Brachiosaurus*, named by Elmer Riggs.

Parks, William A. Authority on Canadian dinosaurs who described *Arrhinoceratops* (1925), *Dyoplosaurus* (1924), *Lambeosaurus* (1923), and *Parasaurolophus* (1923).

Paul, Gregory S. US dinosaurologist who combines original research with detailed illustration. He named a sauropod subgenus *Giraffatitan* (1988), the theropod (bird?) *Avisaurus* and family Avisauridae (1985, with **M. Brett-Surman**), and described the families Coelophysidae and Eustreptospondylidae (1988). Modifying a scheme of **Bakker**'s, in 1988 he suggested dividing dinosaurs into four superorders: paleodinosaurs, herreravians, phytodinosaurs, and theropods (including birds).

Perle, Altangerel Mongolian paleontologist who named *Erlikosaurus* (1980), *Segnosaurus* (1979) and the Segnosauridae (1979). With **R. Barsbold** he named *Enigmosaurus* (1983), *Harpymimus* and the harpymimid family (1984), and the Segnosauria (1980). He also named *Goyocephale* (1982, with **T. Maryańska** and **H. Osmólska**).

Pledge, Neville S. Australian scientist who named *Kakuru* (1980, with **R.E. Molnar**).

Powell, Jaimé E. Argentinian paleontologist who (mainly with **J.F.Bonaparte**) named South American dinosaurs *Aeolosaurus* (1988), *Noasaurus* and the family Noasauridae (1980), *Saltasaurus* (1980), and *Unquillosaurus* (1979).

Raath, Michael A. Rhodesian scientist who named the Zimbabwean dinosaurs *Syntarsus* (1969) and *Vulcanodon* (1972).

Reed, William H. Union Pacific Railroad foreman who, with **W. E. Carlin**, in 1877 discovered Wyoming's Como Bluff dinosaur bone bed, and excavated for **O. C. Marsh**. In 1879 he found an almost complete *Allosaurus* skeleton, now in the Peabody Museum.

Reig, Osvaldo A. Paleontologist who named the early South American dinosaurs *Herrerasaurus* and *Ischisaurus*, both in 1963.

Riabinin, Anatoliy N. Russian scientist who named the Asian dinosaurs *Embasaurus* (1931), *Jaxartosaurus* (1937), and *Mandschurosaurus* (1930).

Rich, Thomas H. and **Patricia Vickers** US husband-and-wife team who, in 1989, named two Australian hypsilophodontids: *Atlascopcosaurus* and *Leaellynosaura*.

Ricqulès, Armand J. de French comparative anatomist whose work on bone structure in the late 1960s and early 1970s suggested dinosaurs had been warm-blooded animals – a claim called into question by others' later studies.

Riggs, Elmer S. US paleontologist who named *Brachiosaurus* (1903) and the family Brachiosauridae (1904), and thought that sauropods had lived on land, a theory ignored for more than 60 years.

Riley, H. Scientist who, with **S. Stutchbury**, co-named the prosauropod *Thecodontosaurus* (1836).

Rodríguez, Jorge Argentinian paleontologist who co-named *Xenotarsosaurus* (1986, with **O. Giménez**, **R. Martínez** and **G. Bochatey**).

Romer, Alfred Sherwood (1894–1973) US paleontologist who wrote major books on vertebrate life. He named *Euhelopus* (1956) and, in 1971, the protodinosaurs *Lagerpeton* and *Lagosuchus*.

Roniewicz, Ewa Polish paleontologist who (with **H. Osmólska**) named *Deinocheirus* (1970), the family Deinocheiridae (1970), and *Gallimimus* (1972, also with **R. Barsbold**).

Rosner, D. E. US paleontologist who, with **C. V. Thompson** and **J. O. Farlow** showed that *Stegosaurus*'s plates lost heat to help their owner stay comfortably cool.

Rowe, Tim US paleontologist who with **Jacques Gauthier** in the late 1980s proposed regrouping theropods in the Ceratosauria and Tetanurae.

Roy-Chowdhury, Tappan K. Indian paleontologist who co-named the primitive sauropod *Barapasaurus* (1975) with **T. S. Kutty, S. L. Jain** and **S. Chatterjee**.

Rozhdestvensky, Anatoly K. Russian paleontologist who named *Aralosaurus* (1968) and *Probactrosaurus* (1966).

Russell, Dale A. Canadian paleontologist who threw new light on ornithomimid dinosaurs, and showed *Gorgosaurus* was *Albertosaurus*. He redescribed *Archaeornithomimus* (1972), named *Daspletosaurus* (1970), *Dromiceiomimus* (1972), and the family Dromaeosauridae (1969), and speculated that *Stenonychosaurus* could have evolved into a "dinosauroid" of almost human form. See too **Spotila, J.**

Santafé, J.-V. Spanish scientist who co-named *Aragosaurus* (1987, with **Buscalioni, Casanovas**, and **Sanz**).

Sanz, J. L. See **Santafé**.

Schlaikjer, Erich M. Scientist who co-named *Pachycephalosaurus* (1943, with **B. Brown**).

Seeley, Harry G. (1839-1909) British paleontologist who split dinosaurs into the orders Ornithischia and Saurischia (1887). He named *Agrosaurus* (1891), *Anoplosaurus* (1878), *Aristosuchus* (1887), *Craterosaurus* (1874), *Macrurosaurus* (1876), *Orthomerus* (1883), *Priodontognathus* (1875), *Rhadinosaurus* (1881), and *Thecospondylus*(1882).

Sereno, Paul US paleontologist who influentially reclassified ornithischian dinosaurs in 1986.

Simmons, D. J. Scientist who named China's *Tatisaurus* (1965).

Spotila, James US biologist. In 1980, with **Dale Russell**, he argued that predator/prey ratios in fossil finds may not show after all that dinosaurs had been warm-blooded as mammals are.

Sternberg, Charles H. New York-born dinosaur hunter, working with sons **Charles M., George**, and **Levi**. They collected largely for **E. D. Cope** and (in Alberta, 1912-17) Canada's Geological Survey.

Sternberg, Charles M. Son of **Charles H. Sternberg** and namer of *Brachylophosaurus* (1953), *Edmontonia* (1928), *Macrophalangia* (1932), *Montanoceratops* (1951), *Pachyrhinosaurus* (1950), *Parksosaurus* (1937), *Stenonychosaurus* (1932), and the family Pachycephalosauridae (1945).

Sternberg, George Son of **Charles H. Sternberg**. In 1908 in Wyoming George found a "mummified" duck-billed dinosaur now in the American Museum of Natural History.

Sternberg, R. M. Scientist who named *Caenagnathus* and the Caenagnathidae (1940).

Sternfeld, R. German scientist who named *Tornieria* (1911) from Africa.

DRAGONS OF THE AIR
AN ACCOUNT OF
EXTINCT FLYING REPTILES

BY
H. G. SEELEY, F.R.S.

WITH EIGHTY ILLUSTRATIONS

Harry Govier Seeley

HUNTING DINOSAURS
IN
THE BAD LANDS OF THE RED DEER RIVER
ALBERTA, CANADA

A SEQUEL TO
THE LIFE OF A FOSSIL HUNTER
BY
CHARLES H. STERNBERG

©DIAGRAM

Charles H. Sternberg

LEHRBUCH DER
PALÄOZOOLOGIE

VON

PROF. DR. ERNST FREIHERR STROMER v. REICHENBACH

II. TEIL: WIRBELTIERE

MIT 254 ABBILDUNGEN

LEIPZIG UND BERLIN
DRUCK UND VERLAG VON B. G. TEUBNER
1912

Title page of a work on prehistoric life by Ernst Stromer von Reichenbach.

Stovall, J. Willis US paleontologist who co-named *Acrocanthosaurus* (1950, with **W. Langston**).

Stromer von Reichenbach, Ernst German paleontologist who named the African dinosaurs *Aegyptosaurus* (1932), *Bahariasaurus* (1934), *Carcharodontosaurus* (1931), and *Spinosaurus* (1915) and the family Spinosauridae (1915).

Stutchbury, Samuel. British paleontologist who, with H. Riley, co-named the prosauropod *Thecodontosaurus* (1836).

Sues, Hans-Dieter German paleontologist who named *Majungatholus* (1979, with **P. Taquet**), and North America's *Ornatotholus* (1983, with **P. Galton**), *Saurornitholestes* (1978), *Stygimoloch* (1983, with **P. Galton**), and *Zephyrosaurus* (1980).

Talbot, Mignon US paleontologist who named the small, early theropod *Podokesaurus* (1911).

Tang Zilu Chinese paleontologist who, with **Dong Zhiming** named *Datousaurus* (1984) and *Xiaosaurus* (1983).

Tapia, Augusto Argentinian paleontologist who named *Notoceratops* (1918), a South American protoceratopsid.

Taquet, Philippe French paleontologist who named *Majungatholus* (1979, with **H.-D. Sues**), *Ouranosaurus* (1976), and *Piveteausaurus* (1977, with **S. P. Welles**).

Thulborn, Richard A. British paleontologist who named *Alocodon* (1973), *Phyllodon* (1973), and *Trimucrodon* (1973), and has studied dinosaur footprints.

Tumanova, Tatiana A. Russian paleontologist who named *Amtosaurus* (1978, with **S. M. Kurzanov**), *Maleevus* (1987), and *Shamosaurus* (1983).

Tyrrell, Joseph B. Canadian pioneer of dinosaur discovery in Alberta's Red Deer River valley, in the early 1880s.

Van Valen, Leigh US scientist, who, with **Robert Sloan**, argued in the 1980s that dinosaurs had died out gradually.

Vince, M. Argentinian scientist who named the sparrow-sized dinosaur *Mussaurus* (1979, with **J. F. Bonaparte**).

Wagner, Johann A. German scientist who named chicken-sized *Compsognathus* (1859).

Walker, Alick D. British paleontologist who, in 1964, named *Eustreptospondylus* and *Metriacanthosaurus*.

Walker, Cyril A. British scientist who named fossil "owls" *Bradycneme* and *Heptasteornis* (1975, with **C. J. Harrison**), later redescribed as dinosaurs.

Walker, William British amateur fossil hunter who discovered the strange theropod *Baryonyx* (1983).

Wall, William P. US scientist who named the bone-headed dinosaur *Gravitholus* (1979, with **P. M. Galton**).

Weishampel, David B. US paleontologist who named nest-building *Orodromeus* (1988, with **J. Horner)**.

Welles, Samuel P. US paleontologist who named *Dilophosaurus* (1970), *Liliensternus* (1984), *Longosaurus* (1984), and *Piveteausaurus* (1977, with **P. Taquet**).

Wieland, G. R. US paleobotanist who named *Hierosaurus* (1909).

William Walker, the discoverer of *Baryonyx*.

Wiffen, Joan First to discover the island-dwelling dinosaurs of New Zealand.

Wild, Rupert West German paleontologist who named the early sauropod *Ohmdenosaurus* (1978).

Williams, M. US scientist who named *Nanotyrannus* (1988, with **R. Bakker** and **P. J. Currie**).

Williston, Samuel W. US fossil collector for **O. C. Marsh**, who found the first known *Diplodocus* (1877) and named *Stegopelta* (1905).

Wiman, Carl Swedish paleontologist who in 1929 named the Chinese duck-billed dinosaur *Tanius* and described the first known Chinese sauropod (*Helopus*, later renamed *Euhelopus*).

Winkley, William US discoverer in Montana in 1940 of the bone-headed dinosaur *Pachycephalosaurus*.

Woodward, Sir Arthur Smith (1864–1944) Major British paleontologist who named Argentina's *Genyodectes* (1901).

Wright, Nelda E. US scientist who named *Anatosaurus* (1942, with **R.S.Lull**).

Yadagiri, P. Indian paleontologist who, with **K. Ayyasami**, co-named the Indian plated dinosaur *Dravidosaurus* (1979).

Yang Zhong-jian See **Young Chung Chien.**

Young Chung Chien Founder of Chinese vertebrate paleontology. He named *Chingkankousaurus* (1958), *Dianchungosaurus* (1982), *Lufengocephalus* (1974), *Lufengosaurus* (1941), *Lukousaurus* (1948), *Mamenchisaurus* (1954), *Omeisaurus* (1939), *Sanpasaurus* (1946), *Sinocoelurus* (1942), *Sinosaurus* (1948), *Tawasaurus* (1982), *Tienshanosaurus* (1937), *Tsintaosaurus* (1958), *Yunnanosaurus* (1942), and the families Mamenchisauridae (1972, with **Zhao**) and Yunnanosauridae (1942).

Zborzewski, Count A. Polish scientist who named the supposed Russian theropod *Macrodontophion* (1834).

Zbyszewski, G. Portuguese geologist who, with **A. F. de Lapparent**, co-named *Lusitanosaurus* (1957).

Zdansky, Otto Austrian paleontologist who made the first find of a Chinese sauropod (*Euhelopus*), in 1922.

Zhang Yihong Chinese paleontologist who, in 1988, named *Protognathus* and showed that at least one sauropod's tail ended in a bony club. With **Dong** and **Zhou**, in 1983 he named *Chungkingosaurus, Gongbusaurus, Shunosaurus,* and *Zizhongosaurus,* and, with **Dong, Zhou,** and **Li**, in 1977, *Tuojiangosaurus.*

Zhao Xijin Chinese paleontologist who named *Chaoyoungosaurus, Megacervixosaurus, Microdontosaurus, Monkonosaurus, Ngexisaurus,* and *Sangonghesaurus* in 1983; and, in 1986, *Chinshakiangosaurus, Dachongosaurus, Damalasaurus, Kunmingosaurus, Lancangjiangosaurus, Oshanosaurus,* and *Xuanhuasaurus.* See also **Young**.

Zhou Shiwu Chinese paleontologist who in 1983, with **Dong** and **Zhang**, co-named *Chungkingosaurus, Gongbusaurus, Shunosaurus* and *Zizhongosaurus* and (with **Dong, Zhang,** and **Li**) *Tuojiangosaurus* in 1977.

Zhow See **Zhou Shiwu**.

Skull of *Tanius*, named by Carl Wiman.

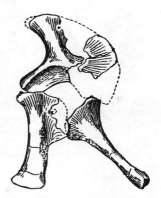

Pelvic bones of *Omeisaurus*, after Young Chung Chien who named it.

Chapter 7

DINOSAURS REVIVED

Wondering what dinosaurs looked like has fascinated everyone from child to scientist since fossil hunters started freeing dinosaur bones from rocks in the 1820s.

Our last chapter looks at past and present notions of the dinosaurs as shown in paintings, models, novels, comics, and motion pictures. Some ignore, others reflect new scientific understanding of the dinosaurs.

We end with tantalizing glimpses of the dinosaurs that might have been, had they continued to evolve instead of dying out.

Above: The first display of lifesize model dinosaurs inspired this mid–1850s cartoon in the British magazine *Punch.* The caption reads: "A visit to the antediluvian reptiles at Sydenham – Master Tom strongly objects to having his mind improved."
Below: A scene from *Gertie the Dinosaur,* an animated cartoon created by Winsor McCay in 1912. *'Gertie'* (a brontosaur), was the first classic character especially designed for an animated cartoon.

Popular misconceptions

Shown here are five
prehistoric reptiles often
misdescribed as dinosaurs.
Dimetrodon dates from
Permian times. The rest
lived in the Age of
Dinosaurs.
1 *Pteranodon*, one of the
flying reptiles known as
pterosaurs.
2 *Dimetrodon*, a predatory
mammal-like reptile.
3 *Ichthyosaurus*, one of the
(aquatic) ichthyosaurs.
4 *Elasmosaurus*, a long-
necked plesiosaur: one basis
for Scotland's Loch Ness
monster legend.
5 *Tylosaurus*, a mosasaur
(marine lizard).

No prehistoric beasts have fascinated people more than dinosaurs,
yet no animals are more misunderstood.

Motion pictures, comics, pulp novels, and newspapers mislead
us by implying that all dinosaurs were huge and included any
outsize long-dead creature and monsters that are myths.
True dinosaurs were the land animals that form the subject of this
book, plus, arguably, birds. They did not include sea monsters,
dragons, the sail-backed prehistoric reptile *Dimetrodon*, those big
swimming reptiles ichthyosaurs, plesiosaurs, and mosasaurs, or
(although close kin to dinosaurs) the skin-winged pterosaurs.

Many tales and motion pictures malign dinosaurs as sluggish

pea-brained brutes. We now know some could probably run faster than a horse and had quite well developed brains.

Confusion also reigns about where dinosaurs slotted into the evolving world of life. In fact they appeared after the first large reptiles had become extinct but before big birds and mammals evolved. Contrary to comic books and motion pictures, no dinosaur survived to frighten early man "one million years B.C." Nor did all dinosaurs live at the same time.

Often ridiculed for dying out, dinosaurs persisted about 165 million years, more than 40 times longer than the time elapsed since our apelike ancestors appeared.

Sea serpent
An old woodcut (*above*) shows a wormlike monster devouring sailors. Sea serpents are imaginary animals perhaps based on giant squid or ribbonfish.

Dragons
An old European woodcut (*left*) and two oriental illustrations (*below*) represent the ancient worldwide belief in dragons. Some pictured dragons look a bit like dinosaurs, and perhaps the dragon legend began with dinosaur bones dug up in China more than 2000 years ago. Some Chinese still value powdered "dragons' teeth" (including those of dinosaurs) as medicines.

©DIAGRAM

Dinosaurs in art

Four artists' views
1 Charles Knight's 1926 drawing of a *Protoceratops* for a mural in the Field Museum of Natural History.
2 A sauropod by Czech artist Zdeněk Burian for *Life Before Man*, with text by Z.V. Špinar (1972).
3 *Allosaurus* by British wildlife artist Maurice Wilson for W.E. Swinton's *The Story of Prehistoric Animals* (1961).
4 The horned dinosaur *Torosaurus* from a Neave Parker Late Cretaceous scene for the *Illustrated London News*.

Most of us see dinosaurs as artists have depicted them since mid nineteenth-century sketches based on scanty fossil evidence.

The American artist **Charles Knight** became the first outstanding painter to depict realistic scenes of prehistoric life. A brilliant draftsman with a keen interest in anatomy, zoology, and paleontology, between the 1890s and early 1940s Knight created drawings, models, and paintings for American museums and publishers. His masterpiece is arguably the set of murals in Chicago's Field Museum of Natural History. Once the most-accurate-ever images of dinosaurs, Knight's paintings set a standard followed everywhere.

After the 1950s, books, magazines, museums – even give-away tea cards – featured impressive works by such European artists as **Zdeněk Burian**, **Neave Parker**, and **Maurice Wilson**.

Meanwhile, in 1925, **Gerhard Heilmann**'s book *The Origin of Birds* had shown dinosaurs (usually considered sluggish reptiles) as active, even running, creatures. This view lay largely dormant until the late 1960s. Then new studies of dinosaur mechanics inspired

1

2

3

4

US paleontologist **Robert Bakker** to draw dinosaurs walking with bodies held erect, and rearing, sprinting, galloping, and scrapping as actively as any living mammal. Most artists now show dinosaurs like that. Fine modern illustrations include **Gregory Paul**'s rapacious theropods in black and white, **John Sibbick**'s beautifully detailed Mesozoic scenes, and the decorative fantasies of **William Stout**.

5

6

Two lively dinosaurs
5 *Deinonychus* at high speed, drawn by paleontologist-artist Robert Bakker in 1969. Bakker's illustrations show dinosaurs as lively, even skittish, creatures unlike the sluggish reptiles of tradition.
6 *Ornithomimus* sprints across a North American landscape in a drawing from paleontologist-artist Gregory Paul's *Predatory Dinosaurs of the World* (1988).

Dinosaurs rebuilt

Three-dimensional dinosaurs first "reappeared" in England. In 1854 **Benjamin Waterhouse Hawkins**' lifesize *Hylaeosaurus*, *Iguanodon*, and *Megalosaurus* invaded what is now London's Crystal Palace Park. They still lurk among its trees – rhinoceros-like concrete curiosities inaccurately based on incomplete remains.

As knowledge grew, improved model dinosaurs of various substances and sizes sprang up in public places. Early landmarks were five realistic lifesize model dinosaurs built for **Carl Hagenbeck**'s zoo which opened in 1907 at Stellingen, near Hamburg, Germany. For Chicago's Century of Progress Exposition in 1933, the Sinclair Refining Company had **P.G. Alen** build six huge galeproof dinosaurs from steel, rubber, and plaster; electric motors gave his *Triceratops* and *Tyrannosaurus* lunging heads.

The mid 1930s saw the opening at Rapid City, South Dakota, of the first permanent US display of lifesize dinosaurs, and of what became the world's largest prehistoric animal park, at Calgary in Canada. In 1964, Sinclair dinosaurs reappeared updated by **Paul Jonas** for the New York World's Fair. This also had Walt Disney's robotic dinosaurs, a nucleus for Disneyland's Primeval World, opening at Anaheim, California, in 1966. That year, too, in California's San Gorgonio Pass, **Claude Kenneth Bell** began work on a twice lifesize *Apatosaurus* – the largest model dinosaur so far.

Models made since 1970 reflect new finds and model-making techniques. Thus in 1975 Chorzow, Poland, opened its Valley of the Dinosaurs, with 18 lifesize restorations of dinosaurs discovered in Mongolia's Gobi Desert. By 1990 museum audiences worldwide enjoyed the sights and simulated sounds of Dinamation's touring prehistoric "zoos," compressed-air powering the nodding heads of half- and full-size dinosaurs. Meanwhile, Cycad's painted fiberglass *Gallimimus* – made for a museum in Taiwan – set new standards in realistic lifesize model dinosaur design.

Model progress
Landmarks in large-scale dinosaur restoration appear plotted on a time- scale (*below*). Numbered items come from three major exhibitions.
1 *Iguanodon* (mistakenly shown with a nose horn).
2 *Stegosaurus* attacked by *Ceratosaurus*.
3 *Struthiomimus* and *Apatosaurus*.

1

2

3

©DIAGRAM

1 | **1854** Crystal Palace Park dinosaurs, London, England

1907 Hagenbeck's zoo opens near Hamburg, Germany. | 2

1850   1860   1870   1880   1890   1900   1910

Meeting *Tyrannosaurus*
Left: A child confronts a lifesize *Tyrannosaurus* head in London's Natural History Museum. In 1989 the museum's visitors also saw big robotic sauropods, and plated, horned, and bone-headed dinosaurs all made by Dinamation. This California-based company exhibited 200 model creatures in 25 "zoos" that toured the world from Denmark to Japan. Dinamation claimed 12 million visitors a year saw its shows in the United States alone.

***Gallimimus* at large**
Left: An ostrich dinosaur takes an outing with its creator, Cycad's director **Roby Braun**. Such beasts begin as a small-scale model based on detailed measurements. Next, experts build a big steel skeleton supporting a body of polystyrene, wire mesh, and Plasticine. They cover with a mold of liquid rubber reinforced by fiberglass-and-resin mesh. From this they make a hollow cast of fiberglass or liquid rubber, let it set, perhaps incorporate robotics, and paint.

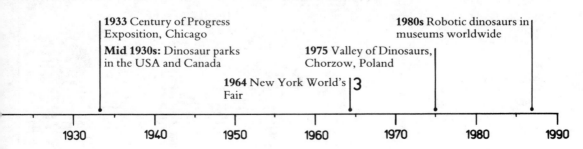

1933 Century of Progress Exposition, Chicago

Mid 1930s: Dinosaur parks in the USA and Canada

1964 New York World's Fair

1975 Valley of Dinosaurs, Chorzow, Poland

1980s Robotic dinosaurs in museums worldwide

3

1930   1940   1950   1960   1970   1980   1990

Dinosaurs in fiction

Mesozoic monsters have prowled through countless novels, novelettes, and short stories since 1864 when an ichthyosaur fought a plesiosaur in an underground lake in **Jules Verne**'s *A Journey to the Center of the Earth*. Dinosaurs arguably came of literary age in 1912 when **Sir Arthur Conan Doyle**'s eccentric Professor Challenger "rediscovered" them alive and well in *The Lost World* alias Roraima – a real, remote, flat-topped mountain in South America. Then, in 1914, supreme American science fantasist **Edgar Rice Burroughs** launched a hugely popular string of stories and sequels teeming with terrifying forms of prehistoric life.

Early stirrings
Numbered items come from influential works of fiction with dinosaurs or dinosaur-like beasts.
1 *A Trip to the Center of the Earth* (1864) by the French writer Jules Verne.
2 *The Lost World* (1912) by Britain's Sir Arthur Conan Doyle.
3 *Tarzan the Terrible* (1921) by American author Edgar Rice Burroughs.

At the Earth's Core (1914), *The Land That Time Forgot* (1918), and *Tarzan the Terrible* (1921) took readers respectively to imaginary, timeless Pellucidar (a world inside our "hollow" planet), the mysterious island Caprona, and Pal-ul-don – a lost land in Africa. Vividly described, these lost worlds provided settings where Tarzan and other heroes survived spine-tingling encounters with dinosaurs or dinosaur-like beasts. Burroughs' rich imagination has since inspired countless pulp-fiction imitators, not to mention comic strips and motion pictures.

Imagined monsters
4 *At the Earth's Core* (illustration from the 1922 hardcover edition) by Edgar Rice Burroughs.
5 Magazine cover for Alexander Phillips' *Death of the Moon* (1929). Here the last *Tyrannosaurus* saves the world from Lunarian invaders.

Space-age dinosaurs
6 Space explorers find dinosaurs still alive on award-winning science fiction writer Anne McCaffrey's *Dinosaur Planet* (1978).

Dinosaurs in comics

Once past children's picture books, readers are most likely to encounter dinosaurs in comic strips and comic books.

The classic humor strip with dinosaurs emerged in 1934 with **V.T. Hamlin**'s *Alley Oop*, a Stone Age tale whose caveman hero rides Dinny, a long-necked dinosaur with a spiny back. Countless adventure comic strips and books have also figured dinosaurs or dinosaur-like monsters. In his *The Dinosaur Scrapbook*, Donald Glut records such creatures cropping up in "illustrated tales of science fiction, fantasy, horror, mystery, jungle, and superhero adventure and even Westerns." Scores of these describe lost worlds where muscular heroes and curvaceous heroines cope with monsters inspired by prehistoric animals of any age within the last 250 million years. Some series, though, stand out for skillful artwork or inventive plots.

Dinosaur humor
Tame dinosaur Dinny shares an umbrella with Alley Oop and his girlfriend Oola on this cover from an Argo Publications comic book of the 1950s, based on the newspaper comic strip begun in 1934.

Dinosaur terror
Crashed warplane pilot Roger Drum meets an angry sauropod. Later he becomes the hero of a tribe who call him Thun'da from the sound his bullets make, fired into a monster.

Here are just a few examples from mid-century, perhaps the heyday of the prehistoric strip. In 1952 artist-author **Frank Fazetta** launched his *Thun'da* strip where World War II pilot Roger Drum crashes in a prehistoric part of Africa inhabited by hostile sauropods. In 1953 one caveman saves another from a carnosaur in **Joe Kubert**'s and **Norman Maurer**'s *Tor*, the first (short-lived) three-dimensional comic book. In 1954 artist **Rex Mason** pitted American Indians against a *Tyrannosaurus* in the first issue of the long-running prehistoric fantasy *Turok, Son of Stone*. In 1960 *The War That Time Forgot* gave a new twist to World War II as US troops fought dinosaurs on remote Pacific islands.

Whatever its contents, many a comic book still sells on the strength of a dinosaur rampaging across the cover.

Man Meets *Triceratops*
One million years ago, astonishingly modern-looking caveman Tor outwits dinosaurs (which long predated people) and coexists with sail-backed reptiles (which lived before the dinosaurs).

Indian fights dinosaur
Poisoned arrows help Turok kill a *Tyrannosaurus*. This incident figured in the first issue of a long-running comic book series where prehistoric Red Indians clash with "dawn-age" prehistoric beasts.

Movie dinosaurs 1

Dinosaurs have stomped, raged, and even simpered across the screen since 1912 saw the first classic animated–cartoon character: **Winsor McCay**'s *Gertie the Dinosaur*. Films like *Dinosaurs . . . the Terrible Lizards* (1970) and *The Animal World* (1956) featured dinosaurs in "factual" dinosaur scenarios, but most movie makers have pitted dinosaurs against human heroes in tales of science fiction and prehistoric fantasy inspired by writers like **Edgar Rice Burroughs**.

Three plot types predominate. Prehistoric people clash with dinosaurs, as in *One Million Years B.C.* (1967). Modern explorers

Live movie monsters
The four pictures below illustrate the variety of methods used by movie makers to bring live "prehistoric monsters" to the screen.
a Animated models such as those created by Ray Harryhausen.
b Real creatures enlarged, such as the iguana lizard used in the film *King Dinosaur* (1955) to portray a *Tyrannosaurus*.
c Real creatures are sometimes dressed-up to resemble dinosaurs. For the film *The Lost World* (1960) an iguana lizard sported added horns.
d Costumed actors portrayed *Ceratosaurus*-like tyrannosaurids in *Unknown Island* (1948).

find prehistoric monsters alive and troublesome in a remote corner of our planet, as in *The Lost World* (1925). Or a monster runs amok in a modern city, as in *The Valley of Gwangi* (1969). Inventive departures from such routines include *The Beast of Hollow Mountain* (1956), a cowboy whodunnit with an *Allosaurus* as killer; and *The Flintstones* (first transmitted 1960), a long-running television animated cartoon character series with a small, puppy-like pet brontosaur. Despite such successful humorous treatment, audiences young and old expect and perhaps prefer their big-screen dinosaurs to arouse pleasing sensations of terror.

Cartoons
Cartoons such as **The Flintstones** are a popular method of portraying dinosaurs, especially with younger audiences. Here Fred Flintstone quarries rock with a sauropod operated as a crane. Dinosaurs often figure in this Stone Age animated cartoon series made for television.

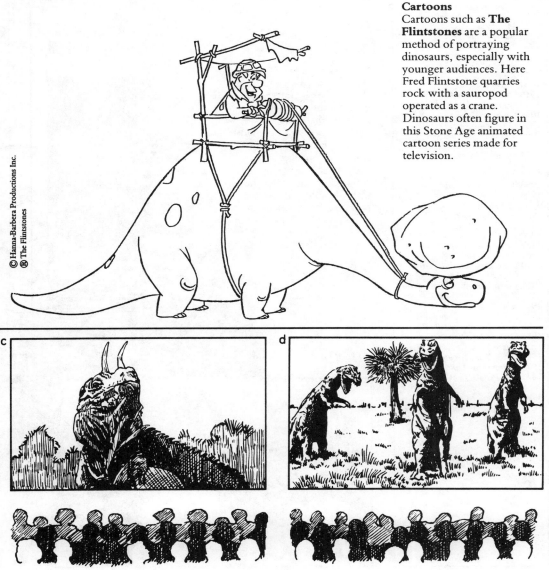

© Hanna-Barbera Productions Inc.
® The Flintstones

c

d

© DIAGRAM

Movie dinosaurs 2

Screen dinosaurs are the brainchildren of model makers, animators, and costume designers – some combining several roles.

Most movie dinosaurs are models. A machine-activated model *Ceratosaurus* appeared in 1914 in **D.W.Griffith**'s *Brute Force*. But prehistoric realism reached new heights with *The Lost World* (1925), among the first feature films with three-dimensional figure animation. Stop-motion photography and special-effects pioneer **Willis O'Brien** brought to life **Marcel Delgado**'s model dinosaurs – built as ball-and-socket skeletons with sponge-rubber muscles and latex hides. O'Brien's successes inspired **Ray Harryhausen**'s jointed rubber models and animation for such famous monster movies as *The Beast From 20,0000 Fathoms* (1952), *The Animal World* (1956), *One Million Years B.C.* (1967)

Some films with dinosaurs

Selected big-screen titles including animated cartoon comedies, but not television movies or non-dinosaur monster movies.

1908 *The Prehistoric Man*
1912 *Gertie the Dinosaur*
1914 *Brute Force*
1916 *The Birth of a Flivver*
1917 *The Dinosaur and the Missing Link*
1917 *R.F.D 10,000 B.C*
1919 *Adam Raises Cain*
1919 *The Ghost of Slumber Mountain*
1923 *Adam's Rib*
1925 *The Lost World*
1926 *Fig Leaves*
1929 *A Stone Age Romance*
1933 *King Kong*
1933 *Son of Kong*
1940 *One Million B.C*
1940 *Fantasia*
1948 *Unknown Island*
1951 *Lost Continent*
1953 *The Beast from 20,000 Fathoms*
1954 *Journey to the Beginning of Time*
1955 *King Dinosaur*
1956 *The Animal World*
1956 *The Beast of Hollow Mountain*
1957 *The Land Unknown*
1960 *The Lost World*
1960 *Dinosaurus!*
1967 *One Million Years B.C*
1969 *The Valley of Gwangi*
1970 *Dinosaurs . . . the Terrible Lizards*
1971 *When Dinosaurs Ruled the Earth*
1974 *The Land That Time Forgot*
1975 *Emilo and His Magical Bull*
1976 *At the Earth's Core*
1976 *One of Our Dinosaurs is Missing*
1976 *When Time Began*
1977 *Planet of the Dinosaurs*
1977 *The People That Time Forgot*
1988 *The Land Before Time*

Model animator
Ray Harryhausen adjusts a realistic flexible model of a giant theropod (*right*). In and after the 1950s Harryhausen won renown for skill in setting small animated models of prehistoric beasts against real backgrounds. For the film *The Valley of Gwangi* he animated models of the dinosaurs *Ornithomimus* and *Allosaurus* (*below*).

and *The Valley of Gwangi* (1969). In these productions, dinosaurs smaller than a rabbit were shot separately from the human action, then both were merged on film so audiences "saw" people fighting giant beasts. Video cameras have since brought even greater realism.

Not all screen dinosaurs are models. *The Animal World* (1956) and the 1960 remake of *The Lost World* included living reptiles dressed up as "dinosaurs." Dinosaur–costumed actors masqueraded as a herd of *Tyrannosaurus* in *Unknown Island* (1948). *Fantasia* (1940) made brilliant use of animated cartoon dinosaurs.

Screen dinosaurs can seem absurd or terrifying – it all depends on a movie maker's ability to get the creatures looking right.

Optical illusion (*below*)
A woman cowers below the terrifying bulk of a sauropod. Filmed scenes like this deceive the eye. Such movie monsters are no bigger than a child's toy.

Dinosaurs old and new

The dinosaurs of paintings, models, movies, books, and comic strips are all based – well or badly – on fossil evidence. Its study has transformed how scientists themselves see dinosaurs.

Scrappy fossil finds at first encouraged errors, and still sometimes do. Scientists misidentified as dinosaurs bits of fossil thecodont, crocodilian, pterosaur, bird – even wood and mollusk borings. Experts have mistaken bits of dinosaur for birds, and named a dinosaur from the jumbled bones of different animals. With few bones to guide him, one paleontologist reconstructed *Iguanodon* with its thumb spike on its nose.

Even when a skeleton was largely known, scientists sometimes failed to realize how its owner stood, or moved, or what it really looked like. They wrongly thought most dinosaurs sprawled, with elbows stuck out at the sides. They believed *Iguanodon* and *Tyrannosaurus* stood upright and walked with tails dragging on the ground. *Hypsilophodon* was thought to be a tree-climber, while the great sauropods wallowed in water because their legs could not support their weight on land. Like theropods, ornithischians supposedly had mouths that ran from ear to ear. Patient probing of old bones disproved these notions and produced the images of dinosaurs depicted in this book.

Build and stance (*right*) illustrations spanning more than 120 years show changing notions of big predatory dinosaurs.
1 *Megalosaurus* shown as a quadrupedal predator. From L. Figuier's *The World Before the Deluge* (1866).
2 *Tarbosaurus* shown bipedally, but with legs stuck out sideways, heavy belly, kangaroo posture, and drooping tail. From Z.V Špinar's *Life Before Man* (1972).
3 *Tyrannosaurus*, with S-curved neck, legs directly below lean body, and horizontal back and tail – a beast combining strength and speed. From this book.

Mode of life (*right*) Past and present illustrations reflect changing views of how sauropods lived.
1 People once thought sauropods needed water to support their weight.
2 Scientists now think they walked on land like elephants and browsed high up like giraffes.
3 Some scientists suppose certain sauropods reared to reach high leafy twigs.

© DIAGRAM

Yet doubts remain. Were dinosaurs warm–blooded just as mammals are? Did any theropods have feathers? Were some dinosaurs born not hatched? What really killed off dinosaurs? We still have much to learn about these most successful backboned animals that ever lived on land.

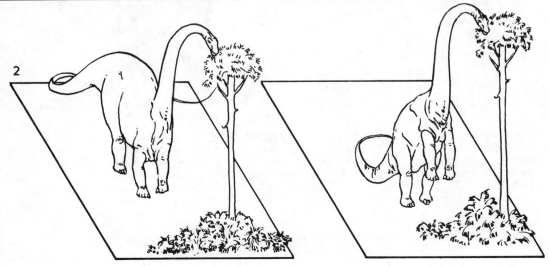

If dinosaurs lived on . . .

Suppose whatever wiped out dinosaurs had never happened. Suppose the dinosaurs lived on and mammals never took their place. What kinds of creatures would now dominate the land?

We can only guess the answers, but our guesses would allow for how some mammals have evolved to meet the challenge of a changing world. In the last 65 million years, splitting and colliding slabs of the Earth's crust have isolated continents and islands, thrust up mountain chains, and diverted ocean currents. This has indirectly frozen regions hoisted high above the sea or carried far from the equator. Meanwhile grasses and other flowering plants have multiplied and spread. Groups of mammals affected by such alterations have changed in ways that helped them to endure harsh climates and exploit new foods and habitats. Dinosaurs might well have altered too.

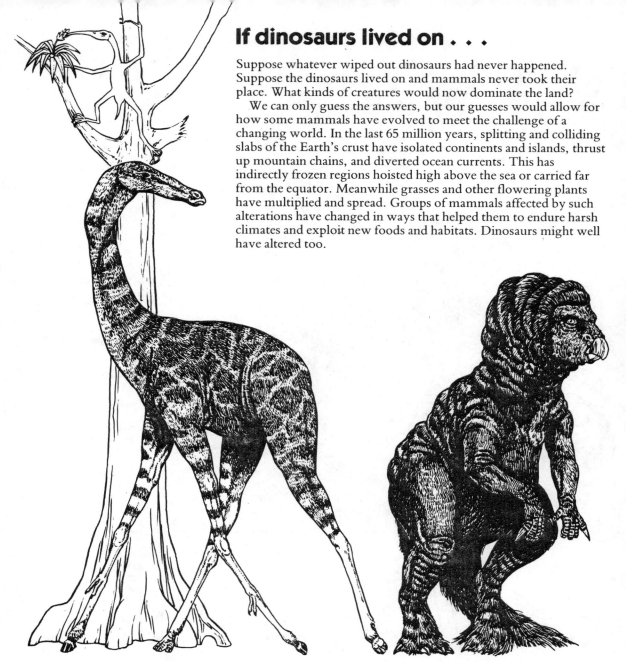

Minidinosaur (*top*)
Evolved from insectivorous dinosaurs, the nectar-eating gimp is a climbing minidinosaur sucking nectar from the flowers with its tube-shaped snout. This is a tropical rainforest dinosaur-that-might-have-been.

Giraffosaur (*above left*)
A grazer tall enough to spot approaching danger, the giraffe-like lank evolved not from dinosaurs but from their near relatives the pterosaurs. It crops grass with a broad snout and long legs carry it away from danger.

Hardy mountaineer
A dinosaur alternative to mountain goats, the fat-insulated and shaggy-coated balaclav eats alpine plants high up in the Rockies. Broad hairy feet and tail give it surefooted grip on slippery glaciers.

High among the tropical rainforest canopy, nectar-sipping and fruit-eating minidinosaurs would play the parts of bats, birds, and insects. Herds of grazing dinosaurs would darken grassy plains. Dinosaurs insulated from the cold by shaggy hair would range high among the Himalayas and perhaps roam frozen Arctic wastes. Dwarfed dinosaurs would dominate small, isolated islands where body size is limited by food supply.

In the last few million years harsh climatic changes arguably set prehistoric apes along the route that led to humankind. The same climatic pressures might equally have given rise to brainy manlike theropods instead.

Had archosaurs not lost their evolutionary grip so long ago, then, animals like those depicted on these pages could be flourishing today. Even the readers of this book would be not people but new-fangled dinosaurs.

Birds possibly excepted, of course no dinosaurs survive. But scientific study of their fossils makes them live again in our imagination, and helps us grasp their role in the evolution of our planet and its life.

Dinosaur fantasies

These pages picture five dinosaurs and one pterosaur-that-might-have-been. The gimp, lank, balaclav, and dwarfed sauropod and megalosaur feature in *The New Dinosaurs: An Alternative Evolution* (1988), by Scottish science writer Dougal Dixon. The dinosauroid, whose model stands in an Ottawa museum, was the 1982 brainchild of leading Canadian paleontologist Dale Russell.

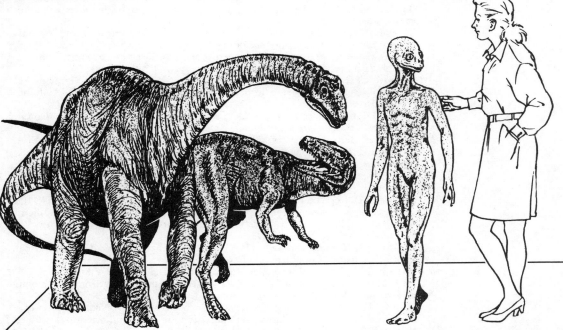

Island dwellers

This dwarf plant-eating titanosaur (*left*) and predatory megalosaur (*right*) inhabit islands cut off from a continent. Limited food supply has stunted these descendants of huge mainland dinosaurs.

Intelligent dinosaurs

Big-brained, with forward facing eyes, upright stance and adaptable hands, the dinosauroid is a product of convergent evolution that transformed *Troodon* into a dinosaur redesigned astonishingly like a man.

©DIAGRAM

Books on dinosaurs

This selection, with brief explanatory notes, gives the general reader an inkling of the wealth of books and articles that feature dinosaurs. Many are English-language publications released separately in the United States and Britain, and some appear in various translations. The list omits books for the very young but includes some key technical examples and outdated publications with evocative illustrations or of historic interest. Items listed under one chapter in this book may include material relevant to others.

General

Carroll, R. *Vertebrate Paleontology and Evolution* W.H.Freeman, 1988. Long-awaited 698-page successor to Romer's *Vertebrate Paleontology* – a major, technical reference work on fossil backboned animals, with dinosaur information of interest to the general reader.

Charig, A.J. *A New Look at the Dinosaurs* Mayflower Books, USA 1979; Heinemann, UK 1983. Updating should keep this leading British paleontologist's book among the best short accounts of current knowledge of the dinosaurs; fully illustrated.

Colbert, E.H. *Dinosaurs: An Illustrated History* Hammond, 1983. Popular account by a major US vertebrate paleontologist, with a glossary of names, pronunciation key, and museums guide.

Colbert, E.H. *Dinosaurs: Their Discovery and Their World* Dutton, USA 1961; Hutchinson, UK 1962. A substantial survey for the general reader; for many years a standard work.

Czerkas, S.J. and Olson, E.C. *Dinosaurs Past and Present* (two volumes) Natural History Museum of Los Angeles County and the University of Washington Press, 1987. Handsomely illustrated, large-format books with articles by experts on aspects of past and present knowledge. Stresses artists' restorations.

Darwin, C. R. *On the Origin of Species by Means of Natural Selection...* London, 1859 (many subsequent editions). This book established the modern theory of biological evolution.

Dixon, D., Cox, B., Savage, R.J.G., and Gardiner, B. *The Macmillan Illustrated Encyclopedia of Dinosaurs and Prehistoric Animals*, 1988. Compendium of prehistoric vertebrates, with a fine text but illustrations based largely on outdated research.

Halstead, L.B. *The Evolution and Ecology of the Dinosaurs* Peter Lowe, 1975. An expert's popular account of dinosaurs, their evolution and lifestyles, attractively illustrated by Giovanni Caselli; some concepts are now controversial or have been superseded.

Lambert, D. and the Diagram Group *A Field Guide to Dinosaurs* Avon, US 1983; *Collins Guide to Dinosaurs* Collins, UK 1983. All then-known dinosaurs classified, described, and illustrated, with sections on dinosaur evolution, lifestyles, discovery, distribution, and museum displays.

Lambert, D. *Dinosaurs* Crown, USA 1978; St. Michael, UK 1978. Large- format, colorfully illustrated popular account of dinosaurs.

McLoughlin, J.C. *Archosauria: A New Look at the Old Dinosaur* Viking Press, USA 1979; Allen Lane, UK 1979. A zoologist/illustrator's popular overview of dinosaurs as warm-blooded (endothermic) creatures.

Moody, R.T.J. *The World of Dinosaurs* Grosset, USA 1977; *A Natural History of Dinosaurs* Hamlyn, 1977. Illustrated popular account by an authority on the subject.

Norman, D. B. and Milner, A. C. *Dinosaur* Dorling Kindersley/Natural History Museum, London, 1989. A popular "Eyewitness Guide" stressing superb, fully captioned color photographs of fossil bones.

Romer, A.S. *Vertebrate Paleontology* Chicago Press, 1966. Monumental survey of fossil backboned animals, with many reconstructed, line-drawn skeletons; a standard students' work still in print after more than 20 years but superseded by Carroll's.

Sheehan, A. (ed.) *The Prehistoric World* Warwick, USA 1975; Sampson Low, UK 1975. Lavishly illustrated compilation covering evolution and prehistoric life.

Simpson, George Gaylord *Tempo and Mode in Evolution* Columbia University Press, 1944. One of several works on evolution by one of the greatest 20th century writers on this subject.

Špinar, Z.V. *Life Before Man* American Heritage Press, USA 1972; Thames and Hudson, UK 1972. Notable for Zdeněk Burian's evocative paintings of prehistoric wildlife and countrysides.

Steel, R. and Harvey, A.P. (eds.) *The Encyclopaedia of Prehistoric Life* Mitchell Beazley, 1979. Cornucopia of experts' alphabetically ordered entries on organisms, time units, places, and personalities, plus evolutionary charts and glossary; mainly black and white illustrations.

Swinton, W.E. *The Dinosaurs* Allen & Unwin, 1970. A leading British paleontologist's substantial work written for the general reader, with maps of British finds.

Tweedie, M. *The World of Dinosaurs* William Morrow, USA 1977; Weidenfeld & Nicolson, UK 1977. Large-format illustrated popular account.

Weishampel, D. et al. *The Dinosauria* University of California Press, 1990. Major scientific work, a "must" for serious dinosaurophiles.

Wilford, J.N. *The Riddle of the Dinosaur* Alfred A. Knopf, USA 1985; Faber & Faber, UK 1986. A *New York Times* Pulitzer Prize winner compellingly recounts highlights in the story of dinosaur discovery since its beginnings.

Notes: News of major discoveries of and about dinosaurs appears in serious newspapers, and in science magazines such as *Nature* and *Science*. Longer scientific papers appear in technical journals such as *Journal of Paleontology*, *Journal of Vertebrate Paleontology*, *Palaeontology*, *Palaeontographica*, and museum and university publications. All items published up to 1983 appear in the *Bibliography of Fossil Vertebrates* published annually by the Society of Vertebrate Paleontology.

Chapter 1: The Age of Dinosaurs

Alvarez, Luis et al. "Extraterrestrial Cause for the Cretaceous-Tertiary Extinction" in *Science*, 208, 6 June, 1980. First generally published report of the theory that asteroid impact killed off the dinosaurs.

Colbert, E.H. *Wandering Lands and Animals* Dutton, USA 1973; Hutchinson, UK 1974. Distributions of prehistoric backboned land animals as influenced by continental drift.

Colbert, E.H. *Evolution of the Vertebrates* Wiley, 1980. Substantial, readable account of the different groups of backboned creatures, described in the order in which they appeared; contains diagrams and line drawings.

Cox, C.B. *Prehistoric Animals* Hamlyn, 1968. Pocket-sized, fully illustrated popular overview by an expert on the subject.

Eldredge, N. and Gould, S.J. "Punctuated Equilibria an alternative to phyletic gradualism" in Schopf, T.J.M. (ed.) *Models in Paleobiology* Freeman, Copper, 1972. Controversial claim that evolution is sometimes not gradual but sudden, occurring as new species arise in isolated populations.

Harland, W.B. et al. *A Geological Time Scale* Cambridge University Press, 1982. Influential revisions show the Triassic Period beginning and ending earlier than formerly believed.

Henbest, N. "Geologists hit back at impact theory of extinctions" in *New Scientist* 28 April 1989. Shows how processes deep inside the Earth could have wiped out dinosaurs.

Kúrten, B. The Age of Dinosaurs McGraw-Hill, USA 1968; Weidenfeld & Nicolson, UK 1968. Readable, 255-page, illustrated account.

Lucas, S.G. and Hunt, A. (eds.) *Dawn of the Age of Dinosaurs in the American Southwest* New Mexico Museum of Natural History, 1989. Technical but fascinating compendium of Late Triassic life.

Padian, K. ed. *The Beginning of the Age of Dinosaurs* Cambridge University Press, 1986. Noted paleontologists' scientific articles on dinosaurs and other aspects of early Mesozoic times and life.

Raup, D.M. *The Nemesis Affair* W.W.Norton, USA and UK 1986; Penguin Books, Canada 1986. A leading paleontologist's own and others' theories that mass extinctions follow periodic impacts by large objects from space.

Stanley, S. *Extinction* W.H.Freeman, 1987. An authoritative survey of mass extinctions, blamed on shifting continents and climatic change rather than on impact by giant meteorites.

Chapter 2: The A to Z of Dinosaurs

Benton, M. *Dinosaurs: An A-Z Guide* Crown, USA 1988; Kingfisher, UK 1988. Popular guide by a British paleontologist. Devotes a page each to more than 80 dinosaurs, with description, full-colour illustration, pronunciation guide, name of namer, year named, map of find(s), and key to museum(s) exhibiting remains.

Buckland, W. "Notice on the *Megalosaurus* or great fossil lizard of Stonesfield" in *Transactions of the Geological Society*, London 1824. First publication of a scientifically named dinosaur.

Chure, D.J. and McIntosh, J.F. *A Bibliography of the Dinosauria (Exclusive of the Aves) 1677-1986* Museum of Western Colorado Press, 1989. An indexed 226-page checklist for paleontologists.

Glut, D.F. *The New Dinosaur Dictionary* Citadel, 1982. Revised, expanded (288-page) version of *The Dinosaur Dictionary*. All genera known to 1982.

Halstead, L.B. and J. *Dinosaurs* Blandford, 1981. A detailed pocket "field guide" including colored restorations of about 100 dinosaurs and a note on likely dinosaur coloration.

Leidy, J. "Remarks concerning *Hadrosaurus*" in *Proceedings of the Academy of Natural Sciences* Philadelphia, 1858. First published account of a North American dinosaur based on more than merely teeth.

Mantell, G. A. "Notice on the *Iguanodon*..." in *Philosophical Transactions of the Royal Society*, London 1825. The second published account of a dinosaur.

Norman, D. *The Illustrated Encyclopedia of Dinosaurs* Salamander Books, 1985. Authoritative, popular, large-format survey with John Sibbick's beautifully detailed full-colour restorations and many captioned skeletal drawings, maps, diagrams, and photographs.

Olshevsky, G. *Mesozoic Meanderings #2* (publication awaited as of early 1990) Updated lists of all dinosaur families, genera, species, synonyms – a mine of data for serious dinosaurophiles. Inquiries to George Olshevsky, PO Box 11021, San Diego, California 92111-0010.

Paul, G.S. *Predatory Dinosaurs of the World* Simon & Schuster, 1988. The first comprehensive account of one dinosaur group – an innovative dinosaurologist's 464-page survey of its evolution, lifestyles, higher groupings, and species, with Paul's own expert black-and-white restorations. Reclassifications open to question.

Sattler, H.R. *The Illustrated Dinosaur Dictionary* Lothrop, Lee & Shepard, 1983. All dinosaurs known by the early 1980s, described in alphabetical order, along with dinosaur-like prehistoric creatures and aspects of dinosaur anatomy; contains line drawings.

Steel. R. (ed. O. Kuhn) *Handbuch der Palaeoherpetologie,* Vols 14, 15 (English edition) Fischer Verlag, 1969. Descriptive classification of dinosaurs; an exhaustive reference work, but lacking the many genera and revisions revealed by subsequent research.

Zeleny, R.O. (ed.) *Dinosaurs!* World Book, 1987 (the 1987 Childcraft Annual). Fully illustrated, 304-page children's book including dozens of feature articles on different dinosaurs, with pronunciation guides, and dinosaur and human silhouettes compared, for scale.

Chapter 3: Dinosaurs classified

Bakker, R.T. See below, under Chapter 4.

Bakker, R.T. and Galton, P.M. "Dinosaur monophyly and a new class of vertebrates" in *Nature*, **248**, 1974. Refuting Seeley's and reviving Owen's claims, this influential article maintained that dinosaurs indeed formed one great group, the Dinosauria, a class with three suborders comprising saurischians, ornithischians, and birds.

Gauthier, J.A. "A cladistic analysis of the higher systematic categories of the Diapsida." PhD dissertation, Department of Paleontology, University of California, Berkeley. 1984. University Microfilms International. Influential redefinition of the dinosaurs.

Olshevsky, G. See above, under Chapter 2.

Owen, R. "Report on British Fossil Reptiles" in *Report of the Eleventh Meeting of the British Association for the Advancement of Science*, 1841. First published appearance of the term Dinosauria and claim that dinosaurs comprised one group of animals.

Paul, G. See above, under Chapter 2.

Seeley, Harry Govier, "On the Classification of the Fossil Animals commonly named Dinosauria" in *Proceedings of the Royal Society of London* Vol 43, 1887. Arguing that dinosaurs were not a natural group, Seeley divided dinosaurs into two orders (Ornithischia and Saurischia) and five suborders (Ornithopoda, Stegosauria, Ankylosauria, Ceratopsia, Theropoda, and Sauropoda) – divisions that commonly persist today.

Weishampel, D. et al. See above, under General.

Chapter 4: Dinosaur life

Alexander, R. McN. *Dynamics of Dinosaurs and other Extinct Giants* Columbia University Press, 1989. Topics include biomechanics involved in dinosaur stance, gaits, and speeds.

Alexander, R. McN. "Estimates of speeds of dinosaurs" in *Nature* 13 May, 1976. Speed estimates based on fossil tracks.

Bakker, R.T. *The Dinosaur Heresies* William Morrow, USA 1986; Longman, UK 1987. The 480-page book restating Bakker's controversial arguments that dinosaurs had been warm-blooded animals as mammals are, and outlining a reclassification.

Desmond, A.J. *The Hot-Blooded Dinosaurs* Blond & Briggs, 1975. Lively account of the evolution of ideas about the dinosaurs – the first book to popularize the theory of warm-blooded dinosaurs championed by Robert Bakker.

Heilmann, G. *The Origin of Birds* London, 1925. Ahead of its time in many fine illustrations showing lively, running dinosaurs.

Hitchcock, E. *Ichnology of New England* William White, 1858. Illustrated account of "bird" footprints left in Connecticut Valley sandstone by what we now know were early dinosaurs.

Horner, R. and Gorman, G. *Digging Dinosaurs* Workman, 1988. Popular account of Horner and Makela's revolutionary discoveries of nesting dinosaurs.

Stout, W. and Service, W. *The Dinosaurs* Bantam Books, 1981. Likely events in dinosaurs' lives graphically pictured and narrated.

Thomas, R.D.K. and Olson, E.C. (eds.) *A Cold Look at the Warm-Blooded Dinosaurs* Westview Press, 1980. Scientific papers for and against the theory that dinosaurs were warm blooded as birds and mammals are.

Chapter 5: Dinosaurs worldwide
(see also bibliography for next chapter)

Andrews, R.C. *The New Conquest of Central Asia (Natural History of Central Asia* Vol 1) The American Museum of Natural History, 1932. The story of American fossil-hunters' expeditions to Mongolia.

Archer, M. and Clayton, G. (eds.) *Vertebrate Zoogeography and Evolution in Australasia* Hesperian Press, Australia 1984. Copiously illustrated 1200-page students' reference work, with details of Australian dinosaurs.

Buffetaut, E. *A Short History of Vertebrate Palaeontology* Croom Helm, 1987. A worldwide survey, mainly of events before 1914.

Croucher, R. and Woolley, A.R. *Fossils, minerals and rocks; collection and preservation* British Museum (Natural History) and Cambridge University Press, 1982. A basic technical guide for beginners and experts alike.

Dong, Z. (English text **Milner, A.C.**) *Dinosaurs from China* China Ocean Press, China 1987; British Museum (Natural History), UK 1988. "The most comprehensive and best illustrated book about Chinese dinosaurs." Many captioned color photographs of reconstructed Chinese dinosaurs and their localities.

Gilbert, J. *Dinosaurs Discovered* Hamlyn, 1979. Includes tales of dinosaur hunters and their finds; illustrations by Guy Michel.

Gillette, D. and Lockley, M. (eds.) *Dinosaur Tracks and Traces* Cambridge University Press, 1989. The first book of its kind: a collection of scientific articles for all dinosaur enthusiasts.

Kielan-Jaworowska, Z. *Hunting for Dinosaurs* MIT Press, 1969. Popular account of Polish-Mongolian dinosaur hunts in Mongolia in the 1960s.

Lanham, U. *The Bone Hunters* Columbia University Press, 1973. Early fossil hunting in North America.

McGinnis, H.J. *Carnegie's Dinosaurs* Carnegie Institute, 1982. Has descriptions and photographs of dinosaurs in Pittsburgh's Carnegie Museum of Natural History.
Ostrom, J.H. and McIntosh, J.S. *Marsh's Dinosaurs. The collections from Como Bluff* Yale University Press, 1966. By two leading paleontologists; with 65 plates.
Quirk, S. and Archer, M. (eds.) *Prehistoric Animals of Australia* Australian Museum, 1983. Features Peter Schouten's lively restorations of Australian dinosaurs in natural settings.
Rich, P.V. and Thompson, E.M. (eds.) *The Fossil Vertebrate Record of Australasia* Monash University Offset Printing Unit, 1982. Includes descriptions of Australian dinosaurs.
Rixon, A.E. *Fossil Animal Remains: Their Preparation and Their Conservation* Humanities Press, 1976. A technical guide for fossils large and small.
Russell, D.A. *A Vanished World: The Dinosaurs of Western Canada* University of Chicago Press, USA 1977; National Museums of Canada, 1977. Beautifully illustrated evocation of dinosaur life in Late Cretaceous Alberta, by a leading Canadian paleontologist.
Russell, D.A. *An Odyssey in Time: the Dinosaurs of North America* University of Toronto Press/National Museum of Natural Sciences, 1989. An acclaimed authoritative account, richly illustrated.
Sternberg, C.H. *Hunting Dinosaurs on Red Deer River, Alberta* World Company Press, 1917. A great fossil hunter's record of Canadian dinosaur discoveries.

Chapter 6: Dinosaurologists

(See also above, under Chapter 5)
Bird, R.T. *Bones for Barnum Brown; Adventures of a Dinosaur Hunter* Texas Christian University Press, 1985. Biography of a great American dinosaur hunter, the Sternbergs' chief rival in Alberta's dinosaur rush.
Colbert, E.H. *The Great Dinosaur Hunters* Dover, 1984. The best general account of worldwide dinosaur discoveries into the mid 1960s.
Gerry, E. *Directory of Palaeontologists of the World* International Paleontological Association, 1976. Lists professional paleontologists, their specialties, and institutions where they work. To be updated.
Sternberg, C.H. *The Life of a Fossil Hunter* Holt, 1909. Reminiscences of one of the great American dinosaur hunters.

Chapter 7: Dinosaurs revived

Czerkas, S.M. and Glut, D.F. *Dinosaurs, Mammoths, and Cavemen* E.P.Dutton, 1982. The Art of Charles R. Knight.
Dixon, D. *The New Dinosaurs: An Alternative Evolution* Salem House, USA; Grafton, UK 1988. Imaginative, colorfully illustrated, yet scientific speculation about how dinosaurs would have evolved had they endured.
Glut, D.F. *Classic Movie Monsters* Scarecrow, 1978. Chapters on King Kong and Godzilla mention dinosaurs or dinosaur-like monsters.
Glut, D.F. *The Dinosaur Scrapbook* Citadel Press, 1980. Pot-pourri of fictional and model dinosaurs, in cartoons, comics, movies, parks, etc.

Index

Notes:
1 Formally named genera are in italics. Genera with informal names only are in quotes. (But see "Ultrasaurus" p. 102)
2 An invalid name is followed by = and the valid name.
3 A genus marked (n) is *nomen nudum* (lacks a formal description).
4 Key text references are in bold type. Main picture references are in italics.

A

Aachenosaurus, **38**
Abel, Roberto, 281
Abelisaurid (-ae, -s), **38**, **129**
  classification, 109, 110
  co-namers of, 269, 281
Abelisaurus, **38**, 129
  co-namers of, 269, 281
Abrictosaurus, **38**, *38*, 150
  namer of, 276
  Sereno's classification, 149
  and winning a mate, 210
Acanthopholis, **38**, *38*, 167, 277
Acid bath, 227
Acrocanthosaurus, **38**, 130, 278, 278, 284
Adasaurus, **38**, *38*, 126, 269
Aegyptosaurus, **38**, *38*, 145, 284
Aeolosaurus, **38**, 282
Aepisaurus, **38**, *38*, 145, *238*, 274
Aetonyx = Massospondylus
Aetosaurs, 18, **39**, *39*
  and dinosaur family tree, 26–27
Afghanistan, 246
African dinosaurs, 261–263
Agathaumas, **39**, 171, **271**, 272
Agrosaurus, **39**, *39*, 138, 283
Air sacs, 178–179
Alamosaurus, **39**, *39*, 145, 275
Albertosaurus, **39**, *39*, 132, *231*
  describer of, 281
  hand, 188
Albisaurus, **39**
Alectrosaurus, **39**, 132, 275
Alen, P.G., *292*
Algeria, 261, 263
Algoasaurus, **39**, 143, 270
Alioramus, **40**, *40*, 132, 277
Aliwalia, **40**, *40*, 113, 274
Allosaurid (-ae, -s), **40**, **130**
  classification, 109, 110
  describer of, 279
Allosaurus, **40**, *40*, *130*, 274, *290*
  and attack, 206
  jaws, 190
  model of, *300*
  in movies, 299

namer of, 278, 279
remains discovered, 273
skull, 180
Alocodon, **40**, *40*, 160, 284
Altispinax, **40**, *40*, 128, 276
Alvarez, Luis and Walter, 268
Amargasaurus (n), **40**
Ameghino, Carlos, 258, 268
Ameghino, Florentino, 258, 260, **268**, *268*
America, *see* North America, South America
Ammosaurus, **40**, *41*, 139, 279
Amphibians, **41**
  and evolution, 14–15
Amphicoelias, **41**, *41*, 146, 272
Amphisaurus = Anchisaurus
Amtosaurus, **41**, *41*, 168, 277, 284
Amygdalodon, **41**, 141
  namer of, 270
  teeth, 191
Anapsids, 16, **41**
Anatosaurus, (= *Edmontosaurus* and "Anatotitan") 278, 285
"Anatotitan," **41**
Anchiceratops, **41**, *41*, 171, 270
  feeding, *205*
Anchisaurid (-ae, -s), **41**, **138**
  classification, 109, 136
  describer of, 279
Anchisaurus, **29**, *29*, *42*, *138*
  Galton's classification, 137
  namer of, 279
Andrews, Roy Chapman, *266*, 246, **268**
Ankylopollexia, Sereno's classification, 149
Ankylosaur (-ia, -s), **42**
  body armor, 208
  brainpower, 183
  classification, 109, 158–159
  and dinosaur family tree, 26–27
  families, 167–168
  in food chain, 204–205
  head size, 180
  namer of, 281
  Sereno's classification, 159
  skin and scales, 196
Ankylosaurid (-ae, -s), **42**, **168**
  classification, 109, 158–159
  namer of, 270
  Sereno's classification, 159
Ankylosaurus, *12*, *42*, 168
  namer of, 270
  tail in combat, *195*
Anodontosaurus = Dyoplosaurus
Anoplosaurus, **42**, 155, 283

Anserimimus, **42**, *42*, 122, 269
Antarctica, 264
Antarctosaurus, **42**, *42*, 145, 276
Anthodon = Paranthodon
Antrodemus (= *Allosaurus*), **42**, 130, 278
Apatodon = Allosaurus
Apatosaurus, **42**, *42*, 146
  brain size, 182
  heart and blood pressure, 178
  lung and heart, 179
  model of, *292*
  namer of, 279
  remains discovered, 273
Araeoscelids, 17
Aragosaurus, **43**, 143, 270, 271, 283
Aralosaurus, **43**, *43*, 156, 283
Archaeopterygid (-ae, -s), **43**, **121**
  classification, 109, 110
  namer of, 277
Archaeopteryx, *24*, 24–25, **43**, *43*, 110, *121*, 121, *273*, 273
  describer of, 280
  feathers, 196–197, *197*
Archaeornis = Archaeopteryx
Archaeornithomimus, **43**, *43*, 122
  namer of, 275
  redescriber of, 283
Archosaur (-ia, -s), 17, 18, **43**
  classification, 20–21
  and dinosaur family tree, 26–27
  and evolution of dinosaurs, 18–19
Archosauromorphs, 17
Arctosaurus, **43**
Argentina, 258, 259, 260
Argyrosaurus, **43**, *43*, 145, 278
Aristosaurus = Massospondylus
Aristosuchus (= *Calamospondylus*), *44*, 283
"Arkanosaurus" (= "Arkansaurus"), **44**
"Arkansaurus," **44**, 122
Armored dinosaurs, **44**, 167–168
  see also Ankylosaur
Arms, 188–189
Arrhinoceratops, **44**, *44*, 171, 282
Arstanosaurus, **44**, *44*, 156
Asian dinosaurs, 246–253
Asiatosaurus, **44**, *44*, 143, 281
Asteroids, and mass extinctions, 34–35
Astrodon, **44**, *44*, 142, 277
Atlantosaurus (= *Apatosaurus*), **44**, *45*, 146, 279
Atlascopcosaurus, **45**, *45*, 151, 282
Atreipus, 230
Attack, 206–207

Attridge, John, 268
Aublysodon, **45**, *45*, 278
Aublysodontid (-ae, -s), **45**
  classification, 109, 110
  describer of, 281
Australasian dinosaurs, 264–265
Austria, 238, 241, 242
Austrosaurus, **45**, *45*, 141, 278
Avaceratops, **45**, 171, 272
Avalonianus, **45**
Avetheropods, Paul's classification, 111
Avimimid (-ae, -s), **45**, **120**
  classification, 109, 110
  namer of, 277
Avimimus, **45**, *45*, *120*, 120, 277
Avipes, **45**, 114, 276
Avisaurid (-ae, -s), **45**, 270, 282
Avisaurus, **46**, 270, 282
Ayyasami, K, **268**, 285
Azendohsaurus, **46**, 273

B

Bactrosaurus, **46**, *46*, 157, 275
Bagaceratops, **46**, 170, 280, 281
Bahariasaurus, **46**, 284
Baird, Donald, 268
Bakker, Robert, 108, **268**, 272, 274, 282, 285, 291
Baldwin, David, 269
Bannikov, Aleksandr Fedorovich, **269**, 277
Baptornis, *25*
Barapasaurid (-ae, -s), **46**
  classification, 109, 136
Barapasaurus, **46**, *46*, 141, *252*
  in cladogram, 137
  co-namers of, 271, 277, 283
Barosaurus, **46**, *46*, 146, 279
Barsbold, Rinchen, 246, **269**, 281, 282, 283
Barsboldia, **46**, 157
  co-describers of, 280, 281
Bartholomai, Alan, **269**, 280
Baryonychid (-ae, -s), **47**, **135**, 280
Baryonyx, **47**, *47*, *135*, 135
  and attack, *207*
  claw, *280*
  co-namers of, 271, 280
  discoverer of, 284
Basutodon, **47**, 47
Beckles, Samuel, 269
Beds, geological, 224
Béland, Pierre, 269
Belgium, 238, 241, 242
Bell, Claude Kenneth, *292*
Bellusaurus, **47**, 141, 272
Benedetto, Juan Luis, 269
Benton, Michael, 21, 137, **269**
Berman, David, **269**, 278
Betasuchus, **47**, *47*, 122, 276
Bird, Roland T., 269
Bird feet, *see* Ornithopods

Bird-hipped dinosaurs, *see* Ornithischians
Birds, **24–25**, 47
Blikanasaurid (-ae, -s), **47**
    classification, 109, 136
    co-namers of, 274, 275
Blikanasaurus, **47**
    classification, 137
    co-namers of, 274, 275
Blood pressures, 178
Bochatey, Graciela, **269**, 275, 280, 282
Body temperature, 200–201
Bohlin, Anders Birger, 269
Bonaparte, José F., 258, **269**, 281, 282, 284
Bone-headed dinosaurs, *see* Pachycephalosaurids and Homalocephalids
Bones, *see* Skeletons
Borogovia, **47**, 127, 281
Borsuk-Bialynicka, Magdalena, 269
Bothriospondylus, **47**, 47, 142, 281
Brachiosaurid (-ae, -s), **48**, **142**
    in cladogram, 137
    classification, 109, 136
    namer of, 282
Brachiosaurus, **48**, 48, *142*, 277
    head size, 181
    namer of, 282
    sense of smell, 185
    spinal bone, 175
    thigh bone, *282*
Brachyceratops, **48**, 171, 275
Brachylophosaurus, **48**, 48, 156, 283
Brachypodosaurus, **48**, 167, 271
Brachyrophus = *Camptosaurus*
Bradycneme, **48**, 48, 126
    co-namers of, 275, 284
    reidentifier of, 270
Brains, 182–183
Braun, Roby, 293
Brazil, 259, 260
Brett-Surman, Michael, **269**, 282
Breviparopus, 262
Brodkorb, Pierce, 270
Brontosaurus = *Apatosaurus*
Broom, Robert, 261, **270**
Brown, Barnum, 230, **270**, 283
Buckland, William, 240, **270**, *270*
Buffetaut, Eric, **270**, 277
Bunzel, Emanuel, 270
Burian, Zdeněk, 290
Burroughs, Edgar Rice, 294–295, 298
Buscalioni, A.D., **270**, 271, 283

C

Cabrera, Angel, 270
Caenagnathid (-ae, -s), **48**, **119**

classification, 109, 110
    namer of, 283
Caenagnathus, **48**, 119, 283
Calamosaurus = *Calamospondylus*
Calamospondylus, **48**, 116, 274, 278
Callovosaurus, **48**, 48, 154, 274
Camarasaurid (-ae, -s), **49**, **143**
    in cladogram, 137
    classification, 109, 136
    namer of, 272
Camarasaurus, **49**, 49, *143*
    claws, 209
    foreleg and shoulder blade, *236*
    namer of, 271
    remains discovered, 273
Camelotia, **49**, 140, 274
Cameroon, 261
Camouflage, 198–199
Camp, Charles L., 270
Camptosaurid (-ae, -s), **49**, **154**
    classification, 109, 148–149
    describer of, 279
Camptosaurus, **49**, 49, *154*
    namer of, 279
    remains discovered, 273
    Sereno's classification, 149
    skull, 180
Campylodon = *Campylodoniscus*
Campylodoniscus, **49**, 145, 277
Canada, 230–231, 233, 235
Cannon, George, 270
Carcharodontosaurus, **49**, 49
    namer of, 284
Cardiodon = *Cetiosaurus*
Carlin, William E., 270, 282
Carnegie, Andrew, 234
Carnosaur (-ia, -s), **49**, 110–111
    brainpower, 183
    classification, 109
    and dinosaur family tree, 26–27
    winning a mate, 210
Carnotaurus, **50**, 50, *129*, 129, 196, 269
Carpenter, Kenneth, 271
Casamiquela, Rodolfo M., 271
Casanovas, M.L., 270, **271**, 283
Casts, 221
Cathetosaurus, **50**, 50, 143
    namer of, 277
    tail as a prop, *195*
Caudocoelus = *Teinurosaurus*
Cauldon = *Camarasaurus*
Cenozoic era, 14–15
Centrosaurus (= *Eucentrosaurus*) 50, 50, 278
Cerapod (-a, -s), **50**
    Sereno's classification, 159

Ceratopia, *see* Ceratopsia
Ceratopid, *see* Ceratopsid
Ceratops, **50**, 171, 279
Ceratopsia (-ns), **50**
    body armor, 208
    brainpower, 183
    classification, 109, 158–159
    describer of, 279
    eggs, 212
    families, 169–171
    in food chain, 204–205
    Sereno's classification, 159
    skin and scales, 196
    winning a mate, 210
Ceratopsid (-ae, -s), **50**, **171**
    classification, 109, 158–159
    describer of, 279
    Sereno's classification, 159
Ceratosaur (-ia, -s), **50**, 111
Ceratosaurid (-ae, -s), **50**, **131**
    classification, 109, 110–111
    describer of, 279
Ceratosaurus, **50**, 50, *131*, 131
    discoverer of, 273–274
    model of, *292*
    in movies, 298–299, 300
    namer of, 279
Cetiosaurid (-ae, -s), **50**, **141**
    in cladogram, 137
    classification, 109, 136
    namer of, 278
Cetiosauriscus, **50**, 146, *276*, 276
Cetiosaurus, **50**, 50, *141*, 141, 281
Chad, 261
Chakravarti, Dhirendra K., 271
Chang, *see* Zhang
Changdusaurus (n), **51**, 166
Chao, *see* Zhao
Chaoyoungosaurid (-ae, -s), **51**
    classification, 109, 158–159
Chaoyoungosaurus, **31**, **51**, 285
Charig, Alan J., 261, **271**, 280
Chasmosaurus, **51**, 51, 171, 277
Chassternbergia, **51**, 51, 167, 268
Chatterjee, Sankar, 252, **271**, 277, 283
"Chendusaurus" = *Changdusaurus*
Cheneosaurus = *Hypacrosaurus*
"Chengdusaurus" = *Changdusaurus*
Chialingosaurus, **51**, 51, 166
Chiayuesaurus, **51**, 51, 143, 269
Chienkosaurus, **52**

Chilantaisaurus, **52**, 52, 130, 276
Chile, 259
China, 248, 249, 254–255
"Chindesaurus," **52**, 112
Chingkankousaurus, **52**, 132, 285
Chinshakiangosaurus, **52**, 52, 140, 285
Chironyms, 37
Chirostenotes, **52**, 52, 119, 119, 274, 275
Chirotherium, 10
Chondrosteosaurus, **52**, 145, 281
Chondrosteus = *Chondrosteosaurus*
Chou, *see* Zhou
Chow, *see* Zhao
Chronometric dating, 225
Chuandongocoelurus, **52**, 116, 275
Chubutisaurid (-ae, -s), **52**
    classification, 109, 136
    namer of, 272
Chubutisaurus, **53**, 272
Chungkingosaurus, **53**, 166, 272, 285
Chure, Daniel, **271**, 278
Cionodon, **53**, 156, 272
Cladeiodon, **53**
Cladistics, 21
Cladogram, of dinosaurs, 21
Claorhynchus = *Triceratops*?
Claosaurus, **53**, 156, 279
Clasmodosaurus, **53**, 53, 268
Classification of dinosaurs, 16–17, 20–21, 108–111
Claws, 209
    and winning a mate, 211
Clevelanotyrannus = *Nanotyrannus*
Cobabe, Emily A., **271**, 273
Coelophysid (-ae, -s), **53**, **114**
    classification, 109, 110–111
    describer of, 282
Coelophysis, **28**, **53**, 53, *114*
    discoverer of, 269
    namer of, 271
    Paul's classification, 111
Coelophysis bauri, 256
Coelosaurus = *Ornithomimus*
Coelurid (-ae, -s), **53**, **116**
    classification, 109, 110
    describer of, 279
Coeluroides, **53**, 53, 116, 276
Coelurosaur (-ia, -s), **54**, 110
    Carnosaurs, 183
    classification, 109
    and dinosaur family tree, 26–27
    Paul's classification, 111
Coelurosauravids, 17
Coelurosaurus, **54**
Coelurus, **54**, 54, 116, 279
Colbert, Edwin H., 271
Colombia, 259
Colonosaurus = *Ichthyornis*
Color, 198–199

Coloradia = *Coloradisaurus*
Coloradisaurus, **54**, *54*, 139
Combat, 206-207, 217
  tails in, 195
  and winning a mate, 210-211
Comics, dinosaurs in, 296-297
Compsognathid (-ae, -s), **54, 115**
  classification, 109, 110
  namer of, 272
Compsognathus, 12-13, *24*, *30*, **54**, *54*, *115*, 115, *172*
  and attack, *206*
  discoverer of, 281
  head, 180
  namer of, 284
Compsosuchus, **54**, 130, 276
Conchoraptor, **54**, 118, 269
Coombs, Walter P. Jr., 271
Cooper, Michael R., 271
Cope, Edward Drinker, 232, 269, **271**, *271*, 275, 278, 279, 283
Coprolites, 220-221
Corro, Guillermo del, 272
Corythosaurus, **54**, *54*, 157
  jaws, 191
  namer of, 270
Cox, C.B., 271
Craspedodon, **54**, 155
Crateomus, **55**, 167
Craterosaurus, **55**, *55*, 166, 283
Creosaurus (= *Allosaurus*), 279
Cretaceous Period, 26-27, **32-33**
Crocodilians, 17, 18, **55**
  and dinosaur family tree, 26-27
Crompton, Alfred W., 268, 271, **272**
Cryptodraco, **55**, 167, 278
Cryptosaurus = *Cryptodraco*
Cumnoria = *Camptosaurus*
Currie, Philip J., 230, 268, **272**, 285
Cuvier, Baron Georges, 272

D

Dacentrurus, **55**, *55*, 166
  describer of, 281
  namer of, 278
Dachongosaurus, **55**, 141, 285
Dachungosaurus = *Dachongosaurus*
Damalasaurus (n), **55**, *55*, 142, 285
Danubiosaurus, **55**, 167, 270
Das-Gupta, H.C., 272
Daspletosaurus, **56**, *56*, 132, 283
Dating dinosaurs, 224-225
Datousaurus, **56**, 141, 272, 284
De Pauw, Louis, 272
Defense, 208-209

Deinocheirid (-ae, -s), **56, 124**
  classification, 109, 110
  co-namers of, 281, 283
Deinocheirus, **56**, *56*, *124*, 124
  arms and hands, 189
  co-namers of, 281, 283
Deinocheirus mirificus, casts of arms, *244*
Deinodon, **56**, 278
Deinonychosaur (-ia, -s), **56**, 110
  classification, 109
  and dinosaur family tree, 26-27
Deinonychus, **56**, *56*, 126, *230*, *281*, *291*
  and attack, *206*
  co-discoverers of, 281
  hand, 188
  jaw muscles, 177
Delgado, Marcel, 300
Denversaurus, **56**, *56*, 167, 268
  skull, *268*
Dianchungosaurus, **56**, 150, 285
Diapsid (-a, -s), 16, **57**
  classification, 20-21
Diceratops = *Triceratops*
Diclonius, **57**, 156, 272
Dicraeosaurid (-ae, -s), **57**, 276
Dicraeosaurus, **57**, *57*
Didanodon = *Lambeosaurus*
Digestive systems, 190-191
Dilophosaurus, **57**, *57*, *235*
  namer of, 284
  swimming, 203
Dimetrodon, *288*, 288
Dimodosaurus = *Plateosaurus*
Dimorphodon, *22*
Dinamation, 292-293
Dinodocus, **57**, *57*, 142, 281
Dinosaur parks, 292-293
Dinosauria,
  classifications, 20-21, 108
Dinosaurs, **57**
  African, 261-263
  arms and hands, 188-189
  arrival of, 18-19
  in art, 290-291
  Asian, 246-253
  in attack, 206-207
  Australasian, 264-265
  and birds, 24-25
  body temperature, 200-201
  bones, 174-175
  brains, 182-183
  cladogram, 21
  classification, 16-17, 20-21, 108-111
  color and camouflage, 198-199
  in comics, 296-297
  in Cretaceous Period, 32-33
  dating fossils, 224-225
  defense, 208-209

digestive systems, 190-191
discovery and excavation, 222-223
droppings, 220-221
eggs, 212-213
errors and doubts concerning, 302-303
European, 238-241
evolution, projected, 304-305
evolution and timescales, 14-19
extinction, 34-35
families classified, 108-109
family tree, 26-27
in fiction, 294-295
fossilization of, 220-221
heads, 180-181
heart-lung systems, 178-179
hips legs and feet, 192-193
inventor of the name, 281
in Jurassic Period, 30-31
key features, 20
life expectancy, 216-217
models of, 229, 292-293, 300
movement, 202-203
in movies, 298-301
muscles, 176-177
North American, 230-233
popular misconceptions, 288-289
rebuilding skeletons, 229
senses, 184-185
skeletons, *see* Skeletons
skin, 196-197
South American, 258-259
tails, 194-195
teeth, 190-191
in Triassic period, 28-29
young, 214-215
Dinosaurus = *Plateosaurus*
Diplodocid (-ae, -s), **58, 146**
  in cladogram, 137
  classification, 109, 136
  describer of, 279
Diplodocus, 12-13, *30*, **58**, *58*, *146*
  claws, 209
  discoverer of, 285
  diseased bones, *216*
  hand, 188
  hip girdle, *106*
  namer of, 279
  remains discovered, 273
  skull and possible trunk, 181
Diplotomodon, **58**, *58*, 133, 278
Diracodon, **58**, 166, 279
Disney, Walt, 292
Dixon, Dougal, 305
Dodson, Peter, **272**, 273

Dolichosuchus, **58**, *58*, 276
Dollo, Louis, 107, 272
Dong Zhiming, 248, **272**, *272*, 278, 284, 285
Doryphosaurus = *Kentrosaurus*
Douglass, Earl, 232, **273**, *273*
Doyle, Sir Arthur Conan, 294
Dracopelta, **58**, 167, 274
Dragons, 289
Dravidosaurus, *33*, **58**, *58*, 166, 268, 285
Dromaeosaurid (-ae, -s), **58, 126**
  classification, 109, 110
  in food chain, 204-205
  namer of, 283
  tails, 194
  and winning a mate, 210, 211
Dromaeosaurus, **58**, 126, 270, 280
Dromiceiomimus, **59**, *59*, 122, 283
Dromicosaurus = *Massospondylus*
Dryomorpha, Sereno's classification, 149
Dryosaurid (-ae, -s), **59, 152**
  classification, 109, 148-149
Dryosaurus, *30*, **59**, *59*, *152*, 152
  namer of, 279
  Sereno's classification, 149
Dryptosaurid (-ae, -s), **59, 133**
  classification, 109, 110
  describer of, 279
Dryptosauroides, **59**, 276
Dryptosaurus, **59**, *59*, *133*, 133, 279
Duck-billed dinosaurs, **59**, 156, 272
  brainpower, 183
  digestive systems, 191
  necks and feeding habits, 187
  skin, 197
  see also Hadrosaurids and Lambeosaurids
Dutuit, Jean M., 273
Dynamosaurus = *Tyrannosaurus*
Dyoplosaurus, **59**, *59*, 168
  describer of, 282
  shoulder and hip muscles, 177
Dysalotosaurus = *Dryosaurus*
Dysganus, **59**, 171, 272
Dystrophaeus, **59**, 141, 272
Dystylosaurus, **60**, 142, 277

E

Eaton, Theodore H. Jr., 273
Echinodon, **60**, *60*, 163
  describer of, 281

discoverer of, 269
Edmontonia, **60**, 167, 283
Edmontosaurus, **60**, *60*, 156
    broad mouth, *205*
    namer of, 277
Efraasia = *Sellosaurus*
Efremov, Ivan Antonovich,
    246, **273**
Eggs, **212-213**
    see also Ooliths
Egypt, 261, 263
Elaphrosaurus, **60**, *60*, 122
Elasmosaurus, *288*
Ellenberger, Paul, 273
Elmisaurid (-ae, -s), **60**,
    119
    describer of, 281
Elmisaurus, **60**, *60*, 119, 281
Elosaurus = *Apatosaurus*
Embasaurus, **60**, 128, 282
England, *see* United
    Kingdom
Enigmosaurid (-ae, -s), **61**
    classification, 109, 136
    namer of, 269
Enigmosaurus, **61**, *61*, 269,
    282
Eoceratops, **61**, *61*, 171, 277
Eolosaurus = *Aeolosaurus*
Eosuchians, 17
Epachtosaurus (n), **61**
Epanterias (= *Allosaurus*?),
    61
Erectopus, **61**, 128, 276
Erlikosaurus, **61**, *61*, 147,
    282
Erythrosuchids, 18
    and dinosaur family
        tree, 26-27
    see also Proterosuchians
Euacanthus = *Polacanthus*
Eucamerotus
    = *Chondrosteosaurus*
Eucentrosaurus, **61**, *61*, 171,
    271, 278
Eucercosaurus
    = *Anoplosaurus*
Eucnemesaurus
    = *Euskelosaurus*
Eudes-Deslongchamps,
    Jacques Amand, 273
Euhelopodid (-ae, -s), **62**,
    144
    classification, 109, 136
Euhelopus, **62**, *62*, *144*,
    144
    describer of, 285
    first finder of, 285
    namer of, 282
Euoplocephalus, *33*, **62**, *62*,
    168
    mouth shape, *205*
    namer of, 277
    shoulder and hip
        muscles, 177
    tail club, *282*
Euornithopoda, **62**
    Sereno's classification,
        149, 159
Euparkeria, 19
    neck curvature, 187
Euparkeriids, **62**

and dinosaur family
    tree,|26-27
European dinosaurs, 238-
    241
Euryapsids, 16-17, **62**
Eurypoda, Sereno's
    classification, 159
Euskelosaurus, **62**, 139, 277
Eustreptospondylid (-ae,
    -s), **62**
    classification, 109, 110
    describer of, 282
Eustreptospondylus, **62**, *62*,
    128, 284
Evolution, 14-19
Extinctions, mass, 34-35

F
Fabrosaurid (-ae, -s), **62**, **160**
    classification, 109, 148
    and dinosaur family
        tree, 26-27
    namer of, 274
Fabrosaurus, *30*, **62**, *62*, *160*,
    275
Family, and classification of
    dinosaurs, 21, 108-109
Farlow, James O., **273**, 283
Fastovsky, David E., 271,
    273
Fazetta, Frank, 297
Feduccia, J. Alan, 273
Feeding, 204-205
Feet, 192-193
Felch, M.P., 273
Fenestrosaurus = *Oviraptor*
Fiction, dinosaurs in, 294-
    295
Figuier, L., 302
Fish, and evolution, 14-15
Formations, geological,
    224
Fossil footprints, *10*, 202-
    203, 221, *275*
Fossil hunter's tools, 223
Fossilization of dinosaurs,
    220-221
Fossils,
    dating, 224-225
    discovering, 222-223
    preparing, 226-227
    understanding, 228-229
Foulke, William P., 274
Fox, Rev. William, 274
Fraas, Eberhard, 60, **274**
France, 238, 241, 242-243
Frenguellisaurus, **63**, 112, 281
"Fukuisaurus," 250
Fulgurotherium, **63**, *63*, 151,
    265, 276
"Futabasaurus," **63**

G
Gadolosaurus
    = *Arstanosaurus*
Gallimimus, **63**, *63*, 122
    co-namers of, 269, 281,
        283
    model of, *293*
Galton, Peter M., 108, 137,
    232, 268, **274**, 275, 277,
    284

Garudimimid (-ae, -s), **63**,
    123
    classification, 109, 110
Garudimimus, **63**, *63*, *123*,
    123
Gasosaurus, **63**, 128, 272
Gasparini, Zulma B., 274
Gauthier, Jacques A., **274**,
    283
Genasauria, Sereno's
    classification, 159
Genus, and classification of
    dinosaurs, 21, 108-109
Genyodectes, **63**, *63*, 285
Geological timescale, 14
Geranosaurus, **63**, 150, 270
Germany, East, 238, 241,
    243
Germany, West, 239, 241,
    243
Gervais, F.L. Paul, 274
Gigantosaurus = *Pelorosaurus*
Gigantoscelus
    = *Euskelosaurus*
Gillette, David, 274
Gilmore, Charles W., 275
Gilmoreosaurus, **64**, 156, 270
Giménez, Olga, 269, **275**,
    280, 282
Ginsburg, Leonard, 275
Giraffatitan, **64**, *64*, 142, 282
Glut, Donald, 296
Gondwana, 28, 30
Gongbusaurus, **64**, 160
    co-namers of, 272, 285
Gorgosaurus, 278, 283
Gow, Chris E., 275
Goyocephale, **64**, *64*, 162
    co-describers of, 280,
        281, 282
Granger, Walter, 275
Gravisaurus, **64**
Gravitholus, **64**, *64*, 161,
    274, 284
Gregory, William K., 275
Gresslyosaurus = *Plateosaurus*
Griffiths, D.W., 300
Griphosaurus = *Archaeopteryx*
Groups, geological, 225
Gryponyx = *Massospondylus*
Grypotholus = *Euhelopus*
Gryposaurus, **64**, 156, 278
Gyposaurus = *Anchisaurus*

H
"Hadrosauravus," **64**
Hadrosaurid (-ae, -s), **65**,
    156
    classification, 109, 148
    namer of, 272
    Sereno's classification,
        149
Hadrosauroidea, Sereno's
    classification, 149
Hadrosaurs, **65**
    and attack, 207
    in food chain, 204-205
    hands, 189
    necks, 187
    skin and scales, 196-197
    see also Duck-billed
        dinosaurs, Hadrosaurids
        and Lambeosaurids

Hadrosaurus, **65**, *65*, *156*
    first description of, 274
    namer of, 278
    vertebrae, *278*
Hagenbeck, Carl, 292
Halticosaurid (-ae, -s), **65**
    classification, 109, 110
    namer of, 276
Halticosaurus, **65**, *65*, 276
Hamlin, V.T., 296
Hands, 188-189
Haplocanthosaurus, **65**, *65*,
    141, 275
Haplocanthus
    = *Haplocanthosaurus*
Harpymimid (-ae, -s),
    co-namer of, 269
Harpymimus, **65**, *65*, 123,
    269, 282
Harrison, Colin J.O., **275**,
    284
Harryhausen, Ray, 300
Hasegawa, Yoshikazu, 250,
    275
Hatcher, John B., **275**, 279
Hatchlings, 214
Haughton, Sydney H., 275
Hawkins, Benjamin
    Waterhouse, 292
Hay, Oliver P., 275
Hayden, Ferdinand V., **275**,
    278
He Xinlu, 275
Heads, 180-181
Hearing, 184-185
Heart-lung system, 178-179
Hecatasaurus
    = *Telmatosaurus*
Heerden, Jacques van, 274,
    275
Heilmann, Gerhard, 173,
    290
Heishansaurus, **65**, 168, 269
Helopus = *Euhelopus*
Hennig, Edwin, 275
Heptasteornis, **65**, 127
    co-namers of, 275, 284
    reidentifier of, 270
Herrerasaur (-ia, -s), **66**, 110
    and classification of
        dinosaurs, 108-109
    and dinosaur family tree,
        26-27
    namer of, 274
Herrerasaurid (-ae, -s), **65**,
    113
    classification, 109, 110
    first describer of, 269
Herrerasaurus, **66**, *66*, *113*,
    282
    in cladogram, 21
    classification, 21
    Paul's classification, 111
Herreravians, Paul's
    classification, 111
Hesperornis, 25
Heterodontosauria, Sereno's
    classification, 149
Heterodontosaurid (-ae,
    -s),**66**, **150**
    classification, 109,
        148-149

and dinosaur family tree, 26–27
namer of, 277
Heterodontosaurus, **66**, *66*, *150*
co-namers of, 271, 272
Sereno's classification, 149
and winning a mate, *210*, 210
Heterosaurus = Iguanodon
Hierosaurus (= *Nodosaurus?*), **66**, 284
Hikanodon = Iguanodon
Hip bones, *106*, 177, 192
and classification of dinosaurs, 108
"Hironosaurus," **66**, 156, *250*
"Hisanohamasaurus," **66**, 146
Hitchcock, Edward B., 231, **275**
Hoffstetter, Robert, 275
Homalocephale, *33*, **66**, *66*, *162*, 280, 281
Homalocephalid (-ae, -s), **66**, **162**
classification, 109, 158–159
namer of, 273
Honduras, 231
Honghesaurus = Yandusaurus
Hoplitosaurus, **66**, *66*, 167, 278
Hoplosaurus = Struthiosaurus
Hopson, James A., 275
Horned dinosaurs, 170–171
see also Ceratopsia
Horner, John R., 232, **276**, 278, 284
Hortalotarsus = Massospondylus
Hotton, Nicholas, III, 276
Hou, 276
Howell, Brazier, 195
Huayangosaurid (-ae, -s), **67**, **165**
classification, 109, 158–159
Huayangosaurus, *31*, **67**, *67*, *165*
namer of, 272
Sereno's classification, 159
Huene, Friedrich von, 239, 248, 252, 259, **276**, *276*
"Hughenden sauropod," **67**, *67*, 142
Hulke, J., 276
Hulsanpes, **67**, 126, 281
Hunt, Adrian P., 276
Huxley, Thomas H., 277
Hylaeosaurus, **67**, *67*, 167, 279
Hypacrosaurus, namer of, 270
Hypselosaurus, **67**, 145
egg, *212*
namer of, 280
Hypsibema, **67**, 272
Hypsilophodon, **67**, *67*, *151*, *274*, 274

eye rings, 185
mistaken ideas respecting, 302
namer of, 277
Hypsilophodontia, Sereno's classification, 149
Hypsilophodontid (-ae, -s), **68**, **151**
classification, 109, 148–149
feeding when young, 214–215
Sereno's classification, 149
Hypsirophus = Stegosaurus

I
Ichnites, 220
Ichthyopterygian, 16
Ichthyornis, *25*, 25
Ichthyosaurs, 16–17, **68**
mass extinction, 34
Ichthyosaurus, *288*
Iguanasaurus = Iguanodon
Iguanodon, *32*, **68**, *68*, *155*, 272, 281
beak and jaws, 191
and defense, 209
first reconstruction of, 272
hand, 188
hip girdle, *106*
mistaken ideas respecting, 302
model of, *292*
namer of, 279
Sereno's classification, 149
tooth, *279*
Iguanodontia, Sereno's classification, 149
Iguanodontid (-ae, -s), **68**, **155**
classification, 109, 148
namer of, 272
thumb claws, 188
Iguanodontoidea, Sereno's classification, 149
Iliosuchus, **68**, 128, 276
India, 252–253, 255
Indosaurus, **68**, 129
Indosuchus, **68**, *68*, 129, 276
Infraorders, classification, 108–109
Ingavat, Rucha, 270, **277**
Ingenia, **68**, *68*, 118, 269
Ingenia yanshini, finger bones, 269
Ingeniid (-ae, -s), **68**
classification, 109, 110
namer of, 269
Inosaurus, **68**, *68*, 116, 278
Intelligence, 182–183
Iran, 246
Ischisaurus, **69**, *69*, 113, 282
Ischyrosaurus = Pelorosaurus
Israel, 246, 247
Italy, 244
Itemirid (-ae, -s), **69**
classification, 109, 110
namer of, 277
Itemirus, **69**, 277

J
Jaekel, O., 277
Jain, Sohan L., 252, 271, **277**, 277, 283
Janensch, Werner, 261, 262, 263, 274, 275, **277**
Japan, 250, 256–257
Jaxartosaurus, **69**, *69*, 157, 282
Jenkins, F.A., 268
Jensen, James A., 195, 232, 274, **277**
Jiangjunmiaosaurus, **69**, 128
Johnston, 277
Jonas, Paul, 292
Jones, Daniel E. and Vivian, 277
Jubbulpuria, **69**, *69*, 116, 276
Jurapteryx, **69**, 276
Jurassic Period, 26–27, **30–31**

K
"Kagasaurus," **69**, 128
Kaijiangosaurus, **69**, 128, 275
Kakuru, **69**, *69*, 116
co-describers of, 280
namer of, 282
Kangnasaurus, **69**, *69*, 152, 275
"Katsuyamasaurus," **70**
Kelmayisaurus, **70**, *70*, 128, 272
Kentrosaurus, **70**, *70*, 166, 275
Kenturosaurus = Kentrosaurus
Kenya, 262
Kermack, Kenneth, 277
Kielan-Jaworowska, Zofia, 246
Kim, Haang Mook, 251, **277**
"Kitadanisaurus," **70**
Knight, Charles, 290
Korea, South, 251
Koreanosaurus, **70**, 126, 277
Kotasaurus, **70**
Kräusel, 277
Kritosaurus, **70**, *70*, 156, *260*, 270
Kubert, Joe, 297
Kuhn, Oskar, 277
Kunmingosaurus, **70**, 141, 285
Kurzanov, Sergei Mikhailovich, 246, **277**, 284
Kutty, T.S., 271, **277**, 277, 283

L
Labocania, **70**, *70*
describer of, 280
Labrosaurus = Allosaurus
Laelaps (= *Dryptosaurus*), 133
Laevisuchus, **71**, 119, *253*, 276
Lagerpeton, namer of, 282
Lagerpetonids, **71**
Lagosuchid (-ae, -s), 19, **71**
classification, 108

and dinosaur family tree, 26–27
gait of, 19
Lagosuchus, 19, *71*
in cladogram, 21
namer of, 282
Lakes, Arthur, 267, **277**, 277, 279
Lambe, Lawrence M., 230, **277**
Lambeosaurid (-ae, -s), **71**, **157**
classification, 109, 148
namer of, 276
and winning a mate, 210
Lambeosaurus, *12*, **71**, *71*, 157, *233*, 272
describer of, 282
and winning a mate, *210*
Lametasaurus, **71**, 71, 145
Lanasaurus, **71**, *71*, 150, 275
Lancangjiangosaurus (n), **71**, 285
Lancangosaurus = Datousaurus
Langston, Wann Jr., **278**, 284
Laopteryx, **72**
Laos, 249
Laosaurus, **72**, 151, 279
Laplatasaurus, **72**, 145, 276
Lapparent, Albert F. de, 261, **278**, 285
Lapparentosaurus, **72**, *72*, 141, 269
Laurasia, 28, 30, 32
Lavocat, Réné, 278
Leaellynosaura, **72**, 151, 282
Legs, 192–193
Leidy, Joseph, 231, **278**
Leipsanosaurus = Struthiosaurus
Leonardi, Giuseppe, 278
Lepidosauromorphs, 17
Lepidosaurs, **72**
Leptoceratops, **72**, *72*, 170, 270
Leptospondylus = Massospondylus
Lesotho, 262, 263
Lesothosaurus, **72**, *72*, 160
co-namers of, 274
Sereno's classification, 159
Lexovisaurus, **72**, *72*, 166, 275
Li, 272, **278**, 285
Likhoelesaurus (n), **73**, *73*, 140, 273
Liliensternus, **73**, 284
Limbs, evolving, *15*
Limnosaurus = Telmatosaurus
Lizard-hipped dinosaurs, *see* Saurischians
Loncosaurus, **73**, *73*, 268
Long, Robert A., 278
Longman, Heber A., 278
Longosaurus, **73**, 114, 284
Lophorhothon, **73**, 156, 278
Loricosaurus, **73**, *73*, 145, 276
Lucas, Frederic A., 278
Lucas, O.W., 232, **278**
Lufengocephalus, **73**, 160, 285

Lufengosaurus, **73**, *73*, 139, 285
Lukousaurus, **74**, 114, 285
Lull, Richard S., 278
Lusitanosaurus, **74**, 164, 278, 285
Lycorhinus, **74**, 150
   namer of, 275
   and winning a mate, *210*
Lydekker, Richard, 278

M

McCaffrey, Anne, 295
McCay, Winsor, 298
McIntosh, John, 269, 271, **278**
Macrodontophion, **74**, 285
Macrophalangia, **74**, *74*, 119, 283
Macrurosaurus, **74**, *74*, 145, 283
Madagascar, 262, 263
Madsen, James H. Jr., 278
Magnosaurus = Megalosaurus
Magyarosaurus
   = (*Titanosaurus?*), 276
Maiasaura, **74**, *74*, 156
   feeding young, 214
   nests, *212*
Majungasaurus, **74**, 129, 278
Majungatholus, **74**, *74*, 161, 284
Makela, Robert, 276, **278**
Malawi, 262, 263
Maleev, E.A., 279
"*Maleevosaurus*," **75**
Maleevus, **75**, 168, 284
Mali, 262
Mamenchisaurid (-ae, -s), **75**, 285
Mamenchisaurus, **75**, *75*, 144, *218*, *248*
   cast, *256*
   namer of, 285
   neck, 186
Mammal-like reptiles, *see* Synapsids
Mammals, **75**
   and evolution, 14–15
Mandschurosaurus, **75**, *75*, 156, 282
Manospondylus
   = *Tyrannosaurus*
Mantell, Gideon A., 240, 272, **279**, *279*
Marginocephalia, **75**
   Sereno's classification, 159
Marmarospondylus
   = *Bothriospondylus*
Marsh, Othniel Charles, 232, 234, 269, 273, 275, 277, **279**, *279*, 280, 282, 285
Marshosaurus, **75**, *75*, 278
Martínez, Ruben, 269, 275, **280**, 282
Maryanska, T., **280**, 281, 282
Mason, Rex, 297
Massospondylus, **75**, *75*, 139, 268, 281
Matheron, Pierre P.E., 280

Mating, **210–211**
Matthew, William D., 280
Maurer, Norman, 297
Megacervixosaurus (n), **75**, 146, 285
Megadactylus = Anchisaurus
Megalosaurid (-ae, -s), **76**, *128*
   classification, 109, 110
   namer of, 277
Megalosaurus, *36*, **76**, *76*, *128*
   first describer of, 270
   lower jaw of, *270*
   mistaken illustration, *302*
Melanorosaurid (-ae, -s), **76**, **140**
   classification, 109, 136
   namer of, 276
Melanorosaurus, **76**, *76*, *140*
   classification, 137
   namer of, 275
Members, geological, 224
Mesozoic Era, 14–15, 16–17, 18
Mesozoic rocks, 222
Meteorites, and mass extinctions, 34–35
Metriacanthosaurus, **76**, *76*, 128, 284
Mexico, 231, 233, 235
Meyer, Grant E., 281
Meyer, Hermann von, 239, **280**
Microceratops, **76**, *76*, 170, *249*, 269
Microcoelus, **76**, 278
Microdontosaurus (n), **76**, 146, 285
Microhadrosaurus, **76**, 156, 272
Micropachycephalosaurus, **77**, 162, 272
Microvenator, **77**, 77, 119, 281
"*Mifunesaurus*," **77**, 128
Milner, Angela, 271, **280**
Minmi, **77**, 77, 167, *265*
   describer of, 280
Mochlodon = Rhabdodon
Molds, 221
Molnar, Ralph E., 264, 265, **280**, 282
Mongolia, 246, 247, 255
Mongolosaurus, **77**, 146, 275
Monkonosaurus, **77**, 166, 285
Monoclonius, **77**, 77, 171, 272
"*Monolophosaurus*"
   = *Jiangjunmiaosaurus*
Montanoceratops, **77**, 77, 170, 283
Morinosaurus = Pelorosaurus
Morocco, 262, 263
Morosaurus = Camarasaurus
Mosasaurs, **78**
"*Moshisaurus*," **78**, *78*, 144
Movement, 202–203
Movies, dinosaurs in, 298–301
Mudge, Benjamin, 279, **280**
Muscles, 176–177
Museums,
   African, 263

   Asian, 254–257
   Australian, 265
   European, 242–245
   North American, 234–237
   South American, 260
Mussaurus, **78**, *78*, 139
   co-namers of, 269, 284
   infant's skeleton, *214*
Muttaburrasaurus, **78**, *78*, 154
   co-describers of, 280
   co-namers of, 269

N

Nagao, 280
Nanosaurus, **78**, *78*, 160, 279
Nanotyrannus, **78**, 132, 268, 272, 285
Nanshiungosaurus, **78**, 272
Necks, 186–187
Nemegtosaurus, **78**, *78*, 146, 281
Neosaurus = Parrosaurus
Neosodon = Pelorosaurus
Netherlands, 239, 241
Neuquensaurus (n), **79**
New Zealand, 265
Newman, Barney A., 280
Ngexisaurus (n), **79**, *79*, 116, 285
Niger, 262, 263
Nigeria, 262, 263
Nipponosaurus, **79**, *79*, 157, 280
Noasaurid (-ae, -s), **117**
   classification, 109, 110
   co-namers of, 269, 282
Noasaurus, **79**, *79*, **117**, 269, 282
Nodosaurid (-ae, -s), *31*, **79**, **167**
   classification, 109, 158–159
   and defense, 208
   describer of, 279
   Sereno's classification, 159
Nodosaurus, **79**, *79*, 279
Nopcsa, Baron Franz, **280**, **281**
Norman, David, 281
North American dinosaurs, 230–233
North American museums, 234–237
Norway, 239
Nothosaur, **79**
Notoceratops, **79**, 170, 284
Novas, Fernando E., 269, **281**
Nowinski, A., 281
Nuthetes, **79**, 116, 281
Nyasasaurus (n), **80**, *80*, 138, 271

O

Oberndorfer, 281
O'Brien, Willis, 300
Ohmdenosaurus, **80**, 141, 285
Oligosaurus = Rhabdodon
Olivero, E., 274

Olsen, George, 281
Omeisaurus, **80**, *80*, 144
   namer of, 285
   pelvic bones, **285**
Omosaurus = Dacentrurus
Onychosaurus = Rhabdodon
Ooliths, 220
   see also Eggs
Opisthocoelicaudia, **80**, *80*, 143, 269
Oplosaurus = Pelorosaurus
Orders, and classification of dinosaurs, 20–21, 108–109
Orinosaurus = Euskelosaurus
Ornatotholus, **80**, *80*, 161, 274, 284
Ornithischia (-ns), **80**
   characteristics of, 108
   classification, 20–21, 108
   and defense, 208
   digestive systems, 190
   and dinosaur family tree, 26–27
   feet, 192
   five suborders, 158–171
   hand, 188
   head size, 180
   hip bones, 175, 191
   mass extinction, 34
   origins, 19
   ornithopods, 148–157
   Sereno's cladogram, 159
   tails, 194
Ornithodira, in cladogram, 21
Ornithoides = Saurornithoides
Ornitholestes, **81**, *81*, 116, 281
   skeleton, *235*
Ornithomerus = Rhabdodon
Ornithomimid (-ae, -s), **81**, **122**
   classification, 109, 110
   describer of, 279
   in food chain, 204–205
Ornithomimoides, **81**, 116, 276
Ornithomimosaur (-ia, -s), 110
   classification, 109
   and dinosaur family tree, 26–27
Ornithomimus, **81**, *81*, *122*, *291*
   model of, *300*
   namer of, 279
   Paul's classification, 111
Ornithopod (-a, -s), **81**, 149
   arms and hands, 188
   brainpower, 183
   classification, 109, 148–149
   describer of, 279
   digestive system, 191
   and dinosaur family tree, 26–27
   eggs, 212
   families, 148
   hip bones, 191
   movement, 203
   Sereno's cladogram, 149
Ornithopsis = Pelorosaurus

Ornithosuchia (-ns), **81**
  in cladogram, 21
Ornithosuchids, **81**
  and dinosaur family tree,
  26-27
Ornithosuchus, *81*
  in cladogram, 21
Ornithotarsus = Hadrosaurus
Orodromeus, **81**, *81*, 151
  co-namers of, 276, 284
Orosaurus = Euskelosaurus
Orthogoniosaurus, **82**, 128,
  272
Orthomerus, **82**, 156, 283
Osborn, Henry F., 281
Oshanosaurus (n), **82**, *82*,
  141, 285
Osmólska, Halszka, 246,
  269, 280, **281**, 282
Ostrich dinosaurs, *172*
  death by drought, 217
  and defense, 208
  see also
      Ornithomimosaurs
Ostrom, John H., 232, 281
Othnielia, **82**, *82*, 151
  co-namers of, 274
  remains discovered, 273
Ouranosaurus, **82**, *82*, 155,
  261
  namer of, 284
  Sereno's classification,
  149
Ouranosaurus nigeriensis, *244*
Oviraptor, **82**, *82*, *118*, 118
  crushing bite, *207*
  describer of, 281
  discoverer of, 268, 281
  head shape, 181
Oviraptorid (-ae, -s), **82**,
  118
  classification, 109, 110
  namer of, 269
Oviraptorosaur (-ia, -s), **82**,
  110
  classification, 109
  and dinosaur family tree,
  26-27
Ovoraptor = Velociraptor
Owen, Sir Richard, 37, 240,
  281, *281*

P

Pachycephalosaur (-ia, -s),
  82
  classification, 158-159
  co-describers of, 280,
  281
  and dinosaur family tree,
  26-27
  families, 161-162
  in food chain, 204-205
  Sereno's classification,
  159
Pachycephalosaurid (-ae,
  -s), **82**, **161**
  classification, 109,
  158-159
  co-namers of, 283
Pachycephalosaurus, **83**, *83*,
  161
  co-namers of, 270, 283
  discoverer of, 285

Pachyrhinosaurus, **83**, *83*,
  171, 283
Pachysauriscus = Plateosaurus
Pachysaurops = Plateosaurus
Pachysaurus = Plateosaurus
*Pachyspondylus
  = Massospondylus*
Padian, Kevin, 23
Palaeopteryx, 83
Palaeoscincus, 83
  discoverer of, 275
  namer of, 278
Paleodinosaurs, Paul's
  classification, 111
Paleopods, 83
Paleotheropods, Paul's
  classification, 111
Paleozoic Era, 14-15
Pangaea, 28, 30, 252, 253
Panoplosaurus, **83**, *83*, 167
  head, 180
  namer of, 278
Paranthodon, **83**, 166, 281
Parasaurolophus, **83**, *83*, *157*,
  272, 282
Parasuchians, **83**
  and dinosaur family tree,
  26-27
  see also Phytosaurs
Parasuchus, 18
Pareiasaur, 16-17
Parker, Neave, 290
Parks, William A., 282
Parksosaurus, **84**, 151, 283
Paronychodon, **84**, *84*, 127,
  272
Parrosaurus, **84**, *84*, 143
Parrot lizards, *see*
      Psittacosaurids
Patagosaurus, **84**, *84*, 141,
  269
Paul, Gregory S., 111, 270,
  282, 291
Peabody, George, 234
Pectinodon = Troodon
Peishansaurus, **84**, *84*, 168,
  269
Pelorosaurus, **84**, 142, *241*,
  279
Pelycosaur, 16
Pentaceratops, **84**, *84*, 171,
  281
Perle, Altangerel, 246, 269,
  280, 281, **282**
Permineralization, 220
Peru, 259
Petrification, 220-221
Phaedrolosaurus, **85**, *85*, 126
Phillips, Alexander, 295
Phyllodon, **85**, 151, 284
Phytodinosauria,
  classification, 108
Phytosaurs, 18
  and dinosaur family tree,
  26-27
  see also Parasuchians
Piatnitzkysaurus, **85**, 130,
  259
  hip bones, *269*
  namer of, 269
Picrodon, **85**
Pinacosaurus, 275
  discoverer of, 268

Pisanosaurus, *29*, **85**, *85*, 150,
  271
  in cladogram, 21
Piveteausaurus, **85**, 128, 284
Plated dinosaurs, *see*
      Stegosaurs
*Plateosauravus
  = Euskelosaurus*
Plateosaurid (-ae, -s), **85**,
  139
  classification, 109, 136
Plateosaurus, **85**, *85*, *139*, *243*
  classification, 137
  describer of, 280
  hand, 188
Pledge, Neville S., 280, **282**
Plesiosaurs, 16-17, **85**
  mass extinction, 34
Pleurocoelus, **86**, *86*, 142, 279
Pleuropeltus = Struthiosaurus
Podokesaurid (-ae, -s), **86**,
  276
Podokesaurus, **86**, *86*, 114,
  284
Poekilopleuron, **86**, 128, 273
Polacanthoides, **86**, 167, 281
Polacanthus, **86**, *86*, 167
  describer of, 281
  discoverer of, 274
Poland, 239, 241, 244
Polyodontosaurus = Troodon
Polyonax = Triceratops
Poposaurids, *see*
      Teratosaurids
Portugal, 239, 241
Powell, Jaimé E., 269, **282**
Prenocephale, **86**, *86*, 161,
  280, 281
Preparators, 226
Price, Llewellyn, 259
Priconodon, **86**, 167, 279
Priodontognathus, **86**, 167,
  283
Probactrosaurus, **87**, 155, *247*
  namer of, 283
  Sereno's classification,
  149
Probactrosaurus gobiensis, *257*
Probactrosaurus mongoliensis,
  244
Proceratops = Ceratops
Proceratosaurus, **87**, 276
Procerosaurus = Iguanodon
*Procheneosaurus see
  Corythosaurus*
Procompsognathid (-ae, -s),
  namer of, 276
  see also Coelophysids
Procompsognathus, **87**, *87*,
  114, 274
Prodeinodon, **87**, *87*, 132, 281
Prosaurolophus, **87**, *87*, 156,
  270
Prosauropod (-a, -s), **87**,
  136-137
  arms and hands, 188-189
  classification, 109
  digestive systems, 190
  and dinosaur family tree,
  26-27
  egg and infant, 214
  eggs, 212
  families, 138-140

Galton's cladogram, 137
  namer of, 276
Proterosuchians, 18, **87**
  and dinosaur family tree,
  26-27
"Protoavis," **88**, 271
Protoceratops, **88**, *88*, *170*,
  290
  co-namers of, 275
  laying eggs, 212-213,
  213
  violent death, 217
Protoceratopsid (-ae, -s), **88**,
  170
  classification, 109,
  158-159
  co-namers of, 275
Protognathus, **88**, 141, 285
Protorosaurs, 17, 18, **88**
*Protorosaurus
  = Chasmosaurus*
Pseudosuchians, **88**
Psittacosaurid (-ae, -s), **88**,
  169
  classification, 109,
  158-159
  namer of, 281
Psittacosaurus, **88**, *88*, *169*,
  271
  color and camouflage,
  199
  describer of, 281
  neck bones, 186
  Sereno's classification,
  159
Pteranodon, *10*, *288*
Pterodactyloid, 23
Pterodaustro, *22*
Pteropelyx, **88**, 157, 272
Pterosaur (-ia, -s), 17, 18,
  22-23, **88**, *88*
  in cladogram, 21
  classification, 108
  and dinosaur family tree,
  26-27
  mass extinction, 34
Pterospondylus, **88**, 114, 277
Pyrite disease, 227

Q

Quaesitosaurus, **88**, 146, 269,
  277
Quetzalcoatlus, *23*, 33

R

Raath, Michael A., 282
Radiometric dating, 225
Rapator, **89**, 276
Rauisuchians, 18, **89**
  and dinosaur family tree,
  26-27
Rebbachisaurus, **89**, *89*, 142,
  278
Reed, William H., 232, 270,
  279, **282**
Regnosaurus, **89**
Reig, Osvaldo A., 282
Reproduction,
  eggs, 212-213
  winning a mate, 210-211
Reptiles (Reptilia), **89**, 108
  and classification of
  dinosaurs, 20-21

and evolution, 14–15, 16–17
Revueltosaurus, **89**, *89*, 276
Rhabdodon, **89**, *89*, 151, 280
Rhadinosaurus, namer of, 283
Rhamphorhynchoids, 22
Rhodanosaurus = *Struthiosaurus*
Rhoetosaurus, **89**, *89*, 141, 278
Rhynchosaurs, 17, 18, **90**
Riabinin, Anatoliy N., 282
Rich, Thomas H., 264
  and Patricia Vickers, **282**
Ricqulès, Armand J. de, 282
Riggs, Elmer S., 282
Riley, H., 282
Riojasaurus, **90**, *90*, 140, 269
Roccosaurus(= *Melanorosaurus*), 275
Rodríguez, Jorge, 269, 275, 280, **282**
Romania, 239, 241
Romer, Alfred Sherwood, 282
Roniewicz, Ewa, 269, 281, **282**
Rosner, D.E., 273, **283**
Rowe, Tim, 283
Roy-Chowdhury, Tappan K., 271, 277, **283**
Rozhdestvensky, Anatoly K., 283
Russell, Dale A., 230, 269, **283**, 283, 305

S
Saichania, **90**, 168, 280
Saltasaurus, *32*, **90**, *90*, *145*, 269, 282
Saltopus, **90**, *90*, 114, *240*, 276
"Sanchusaurus," **90**, 122
Sangonghesaurus (n), **90**, 285
Sanpasaurus, **90**, 285
Santafé, J.-V., 270, 271, **283**
Sanz, J.L., 270, 271, **283**, 283
Sarcolestes, **90**, *90*, 167, 278
Sarcosaurus, **91**, *91*, 131
Sattler, W.B., 274
Saudi Arabia, 247
Sauraechinodon = *Echinodon*
Saurischia (-ns), **91**, 108
  characteristics of, 108
  classification, 20–21, 108–109
  and dinosaur family tree, 26–27
  hand, 188
  hip bones, 175, 191
  mass extinction, 34
  origins, 19
  sauropodomorphs and segnosaurs, 136–147
  theropods (with Herrerasaurs), 110–135
Saurolophus, **91**, 156
  hearing and voice, 185
  namer of, 270
Sauropelta, **91**, *167*, 281
Saurophagus = *Allosaurus*

Sauroplites, **91**, *91*, 168, 269
Sauropod (-a, -s), **91**, 136, *301*
  arms and hands, 188–189
  body temperature, 200–201
  brain size, 182–183
  classification, 109
  colour and camouflage, 199
  death from drought, 217
  and defense, 209
  describer of, 279
  digestive systems, 190–191
  and dinosaur family tree, 26–27
  families, 141, 146
  feeding, 204
  giant femur, *174*
  head size, 180
  hip bones, 191
  life expectancy, 216–217
  mistaken ideas respecting, 302
  model of, *301*
  necks, 186
  skin and scales, 196
  and their young, 215
  tracks, 202–203
Sauropodomorph (-a, -s), **91**
  in cladogram, 137
  classification, 108, 109
  infraorders and Segnosaurs, 136–137
  namer of, 276
Sauropterygian, 16
Saurornithoides, **91**, 127
  describer of, 281
  discoverer of, 268
Saurornithoidids, 127
  see Troodontids
Saurornitholestes, **92**, *92*, 126, 284
Scales, 196–197
Scasso, R., 274
Scelidosaur (-ia, -s), body armor, 208
  classification, 109, 158–159
  and dinosaur family tree, 26–27
  families, 163)164
Scelidosaurid (-ae, -s), **92**, **164**
  classification, 109, 158–159
  namer of, 272
Scelidosaurus, *31*, **92**, *92*, *164*
  describer of, 281
  foot, *36*
  Sereno's classification, 159
Schlaikjer, Erich M., 270, **283**
Scleromochlus, **92**
Scolosaurus = *Dyoplosaurus*? and/or *Euoplocephalus*
Scutellosaurid (-ae, -s), **92**, **163**
  classification, 109, 158–159

Scutellosaurus, **92**, *92*, *163*, 163
  namer of, 271
  Sereno's classification, 159
Sea serpents, 289
Secernosaurus, **92**, 156, 270
Seeley, Harry Govier, 268, **283**, *283*
Segisaurid (-ae, -s), namer of, 270
Segisaurus, **92**, *92*, 114
  limb bones, *270*
  namer of, 270
Segnosaur (-ia, -s), **93**, 136–137
  in cladogram, 137
  classification, 109
  co-namers of, 269, 282
  and dinosaur family tree, 26–27
Segnosaurid (-ae, -s), **93**, **147**
  classification, 109, 136
  namer of, 282
Segnosaurus, *32*, **93**, *93*, *147*, *246*, 282
"Seismosaurus," **93**, 146, 274
Sellosaurus, **93**, *93*, 138, 276
Sereno, Paul, 148, 149, 159, **283**
Shamosaurus, **93**, 284
Shanshanosaurus, **93**
  namer of, 272
  skull, *272*
Shantungosaurus, **93**, *93*, 156, 276
Shoulders, 177
Shunosaurus, **93**, *93*, 141
  co-namers of, 272, 285
  and defense, 209
Shuosaurus = *Shunosaurus*
Siamosaurus, **94**, 134
  co-namers of, 270, 277
Sibbick, John, 291
Sight, 184–185
Silvisaurus, **94**, *94*, 167, *273*, 273
Simmons, D.J., 283
Sinclair Refining Company, 292
Sinocoelurus, **94**, 116, 285
Sinosaurus, **94**, 113, 285
Skeletons, 174–175
  and age, 215
  ankle joints, 193
  arms and hands, 188–189
  of birds, 24–25
  and classification of dinosaurs, 20–21
  diseased bones, 216
  evolving limbs, *15*
  and eyes, 185
  hip bones, 175
  hips legs and feet, 192–193
  jaws, 180, 190–191
  key features, 20
  and muscles, 176–177
  necks, 186–187
  of pterosaurs, 23

skulls, 16–17, 180, 190–191
  and speed, 208
  tails, 194–195
  toe and thumb claws, 209
  wings, 25
Skin, 196–197
Skulls, 16–17, 180, 190–191
Sloan, Robert, 284
Smell, 184–185
South Africa, 262, 263
South American dinosaurs, 258–259
South American museums, 260
Spain, 239, 241, 244
Species, and classification of dinosaurs, 21
Sphenodonts, 17
Sphenospondylus = *Iguanodon*
Špinar, Z.V., 290, 302
Spinosaurid (-ae, -s), **94**, **134**
  classification, 109, 110
  namer of, 284
Spinosaurus, *12-13*, **94**, *94*, *134*, 134
  body temperature, 201
  namer of, 284
Spotila, James, **283**
Stagonolepis, *18*
Staurikosaurid (-ae, -s), **94**, **112**
  classification, 109, 110
  namer of, 274
Staurikosaurus, *28*, **94**, *94*, *112*, 112, *258*
  in cladogram, 21
  namer of, 271
  Paul's classification, 111
Stegoceras, **94**, *94*, 161, 278
Stegopelta (= *Nodosaurus*), 285
Stegosaur (-ia, -s), **95**
  body armor, 208
  brainpower, 183
  classification, 109, 158–159
  describer of, 279
  and dinosaur family tree, 26–27
  families, 165, 166
  Sereno's classification, 159
Stegosaurid (-ae, -s), **95**, **166**
  classification, 109, 158–159
  describer of, 279
  Sereno's classification, 159
Stegosaurides, **95**, 168, 269
Stegosaurus, *12-13*, **95**, *95*, *166*, *232*, 273
  brain size, 182
  model of, *292*
  namer of, 279
  remains discovered, 273
  tail in combat, *195*
Steneosaurus, *10*
Stenonychosaurus (= *Troodon*), 272, 283
Stenopelix, **95**, *95*, 169, 280

Stenotholus = Stygimoloch
Stephanosaurus
   = Lambeosaurus
Stereocephalus
   = Euoplocephalus
Sternberg, Charles H., 230,
   283, *283*
Sternberg, Charles M., **283**
Sternberg, George, 283
Sternberg, Levi, 283
Sternberg, R.M., 283
Sternfeld, R., 283
Sterrholophus = Triceratops
Stokesosaurus, **95**, *95*, 130,
   278
Stout, William, 291
Stovall, J. Willis, 278, **284**
Stratigraphy, 224
Strenusaurus = Riojasaurus
Stromer von Reichenbach,
   Ernst, 261, **284**
Struthiomimus, **95**, *95*, 122
   describer of, 281
   model of, *292*
Struthiosaurus, **96**, *96*, 167,
   239, 270, *280*
Stutchbury, Samuel, 282,
   284
Stygimoloch, **96**, 161, 274,
   284
Styracosaurus, **96**, *96*, 171,
   237
   namer of, 278
   and winning a mate, *211*
Styracosterna, Sereno's
   classification, 149
Subclasses, and classification
   of dinosaurs, 20–21
Subgroups, geological, 225
Suborders, and classification
   of dinosaurs, 21, 108–109
Sues, Hans-Dieter, 274,
   284, 284
"Sugiyamasaurus," 250
Supergroups, geological,
   225
Superorders, and
   classification of dinosaurs,
   20–21
Supersaurus, **96**, *96*, 146
   discoverer of, 277
shoulder blade, *277*
Sweden, 239, 244
Swinton, W.E., 290
Switzerland, 239, 241, 244
Symphyrophus
   = Camptosaurus
Syngonosaurus
   = Anoplosaurus
Syntarsus, **96**, *96*, 114
   feathers, *197*
   namer of, 282
Syria, 247
Syrmosaurus = Pinacosaurus
Szechuanosaurus, **96**, 130

T
Tails, 194–195
   and defense, 209
   and movement, 202
Taiwan, 255
Talarurus, **97**, *97*, 279
Talbot, Mignon, 284

Tang Zilu, 272, **284**
Tanius, **97**, 156
   namer of, 285
   skull, **285**
Tanystrosuchus
   (=Halticosaurus?), 277
Tanzania, 262, 263
Tapia, Augusto, 284
Taquet, Philippe, 261, **284**,
   284
Tarbosaurus, **97**, *97*, 132
   arms and hands, 189
   describer of, 279
   mistaken illustration,
   302-303
   skeleton, *257*
Tarchia, **97**, *97*, 168, 280
Tatisaurus, **97**, 163, 283
Tawasaurus, **97**, 138, 285
Technosaurus, 29, **97**, *97*,
   160, 271
Teeth, 190–191
Teinchisaurus = Tenchisaurus
Teinurosaurus, **97**, 116, 281
Telmatosaurus, **98**, *98*, 156,
   281
Temperature, 200–201
Tenantosaurus
   = Tenontosaurus
Tenchisaurus (n), **98**, 168
Tenontosaurus, **98**, *98*, 151
   namer of, 281
   Sereno's classification,
   149
Teratosaurids, see
   Rauisuchians
Teratosaurus, **98**, *98*
Testudinates, 16, **98**
Tetanurae, **98**, 111
Tetragonosaurus
   = Corythosaurus
Thailand, 249
Thalattosaurs, 17
Thecocoelurus
   (= Calamospondylus), 116,
   276
Thecodontosaurus, 29, **98**-
   classification, 137
   co-namers of, 282, 284
   teeth, 191
Thecodonts, 17, 18, **98**
and dinosaur family
   tree, 26–27
   and evolution of
   dinosaurs, 18–19
   gait of, 19
   neck curvature, 187
Thecospondylus, **98**, 283
Therapsids, 16, **99**, *99*
Therizinosaurid (-ae, -s), **99**,
   125
   classification, 109, 110
   describer of, 279
Therizinosaurus, *125*, 125,
   279
Theropod (-a, -s), **99**, 110
   arms and hands, 188–189
   in attack, 206
   body temperature, 200
   classification, 20–21, 109
   describer of, 279
   digestive systems,
   190–191

and dinosaur family tree,
   26–27
families, 114–135
food requirements, 205
head size, 180
infraorders, and the
   Herrerasauria, 110–111
movement and tracks,
   202–203
necks, 186
Paul's classification, 111
tails and balancing, 194
Therosaurus = Iguanodon
Thescelosaurid (-ae, -s), *153*
   classification, 109,
   148–149
Thescelosaurus, **99**, *153*, 153
   namer of, 275
   Sereno's classification,
   149
Thespesius, **99**, 156, 278
Thompson, C.V., 273, 283
Thotobolosaurus (n), **99**, *99*,
   140, 273
Thulborn, Richard A., 284
Thyreophora (-ns), **99**
   Sereno's classification,
   159
Tianchungosaurus, **99**
Tichosteus (= Othnielia),
   272
Ticinosuchus, 18
Tienshanosaurus, **100**, *100*,
   144, 285
Titanosaurid (-ae, -s), **100**,
   145
   in cladogram, 137
   classification, 109, 136
   namer of, 278
Titanosaurus, **100**, *100*, 145,
   278
Tomodon = Diplotomodon
Tools, for fossil hunters,
   223
Tordorff, H.B., 273
Tornieria, **100**, 146, 283
Torosaurus, *33*, **100**, *171*,
   275, *290*
   head size, 181
   namer of, 279
Torvosaurid (-ae, -s), **100**
   classification, 109, 110
   namer of, 277
Torvosaurus, **100**, *100*, 274,
   277
Trace fossils, 221
Trachodon, **100**, 156, 278
Trexler, David and Laurie,
   276
Triassic Period, 26–27, **28-**
   29
Triceratops, *12-13*, **100**, *100*,
   171
   and attack, *206*
   and defense, 209
   head, *235*
   heart and blood
      pressure, 178
   namer of, 279
   skull, *279*
Triceratops alticornis, 270
Trilophosaurs, **101**

Trimucrodon, **101**, 163, 284
Troodon, **101**, *101*, 127, 272
   brain size, 183
   claws, 189
   discoverer of, 275
   eyes, *184*, 184–185, *185*
   namer of, 278
Troodontid (-ae, -s), **101**,
   127, 275
   classification, 109, 110
Tsintaosaurus, **101**, *101*, 156,
   285
Tugulusaurus, **101**, 116, 272
Tumanova, Tatiana A., 277,
   284
Tunisia, 262, 263
Tuojiangosaurus, **101**, *101*,
   166
   co-namers of, 272, 278,
   285
Tylocephale, **101**, *101*, 161
   co-describers of, 280,
   281
Tylosaurus, 288
Tylosteus
   = Pachycephalosaurus
Tyrannosaur, skeleton, *174-*
   175
Tyrannosaurid (-ae, -s),
   102, *132*
   changing proportions,
   215
   classification, 109, 110
   in food chain, 204–205
   movement, 203
   namer of, 281
   scales, 196
Tyrannosaurus, *12*, *32*, **102**,
   102, *132*, 280
   and attack, 206–207, *207*
   brain, 182–183, *184*
   describer of, 281
   digestive systems, 191
   hind limbs, *20*
   mistaken ideas
      respecting, 302
   mistaken illustration,
   302-303
   model of, *293*
   in movies, 295, 297,
   298–299, 301
   Paul's classification, 111
   scales, *196*
Tyrrell, Joseph B., 230, **284**

U
Ugrosaurus, **102**, 171, 271,
   273
Uintasaurus = Camarasaurus
Ultrasaurus, **102**, 142, *251*,
   277
"Ultrasaurus," *12-13*, **102**,
   102, 277
United Kingdom, 240, 241,
   245
United States of America,
   231–237
Unquillosaurus, **102**, *102*,
   282
Uruguay, 259
USSR, 240, 241, 245, 247

V

Valdosaurus, **102**, *102*, 152, 274
Van Valen, Leigh, 284
"Vectensia," **103**
Vectisaurus, **103**, *103*, 155, 276
Velocipes, **103**, 114, 276
Velociraptor, **103**, *103*, *126*
  describer of, 281
  discoverer of, 268
  neck curvature, 187
  skull, *281*
  violent death, *217*
Vertebrates, evolution of, 15
Vickers, Patricia, 282
Vince, M., 269, **284**
Volcanoes, and mass extinctions, 34–35
Volkheimeria, **103**, *103*, 141, 269
Vulcanodon, **103**, *103*, 271, 282
Vulcanodontid (-ae, -s), **103**, 271
  classification, 109, 136

W

Wagner, Johann A., 284
Walgettosuchus (= *Rapator?*), 276
Walker, Alick D., 284
Walker, Cyril A., 275, **284**
Walker, William, 284
Walkeria, **103**, *103*, 113, 271
Wall, William P., 274, **284**
Wannanosaurus, **104**, 162, 276
Weishampel, David B., 276, **284**
Welles, Samuel P., **284**, 284
Wellnhofer, Peter, 23
Wieland, G.R., 284
Wiffen, Mr and Mrs, 280
Wiffen, Joan, 265, **285**
Wild, Rupert, 285
Williams, M., 268, 272, **285**
Williston, Samuel W., 279, **285**
Wilson, Maurice, 290
Wiman, Carl, 285
Winkley, William, 285
Woodward, Sir Arthur Smith, 285
Wright, Nelda E., 278, **285**
Wuerhosaurus, **104**, *104*, 166, 272

X

Xenotarsosaurus, **104**, 129
  co-namers of, 269, 275, 280, 282
Xiaosaurus (n), **104**, 160
  co-namers of, 272, 284
"Xiphosauridae," Sereno's classification, 149
Xuanhanosaurus, **104**, *104*, 272
Xuanhuasaurus, **104**, 285

Y

Yadagiri, P., 252, 268, **285**
Yaleosaurus = *Anchisaurus*
Yandusaurus, **104**, *104*, 151, 275
Yang, Seong Young, **251**
Yang Zhong-jian, *see* Young Chung Chien
Yangchuanosaurus, **104**, *104*, 131, 272
Yaverlandia, **105**, *105*, 161, 274
Yaxartosaurus = *Jaxartosaurus*
Yingshanosaurus (n), *105*, 166
Young Chung Chien, 248, 285
Yubasaurus, **105**
Yunnanosaurid (-ae, -s), **105**
  classification, 109, 136
  namer of, 285
Yunnanosaurus,
  classification, 137
  namer of, 285

Z

Zapsalis = *Paronychodon*
Zborzewski, Count A., 285
Zbyszewski, G., 278, **285**
Zdansky, Otto, 285
Zephyrosaurus, **105**, *105*, 151, 284
Zhang Yihong, 272, 278, **285**
Zhao Xijin, 285
Zhou Shiwu, 272–273, 278, **285**, 285
Zhow, *see* Zhou Shiwu
Zigongosaurus (= *Omeisaurus?*), 144
Zimbabwe, 262, 263
Zizhongosaurus, **105**, *105*, 141, 272, 285